People and Place

Also by Michael S. Horton

Covenant and Eschatology: The Divine Drama
Lord and Servant: A Covenant Christology
Covenant and Salvation: Union with Christ

People and Place:
A Covenant Ecclesiology

Michael S. Horton

Westminster John Knox Press
LOUISVILLE • LONDON

Unless otherwise indicated, Scripture quotations are from the New Revised Standard Version of the Bible and are copyright © 1989 by the Division of Christian Education of the National Council of the Churches of Christ in the U.S.A. Used by permission.

Scripture quotations marked KJV are from the King James Version of the Holy Bible.

Scripture quotations marked NKJV are from The New King James Version. Copyright © 1979, 1980, 1982, Thomas Nelson Inc., Publishers. Used by permission.

Scripture quotations marked ESV are from The Holy Bible, English Standard Version, and are copyright © 2001 by Crossway Bibles, a division of Good News Publishers. Used by permission. All rights reserved.

Scripture quotations marked NASB are from the *New American Standard Bible*. Copyright © 1960, 1962, 1963, 1968, 1971, 1972, 1973, 1975, 1977, 1995 by the Lockman Foundation. Used by permission.

Book design by Sharon Adams
Cover design by Eric Walljasper/Teri Vinson

First edition
Published by Westminster John Knox Press
Louisville, Kentucky

This book is printed on acid-free paper that meets the American National Standards Institute Z39.48 standard. ∞

PRINTED IN THE UNITED STATES OF AMERICA

08 09 10 11 12 13 14 15 16 — 10 9 8 7 6 5 4 3 2 1

Library of Congress Cataloging-in-Publication Data

Horton, Michael Scott.
    People and place : a convenant ecclesiology / Michael S. Horton. — 1st ed.
      p. cm.
    Includes index.
    ISBN 978-0-664-23071-5 (alk. paper)
    1. Church.   2. Covenant theology.   I. Title.
    BV600.3.H67 2008
    262—dc22

                                                  2007052374

Contents

Abbreviations   vii

Introduction   ix

Chapter 1: Real Absence, Real Presence:
Ecclesiology and the Economy of Grace   1

Part One: Origin: Theater of Grace   **35**

Chapter 2: *Creatura Verbi*: The Sacramental Word   37

Chapter 3: A Liberating Captivity: The Word
as Canon   72

Chapter 4: Signs and Seals: Ratifying the Treaty   99

Chapter 5: "This Is My Body":
Reformed Eucharistic Theology   124

Part Two: Identity: Figuring the Body   **153**

Chapter 6: *Totus Christus*: One and Many   155

Chapter 7: Catholicity and Holiness: "Sanctify Them
in the Truth"; Your Word Is Truth" (John 17:17)   190

Chapter 8: Apostolicity: Historical Institution
and Eschatological Event   221

Part Three: Destination: Royal Procession to Zion   **257**

Chapter 9: Holy Land, Holy War: Preparing a Place   259

Chapter 10: Consummation: The Eucharistic Liturgy
of the Kingdom That We Are Receiving   289

Index of Subjects and Names   309

Abbreviations

ARV   American Revised Version. 1901.

BC   *The Book of Confessions.* Louisville, KY: Office of the General Assembly, Presbyterian Church (U.S.A.), 1991.

CD   Karl Barth. *Church Dogmatics.* Edited by G. W. Bromiley and T. F. Torrance. Translated by G. T. Thomson. 5 vols. in 14. Edinburgh: T&T Clark, 1936–77.

CO   John Calvin. *Calvini opera.* 59 vols. in CR, vols. 29–87. Brunsvigae (Braunschweig): Schwetschke, 1863–1900.

CR   Corpus reformatorum. Edited by C. G. Bretschneider, H. E. Bindseil, et al. 101 vols. Halis Saxonum (Hall): Schwetschke; et al., 1834–1963. Reprinted, New York: Johnson, 1964.

ESV   English Standard Version. 2001

Institutes   John Calvin. *Institutes of the Christian Religion.* Edited by J. T. McNeill. Translated from the 1559 edition by F. L. Battles. 2 vols. Philadelphia: Westminster, 1960.

KJV   King James Version. 1611.

LW   Martin Luther. *Luther's Works.* Edited by J. Pelikan and H. T. Lehmann. 55 vols. St. Louis: Concordia Publishing House; Philadelphia: Fortress Press, 1955–86.

NASB   *New American Standard Bible.* 1960, 1995.

NKJV   *New King James Version.* 1982

NRSV   New Revised Standard Version. 1989.

OS   *Johannis Calvini opera selecta.* Edited by P. Barth and G. Niesel. 5 vols. Munich: Chr. Kaiser, 1926–52.

RSV   Revised Standard Version. 1946, 1952.

SC   Dietrich Bonhoeffer. *Sanctorum Communio: A Theological Study of the Sociology of the Church.* Vol. 1 of *Dietrich Bonhoeffer Works.* Original edited by Joachim von Soosten. English edition edited by Clifford J. Green. Translated by Reinhard Krauss and Nancy Lukens. Minneapolis: Fortress Press, 1998.

Introduction

With this volume I draw to a close a four-volume series exploring the potential of covenant theology for a renewal of theology that is conscious of its biblical-theological context and horizon. Along the way, I have suggested that this approach helps us to navigate between extremes currently on offer. Borrowing on Paul Tillich's contrasting paradigms for the philosophy of religion—"overcoming estrangement" versus "meeting a stranger"—and adding a third type, "the stranger we never meet," I have opted for the second view as the corollary of a covenantal ontology. Further, this project has consistently defended an analogical account of theological statements, appealing to the metaphor of drama to express the dynamic interplay between eschatology and history in the diverse covenantal administrations. So the prolegomenon, *Covenant and Eschatology*, attempted to show how this approach can help us reintegrate the rhetoric of redemption in a postmodern situation. Elaborating the paradigm of "meeting a stranger," *Lord and Servant* sought to transcend the false choice of an impersonal and a dependent God, Christologies from above and below, the legal and the relational, and vicarious atonement and Christus Victor. *Covenant and Salvation* challenged the choice between forensic-extrinsic and effective-participatory soteriologies.

Picking up where *Covenant and Salvation* left off, *People and Place* highlights the inextricable connection between union with Christ (soteriology) and the communion of saints (ecclesiology). After plotting ecclesiology on the map of the redemptive-historical economy (ascension, Pentecost, and Parousia), I explore the source or origin of the church in proclamation and sacrament (part 1), its consequent identity and mission (part 2), with two concluding chapters on the destiny of God's pilgrim people in their royal procession to Zion (part 3). As I have tried to do throughout this series, in this work I interact at some length with alternative proposals.

"The Church as Covenant" is Veli-Matti Kärkkäinen's label for Reformed ecclesiology.[1] Of course, the Reformed tradition hardly has a patent on this widely attested biblical motif. However, it has been distinguished by the extent to which covenantal thinking structures its thinking about the church and, as I

---

1. Veli-Matti Kärkkäinen, *An Introduction to Ecclesiology: Ecumenical, Historical and Global Perspectives* (Downers Grove, IL: InterVarsity Press, 2002), chap. 4.

have argued throughout this series, much else besides. Rooted in the history of Israel, the covenant of grace provides the proper context for situating a New Testament ecclesiology. Given the current challenges presented by contractual theory and praxis in our culture, along with overcorrections currently on offer, a covenantal approach is especially relevant for current reflection.

Taking its coordinates from the economy of grace as determined by the ascension, Pentecost, and the Parousia, each chapter offers an alternative to two apparent extremes in contemporary ecclesiological proposals. The first tendency is to conflate head and members in a single subject: the whole Christ (*totus Christus*). This trajectory often presupposes a panentheistic ontology, a synergistic soteriology, and assimilates Christology to ecclesiology. The result, I argue, is the metaphysical paradigm of overcoming estrangement and the ascent of mind applied to ecclesiology: there is no need for Christ to return bodily, since he has already returned in and as the church. The second trajectory distinguishes the true body of Christ from the visible church as a historical institution, even to the point of setting them in opposition.

These divergent trajectories continue to suggest themselves in consideration of the church's unity, holiness, catholicity, and apostolicity. Through this section I elaborate a view of the church as simultaneously unity and plurality, united to yet distinct from Christ, justified and sinful, eschatological event and historical institution, mother of the faithful and missionary to the world, participating already through Word and sacrament in the powers of the age to come while constantly on the verge of being assimilated back into this passing age. In this volume my goal is to demonstrate the potential of a covenantal model for integrating the critical and mutually dependent themes of the church as people and as place, with an urgent concern for contemporary practice as well as theory.

Along with those for whom I have expressed gratitude throughout this series, I would especially repeat my appreciation for the team at Westminster John Knox, especially Donald McKim, Daniel Braden, and Julie Tonini. Thanks also to friends who looked this manuscript over to offer suggestions for its improvement, especially Brannan Ellis and Ryan Glomsrud. Amazingly, my wife, Lisa, has not left me during this project (which I began before we were married), but in fact has been a constant source of encouragement and exhortation. I am also grateful to my four children who constantly remind me that the covenant is a living reality and to Christ United Reformed Church in Santee, for exhibiting in concrete ways what it means to be a local expression of that one holy, catholic, and apostolic church.

Chapter One

Real Absence, Real Presence

Ecclesiology and the Economy of Grace

The resurrection and ascension of Jesus generate a remarkable paradox. Right at the place where the Suffering Servant has been exalted as conquering Lord, the firstfruit of a new creation, and the head of a body, he disappears. However, precisely in that place that is vacated by the one who has ascended, a church emerges. Endeavoring to locate ecclesiological reflection on the map of the Trinitarian economy of grace, this chapter fleshes out the redemptive-historical context for the rest of the volume.

THE ASCENSION OF CHRIST
IN REDEMPTIVE-HISTORICAL CONTEXT

The most direct ascension account comes from Luke. Meeting two of his disillusioned disciples on the road, the recently risen (though as yet unrecognized) Jesus pushes them regarding their knowledge of the Scriptures: "'Was it not necessary that the Messiah should *suffer these things* and *then enter into his glory?*' Then beginning with Moses and all the prophets, he interpreted to them the things about himself in all the scriptures" (Luke 24:13–27, emphasis added). Commanded to

1

remain in Jerusalem until the promised Spirit is given, so that they might be "clothed with power from on high," we read, "Then he led them out as far as Bethany, and, lifting up his hands, he blessed them. While he was blessing them, he withdrew from them and was carried up into heaven. And they worshiped him, and returned to Jerusalem with great joy; and they were continually in the temple blessing God" (vv. 50–53).

Acts 1 reprises this episode in its opening verses. The promise of the Holy Spirit to endow them for their witness to the ends of the earth is reiterated, followed by the ascension report:

> When he had said this, as they were watching, he was lifted up, and a cloud took him out of their sight. While he was going and they were gazing up toward heaven, suddenly two men in white robes stood by them. They said, "Men of Galilee, why do you stand looking up toward heaven? This Jesus, who has been taken up from you into heaven, will come in the same way as you saw him go into heaven." (Acts 1:6–11)

Thus the ascension (and Parousia) now became part of the gospel itself. Not only was Jesus crucified and raised according to the prophets, Peter preaches, but the Messiah will be sent again, "that is, Jesus, who must *remain* in heaven *until the time of universal restoration* that God announced long ago through his holy prophets" (Acts 3:20–21, emphasis added).

As they were taught by Jesus in the Olivet and Upper Room discourses (Matt. 24–25 and John 14–16, respectively) and on the road to Emmaus (one can presume, in the rest of the days leading up to the ascension itself), the apostolic preaching that we find in Acts follows the familiar pattern of descent-ascent-return, justifying the confession in the eucharistic liturgy, "Christ has died, Christ is risen, Christ will come again." His departure is as real and decisive as his incarnation, and he "will come [again] in the same way as you saw him go into heaven" (Acts 1:11)—that is, in the flesh. In the meantime, he is absent in the flesh. And yet, in this interim, the Spirit causes the Word to spread and bear fruit, through preaching, baptism, and the Supper. It is this eucharistic tension, occasioned by the ascension, that begins to rearrange our questions, not to mention our answers, with respect to the identity, mission, marks, and ministry of the church.

In the Epistles, the ascension marks the present heavenly work of Jesus Christ on behalf of his church (Rom. 8:33–34; Eph. 4; 1 John 2:1), as the firstfruits of the harvest (1 Cor. 15), who will return from heaven (1 Thess. 4:13–5:11) in judgment and salvation to fulfill the "Day of the Lord" (Rom. 2:5; 1 Thess. 5:2; cf. Heb. 10:25; Jas. 5:3; 2 Pet. 3:10). The ascension is attested in Stephen's vision as he was martyred, not to mention Paul's on his way to Damascus. United to Christ, believers have been seated with him in the heavenly places (Eph. 2:6–7), and there is explicit mention of the ascension (interpreting Ps. 68:18) as the source of the gifts being poured out on the church (Eph. 4:7–10). The writer to the Hebrews appeals to the ascension as part of the contrast between old and new covenant worship (Heb. 7:23–26; 9:25). A further contrast in chapter 10 is that whereas the Levitical priests never sat down during their liturgical service in the sanctuary, "when Christ had offered for all time a single sacrifice for sins, 'he sat down at the right hand of God,' and since then has been waiting until his enemies would be made a footstool for his feet" (vv. 11–13).

More than any work I have come across in recent years, Douglas Farrow's *Ascension and Ecclesia* has sought to remedy the apparent marginalization of the ascension in theology, seeing it as "the point of intersection in Christology, eschatology, and ecclesiology."[1] This is a critical claim, since much of twentieth-century theology has demanded a false choice between history and eschatology. Farrow follows Eric Franklin's suggestion "that the ascension is used by Luke not to *abandon* eschatology for history, as the 'delay of the parousia' scholars would have it, but to bring history into the *service* of eschatology."[2] Only if we misunderstand the nature of this kingdom do we miss the wonder of its inauguration.

However, one problem in the history of interpretation has been to treat the ascension as little more than a dazzling exclamation point for the resurrection rather than as a new event in its own right. The conflation of resurrection and ascension "puts in jeopardy the continuity between our present world and the higher places of the new order established by God in Christ," says Farrow.[3]

Giving the ascension a "docetic" interpretation not only separates this event from Old Testament expectations; it also "eventually rebounds on the doctrine of the resurrection itself—if indeed it is not already the sign of a docetic version of that doctrine—and binds it closely to an otherworldly eschatology that has little in common with that of scripture." "Resurrection comes to mean 'going to heaven,' which in some theologies makes it rather hard to distinguish from dying!" The promise of the angels that "this same Jesus" will return in the flesh simultaneously affirms the *continuity* between our resurrection and Christ's and the *dis*continuity between Jesus-history and the common history of this passing age. Apart from this discontinuity, we substitute "our own story (the story of man's self-elevation) as the real kernel of salvation history in the present age."[4] Christ's pattern of coming, going, and returning in the flesh keeps us from turning Jesus-history into an allegory for the ascent of the mind.

As I argued in *Covenant and Eschatology*, Paul's "two ages" rather than Plato's "two worlds" dominates the cosmological and eschatological horizon.[5] Not the world itself, but "the present form of this world is passing away" (1 Cor. 7:31): its bondage to sin and death.

As for Hebrews, Farrow observes, "the unhappy notion" that it is "a work of Christian Platonism" has been decisively refuted. Rather, this epistle is "the classic

---

1. Cited by Douglas Farrow, *Ascension and Ecclesia* (Edinburgh: T&T Clark, 1999), 16, citing R. Maddox, *The Purpose of Luke-Acts* (Edinburgh: T&T Clark, 1982), 10.
2. Farrow, *Ascension and Ecclesia*, 17.
3. Ibid., 29.
4. Ibid.
5. Michael S. Horton, *Covenant and Eschatology: The Divine Drama* (Louisville, KY: Westminster John Knox Press, 2002), chap. 1.

Christian restatement (in the context of, and over against, an educated *diaspora* Judaism) of the Old Testament journey motif. The journey in question is the exodus, viewed here as a pilgrimage into 'the world to come.'"[6] Psalms 8 and 110, along with Daniel 7, are echoed in the language about Jesus: "namely, that 'he sat down' in the presence of God as the Melchizedekian priest-king. This bit of ascension theology, repeated at key intervals, is the focal point which holds Hebrews together."[7] Thus, "his whole life is seen as an act of self-offering that culminates in the cross. In the ascension this offering is received on high. . . . The reference therefore is not to an ideal or supra-sensual realm but to the divine Rest from which the present creation has been barred, but which Jesus has entered."[8]

Thus the "earthiness" of the redeemed creation in the consummation depends entirely on whether the ascension was a historical, bodily, and pneumatologically constituted event. If Jesus is the firstfruits, a docetic ascension requires a docetic consummation. At the same time, the ascension cannot be reduced to history; it reveals the power of new, eschatological life, not simply of picking up where he left off in his historical existence. With Jesus' resurrection and ascension, a new power is introduced into the matrix of natural and historical existence that could not be produced immanently within it—even within the possibilities of Israel, since Israel too had ended up with the rest of the world, "in Adam."

As the firstfruits of the new creation, Jesus in his ascension does not abandon history but redefines all that has preceded it as the old age of sin and death, subjecting it to judgment. The history of human misery and pomp, presumed autonomy and strife, which can only yield the fruit of condemnation, is now passing away—becoming obsolete. Even now the "age to come" is reconfiguring reality around its glorified head. The time that the church thus occupies because of the ascension is defined neither by full presence nor full absence, but by a eucharistic tension between "this age" and "the age to come." Again Farrow frames the issue nicely:

> The comfort of the *Christus praesens* is clearly grounded in the stubborn and troubling fact of the *Christus absens*. . . . Covenant history and world history have divided in this departure, for in and with Jesus the former has already reached its goal. In the resulting gap a place has opened up for the eucharistic community as a genuinely new entity within world history, albeit a peculiar one with its own peculiar view of the way things are.[9]

Farrow indicates the hermeneutical significance of the "two histories" that arises after the resurrection in the light especially of the breaking of the bread with his disciples. "'Where I am going you cannot come.' It is the divergence of Jesus-

---

6. Ibid., 33; cf. L. D. Hurst, *The Epistle to the Hebrews: Its Background of Thought*, Society for New Testament Studies Monograph Series 65 (Cambridge: Cambridge University Press, 1990); Barnabas Lindars, *The Theology of the Letter to the Hebrews* (Cambridge: Cambridge University Press, 1991).

7. Ibid., 33, referring to Heb. 1:3; 8:2; 10:12; 12:3.

8. Ibid., 34–35.

9. Ibid., 37, 40

history from our own that gives to the ecclesia its character and its name. It is the divergence of Jesus-history from our own that calls for a specifically *eucharistic* link: for the breaking and remoulding, the substantial transformation of worldly reality to bring it into conjunction with the lordly reality of Jesus Christ."[10]

Christ's repatriation in our exalted humanity is a radical *detour from* the form of this present age, ensuring that it is passing away and therefore does not have the last word. Yet because it is *Christ's* repatriation, this detour is not away from this world as nature and history, but *toward its future consummation* beyond sin and death.

THE SIGNIFICANCE OF THE ASCENSION IN CHRISTIAN THOUGHT

This doctrine of the ascension radically challenged Platonism, but it also burst the wineskins of early Jewish eschatology and cosmology.[11] Nevertheless, the church has frequently looked away from the ascension of Christ in the flesh, resolving the eschatological tension by appeal to his omnipresent deity or the notion of a ubiquitous flesh or by substituting the church in the place of its absent Lord.

It was the second-century bishop Irenaeus who, in the face of Gnosticism, particularly stressed the descent of the Son in the flesh, his recapitulation of our fallen existence during his life and his atoning sacrifice in his death, together with the resurrection, ascension, and return in the flesh. He saw the "deification" of believers as their true *humanization*, another inbreathing of the Spirit to make a new creation, alive in Christ, although later writers like Athanasius would say that "God became man that man might become *God*" (emphasis added).[12] So in the history of Christian interpretation, there is the Irenaean concentration on the historical-eschatological economy of grace on one end, and Origen's rationalization and interiorization, away from matter and history. No longer conceived eschatologically (the two ages), the antithesis for Origen was between embodiment and spiritual existence. If Jesus Christ's own glorification was, as Origen said, "more of an ascension of the mind than of the body,"[13] then it follows that ours is as well.

This ascent of mind (from purgation to illumination to contemplation) became a chief source of docetizing tendencies in monasticism and early Christian theology generally. While affirming the ascension in the flesh, Augustine and Athanasius do not seem to have allowed it to have the constitutive role for their cosmology that the incarnation and atonement occupy. They speak of the ascension finally allowing the disciples to concentrate on Jesus' divinity rather than on his humanity.[14] So now the ascension is chiefly a proof of his deity more than his

10. Ibid., 10.
11. Ibid., 35.
12. Ibid., 61.
13. Ibid., 97, citing Origen's *First Principles* 23.2.
14. Ibid., 119–20, citing Augustine, *Sermones* 264; cf. *The Trinity* 1.18.

exaltation as the last Adam. Jesus' being removed from us "exteriorly" in his ascension, says Augustine, allows finally for his filling us up "interiorly," which refers to the divine essence per se rather than to the Spirit. Christ's humanity is necessary "only 'for our weakness.'"[15]

Like Augustine, Athanasius affirms the ascension in the flesh, but neither theologian—particularly when it comes to their mystical and ascetic works—is as thoroughly reshaped as was Irenaeus by the historical economy.[16] The metaphysical apparatus of Platonic ascent was never dismantled, and as a result "the church's sense of its eucharistic precariousness naturally began to fade."[17]

Even as sympathetic a patristics scholar as Hans Urs von Balthasar offered a similar summary of this tendency, especially in "its asceticism and mysticism, . . . a movement of the ascending, step-by-step return of the world potencies into God, unambiguously away from the material to the spiritual. Spiritualization, presented in a thousand different colorations, is the basic tendency of the patristic epoch," with early monasticism in some respects already exhibiting "the peril of this movement."[18]

Looking away from the absence of Jesus of Nazareth, the church as the body of Christ could easily come to see itself as his visible and earthly replacement, Farrow notes, "a mirror of Christ's heavenly triumph."[19] Augustine spoke of a *totus Christus*, the whole Christ consisting of its head and its members. "The *totus Christus* notion combines with a Nestorianizing analysis of the ascension to allow what belongs to Jesus to pass more or less directly into the church."[20] For Augustine, the church is now "'the ladder of heaven on which God descends to earth' and the one [ladder] 'through whom we ascend to him who descended through her [the church] to us.'"[21]

In other words, that which is human about *Jesus*—visibility, temporality, fleshiness—is now transferred to the *church* as a historical body. Jesus proclaimed himself as Jacob's ladder (John 1:50–51), but in his bodily absence the church offers itself for that mediation. The history of Jesus in the flesh is at least implicitly replaced by the history of the church as the kingdom of God. The deity of Christ remains transcendent, but his incarnate existence is "fleshed out" by and as the church.

At the same time, this move can easily lead to a subjective individualism with respect to the Eucharist that denies the social and corporeal nature of the event.[22]

---

15. Ibid., 120, citing Augustine, *Serm.* 264, 270.
16. Ibid., 106.
17. Ibid., 114. Cf. Boethius, *Opuscula sacra*, 4:69: After his resurrection, Jesus "ascends into heaven whence we know that he was never absent, because he is Son of God."
18. Hans Urs von Balthasar, "Patristik, Scholastik, und wir," *Theologie der Zeit* 3 (1939): 88, translated by Edward T. Oakes, *Pattern of Redemption: The Theology of Hans Urs von Balthasar* (New York: Continuum, 2005), 120.
19. Farrow, *Ascension and Ecclesia*, 122.
20. Ibid., 123.
21. Ibid, 154 n. 257.
22. Ibid.

The humanity-divinity dualism is carried over into ecclesiology in "a damaging dichotomy between the church as an institution and the church as the people of God, a dichotomy which still troubles us today. . . . *The eucharistic tension, and the church with it, appears to have broken down into vertical and horizontal, interior and exterior, components*" (emphasis added).[23] Thinking more in terms of a metaphysical rather than eschatological dualism, the church increasingly settled for a less ambiguous and more realized presence of Christ not only *with* but *as* the church.

The substitution of individual and ecclesial ascent for the descent-ascent-return of Christ in the flesh became even more thoroughly secured in the Christian Neoplatonism of Pseudo-Dionysius. Dionysian cosmology is incorporated into Byzantine theology through Maximus and in Western theology mostly by Thomas Aquinas. Although Christ is the summit of the Dionysian hierarchy, this is less the historical Christ than the "divine mind" transcending all flesh and history—ensuring the virility of Origen's ascent of mind in the medieval era.[24] "Luther's judgment in *The Babylonian Captivity of the Church* that Denys 'platonizes more than he Christianizes' is not easily dismissed."[25] Although the descent and ascent in the flesh are affirmed, the ascent that really matters is that of the individual soul. "It means, as usual," Farrow judges, "a turning from the earthly Jesus to the cosmic Christ," whom we imitate in our own ascension of mind.[26]

For Thomas, Christ had bodily ascended, yet the omnipresent Logos could generate a eucharistic body that was nevertheless nonspatial, further undermining the true humanity (and therefore real absence) of Jesus Christ.[27] On one hand, this represents an overrealized eschatology; at the same time, however, "as Calvin noticed long ago," what is "realized" is something less than "his specificity as a particular man. Christ everywhere really means Jesus of Nazareth nowhere." The course of Christ's descent-ascent-Parousia in the flesh is transformed into the soul's intellectual and moral ascent: transcending creation and history instead of redeeming it. "In other words, just when the gospel has taught us to think of salvation in the most concrete terms, as an act of God in the flesh and for the flesh, the story of Jesus is turned against itself. His humanity is betrayed and marginalized after

23. Ibid., 125, 127.
24. This interpretation is especially revived in Radical Orthodoxy. John Milbank and Catherine Pickstock, in *Truth in Aquinas* (London: Routledge, 2001), explain, "Aquinas details God's presence to creatures, under the heading of divine substance. This drastically indicates that God's omnipresence simply is God himself, and that there cannot really be any being 'other' than God. . . . God is in himself the repletion of being. . . . Thus at the heart of this chiasmic reversal—Creation and humanity dealt with under divine substance—grace appears for the first time. . . . One could interpret this to mean that, for Aquinas (and here we press perhaps beyond the *nouvelle theologie*), all creatures subsist by grace in the sense that they only subsist in their constant 'return' to full divine self-presence, while intellect simply is the consciousness of this return. Thus not only is the intellect grace; it [also] is in a sense simply the site of manifestation of the creature, and so of grace. Because we are mind, humans specifically are destined to be deified" (37–38).
25. Farrow, *Ascension and Ecclesia*, 127.
26. Ibid., 144.
27. Ibid., 156.

all."[28] Consequently, Farrow contends, "ecclesiology also deteriorates into the impersonal and, indeed, the irrelevant."[29]

Down the church's hierarchical pyramid flowed all heavenly grace, which was no longer disruptive but elevating; no longer coming to the church from outside but oozing from the church's pores. The life of the monk reflected on an individual level the ascent of mind, to which the church was devoted, as it built towers to the heavens. It was the Mass, culminating in the ringing of the bell announcing the transubstantiation, that visually enacted this cosmology, with the focus on the church's atoning offering to God rather than on God's communication of Christ and all his benefits to his people. In fact, the laity were mere spectators, receiving the bread without the cup—and that, only twice a year.

As Farrow reminds us, the growing dominance of icons was also driven by the desire to overcome the absence of Jesus. By rendering the host iconic, it negated the real absence in an "over-realized eschatology, to which the likelihood of a churchly substitute for Jesus always attaches." Thus, the triumph of icons "was not so clear a victory for incarnational theology as it is usually made out to be," since it confused "a Platonic participation and transformation with an eschatological one."[30] Even icons of the ascension "rapidly became icons of the Virgin more than icons of Christ. For it is these which provide the most eloquent testimony to a diminishing Jesus and a larger-than-life church."[31]

The church's panoply of "sacred images on a graduated scale: saints lesser and greater, the holy angels, Mary, Christ, the Trinity—a veritable Jacob's ladder with humanity at one end and divinity at the other, and those whom it wished to honour somewhere in between"—created a pyramid of grace that one could ascend even from the lowest rung.[32] The space between the ascended Christ and his ecclesial body was increasingly filled by ecclesiastical accessories.

With the natural body of Jesus despatialized in Thomas's formulation, the miracle of transubstantiation "placed Christ fully in the church's possession," notes Farrow. "Indeed, it meant that the church now controlled the parousia. At the ringing of a bell the *Christus absens* became the *Christus praesens*. . . . Seated comfortably with the Christ-child on its lap, the church soon became his regent rather than his servant. In short, its Marian ego, already out of control at the beginning of the eucharistic debates, afterwards knew no bounds."[33] This totalizing and absolutizing trend is evident in the bull of Pope Boniface VIII, *Unam Sanctam* (1302), which consolidated papal power over all souls and bodies, both the ecclesiastical and civil spheres, requiring submission as necessary for salvation.

Henri de Lubac traces this path from Boniface to Trent. As he reminds us, the earlier Middle Ages recognized a *corpus triforme*: a threefold body that included

---

28. Ibid., 13.
29. Ibid., 14.
30. Ibid., 150–51.
31. Ibid., 152.
32. Ibid.
33. Ibid., 157.

the natural, eucharistic, and mystical bodies. The mystical body referred to the church during this era, but at the Council of Trent, it came to refer to the Eucharist.[34] Increasingly, the church as a communion generated by the Eucharist was replaced with a legalistic model of the church as a social institution with juridical power. Karl Rahner points out,

> This led theologians to concentrate in the definition of the Church on its juridical and visible reality and to give less prominence to the reality of grace. With Bellarmine the juridical power of the Pope enters into the definition of the Church, as does the magisterium into that of tradition. But there is no longer any mention of the relation of the Eucharist to the Church.[35]

Nominalism as well as reaction against the Reformation and Jansenism deepened the late medieval emphasis on the church as a juridical institution.[36] "Of the notion of the mystical body there remained above all the external and socially organized aspect of the Church," says Rahner. "The pneumatological aspects, the life of the faithful, the Eucharist, and the communion between the local Churches, were passed over practically in silence."[37]

"Where the church is seen as the express image of an ascending Christ who is all but absorbed into the divine Reason," Farrow judges, "ecclesiology is bound to move along an absolutist course."[38] As a result, the church itself is no longer placed under the judgment of its Lord. The ecclesial substitution is not only *occasioned* by the bodily absence of its Lord. Farrow goes so far as to suggest,

> Western ecclesiology . . . *requires* a completely absent Christ if it is to provide instead that miraculous eucharistic one who will underwrite the programme of the church, a programme always in danger of becoming fully immanentist, and hence absolutist, in nature. . . . With Duns Scotus, who applied his famous maximalism to Christ and Mary alike, the west began to look towards the idea of the Logos incarnate in all things, and to explore more confidently a ubiquitarian Christology. His lead was followed by Nicholas of Cusa, who situated the ascended Christ in a place that cannot really be defined in terms of place, but is at once "the centre and the inclusive periphery of all spiritual beings," and thus also of the cosmos as such. The resurgence of neoplatonism and even of Hermeticism, that *prisca theologia* which the later Middle Ages shared with the Renaissance, must also be taken into account here. It testifies to the tenacity of a pre-Christian sacramentalist worldview, of panentheism. That was a worldview naturally resistant to the hard edge of biblical eschatology, but quite comfortable with a hidden Christ who is always ascending and a Mary who is always bringing him down again; with an endless liturgical rhythm in which the

---

34. See Henri de Lubac, *Corpus Mysticum*, 2nd ed. (Paris: Aubier, 1949), esp. 281–88; idem, *The Splendour of the Church*, trans. Rosemary Sheed (London: Sheed & Ward, 1956).

35. Karl Rahner, "The Church," in *Sacramentum Mundi: An Encyclopedia of Theology*, ed. Karl Rahner SJ et al., vol. 1 (New York: Herder & Herder, 1968), 315–16.

36. Ibid., 317.

37. Ibid.

38. Farrow, *Ascension and Ecclesia*, 159.

parousia (not unlike the philosophers' stone) is always within reach yet forever receding.[39]

The church in its historical visibility was unambiguously identified with the eschatological (so-called "invisible") church of the elect. Similarly distinctions between Christ (glorified head) and body (awaiting glorification) as well as Christ's work and ecclesial agency were barely legible. The church, according to post-Tridentine theology, was an unambiguous, juridical, fully realized and wholly immanent form of the kingdom of God, with absolute power located in the earthly-historical *vicar* (substitute) of Christ.

Farrow suggests that Calvin, like Irenaeus, brought attention back to the economy and thus to the *problem* of Christ's absence. "'But why,' asked Calvin, 'do we repeat the word "ascension" so often?' To answer in our own words, it was because he found it necessary to reckon more bravely than the other reformers with the absence of Christ as a genuine problem for the church." Apart from the ascension in the flesh, says Calvin, we are robbed of Christ's likeness to us; we lose the significance of the Spirit's role in uniting us to the ascended Christ, and the reality of Christ's bodily return is called into question. More like Irenaeus, then, Calvin returns our focus to the economy of redemption: the actual history of Jesus of Nazareth from descent (incarnation and his earthly ministry of redemption), to his ascension and heavenly ministry, to the Parousia at the end of the age.

> To maintain a real absence is also to maintain a real continuity between the saviour and the saved. All of this demonstrates that Calvin had a better grasp on the way in which the Where? question is bound up with the Who? question. That indeed was his critical insight into the whole debate. Calvin saw that neither a Eutychian response (Jesus is omnipresent) nor a Nestorian one (absent in one nature but present in the other) will do, since either way Christ's humanity is neutralized and his role as our mediator put in jeopardy. It is the God-man who is absent and the God-man whose present we nevertheless require. . . . A "species of absence" and a "species of presence" thus qualify our communion with Christ, who remains in heaven until the day of judgment. It is *we* who require eucharistic relocation.[40]

Instead of moving from Eucharist to ascension, Calvin moved in the other direction, and this led him to stress "the particularity of Jesus without sacrificing sacramental realism." This "forced him to seek a *pneumatological solution* to the problem of the presence and the absence" (emphasis added).[41] Despite all of these advances, Farrow rightly points out that despite directing attention to the Parousia, Calvin treats the presence-absence dialectic in almost exclusively spatial terms.[42] Pushing this account in a more eschatological direction will be one of my goals in chapters 7 and 8.

39. Ibid., 163.
40. Ibid., 176–77.
41. Ibid., 177–78.
42. Ibid., 178.

As the Enlightenment rejected in principle any external authority that might judge or save, the ascent of mind (interiorization) was taken to remarkable extremes. Joachim of Fiore's vision of a "third age"—the Golden Age of the Spirit, when no one would need external aids (including the church and its public ministry) but know everything immediately and intuitively—sparked medieval and early modern apocalypticism that can be discerned in ecstatic movements (both Roman Catholic and Protestant) all the way to the present.[43] Lessing appropriated for the Enlightenment the Joachite prophecy of a "third age" when the inner light of reason would transcend any need for external authority or its mediation to us in creaturely forms.[44] The vertical ascent of mind also became a horizontal ascent of historical progress. The Irenaean trajectory seemed to be almost entirely overwhelmed by the Origenist and even gnostic triumph of spirit (universal idea) over matter (particular actualization).

When pure religion (i.e., morality), Absolute Spirit's unfolding self-consciousness, or God-consciousness, is made the central theme of religion, the last thing that one is concerned about is the whereabouts of Jesus in the flesh. As Farrow notes, Schleiermacher collapsed "the spatial distance on which Calvin had insisted into something radically Lutheran, that is, to render it in strictly existential terms."[45] Now the church itself became the topos of Jesus. "Pursuing Augustine's line, Schleiermacher argued that it was altogether necessary for Christ's visible presence to come to an end, that his invisible and spiritual work in human society might succeed."[46] In his theology, the "ecclesial substitution for

43. On Joachim of Fiore's "three ages," see especially Marjorie Reeves, *Joachim of Fiore and the Prophetic Future: A Medieval Study in Historical Thinking* (London: SPCK, 1976); Bernard McGinn, *The Calabrian Abbot: Joachim of Fiore in the History of Western Thought* (New York: Harper & Row, 1985); Delno C. West and Sandra Zimdars-Swartz, *Joachim of Fiore: A Study in Spiritual Perception and History* (Bloomington: Indiana University Press, 1983). Radical Anabaptists like Thomas Müntzer saw their movement as a fulfillment of the Joachite prophecy. This significance of Joachim for Hegel's thought is treated in fascinating detail by Cyril O'Regan, *The Heterodox Hegel*, SUNY Series in Hegelian Studies (Albany: State University of New York Press, 1994), 270–85. In that work, O'Regan also provides tremendous insight into Hegel's dependence on ancient Gnosticism and its trajectory to the modern era. Amos Yong, *The Spirit Poured Out on All Flesh* (Grand Rapids: Baker Academic, 2005), 248–49, points out the adaptation of Joachim's thesis by Wesley's successor, John Fletcher, with the dispensation of the Father corresponding to God's work among nonbelievers; the dispensation of the Son corresponding to God's work among Jews, Gentile monotheists, and the disciples of Jesus ("carnal" and "imperfect" during Jesus' ministry); and the dispensation of the Spirit, which makes perfection possible through the baptism of the Spirit. Yong even points out the similarities with Joachim's speculations (249) and draws on Fletcher's view that "Deists, Socinians, Unitarians, and even Arians," as well as adherents of other religions, are also children of God in whom the Spirit is at work (248–50). Explicit appeals to Joachim's Trinitarian apocalyptic (however revised) are remarkably plentiful in contemporary theologies, especially those that display a creative reappropriation of Hegelian thinking. Jürgen Moltmann displays this interest throughout his remarkable series of studies in dogmatics, and on the dust jacket of *History and the Triune God* (New York: Crossroad, 1992) is reproduced Joachim's chart of the three ages.

44. Lessing adopted the Joachite prophecy of the third age of the Spirit for the Enlightenment ("The Education of the Human Race," in *Lessing's Theological Writings*, selected and translated by Henry Chadwick (1956; repr., Palo Alto, CA: Stanford University Press, 1967), 96–97.

45. Farrow, *Ascension and Ecclesia*, 182.

46. Ibid., 182–85.

Jesus is finally perfected."[47] Hegel put it even more boldly: "Christ dies; only as dead is he exalted to Heaven and sits at the right hand of God; only thus is he Spirit. He himself says: 'When I am no longer with you, the Spirit will guide you into all truth.'"[48] Thus, Farrow observes,

> Christology had become a discourse on the dead Christ. To combine an ascension theology with a *theologia crucis* was Irenaeus' achievement against the Gnostics; to make them one and the same thing was the achievement of Hegel, who did much to translate Gnosticism into a modern idiom. "The history of the resurrection and ascension of Christ to the right hand of God," he insisted, began at the point where the history of the crucified received "a spiritual interpretation."[49]

Hegel's dialectic is Dionysian differentiations and unions.[50] "With Hegel, then, we appear to stand in close proximity to the end of a long and troubled tradition of immanentism."[51] Finally, with Hegel's left-wing disciples such as Feuerbach and Nietzsche, it is the flip side: "sheer absence."[52]

Yet today a revived Hegelianism gives us the "cosmic Christ," a *totus Christus* that merges Christology into ecclesiology. As I will point out in greater detail in part 2, its effects can be seen across the ecclesiastical spectrum today, from Radical Orthodoxy to the Emerging Church movement within evangelicalism.[53] The upshot of such proposals is the identification of Christ's person and work with the historical development of the church—and through the church's extension of Christ, with the whole cosmos itself. In effect, the incarnation undoes the ascension by replacing it. Liberated from all restrictions of time and space, this version of the ascension redefines the historical Jesus as someone who has never really left us, but at the price once again of putting his actual existence as a historical person into question.[54] In the place of his historical life stands the church in all of its (or rather, his) glory. As Christ and his work are assimilated to the church and its work, similar conflations emerge between the gospel and culture, the Word of God and the experience of our particular group, the church's commission and the transformation of the kingdoms of this age into the kingdom of Christ.[55]

47. Ibid., 186.
48. Ibid.
49. Ibid., 187.
50. Ibid., 188.
51. Ibid., 189.
52. Ibid., 191. Obviously, this narrative stands in some contrast with that of Radical Orthodoxy (esp. John Milbank), which regards modernity as the consummation of nominalism, entirely away from Christian Platonism.
53. For the extent to which this has become a dominant theme in more popular versions of the movement, see, e.g., Brian McLaren, *A Generous Orthodoxy* (Grand Rapids: Zondervan, 2004), 245–66. However, it has been a staple in mainstream evangelical theology and missiology for decades. For an evenhanded critique, see Todd Billings, "'Incarnational Ministry': A Christological Evaluation and Proposal," *Missiology: An International Review* 32, no. 2 (April 2004): 187–201.
54. Farrow, *Ascension and Ecclesia*, 195, quoted in *The Tablet*, May 30, 1992.
55. Among myriad examples, one could cite Karen Baker-Fletcher and Garth Kasimu Baker-Fletcher, *My Sister, My Brother* (Maryknoll: Orbis Books, 1997), 275–76, where the church's kingdom-establishing work here and now yields a "ONEness" between the divine and human as well as the church and the world.

Thus, we might say, if the answer to *Where?* is "Everywhere," then the answer to *Who?* is "Everything." As Farrow concludes, all of these views claim to be Irenaean, "incarnational," and antignostic, but in truth they are much closer to Gnosticism.[56] "Its chief theological characteristics are to be found in its universalism, its synergism, and its panentheism, all of which justify us in labeling it as Origenist rather than Irenaean."[57] To my mind, Farrow is justified in concluding, "To perpetuate a discourse on the dead Christ by renaming him the cosmic Christ, bold though it may be, gives every appearance of being a bluff—an evasion of Nietzsche's challenge, not an answer to it. It looks, that is, like an attempt to excuse ourselves from any direct encounter with the real absence."[58]

It is the church's recurring temptation to look away from the absence—toward a false presence, often substituting itself as an extension of Christ's incarnation and reconciling work—that distracts it from directing the world's attention to the Parousia in the future. Yet a church that does not acknowledge Christ's absence is no longer focused on Christ but is tempted to idolatrous substitutions in the attempt to seize Canaan prematurely. The parallel with Moses is striking: "When the people saw that Moses delayed to come down from the mountain, the people gathered around Aaron, and said to him, 'Come, make gods for us, who shall go before us; as for this Moses, the man who brought us up out of the land of Egypt, we do not know what has become of him'" (Exod. 32:1).

REAL PRESENCE: PENTECOST AND THE DIVINE DISRUPTION OF THIS AGE

Having underscored the importance of meeting the *absence* of Christ with the appropriate anxiety and tension of the disciples themselves, we turn our attention now to the *presence* of Christ, mediated by the Spirit.

The Spirit of Promise

Beginning with the intra-Trinitarian covenant of redemption in eternity, classic covenant theology underscored that not even election can be attributed to the Father apart from the Son and the Spirit. Dividing the works of creation, redemption, and ecclesiology between the divine persons, even for heuristic reasons, implicitly detracts from the affirmation that the works of the Godhead *ad extra* are undivided (*opera trinitatis ad extra sunt indivisa*). In every work of the Trinity, the new creation as well as the old, the Spirit brings about the perlocutionary effect of the Father's speaking in the Son.

In the flood narrative, we encounter the first instance of the Spirit in avian form, announcing the appearance of dry land. Exodus 19 echoes Genesis 1 and

56. Farrow, *Ascension and Ecclesia*, 198.
57. Ibid., 220–21.
58. Ibid., 221. Cf. my opening chapter in *Covenant and Eschatology*, "Eschatology after Nietzsche."

2, with the Spirit descending, hovering over the waters, to separate them in order for dry land to appear, and then to lead by pillar and cloud to the Sabbath rest.[59] In Exodus 19, this descent of the Spirit is represented by the sound of winged creatures in a moving cloud, a theme that will return at Pentecost. To the Spirit particularly is attributed the dignity of transforming created space into covenantal place: a home for communion between Creator and creatures, extending to the ends of the earth in waves of kingdom labor. In the prophets, the Spirit is associated with a glory-cloud (Isa. 63:11–14; Hag. 2:5) and wind—*ruach*, the same Hebrew word for spirit/the Spirit (Ps. 104:1–3). It is by this Spirit that all things are created and renewed (v. 30). This *ruach* creates a place for covenantal communion in creation, descends in judgment at various points in redemptive history, and parts the waters of the exodus. In the new creation, this same Spirit descends above the incarnate Son in approving judgment with the Father.

Like our own breath, the Spirit carries the word spoken by the Father in the Son to its recipient, constituting the creature's identity. All of these passages find their echo in the vivid description of Pentecost, as we will see. Creation and new creation are interdependent themes, especially with the unifying theme of the procession of creation into the "seventh-day" consummation led by the creature bearing the Creator's image and likeness.

Parallel to the image-of-God motif, there is a close connection not only with *glory* but also with the role of the Spirit as divine *witness*.[60] In creation, exodus, conquest, even in exile, the Spirit preserves a cloud of witnesses in the cosmic courtroom. Yet from the very beginning this witness of the Spirit involves judgment as well as salvation (Gen. 3:8).[61] The Son is the archetypal *imago Dei*, and the Spirit is both the one who upholds Christ in his earthly work and clothes him with eschatological glory in the resurrection as a legal verdict with moral, aesthetic, and ontological effects.[62]

The character of the Spirit as divine witness is closely related to "the Angel of the Presence" (Isa. 63:9–14; Exod. 33:2, 12–15). In the prophets, being taken into Yahweh's council-chamber, where they receive their court brief, is identified with being "in the Spirit." All of these judicial missions anticipate the New Testament events. Kline notes,

> Yet the Glory is not a static structure, but mobile, for the throne is a char-
> iot-throne, Spirit directed and propelled through the winged beings, a vehi-
> cle of divine judgment, moving with the swiftness of light to execute the

59. M. G. Kline, *Images of the Spirit* (1980; repr., S. Hamilton, MA: self-published, 1986), 14–15.
60. See M. G. Kline, "The Holy Spirit as Covenant Witness" (ThM thesis, Westminster Theological Seminary, 1972).
61. God came "in the cool of the day" is a less likely rendering than "in the Spirit of the day." Although *ruach* can be variously translated as wind or spirit, the sense (esp. in the obvious context of judgment) seems to favor the Spirit coming in the day of judgment. See Kline, *Images of the Spirit*, chap. 4; cf. M. G. Kline, *Kingdom Prologue: Genesis Foundations for a Covenantal Worldview* (Overland Park, KS: Two Age Press, 2000), 128–29.
62. Kline, *Images of the Spirit*, 16.

sentence of the King. . . . Also, the dual columnar formation assumed by the Glory-cloud as pillar of cloud and pillar of fire is conceptualized in the Bible as the feet of God standing as divine witness.[63]

He adds, "The ark of the covenant located beneath the enthroned Glory is accordingly called God's footstool (Isa. 60:13)."[64] We see then the "covenantal cast of the whole creation narrative." The Glory-cloud standing as covenantal witness in Genesis 1:2 reappears in the exodus re-creation in the promise of a latter-day temple more glorious than the first temple (see Hag. 2:5), and in the new creation with the baptism of Jesus, descending as a dove. Finally, in Revelation 10:1–11, "the Glory-figure is seen clothed with a cloud, rainbow haloed, with face like the sun and feet like pillars of fire, standing astride creation with his hand raised in oath to heaven, swearing by him who on the seventh day finished his creating of the heaven, the earth, the sea, and all their hosts that in the days of the seventh trumpet the mystery of God will be finished."[65]

The Creator Spirit is, even in the very beginning, a divine witness to the goal of creation: the consummation.[66] Thwarted by Adam in the first creation, this goal is finally achieved by the last Adam in the new creation. No wonder, then, that the outpouring of the Spirit is identified with the "last days" and the age to come. Already in creation, therefore, we meet the Spirit of promise: the one who propels creation toward its goal, which is nothing less than the consummation at the end of the trial. This interpretation of the relationship between the Spirit of Glory and judgment is especially supported by 2 Corinthians 3 and 4. In Christ, the veil that prevents us from seeing the glory of God in the face of Christ is now removed (2 Cor. 3:1–6).

The Spirit who clothed Christ in our flesh and in consummated glory now clothes us with Christ. In all of these various ways, the appeal is to the old covenant history of royal investiture that begins in Eden, with the Spirit's in-breathing, followed by all of the priestly imagery of glorious vestments and the event of Christ breathing on his disciples. "When the investiture figure is used," writes Kline, "what is 'put on' is the new man created in the image of God (Eph. 4:24; Col. 3:10), or Christ the Lord (Rom. 13:14; Gal. 3:27; cf. Eph. 2:15; 4:13), or the resurrection glory of immortality (I Cor. 15:53; II Cor. 5:2ff.). . . . In the vocabulary of Peter, 'partakers of the divine nature' expresses renewal in the image of God (II Peter 1:4)."[67] Believers are now, in Christ, "the image and glory of God" (1 Cor 11:7).

Having filled the earthly sanctuary, this Spirit of glory now fills the eschatological end-time temple: the church as Christ's body. If the Son is the place in God where covenant community is created, then the Spirit is the one who turns

---

63. Ibid., 18–19.
64. Ibid., n. 21.
65. Ibid., 19.
66. Ibid., 20.
67. Ibid., 29.

a house into a home. This is why the Spirit is especially identified with sanctification: consecrating natural, creaturely reality—people, places, and things. Not only created to worship God, humanity was created to be the temple of God filled with the Spirit of Glory. The inbreathing of the Spirit that makes humanity a living being in Genesis 2:7 reappears throughout redemptive history, as in the temple-filling episode in Ezekiel 37, as well as Mary's annunciation (Luke 1:35), culminating in the prophetic anticipation of Pentecost, when Jesus breathed on the disciples and issued his performative utterance, "Receive the Holy Spirit" (John 20:22).

Echoing the original creation, the Father and the Spirit issue their heavenly benediction on Jesus in his baptism (Mark 1:11), repeated by the Father at the transfiguration (9:7), testifying from heaven. Yet as encouraging as this verdict was for Jesus, given the stubborn opposition of the world (often including the covenant people) to Christ, a further stage of redemptive history was required. The witness of mortals on earth would have been insufficient in winning our consent. The world (even the disciples themselves) required not only a divine witness from heaven *to* us, but a vital testimony on earth, *within* us, bringing about the "Amen" of the covenant partner. In the cosmic courtroom, the Spirit is the archetypal Cloud of Witness, whose animating agency creates a cloud of witnesses.

We recognize this close connection between the Spirit and judgment in Peter's Pentecost sermon, where he announces the fulfillment of Joel's prophecy, which itself is unmistakably judicial in character. As Raymond Dillard comments, Joel 3:1–5 (2:28–32E) is a gloss on Numbers 11:1–12:8. The plea of a weary Moses that God would pour out his Spirit on all of God's people is explicitly promised in Joel's prophecy. Both texts affirm that "God's people will prophesy" (Num. 11:25–29; Joel 3:1 [2:28E]) and "the outpouring of God's Spirit will not be the experience of [only] the few (Num 11:25; 12:6), but rather the experience of all (Joel 3:1 [2:28E])."

> Both contexts also reflect a judicial function in the possession of the Spirit. The seventy elders are to be Moses' surrogates and to serve as judges (Num 11:17; cf. Exod 18:13–27); in Joel, the eschatological outpouring of prophetic enduement is conjoined with the Lord's coming in judgment on the nations (Joel 3:4 [2:31E]; 4:12 [3:23E]). Multitudes come not to *make* a decision, but to *hear* the decision of God (4:14 [3:14E]). (emphasis added)[68]

Pentecost inaugurates the day of reckoning—not the final day of judgment, but its prolepsis, as Israel and the nations are gathered to be judged and justified in these last days before the last day, in which only judgment will prevail.

Before they speak, they must hear. Before they act, they must be acted upon. Before they are made witnesses, they must themselves be saved by the proclamation of the gospel. "You are witnesses of these things," Jesus told the disciples

---

68. Raymond B. Dillard, "Intrabiblical Exegesis and the Effusion of the Spirit in Joel," in *Creator, Redeemer, Consummator: A Festschrift for Meredith G. Kline*, ed. Howard Griffith and John R. Muether (Greenville, SC: Reformed Academic Press, 2000), 90.

before his ascension. "And see, I am sending upon you what my Father promised; so stay here in the city until you have been clothed with power from on high" (Luke 24:48–49). Dillard points out the parallels between the Spirit's judicial missions in the Old Testament and at Pentecost: "Both contexts also include a fire theophany appearing in judgment (Num 11:1–3; Joel 1:19–20; 2:3, 5; 3:3 [2:30E]). In each the outpouring of the Spirit is in a context which includes judgment for some in Israel (Num 11:31–35; 12:9–15; Joel 3:5 [2:32E]); not all survive."[69] However, at Pentecost God manifests himself not in a devouring fire (Acts 2:3–4); rather, the Shekinah glory of God divides and takes up residence within individuals; the divine presence will not dwell *above* the Most Holy Place, but *within* his people, who have become his temple (Acts 2:3; 1 Cor. 3:16–17; 6:19; 2 Cor. 6:16; Eph. 2:19–22), making them all witnesses. Just as the Spirit upheld Jesus in his trial as the last Adam—"the true and faithful witness," so he is sent to indwell us (individually and corporately) as a cloud of witnesses.

Before arriving at the event of Pentecost itself, it may be worth recalling that the Sinaitic economy knew three major feasts. The first, Passover, held on the fourteenth day of the first month, commemorated the exodus (Exod. 12; Lev. 23:5–8; Num. 28:16–25; Deut. 16:1–8). This was followed fifty days later by the Feast of Weeks (also known as the Feast of Harvest, Firstfruits, and Pentecost), which marked the end of the grain harvest (Exod. 23:16; 34:22; Lev. 23:15–22; Num. 28:26–31; Deut. 16:9–12). In *Jubilees* 6:17–22, Pentecost is actually raised to the level of the Sabbath itself and is designated the "Feast of the Covenant-oath." In the seventh month, the Feast of Tabernacles celebrated the end of the agricultural year and God's leading of Israel through the wilderness (Lev. 23:39–43; Num. 29:12–38; Deut. 16:13–15).

It was at the Feast of Tabernacles where Jesus, during the water-drawing ceremony commemorating the provision of water in the wilderness and the lamp-lighting ritual, offered himself as the fountain of living water. "Now he said this about the Spirit, which believers in him were to receive; for as yet there was no Spirit [given] because Jesus was not yet glorified" (John 7:37–39). Notice the close connection again between Jesus-history and the Spirit's work in the economy of grace. Until the head is glorified, there is no archetypal image or exalted and consummated state for the ecclesial body to share, even proleptically.

Then, soon after he makes his triumphal entry into Jerusalem for Passover—exactly where and when the disciples' triumphalism was at its peak, Jesus began to prepare them for his departure: the triumphal entry into the heavenly sanctuary (John 14–16). Jesus, the greater Joshua, passed through the waters of judgment and entered triumphantly into the promised land, having conquered all opposition. And now the Spirit directs the Jesus-led procession of his people into the homeland being prepared for them. Yet, from the perspective of the disillusioned disciples, right where it would appear that the kingdom would proceed from glory to glory, there is a jarring interruption with the cross, resurrection,

69. Ibid., 91.

and ascension standing between Palm Sunday and Christ's return. It is this space—the "epicletic interim," that the church would occupy in this age, so Jesus introduces the disciples to the Holy Spirit.

The Spirit at Pentecost

Acts 1 marks the transition from the ascension to Pentecost. Ordered by Christ to remain in Jerusalem "for the promise of the Father": the baptism with the Holy Spirit "not many days from now" (Acts 1:1–5). About 120 people were gathered in the upper room, near the temple, where pilgrims had gathered for the feast from far-flung regions.

> When the day of Pentecost had come, they were all together in one place. And suddenly from heaven there came a sound like the rush of a violent wind, and it filled the entire house where they were sitting. Divided tongues, as of fire, appeared among them, and a tongue rested on each of them. All of them were filled with the Holy Spirit and began to speak in other languages, as the Spirit gave them ability. (Acts 2:1–4)

Astonished that uneducated Galileans were proclaiming the gospel in their own languages, the visitors' reactions ranged from "amazed and perplexed" to outright incredulity: "They are filled with new wine" (vv. 12–13).

The consequence of this amazing event was not unrestrained pandemonium but the public proclamation of the gospel by Peter, with the other apostles standing at his side (vv. 14–36). The one who had cowardly denied Christ three times was now risking his life for the message that the one who had been crucified a short distance from there had been raised and was at God's right hand, returning to judge the earth. Stringing together a series of citations from the prophets and the Psalter, Peter proclaimed Christ and this remarkable descent of the Spirit as the fulfillment of everything the Scriptures had foretold. "Cut to the heart," three thousand people embraced Peter's message and were baptized (vv. 37–41). The Spirit was accomplishing inwardly the perlocutionary effect of the illocutionary speech publicly proclaimed by Peter. United to the true and faithful witness in heaven, and empowered by the indwelling Spirit as witnesses, the rest of Acts can be summarized by the theme "The word of God spread."

When we refuse to collapse the resurrection, ascension, and Parousia into one event, a pneumatological space appears for the time between the times. The Spirit is the mediator of, not the surrogate for, Christ's person and work. The redeeming work of Christ lies behind us, but the perlocutionary effect of that Word is at work in "these last days."

The Spirit and Jesus

Pentecost exhibits all of the marks that Jesus described in John 14–16 with respect to the advent of the Spirit. The Spirit will testify of Christ, convicting the world of sin and judgment, producing faith in Christ as the Messiah of God. Pentecost was at last the beginning—firstfruits—of the harvest of the last days, the real Feast of Firstfruits for which all previous Pentecost feasts had been mere dress rehearsals.

First, Jesus is the Spirit's gift. Before Jesus gave us the Spirit, the Spirit gave us Jesus. Not only conceived by the Holy Spirit, Jesus also was empowered and sustained by the Spirit in his obedient life, miraculous signs, death, and resurrection. Before being sent to bring about our "Amen" to the work of the Son, the Spirit had already strengthened Jesus to fulfill all covenantal righteousness—the decisive "Amen" that restored communion between God and humans.[70]

This coinherence of the work of Jesus and the Spirit restores the covenantal liturgy because it is not merely God talking to himself, but actually a representative human reply to the summons of the Covenant Lord. At last there is a human representative who listens to the Father's word and faithfully follows the Spirit through the wilderness of temptation to the victory that overcomes the world. Both recapitulating Israel's history and raising it to a new (eschatological) stage, from glory to glory, his ministry begins with the announcement, "Then Jesus returned in the power of the Spirit to Galilee, and news of Him went out through all the surrounding region. . . . So He came to Nazareth, where He had been brought up" (Luke 4:14, 16 NKJV). And when handed the scroll in the synagogue on the Sabbath, he read Isaiah 49:8–9: "The Spirit of the LORD is upon me, because he has anointed me to preach the gospel to the poor" (Luke 4:18 NKJV). "Today," he told them, "this Scripture is fulfilled in your hearing" (Luke 4:14–21; cf. Matt. 12:18–21, quoting Isa. 42:1–4).

In Jesus Christ, we recognize both the Lord who speaks and the servant who answers back, in the Spirit, "Here I am." "For in him every one of God's promises is a 'Yes.' For this reason it is through him that we say the 'Amen,' to the glory of God" (2 Cor. 1:20). The equivalent of the divine benediction on the first creation ("God saw everything that he had made, and indeed, it was very good"; Gen. 1:31) is repeated at Jesus' baptism, with the descent of the Spirit in avian form and the Father's speech. After Jesus accepted his commission ("Let it be so now; for it is proper for us in this way to fulfill all righteousness"), "a voice from heaven said, 'This is my Son, the Beloved, with whom I am well pleased" (Matt. 3:13–17). Even his passive obedience is linked to the Spirit. The writer to the Hebrews tells us that Christ's blood sanctifies us in that Christ "through the eternal Spirit offered Himself without spot to God" (Heb. 9:14 NKJV).

Because the promised Spirit has been sent, there are two histories: one defined by this present age, under sin, death, and judgment; and another defined by the age to come. Noting the close relationship between the Spirit and eschatology, Edmund Clowney writes, "The Spirit is with us because we are in the last days (Ac

---

70. When Christology marginalizes the humanity of Christ as the second Adam, it not only loses its connection to the actual history of Israel and Christ's active obedience, but also downplays the work of the Spirit in bringing the Word's life and work to fruition by attributing all saving action to the Son's divinity. I develop this point in *Lord and Servant: A Covenant Christology* (Louisville, KY: Westminster John Knox Press, 2005), 167–69.

2:17; 3:24; 1 Pet 1:10–12)."[71] Just as the Logos can only become flesh by the work of the Spirit, we cannot say "'Jesus is Lord' except by the Holy Spirit" (1 Cor. 12:3).

So, together with the Father, the Spirit is still giving us Jesus Christ, after having given him once and for all in the incarnation. By his Spirit, Christ is accessible to us everywhere without having to redefine his natural body or look away from his going-and-coming in the flesh. It is the Spirit who keeps the history of Jesus and the history of this age in constant contact—and conflict—without allowing the former to become assimilated to the latter. The Spirit, then, is not sent to complete Christ's work. Nor, on the other hand, is the Spirit a latecomer to the scene. All along, the Spirit has brought redemptive history—and its central character, Jesus Christ—to its denouement. That is what it means to live in these last days, the age of the Spirit.

Second, then, the Spirit is Jesus' gift. If it is true that Jesus Christ is the gift of the Father and the Spirit, it is also true that the Spirit is the gift of the Father and the Son. All that I have argued thus far finds its exegetical lodestar in John 14–16, and we will concentrate especially on chapter 15.

What did Jesus teach the disciples that, although they did not recognize it at the time, prepared them for Pentecost? In John 14:26, Jesus announces the imminent arrival of another Paraclete. Not simply "Helper" or "Comforter," as in some translations, *paraklētos* is more accurately translated "Advocate" (as in the NRSV). It is a legal term, equivalent to an attorney, like the prophets of old. Yet in this case, the prophet is not simply a representative of Yahweh but Yahweh in person, while also being the representative of the people. Both Lord and Servant, Jesus Christ promises to send another Advocate, not for determining the outcome of the cosmic trial itself (since this is Jesus' work to do), but to prosecute God's case against the world (bringing conviction of unrighteousness) and intercede for the accused. He will bring about the ultimate *rib* (the Hebrew term for the covenant lawsuit in the prophets), but this time it will lead not simply to another renewal of the Sinai covenant; it will finally deal with sin through Christ's cross and issue in a new heart through the Spirit's regenerating work (Jer. 31:30–33).

It is with this background that Jesus refers to the Spirit as "*another* Advocate," whom the Father will send. The Spirit of Christ is neither the deity nor the soul of Christ, but a distinct person. By trading places with the Spirit, the church's prayer will be answered: "Thy kingdom come. Thy will be done on earth, as it is in heaven" (Matt. 6:10 KJV). The Spirit leads us to die to ourselves (mortification) and live to Christ (vivification), clinging to the promise that our heavenly Advocate is "the propitiation for our sins" (1 John 2:1–2 NKJV). So because of the Spirit's gift of Jesus Christ and Jesus Christ's gift of the Spirit, there are two divine covenant attorneys interceding, testifying, and witnessing: one in the heavenly courtroom, the other in the earthly courtroom—until God's will is done on earth as it is in heaven.

71. Edmund P. Clowney, *The Church: Contours of Christian Theology* (Downers Grove, IL: Inter-Varsity Press, 1995), 66.

It is one thing to be judicially convicted of a crime and sentenced for it, and another to be subjectively convinced of guilt. Christ's work accomplished once and for all is the ground of our forgiveness, reconciliation, justification, and adoption, but it cannot by itself yield repentance, friendship with God, faith, and the filial cry, "Abba, Father!" Upheld by the Spirit, Jesus fulfilled perfectly all that was his alone to achieve. Filled with the same Spirit, we render our imperfect response. Through the Spirit, all that is done by Christ for us, outside of us and in the past, is received and made fruitful within us in the present. In this way, the power that is constitutive of the consummation (the age to come) is already at work now in the world. Through the Spirit's agency, not only is Christ's past work applied to us but his present status in glory also penetrates our own existence in a semirealized manner. The Spirit's work is what connects us here and now to Christ's past, present, and future. As the perfecting power of the Godhead's speech, the Spirit shapes creaturely reality according to the archetypal image of the Son.

Apart from the new birth by the Spirit, one cannot recognize or enter the kingdom of Christ (John 3:3). Not even the external signs that Jesus performed as the true and faithful witness could by themselves bring about faith. Even the religious leaders would not "be convinced even if someone rises from the dead" (Luke 16:30–31). Nothing can be added to Christ's person and work as the ground of redemption, and yet something further must be done in order to bring the ungodly into a living relationship to it. With Christ's glorification, the gates of paradise are open wide, but if he is not to be alone in his exaltation—a head without a body, a vine without branches, or the firstfruits without the harvest—then the new creation must be attended by a power to raise its citizens from spiritual and, finally, physical death. This is why John the Baptist yields to the greater authority of the one who will baptize not only with water but also with the Spirit and with fire (John 1:29–34). Although John was the greatest in the distinguished line of prophets, he is—by virtue of where he stood in redemptive history—the least in the kingdom inaugurated by Christ (Matt. 11:11).

The Spirit's presence announces that the epochs are turning: this present age is giving way to the age to come. The outpouring of the Spirit will guarantee a believing community in "these last days," one that not only remembers Christ's completed work, but is actually inserted into the covenantal history (and eschatology) of its glorified head. As Paul teaches, the Spirit is not only sent *among* believers but *into* them, to indwell them, as a deposit (*arrabōn*) of their final redemption. Even the prophets are said to have been "in the Spirit" from time to time, in the event of revelation, but in these last days every believer is indwelled by the Spirit of prophecy, assuring us of adoption in the present and glorification in the future (Rom. 8:14–16). The prophets themselves anticipated the day when the whole congregation of Israel would be made alive in the Spirit (Ezek. 37).

It is precisely because we "have the firstfruits of the Spirit" that "even we ourselves groan within ourselves, eagerly waiting for the adoption, the redemption of our body" (Rom. 8:23 NKJV; cf. Gal. 4:6). As the *arrabōn* (down payment) of our final redemption, the Spirit gives us the "already" of our participation in

Christ as the new creation, and it is the Spirit within us who gives us the aching hope for the not-yet that awaits us in our union with Christ (Rom. 8:18–28; cf. 2 Cor. 1:22; 5:5; Eph. 1:14).

The *more we receive* from the Spirit of the realities of the age to come, the *more restless we become.* Yet it is a restlessness born not of fear but of having already received a foretaste of the future. Only when we have caught the scent of ever-lasting life and joy that pervades the atmosphere of the consummation does the air of this present age seem stale and redolent of death. Having tasted morsels of the heavenly feast, we no longer find the rich banquets of this age as satisfying. The Spirit's presence always tantalizes us with the more still to be enjoyed, which makes Christian suffering different from either a nihilistic and cynical fate to be accepted with Stoic indifference or a reality to be denied in a spirit of tri-umphalism. Those who are filled with the Spirit are characterized by struggle more than by victory, since it is the Spirit's presence that draws the two ages into conflict and draws out the insurgents of this present evil age to defend their new contested terrain. Where the Spirit indwells, there is peace with God and con-flict within, with the powers of sin and death within us and in the world.

It is therefore crucial to recognize that the Spirit is not a replacement for Jesus nor a parallel redeemer. The Spirit does not fill up the gap between the Jesus his-tory and our history; on the contrary, the Spirit's presence causes us to deeply sense that difference precisely to the degree that the Spirit generates communion with Christ. The Spirit's work both measures and mediates the eschatological dif-ference between the head and his members.

My interpretation thus far calls into question recent attempts to identify the presence of the Spirit "in these last days" with a fully realized eschatology. Although John Zizioulas helpfully reminds us that the Holy Spirit is the one who makes the Jesus history actual in the first place and creates *ecclesia* in the eucharis-tic event, he draws illegitimately from this the following conclusion: "Between the Christian truth and ourselves there is no gap to fill by the means of grace. . . . All separation between Christology and ecclesiology vanishes in the Spirit" (emphasis added).[72] This is consistent with his view that in the Eucharist the *totus Christus* (Christ and the church) becomes a fully realized eschatological event, although with Miroslav Volf, I can only conclude that this represents an overre-alized eschatology.[73]

The problem is to be located not in Zizioulas's suggestion that the Eucharist most clearly manifests the intersection of Christology, pneumatology, and eccle-siology, but in his overrealized eschatology of the Eucharist, which actually undermines the eschatological tension that this event highlights rather than resolves. Church, Spirit, and Jesus all seem to merge. When the Spirit is appealed to as merely the solution to the problem of Christ's absence, and not also as the

72. John Zizioulas, *Being as Communion: Studies in Personhood and the Church* (Crestwood, NY: St. Vladimir's Seminary Press, 1985), 110–11.
73. Miroslav Volf, *After Our Likeness: The Church as the Image of the Trinity* (Grand Rapids: Eerd-mans, 1998), 141.

one whose very presence constantly provokes our sense of the "more" of the Parousia, we are no longer speaking of the Spirit's mediation so much as the Spirit's replacement of Jesus Christ.

There are other examples in contemporary theology of a tendency to treat the Spirit as a substitute for the absent Christ more than the one who negotiates the eschatological tension.[74] Along lines similar to the controversial Russian Orthodox theologian Sergei Bulgakov, John Milbank goes so far as to speculate that the Spirit as well as the Son must become incarnate. Milbank calls for an alternative Protestantism and a reformed Catholicism that, encouraged by "the Charismatic and Holiness movements," draws us along "in a much more Catholic direction, accepting the continued and unlimited power of the Spirit in the church and in the world." He adds, "If miracles did not end with the apostolic times, then surely despite supposedly orthodox tradition, neither did revelation, even though the continued revelation of the Spirit in the human only shows us once again Christ. (So I am not being Joachite here, even if the Calabrian abbot caught a distorted glimpse of something missing.)"[75]

According to Milbank, the incarnation of the Son is predicated on the prior incarnation of the Spirit—*as the church.*[76] The conflation of the Spirit (via incarnation) with the Son serves as a pathway to Milbank's full identification of the church with both. There must be "a different sort of enhypostasization, that is, collective humanity (ecclesia) by the Holy Spirit," he says, adding:

> To be possible, incarnation must be not only of the logos, but [also] of Sophia or of the *Verbum-Donum* hypostatic interaction. This interaction indeed also transfigures the past into a kind of identity with the "prehistorical" Father—as Augustine's linking of Father with memory already suggests. In this way a more complete orthodoxy of the future, which acknowledges continued revelation, will need to speak in a sense of *a triple incarnation of the entire Trinity.* (emphasis added)[77]

Extrapolating Augustine's famous (or infamous) psychological analogy for the Trinity well beyond the Bishop of Hippo's imagining, Milbank (despite his protestations to the contrary above) not only echoes but also radicalizes the speculations of Joachim of Fiore.

Where the Spirit is separated from Christ—and not a cosmic Christ, but the incarnate Word—the gospel is easily surrendered to general experience of "the sacred" and the church to the history of religions. No longer the Spirit of Jesus, but a generic name for divinity (*Nous*, World-Soul, the Great Spirit, *Geist*), the

---

74. Yves Congar points out that the late nineteenth-century Roman Catholic theologian M. J. Scheeben, among others, called the church a "kind of incarnation of the Holy Spirit" (*I Believe in the Holy Spirit* [New York: Crossroad, 1999], 155).

75. John Milbank, "Alternative Protestantism," in *Radical Orthodoxy and the Reformed Tradition: Creation, Covenant, and Participation*, ed. James K. A. Smith (Grand Rapids: Baker Academic, 2005), 38.

76. Ibid., 38–39.

77. Ibid., 39.

third person of the Trinity loses specificity. Not surprisingly, Milbank's notion of an enhypostasis of the Spirit leads to a resacralized cosmos.[78]

In all of these ways, the eschatological difference between this age and the age to come is marginalized in favor of reconciling ontic binaries as being strives upward. For all the talk of mediating binaries and overcoming dualism, these substitutions of church and Spirit for Jesus Christ leave nothing to actually be mediated, no difference to be negotiated. When the Spirit is no longer as easily recognized as the mediator of Christ's presence and therefore the pledge of our future inheritance as much as expected to be the immanent *Geist* (Absolute Spirit), then the "spirit of the community" or the presence of Jesus in the heart of individual believers compensates for the loss of his absence in the flesh. Just as the historical Jesus is absorbed into the historical church divinized by a cosmic Christ, eschatology (the two ages) is lost to philosophy (Plato's two worlds).

If we follow the logic of Jesus' discourse in John, however, what is promised is not another enhypostasis of deity in time and space, but "another Paraclete" who directs us not to ourselves and our inner experience nor to the church, and not even to the Spirit, but *to the Lord from heaven*. This other Paraclete is sent not on a freelance mission, but on an embassy to bring about the end-time gathering (*ekklēsia*) through the one revelation of God in Christ.

Rather than being somehow in control of the Spirit by means of its official ministry or becoming assimilated to the Spirit as an ongoing incarnation, the church must yield to the Spirit, who operates within human beings through these outward means, and through them brings about both crisis and continuity in the life of the church. The Spirit's presence in our hearts binds us to the "then and there" of Christ's work (anamnesis), the "here and now" of our own justification, renewal, fellowship, and witness (epiclesis), and the joyful expectation of Christ's return (*epektasis*). If these tenses are simply run together, we lose the already/not-yet tension that the Spirit's presence actually highlights.

From John 14–16 we also see that the Spirit brings about the perlocutionary effect of the threefold office of Christ in these last days. As *prophet*, the Spirit bears the covenant word of judgment and justification, conviction of sin and faith-creating promise. This is what it means for the Spirit to be poured out on all flesh (Joel 2). As Barth famously put it, "The Lord of speech is also the Lord of our hearing."[79]

Furthermore, the Spirit is not merely a bonding agent between the Father and the Son, but also an equal actor in the economy of grace. Although the external works of God are undivided, the agency of each person is distinct. The one Word is spoken by the Father and reaches its creaturely goal through the perfecting power of the Spirit. As the Spirit is different from the Son ("another Paraclete"), Pentecost is a genuinely new episode in the economy of grace. The Spirit "translates" for us and within us the intra-Trinitarian discourse concerning us (election,

78. Milbank, "Alternative Protestantism," 40.
79. Karl Barth, *CD* 1/1:182.

redemption, and renewal in Christ). The content of the Spirit's teaching ministry is Christ (John 15:26b)—not another Word, but its inward effect in our hearts, provoking our "Amen!" As one sent by the Father in the name of Christ, the Spirit preaches Christ, gives faith to hearers, and thereby unites them to Christ as members of his mystical body.

As "another Advocate," the Spirit also ministers within us that *priestly* office that Christ holds objectively outside of us (John 27–28). The Spirit is not our high priest, but applies the benefits of Christ's completed work to us and unites us to Christ himself. Apart from the Spirit's agency, we would remain "dead in trespasses and sins," refusing the Gift, without any vital connection to Christ's person and work (Eph. 2:1–5 NKJV). We have already been reconciled to God in Christ even "while we were [still] enemies" (Rom. 5:10), but the Spirit comes to make us friends and children of God (Rom. 8:1–27). As a covenant attorney, the Spirit makes more than a *truce*—a mere cessation of hostilities—and brings about a state of *union*.

Mediating Christ's *royal* ministry, the Spirit subdues unbelief and the tyranny of sin in the lives of believers, creating a communion of saints as a body ruled by its living head through the prophets and apostles, evangelists, pastors, and teachers that Christ has poured out as the spoils of his victory (Eph. 4:11–16). The Spirit makes Christ's rule effective in us and among us by inspiring the scriptural canon and by creating a people who will be constituted by it. Jesus Christ had already appointed apostles as Spirit-inbreathed witnesses, but now at last through the ordinary ministry of pastors, teachers, and other officers in the church, Moses' request in Numbers 11:29 ("Would that all the LORD's people were prophets, and that the LORD would put his Spirit on them!") will be fulfilled beyond his wildest dreams. Not only the seventy elders, but also the whole camp of Israel is made a Spirit-filled community of witnesses. The charismata bestowed on the whole body are orchestrated by the Spirit through the ordained office-bearers, who differ only in the *graces* (vocation), but not in the *grace* (ontic status) of the Spirit. Thus, the mission of the Twelve in Luke 9:1–6 widens to the seventy in chapter 10. Yet this was but a prelude to the commissioning ceremony of Pentecost.

Trading Places (John 16)

The coming-and-going of the Son and the Spirit as we find it in John 16 highlights the paradox with which I introduced this chapter. Especially in verses 5–7, we discern, on one hand, the real absence: Jesus Christ is gone, but his departure signals his ascension to the Father's right hand to intercede for us and beat down all of his and our common enemies under his feet. He had earlier said, in 14:28–29, "You heard me say to you, '*I am going away, and I am coming to you.*' If you loved me, you would rejoice that I am going to the Father, because the Father is greater than I. And now I have told you before it occurs, so that when it does occur, you may believe" (emphasis added). He is going *and* coming: that is the paradox. Here the reference to his "coming" is not first of all at least to his second coming, but to the coming of the Spirit. His going is a real going—a bodily departure. At the same time, his coming is a real coming—the sending of his Spirit.

So closely identified is the Spirit with Christ that wherever the Spirit is said now to be present, Christ is present. Neither magisterium nor conventicle, sacramental system nor pious believer, but the divine Spirit alone dispenses the spoils of Christ's victory. Behind every human representation—such as the official ministry in the church—stands the Spirit, the divine witness at work in every human witness. It is not the church that stands between heaven and earth, between this age and the age to come, but Christ. And precisely because it is his Spirit—the other Advocate—who mediates his presence and activity in this age, Christ's unique heavenly session is guaranteed success until his return in the flesh. It is the Spirit now who trades places, as it were, and leads the ground campaign with our enthroned head directing it from the Father's right hand. The Son goes through the cross to the resurrection and is exalted in the ascension, breaking open the treasure houses of heaven to be distributed by the Spirit to his coheirs. The Spirit has been sent from the Father (14:26); now it is added, "But if I go, I will send him to you" (16:7 ESV).

First, elaborating his earlier remarks, Jesus says in chapter 16 that the Spirit inwardly convicts. The Spirit is sent not only to announce the coming judgment, but "to prove the world wrong about sin, righteousness, and judgment," with unbelief in Christ as the focus of that conviction (v. 8, emphasis added). We are reminded in Acts 2:37 of the empirical reality that Jesus here foretells, as those who heard Peter's Pentecost sermon were "cut to the heart and said to Peter and to the other apostles, 'Brothers, what shall we do?'" The Spirit will not speak another word, but will inwardly renew, convicting and persuading us of our guilt and Christ's righteousness.

Second, as the Son is the sole embodiment of all truth, the Spirit will be sent "to guide you into all truth" (John 16:13). The Spirit is the guide, while the Son is the destination. Just as the Son did not speak on his own authority, but related everything he himself heard from the Father, the Spirit "will not speak on his own, but will speak whatever he hears, and he will declare to you the things that are to come" (v. 13). The Spirit is the one who "does not in fact present himself but the absent Jesus," as Farrow notes.

> This is the Spirit who through word and sacrament also unites us to the absent Jesus, so that it is we who are grasped or seized, ἐκ τοῦ κόσμου. The Spirit's work is an infringement on our time, an eschatological reordering of our being to the fellowship of the Father and the Son, and to the new creation. That gracious infringement is what the man of the world, and the church which has become worldly, falsify with talk of grasping the divine as it presents itself to us in time.[80]

The upper room discourse underscores the point that the Spirit comes not to verify our religious experience or assist us in our enthusiastic efforts to establish the

---

80. Farrow, *Ascension and Ecclesia*, 257.

ethical kingdom in the world, but to convict us of guilt and righteousness and judgment.

The ascension requires us to look away from ourselves and our actions, aspirations, programs, and experiences—to look to the stranger whom the Spirit has enabled us to recognize as the Advocate at the Father's right hand, and Pentecost inaugurates this recognition. Only the Spirit can keep us aware simultaneously of the otherness of Jesus and our communion with and in him. His personal history must be for us a distant and fading memory, except for the Spirit's work of ushering us into the courtroom where even now Christ pleads on behalf of his witnesses on earth and prepares a place for them.

Yet this means conflict, not conquest. Confusing itself with its glorified head, the church forgets its being *simul iustus et peccator* (simultaneously righteous and sinner) and loses sight of the fact that its visibility is recognized chiefly in its confession of its sin and of its faith in the gospel. Like Jesus in his earthly humiliation, the church militant is a witness (*martys*, from which we get the word "martyr"): it is the part of the world that, seized by the Spirit in the powers of the age to come, issues an "Amen" to Christ that contradicts the "No!" of the powers and principalities of this age. The church would always prefer to reign with Christ now (or in his absence, here below) than to be witnesses. When it is no longer content to be visible as the eucharistic community, gathered in the upper room to be scattered in witness and martyrdom, the church begins to resemble more the disciples on their way to Jerusalem before the solemn events that unfolded there, expecting Jesus to restore the earthly theocracy to its visible splendor. When, just before ascending, the resurrected Jesus told his disciples to go to the upper room and wait for the Spirit's baptism, they ask, "Now are you going to restore the kingdom to Israel?" (cf. Acts 1:4–6).

Only after Pentecost—and even then, only through considerable controversy and birth pangs—would they understand Jesus' answer. If Jesus had answered affirmatively, his ascension and the sending of the Spirit would have been rendered moot. In this interim, the Spirit inwardly convicts the guilty and conveys forgiveness by making them hearers of the Word. Even the Spirit is a hearer of the Word. The statement that the Spirit "will speak whatever he hears" (John 16:13) is intriguing in that connection. Just as the Son did not speak on his own authority, but only delivered the Word of the Father, the Spirit will be the missionary sent from the Father and the Son.

Ever since the first temptation, the human partner in the covenant has always suppressed the truth by taking the bait of the archetypal false prophet: "Has God *really* said . . . ?" (cf. Gen. 3:1). The false prophets in Jeremiah 23 are excoriated for presuming to speak for God (always "positive preaching") even though they have not stood in his council. By contrast, the Spirit's role is not to say something else, but to answer back within our heart, "Yes, he has indeed said . . . !" This is the inner testimony of the Spirit. The Spirit "gossips," relaying what he has heard. The Spirit has not only stood in the council of Yahweh as a witness, like the prophets and apostles, but is one with the Father and the Son. The one by whom the Word was conceived in the flesh is the source and the interpreter of the word concerning him. And he will not only tell the truth about the past (what God *has* done in Christ), but also about the future (what God *will do* in Christ): "and he will declare to you things that are to come" (John 16:13).

Notice again how the Spirit's work will concentrate on revealing the economy of grace more than on the psychology of religious experience. The Spirit's ministry is not only concerned with making the church remember what Christ has accomplished (anamnesis), but also to give conviction of sin, faith, and righteousness in the present (epiclesis) as well as to anticipate the next act in the divine drama (*epektasis*). Drawing us outside of ourselves to focus on this economy is something that only the divine Spirit could possibly achieve. The Spirit is an extrovert, always going forth on missions with his Word, creating an extroverted community that can at last look up to God in faith and out to the world in love, witness, and service.

The Son has created a redeemed community, and the Spirit is creating a repentant and believing community, with the fruit of love and hope. We see the first impact of this promise at Pentecost, with the proclamation of Christ as the fulfillment of all prophecy. And here in John 16, the Spirit who led Christ to his destiny leads us also. In this discourse, Reinhard Hütter wisely reminds us, the Spirit's leading "into all truth" is not a vague sentiment about a supposedly direct and immediate "in-spiration of Spirit into individual religious consciousnesses, but in the form of concrete church practices which as such are to be understood as the gifts of the Spirit in the service of God's economy of salvation."[81] The Spirit leads into all truth by creating a church in time that baptizes, catechizes, preaches, communes, and guards the flock. In doing so, the Spirit keeps our eyes fixed on Christ.

Third, Jesus says concerning the Spirit, "He will glorify me" (John 16:14). This surely denotes the point of the Spirit's testimony, just as verses 14b and 15 underscore this mutuality (perichoresis) between the Son and the Spirit in the covenant of redemption: the Spirit and the Son share a common treasure, a treasure that they together with the Father intend to share also in common with us. This comes to fullest expression perhaps in Jesus' prayer in John 17. In Jesus' earthly ministry, he glorified the Father; on the eve of his crucifixion, he invokes the Father to glorify him, and in the upper room discourse he assures his disciples that the Spirit will do so also.

Therefore, Jesus prepares the disciples for his real absence—an absence that is itself a further work of salvation for them; it is not a departure from the site of their redemption, but a relocation in that great service. "In my Father's house there are many dwelling places. If it were not so, would I have told you that I go to prepare a place for you? And if I go and prepare a place for you, I will come again and will take you to myself, so that where I am, there you may be also"

---

81. Reinhard Hütter, *Suffering Divine Things: Theology as Church Practice* (Grand Rapids: Eerdmans, 2000), 127.

(John 14:2–3). Because Jesus still has a history, so do we, and because he has a place, we will have one also—where he is. And he will come again to take us there.

In the meantime, his departure opens a fissure in history where the Spirit—for the first time in redemptive history—will not only lead, guide, and be light above or upon the temple-people, but will permanently indwell them.

> And I will ask the Father, and he will give you another Advocate, to be with you forever. This is the Spirit of truth, whom the world cannot receive, because it neither sees him nor knows him. You know him, because he abides with you, and he will be in you. I will not leave you orphaned; I am coming to you. (John 14:16–18)

Jesus Christ indwells believers and the church, but by his Spirit, not immediately in the flesh (2 Cor. 1:22; cf. Rom. 8:16, 26; 1 Cor. 3:16; Gal. 4:6; Eph. 5:18). For this immediate presence, nothing short of Christ's bodily return is required. Because of the ascension, the church on earth is not triumphant and must wait for the bodily return of its head in the future, for the renewal of all things. Yet Christ's bodily absence does not leave the church orphaned, because in one sense at least, the Spirit makes Christ more present than he was even to the disciples. They may have seen him in the flesh, but we see him in the Spirit through the proclamation that is authorized by the Son and inspired by the Spirit. The disciples saw him in the flesh, but they did not recognize him as their redeemer until the Spirit opened their eyes (Matt. 16:17). Their relationship with Jesus was conditioned (both for Jesus and for them) by the realities of "this age" that came crashing down upon the Savior at Golgotha, but their saving relation to Christ came from the realities of the age to come, on the other side of the death that could not hold him.

If this is true, then John the Baptist was actually less a contemporary of Jesus than believers today. In fact, the personal lives of the disciples themselves fell into two halves: before and after recognition of Christ's identity. In a real sense, the "distance" between Peter-the-Disciple and Peter-the-Apostle is far greater than that between Peter and us. After all, Peter-the-Apostle lived on this side of "these last days," as do we—and all because the Father and the Son fulfilled their promise to send the Spirit. A covenant child today recognizes Jesus in his saving office more fully than did Jesus' own brothers during his earthly ministry. This is because we live with the Apostle Peter on this side of Pentecost, where the age that Jesus inaugurated is at work, disrupting the powers and principalities that keep us from recognizing him. We know him now not simply as a historical figure or a model to be emulated, but as the firstfruits of the harvest to which we belong. It is the Spirit who causes us to recognize the Jesus of history as the Christ of faith (2 Cor. 5:16–17).

Because the church is neither the Son nor the Spirit, it is always the object rather than the subject of redeeming action. Ascension and Pentecost work together, therefore, to keep us attentive both to the differences and affinities between Christ and his church. Apart from Pentecost, ecclesial performance of this script could only be on the order of *imitatio Christi*, a hopeless series of attempts to re-create the original work or translate it into a contemporary idiom. Holding on to a few scraps of "sayings" (always ethical), we might focus all of our energies on answering the question, "What would Jesus do?" but then we would have no connection to what Jesus has done, is doing, and will do for the ungodly. The church would then be our work, inspired by Jesus, but our work nonetheless.

But because of Pentecost, even we who were previously aimless characters in the dead-end and insignificant plots of this passing age become part of the growing cast in the supporting role of witnesses to the God of promise. Because of the Spirit, the church's performance here and now is not "based on a true story," but is part of it: a living liturgy of covenantal action and response. It originates in the heart of the Father, unfolds in the life of the Son, and is brought to fruition by the graciously disruptive power of the Spirit.

This Spirit bridges the eschatological distance between the already-consummated Jesus history (the age to come) and our existence in the last days of this present age. Nevertheless, the church is part of that story always *at a different place* than its lead character. He is ahead of us, in the last act, yet is keeping our history moving toward him by his intercession and the work of his Spirit.

In John 14–16, this intra-Trinitarian unity-and-difference is given clear expression: the real bodily absence of the Son is not a break in the saving presence of God in the world, but a new kind of presence. The Father speaks the liturgy of grace, while the Son is himself its embodiment, and the Spirit then works in "the children of disobedience" (Eph. 2:2 KJV) to create a choir of antiphonal response that answers back its appropriate "Amen" behind its glorified forerunner (2 Cor. 1:19–22). "He who has prepared us for this very thing"—immortality—"is God, who has given us the Spirit as a guarantee" (2 Cor. 5:5).

A NEW KIND OF PRESENCE: THE EXALTED KING DISPENSES GIFTS TO COHEIRS

Ephesians 4 provides a lodestar for the integration of Christology, pneumatology, and ecclesiology, which I have been pursuing in this chapter. Making us alive while we were dead, the Spirit has "seated us with [God] in the heavenly places in Christ Jesus, so that in the ages to come he might show the immeasurable riches of his grace in kindness toward us in Christ Jesus" (Eph. 2:4–7). Therefore, even the bodily absence of Jesus Christ is a productive interim in the economy of grace.

First of all, ascension and Pentecost conspire, each in its own way, to transform anonymous people into a covenantal place: the body of Christ.

> Therefore it is said, "When he ascended on high he made captivity itself a captive; he gave gifts to his people." (When it says, "He ascended," what does it mean but that he had also descended into the lower parts of the earth? He who descended is the same one who ascended far above all the heavens, so that he might fill all things.) (Eph. 4:8–10)

In this ascension, he poured out his *grace* on all of his people and bestowed specific *graces*: pastors, evangelists, and teachers whose ministry will bring the whole body to maturity in Christ (Eph. 4:8–16).

This unity is a gift already given, not a goal for us to attain. With the two hands of Word and Spirit, the Father creates a body of which his Son is the head. That unity is already lodged in God's election, redemption, calling, and sealing elaborated in Ephesians 1. Preserving the visible unity of this body in the concrete historical existence of the visible church is a task (Eph. 4:3), but it rests on the triumphant indicative: we belong, by God's grace alone, to one body and one Spirit, called in one hope, with "one Lord, one faith, one baptism; one God and Father of all, who is above all and through all and in all" (4:4–6).

The ascended Lord of the covenant distributes the spoils of his conquest. Interpreting Psalm 68, verses 7–10 of Ephesians 4 explain that in the incarnation, the Son of God "descended into the lower parts of the earth," and now he ascends "above all the heavens"—far above all power, rule, and authority. Psalm 68 is a psalm of ascent, as Israel's king returned from conquest in triumphal procession with his spoils.[82] Ephesians 4:7, 8, and 11 repeat the reference: "was given," "Christ's gift," "he gave gifts," and "the gifts he gave." The church is always on the receiving end in its relationship to Christ; it is never the redeemer, but always the redeemed; never the head, but always the body; never the ruler, but always the ruled. In his ascension, "he led a host of prisoners captive" (cf. v. 8a). Once again, this is common to all believers.

"He gave gifts to his people" (v. 8b). The *gifts* (plural) being distributed here by Christ in his ascension refer specifically to offices in the church. This involves giving graces (charismata) to those who hold such offices for their work. However, in this passage the pastors, teachers, and evangelists are the gifts he gives to his church. Although there are references to the act of shepherding, as with *poimainō;* its cognate noun, *poimēn*, "shepherd, pastor," is used only of Christ in the NT (John 10:11, 14; Heb. 13:20; 1 Pet. 2:25), with this verse being the only exception.[83] Although ministers are not the only gifts in the body (see Rom. 12 and 1 Cor. 12 for a more extensive list), the focus here is on the ministry of the Word that creates, nourishes, matures, and expands the ecclesial body.

Second, as a consequence of this trading places highlighted by ascension and Pentecost, the Spirit transforms the mission field into the missionary. The eschatological

---

82. G. H. P. Thompson, *The Letters of Paul to the Ephesians, Colossians, and to Philemon*, Cambridge Bible Commentary (Cambridge: Cambridge University Press, 1967), 67.

83. Andrew Lincoln, *Ephesians*, Word Biblical Commentary 42 (Dallas: Word, 1990), 250. The term was widely used in association with the overseer or leader (shepherd) in the Qumran community, and in Acts 20:28 the ministers of the Ephesian church are called to "shepherd the church of God." "It is probable, then, that the pastor of Eph 4:11 fulfills the functions denoted in Paul's writings by such terms as προΐστημι, 'to rule, manage' (1 Thess 5:12; Rom 12:8), κυβέρνησις, 'administration' (1 Cor 12:28), and ἐπίσκοπος, "bishop, overseer" (Phil 1:1). Ἐπίσκοπος was a term taken from the Hellenistic world, but because the general notion of overseeing had close associations with the shepherd in Jewish thought, it is understandable that the term 'pastor' could become interchangeable with 'bishop' in the Christian movement. It is the equivalent to πρεσβύτερος, "elder," of Acts 14:23; 20:17; 1 Tim 4:14; 5:17, 19; Titus 1:5; 1 Pet 5:1, 5; Jas 5:14" (251).

interim between Pentecost and Parousia is not only a period of marking time; rather, "Today" is "the day of salvation." Pentecost generates a whole community of Spirit-empowered testimony, prophets of good news, not a closed circle of the spiritually sensitive, morally aggressive, or doctrinally self-confident. This community gathers to receive its ecclesial being and is scattered to live it out in the world. As such, the church does not *engage* in mission; it *is* a mission, God's embassy in the world.

Unlike the general awareness of God and his righteous will and judgment, the gospel is not a *logos spermatikos*—an inner, immanent word that we find shot through all of creation; it must be *brought* to the world. Since all authority is given to the risen and ascended Christ, going, preaching, baptizing, and teaching is the very essence of Christ's ecclesial body. Nothing that the church does in this matter belongs to the indicative that Christ claims for himself alone; the imperative is the consequence of his achievement.

Jesus promises that those who believe in him "will do greater works than these" miraculous signs that he has performed in his ministry (John 14:12). After all, these are *signs* of the kingdom, but when Christ rules from heaven and the Spirit rules in the hearts of his people, the *reality* of the kingdom will become more fully manifest. He has given these heirs his Word, and despite the world's opposition, this witness will endure (John 17:14–19). The powers and rulers of this present darkness had to have their way with Jesus for our redemption to be secured, yet the descent of the Spirit ensures that now the saving ministry of Jesus will reach the ends of the earth and "the gates of Hades will not prevail against it" (Matt. 16:18). The analogical and covenantal sharing of these earthly witnesses in the life of the Trinity will generate a unity of witness, "so that the world may know that you have sent me and have loved them even as you have loved me" (John 17:23).

As the Father sends the Son into the world, the Father and the Son send the Spirit, and the Trinity in unison sends the community of redeemed witnesses. The pattern of receiving gifts and passing them on extends in concentric circles from the Godhead to the ends of the earth. And although it is the Spirit's presence itself that testifies to the Son and creates a longing for the return of the bodily ascended Jesus, it is also through that presence that Jesus keeps his promise, "And remember, I am with you always, to the end of the age" (Matt. 27:20).

UNTIL HE COMES AGAIN

Ephesians 4 does not end with the ascension. For the time being, Christ's universal kingship hardly captures the world's headlines. Yet the goal toward which the body of Christ walks is nothing less than the vision of the One who "ascended far above all the heavens, *so that he might fill all things*" (v. 10, emphasis added). This is the ultimate goal for which these gifts are now given. They are not given for private use, but for the common good of the whole body.

This extroverted orientation created by the Spirit pertains not only to the communion of the visible body, but also to the church's relationship to the world. As Christ's embassy among the fading kingdoms of this age, the church lives not for itself but for the world, in the confident expectation that Christ's triumph and return in glory will bring about a restored cosmos, of which the church is now the sign. The church does not create a transformed world; rather, the church is that part of the world that God has newly created in anticipation of the renewal of the world itself at the end of the age. Already, election and redemption are completed events (Eph. 1). Already, Christ is raised and rules in heaven, beyond the reach of death, and is raising those spiritually dead to everlasting life (Eph. 2). Already, the two hostile enemies—Jews and Gentiles—have been united in one body (Eph. 3).

Yet there is more to come. We are living in the parenthesis between the ascension and the return of Christ. By his Word and Spirit, Christ is creating a historical community, but precisely because they are *his* Word and Spirit, they always put that community in question, breaking up its presumptuous autonomy, so that the event of Christ's action among us will not be assimilated to the history of this passing age.

Because he has sent the Spirit, the risen Lord is present in the world *through* the community, though not *as* the community. As the Spirit "creates recognition, establishes knowledge, calls to confession and therefore quickens the dead," says Barth, "the existence of the community begins and endures."[84] Therefore, if the church exists at all, it is because it is called and controlled by Jesus Christ through the Spirit in his Word, not because it controls either this reality or itself.[85] It exists only because it is *his* property, branches of his vine, apart from whom it can do nothing (John 15:5). It exists because it was elected to belong to Christ as his body, of which he alone is its head.[86] It is holy because it is in Christ.

As Barth reminds us, the existence of Jesus does not depend on the existence of his body, as Schleiermacher offered, but vice versa; not by its works, but by Christ's. "No, the community exists only as He exists. 'Because I live, ye shall live also' (Jn. 14:19), is the right order. . . . He alone is who and what He is. But He is not alone as who and what He is."[87] He alone is our redemption, justification, and sanctification, the resurrection from the dead, and the Word of God. He is all of this for us.

> But He is not these things together with humanity nor together with His community. He was all these things in His once-for-all enacted work, in His person; and He is them now, in the time after His first parousia and before His second, up above in heaven at the right hand of the Father—He alone, i.e., with God alone, hidden in God, accessible to no aggression nor control from below on the part of the creaturely world, distinct from the being of

84. Barth, *CD* IV/3.2:752.
85. Ibid.
86. Ibid., 753.
87. Ibid., 754.

humanity and His community as the Creator and creature are distinct. . . .
To Him in this form of His existence, [the church] can only look and
move as, "absent from the Lord" (2 Cor. 5:6), it waits with all creation
for His appearance from heaven, for His coming forth from the hiddenness
of God.[88]

In itself, this community is as helpless, fallen, stupid, and defiant as the rest of
the world, but the Holy Spirit clothes the infant with Christ, says Barth, alluding to the moving analogy of Ezekiel 16:4–14.[89] It is the Spirit who secures and
guarantees this genuine yet often empirically ambiguous unity of the *totus Christus*.[90] Through the Spirit, Jesus can be regarded as simultaneously "the Head at
the right hand of the Father and as the body in the being of the community in
its temporal and spatial present and situation, and therefore as the *Kyrios* in His
totality."[91] The Spirit holds together that which is different.[92]

Minimally, the church is, therefore, that place—wherever it is in the world—
where Jesus Christ is faithfully heard as God's "Yes," generating the "Amen" of
faith to the ends of the earth. Yet where does such faith—and therefore, the
church itself—come from? It is to that question that we turn in the first section.

88. Ibid., 755.
89. Ibid., 760.
90. Ibid.
91. Ibid., 760–61.
92. Ibid., 761.

PART ONE
ORIGIN
Theater of Grace

Chapter Two

Creatura Verbi

The Sacramental Word

With the towering peaks of Christ's ascension and Pentecost as our landmarks, we turn first to the origin of the church: not only its beginning, but also the perpetual source of its identity. Nuclear to Lutheran and Reformed ecclesiologies, the notion of the church as *creation of the Word* has received renewed attention in ecumenical discussions, as in the Reformed–Roman Catholic dialogue that nicely summarizes the theme:

> The church existing as a community in history has been understood and described in the Reformed tradition as a *creatura verbi*, as "the creation of the word." God is eternally Word as well as Spirit; by God's Word and Spirit all things were created; reconciliation and renewal are the work of the same God, by the same word and Spirit. . . . This is why the Reformed tradition has insisted so emphatically that the preaching, teaching and witness of the church through the centuries—the church's dogma and tradition—are always to be subordinated to the testimony of the Bible, that scripture rather than Tradition is "the word of God written" and "the only infallible rule of faith and practice." . . . The church, like faith itself, is brought into being by the hearing of God's word in the power of the Spirit; it lives *ex auditu*, by hearing. This emphasis upon hearing the word of God has been of central importance in Reformed theology since the sixteenth century. This is

why the Reformed have stressed "the true preaching of the word" together with "the right dispensing of the sacraments according to the institution of Jesus Christ" as a decisive "mark of the true church."[1]

The dialogue adds, again from the Reformed side,

> Against the appeal to continuity, custom and institution, the Reformed appealed to the living voice of the living God as the essential and decisive factor by which the church must live, if it will live at all: the church, as *creatura verbi*. . . . The church is the creation of the word because the word itself is God's creative word of grace by which we are justified and renewed. . . . The community of faith is thus not merely the community in which the gospel is preached; by its hearing and responding to the word of grace, the community itself becomes a medium of confession, its faith a "sign" or "token" to the world; it is itself part of the world transformed by being addressed and renewed by the word of God.[2]

As inherently social in both its act and effects, proclamation of the gospel cannot be set over against the church, as other defining practices often are in more individualistic and experiential approaches to spirituality. As living speech, it cannot be reduced to a timeless body of doctrine or ethics, yet as the speech of God, who is other than us, individually or collectively, it always arrives as an external word (*verbum externum*) with the sovereign authority to define and redefine the church's existence. Conceived in the event of hearing, the church always remains on the receiving end of its redemption and identity. Articulating this motif, especially with respect to the significance of hearing, is the goal of this chapter and the next.

LIVING AND ACTIVE: THE SACRAMENTAL WORD

First and foremost, the Word is the second person of the Holy Trinity: the eternal Son, by whom all things were created and in whom they hold together, including the church (John 1:1–16; Col. 1:15–23; Heb. 1:1–4; Rev. 19:13). Yet Scripture also refers to specific instances of the Father's speaking in the Son by the power of the Spirit, who brings about its intended effect. In this sense, God's word is God's *working*. As our own words spread out our intentions and influence without spreading out our persons, God's Word in this sense is not an extension of the divine essence, but the effect of personal presence and lively activity. The human words do not simply coincide at certain points with God's Word, but are actually God's "breath" (2 Tim. 3:16). Borrowing on J. L. Austin, we may say

---

1. "Lutheran–R.C. Dialogue," in *Growth in Agreement II: Reports and Agreed Statements of Ecumenical Conversations on a World Level, 1982–1998*, ed. Jeffrey Gros (FSC) Harding Meyer, and William G. Rusch (Geneva: World Council of Churches; Grand Rapids: Eerdmans, 2000), 802. For the Lutheran–Roman Catholic Dialogue on this point, see 495–98.

2. Ibid., 803.

that *God does things with words.*[3] Although the divine essence does not emanate, God's words do truly "go forth" and are "sent" on their missions. The Word is that living and active energy that creates and re-creates. It may harden hearts or melt them, but it is never inert, since it is the Word of the Father, spoken in the Son, made effectual by the Spirit.

Not by silent thoughts or ideas in the divine mind, but "By the word of the LORD the heavens were made, and all their host by the breath of his mouth" (Ps. 33:6). "We are used to thinking that it was light that broke the primordial darkness," writes Stephen H. Webb, "but it was really God's voice that shattered the silence. This is the significance of God's appearance to Moses in the fire. Moses hears the words but sees no form: 'there was only a voice' (Deut. 4:12). The words illumine, not the flame."[4] Although the phrase *word of God* has various meanings in Scripture, notes Bavinck, "it is always a word of God which means: never simply a sound, but a power, no mere information but also an accomplishment of His will, Isa. 55:11; Rom. 4:17; 2 Cor. 4:6; Heb. 1:3; 11:3. By this word Jesus quiets the sea, Mk. 4:38; heals the sick, Mt. 8:16; casts out demons, 9:6; raised the dead, Luke 7:14; 8:54; John 5:25, 28; 11:43."[5] As in the former creation and exodus, so in the new, God's performative utterance brings a world into being (Isa. 55:10–11). Wherever the Father speaks, the Son is spoken, and the Spirit creates hearers, a mass of individuals become the covenant people, and anonymous space becomes "a broad place" of lavish abundance and freedom, where the Lord dwells in the midst of Zion (Ps. 18:19).

The alternative to a theocentric and Trinitarian conception of the word is not autonomy, but captivity to other lords, who cannot liberate. When this conception is given priority, there is a proper place for experience and doctrine. Although this canon is also a written norm and constitution, it is also "the implanted" Word (Jas. 1:21) that "abides in you" (1 John 2:14) and is to "dwell in you richly" (Col. 3:16). Because it comes to us from outside of ourselves, either as pious individuals or a magisterium, this Word creates, renews, judges, and justifies the church; yet because it comes to us in the power of the Spirit, this Word wins our consent and makes one body out of many.

The notion that the church is the creation of the Word arises from the repeated assumption in Scripture itself that God's *speaking* is *acting*, and this acting is not only descriptive and propositional; it is also creative and performative. God's Word is not only authoritative because it communicates doctrinal and ethical

---

3. It is striking how many contemporary theologians observe the similarities between the Reformers' theology of the Word and speech-act theory, especially J. L. Austin's *How to Do Things with Words*, 2nd ed. (Oxford: Clarendon, 1975). See, for example, Oswald Bayer, *Theologie*, Handbuch Systematischer Theologie 1 (Gütersloh: Gütersloher Verlagshaus G. Mohn, 1994), 441ff.; Reinhard Hütter, *Suffering Divine Things: Theology as Church Practice* (Grand Rapids: Eerdmans, 2000), 82–94.

4. Stephen H. Webb, *The Divine Voice: Christian Proclamation and the Theology of Sound* (Grand Rapids: Brazos, 2004), 47.

5. From chap. 10 (sec. 56) of Herman Bavinck's *Gereformeerde Dogmatiek*, 3rd unaltered ed., vol. 4 (Kampen: J. H. Kok, 1918); this excerpt was translated by Nelson D. Kloosterman as "Law-Gospel Distinction and Preaching," http://auxesis.net/bavinck/law gospel distinction and preaching.php, p. 2.

truth—although these are not to be denied—but chiefly because it is *God's* truthful praxis: God at work in bringing about the new creation. It not only tells us what God has done; it also does what God tells. Any theory of language that allows only a referential function for signs will miss some of the most interesting descriptions of the Word's activity in the biblical drama.[6] Preaching involves teaching, but it is much more than that. Even this important didactic aspect becomes more valuable when it is comprehended under the category of the sacramental Word: "The dogma is the drama," as Dorothy Sayers put it.[7]

In a covenantal context of a living relationship, doctrine and life, theory and practice, creed and deed are inextricably connected. It is the drama of redemption itself—God's activity in the world—that keeps the dogma from degenerating into mere propositionalism and the praxis from degenerating into mere moralism. A merely intellectual view of the Word will yield a merely intellectual view of faith. However, as life-giving as well as informative news, the gospel *creates* knowledge, assent, and trust.

Given the way in which the "sacramental" is often marginalized by a purely pedagogical and regulative understanding of the concept, it is no wonder that the Word written and preached is often treated as a dead letter that must somehow be supplemented by something else: either a living community or Spirit-filled individuals. When doctrine is conceived merely as timeless propositions, then faith and practice, preaching and experience, drift apart, and there is pressure on ministers to find a way to make the Bible relevant, practical, applicable, and effectual.

On the other hand, B. A. Gerrish observes, "Calvin felt no antagonism between what we may call the 'pedagogical' [teaching] and the 'sacramental' functions of the word."[8] Life is found only in God, located in Christ, mediated by his Word.[9] "God's word, for Calvin, is not simply a dogmatic norm; it has in it a vital efficacy, and it is the appointed instrument by which the Spirit imparts illumination, faith, awakening, regeneration, purification, and so on. . . . Calvin himself describes the word as *verbum sacramentale*, the 'sacramental word,'" which gives even to the sacraments themselves their efficacy.[10] "It is crucial to Calvin's inter-

---

6. No less an evangelical theologian than Carl F. H. Henry asserted that doctrines are "the theorems derived from the axioms of revelation" (*God, Revelation, and Authority* [Waco: Word, 1979], 1:234; see also 4:105–9, 113, 120). Scripture's two primary functions are, says Henry, to give us "propositional truths about God and his purposes" as well as "the meaning of divine redemptive acts" (Carl Henry, "Narrative Theology: An Evangelical Appraisal," *Trinity Journal* 8 [1987]: 3). Henry reflects an enormous debt to his mentor, Gordon Clark, who argued that biblical language is "inadequate" until distilled in propositional language (Gordon Clark, *Religion, Reason, and Revelation* [Nutley, NJ: The Craig Press, 1978], 143). Elsewhere, Clark wrote, "Truth is a characteristic of propositions only. Nothing can be called true in the literal sense of the term except the attribution of a predicate to a subject" (Gordon Clark, "The Bible as Truth," *Bibliotheca Sacra* [April 1957]: 158). After centuries of a Kantian moratorium on claims to constitutive knowledge of God (i.e., theology) and anti-intellectual dismissals of propositions, Henry's reaction was understandable. However, it is often just such views as those defended by Henry and Clark that keep the epistemological pendulum swinging.

7. Dorothy Sayers, *Creed or Chaos?* (New York: Harcourt, Brace, 1949), 3.

8. B. A. Gerrish, *Grace and Gratitude: The Eucharistic Theology of John Calvin* (Minneapolis: Augsburg Fortress Press, 1993), 84.

9. Ibid., 85; cf. John Calvin, *Petit tracté de la sancta Cene* (1541), in *OS* 1:504–5.

10. Ibid., 85, referring to Calvin, *Institutes* 4.14.4.

pretation that the gospel is not a mere invitation to fellowship with Christ, but [also] the effective means by which the communion with Christ comes about. . . . It therefore makes good sense to us when we discover that in Theodore Beza's (1519–1605) edition of the Geneva Catechism the fourth part, on the sacraments, actually begins with the heading 'On the *Word* of God.'"[11] As with baptism and the Supper, the Spirit creates a bond between the sign (proclamation of the gospel) and the reality signified (Christ and all his benefits). The Word is a ladder, to be sure, but like the incarnation, one that *God* always *descends* to us (Rom. 10:6–17).

Specifically, the *gospel* is that part of God's Word that gives life. While everything that God says is true and full of impact, not everything that God says is *saving*. Sometimes God's speech brings judgment, disaster, fear, warning, and dread, Calvin reminds us.[12] "For although faith believes every word of God, it rests solely on the word of grace or mercy, the promise of God's fatherly goodwill," which is only realized in and through Christ.[13] "For in God faith seeks life," says Calvin, "which is not to be found in commandments or the pronouncement of penalties, but in the promise of mercy—and only a free promise."[14] The only safe route, therefore, is to receive the Father through the incarnate Son. Christ is the saving content of Scripture, the substance of its canonical unity.[15] "This is the true knowledge of Christ: if we take him as he is offered by the Father, namely, clothed with his gospel. For as he himself has been designated the goal of our faith, so we shall not run straight to him unless the gospel leads the way."[16]

Just as creation begin with a command, "Let there be . . . , And there was . . . ," so too does the new creation originate in the womb of the Word. The Spirit does not eliminate the need for earthly means, but consecrates them in the service of uniting us to the ascended Christ so that our life is "now hidden with Christ in God" (Col. 3:3).

This Word, then, is not only the source or norm that we appeal to in order to get *hearers* to do something or become something, but is also the means through which *God* communicates here and now the benefits of a redemption achieved then and there. We and all other creatures exist because God *told* us to exist. While God's Word certainly "tells it like it is," it is also the act by which God makes things what they are and the way that they are in the first place.[17] God's Word not only warns and promises, but also brings about in history that which is threatened and assured: "The Lord sent a word against Jacob, and it fell on

---

11. B. A. Gerrish, *Grace and Gratitude*, 84, referring to Calvin, *Institutes* 3.5.5.

12. Calvin, *Institutes* 3.2.7; 3.2.29.

13. Ibid., 3.2.28–30.

14. Ibid., 3.2.29.

15. Ibid., 1.13.7.

16. Ibid., 3.2.6.

17. The demand that theological statements have meaning only if they refer to an extralinguistic reality therefore seems to reflect a more Platonist than Hebraic worldview. Instead of transcending the finite creation, of which words are like the bodily carapace that is shrugged off on the way up the ladder of contemplation, from Gen. 1 on, all that there is to know is "worded" by God in creation, providence, redemption, and consummation. This linguisticality has its deepest ontological source in the Trinity itself, with the Son as the archetypal Word eternally begotten of the Father. Thus, to get behind or above language, one would have to get behind or above God.

Israel" (Isa. 9:8). Far from being a dead letter, the word of God "gets around." Like the God who utters it, this word is restless until it accomplishes the reality it describes. To put it simply, the word not only *sets* forth; it also *brings* forth. The word not only explains, describes, asserts, and proposes; it also *arrives*. J. A. Moyter asks, "How did the prophet receive the message which he was commissioned to convey to his fellows? The answer in the vast majority of the cases is perfectly clear and yet tantalizingly vague: 'The Lord came. . . . '"[18] Indeed, "the word of the Lord came to me, *saying, . . .* " is also a common expression in the prophets. The Lord came in the energy of his word, delivered through the prophets and now consummately in the One who is the Word of God, not only in energy but also in essence (Heb. 1:1–3).

Unlike the hypostatic Word, the sacramental word is not an eternal event that is necessary to God's very being. Rather, it is freely spoken in time—always new and yet connected to the words that have preceded it; in one sense, contingent (God could have spoken otherwise), yet never arbitrary because it always reveals God's self-consistent character. It is a word that is never lost to the ebb and flow of history—not because it does not really enter into it, but because it actively shapes its course and brings it to its appointed end. "The grass withers, the flower fades; but the word of our God will stand forever" (Isa. 40:8; cf. Matt. 24:35). And that appointed end is a covenantal relationship with the only suzerain worthy of our trust and worship: "Turn to me and be saved, all the ends of the earth! For I am God, and there is no other. By myself I have sworn, from my mouth has gone forth in righteousness a word that shall not return: 'To me every knee shall bow, every tongue shall swear'" (Isa. 45:22–23).

The prophet's role can be reduced neither to that of mere witness nor to a mere recorder of divine utterances; instead, the prophet is the ambassador who is authorized and commissioned to speak the living and active word that brings about a new state of affairs in history: "I have put my words in your mouth" (Isa. 51:16). Significantly, it is the mouth that is sanctified and commissioned, just as it is the ears of the hearers that are opened to receive judgment and justification, underscoring the priority of proclamation in the history of God's covenantal communication. Although Isaiah himself is "undone" in the presence of the Holy One, recognizing that he as well as the people have "unclean lips," the burning coal is pressed to his lips so that he will be able to speak God's word faithfully to God's covenant people (6:5–9).

As will become especially important for my interaction in later chapters, there is a distinction, but no contrast drawn here, between divine and human action: the human signs are sanctified as divine signs that communicate the reality signified. Once again the covenant, not abstract theories of philosophical realism or constructivism, provides the context for the prophet's actions. The prophetic word has its source in neither the prophet's person nor in the community's judg-

---

18. J. A. Moyter, s.v. "Prophecy," *The New Bible Dictionary*, ed. J. D. Douglas (Grand Rapids: Eerdmans, 1962), 1039.

ment, but in God (2 Pet. 1:20). At the same time, the prophet's personal characteristics are never circumvented or overwhelmed.

Yahweh's word in human words is compared to the rain that descends and brings forth fruit: "So shall my word be that goes out from my mouth; it shall not return to me empty, but it shall accomplish that which I purpose, and succeed in the thing for which I sent it" (Isa. 55:10–11). The same word goes forth from God's mouth and the prophet's mouth. Although it brings him nothing by reproach, this word is like a burning fire in Jeremiah's bones, compelling him to bring it to the covenant people day and night (Jer. 20:9). "Is not my word like fire, says the LORD, and like a hammer that breaks a rock in pieces?" (Jer. 23:29).

God's words are event-generating discourse; they are not only enlightening or informative, but are also *fulfilled* (Ezek. 12:28). The scene of the prophet preaching to the valley of dry bones in Ezekiel 37 vividly portrays this living and active word, which creates the reality of which it speaks. Only because the words of the prophets and apostles share in the energetic light of the hypostatic Word, and precisely because they do, they are the very word of God. Christ is the Word who upholds all of creation for the good of his church (Col. 1:15–20) and gives us his word to dwell in us richly (3:16).

With their sharp antithesis between outer and inner, visible and invisible, divine and human, enthusiasts through the ages have appealed to John 6:63 for an alleged contrast between the Spirit and the word, as if the latter were a "dead letter": "It is the Spirit that gives life; the flesh is useless." And yet, Jesus immediately adds, "The *words* that I have spoken to you are Spirit and life." The Spirit's role is to make the external word an inwardly experienced and embraced reality, not to offer a gnosis superior to the word itself. The Thessalonians are acknowledged as fellow saints, chosen in Christ, "because our message of the gospel came to you not in word only, but also in power and in the Holy Spirit and with full conviction" (1 Thess. 1:5). Nevertheless, the object and matter of the Spirit's testimony and conviction within us remains the Word of Christ externally proclaimed to us.

So the Word of God written and proclaimed is not an impersonal body of timeless doctrine or ethics, but is grounded ultimately in the Son as the climax of the Father's revealing and redeeming speech in a gradually unfolding history (Heb. 1:1–3), and in the Spirit as its perfecting power: the source of its perlocutionary effect. "Indeed, the word of God is living and active," exposing and judging our hearts (Heb. 4:12–13). According to James 1:21, the Word is an implanted seed "that has the power to save your souls." First Peter 1:23–24 adds, "You have been born anew, not of perishable but of imperishable seed, through the living and enduring word of God." Furthermore, it is not the word in general but the gospel in particular that is credited with this vivifying effect: "That word is the good news that was announced to you" (v. 25).

Similarly, Paul says that "faith comes by hearing . . . the word of God" (Rom. 10:17 NKJV), specifically, the word of gospel or good news (vv. 8, 15). Salvation is not something that one has to actively pursue, attain, and ascend to grasp, as if it were far away, but is as near as "the word of faith that we proclaim" (v. 8). We do not have to bring Christ up from the dead or ascend into heaven to bring him down, since he addresses us directly in his Word (vv. 6–9). The Word of God is the source not only of creation, but also of the events of judgment and redemption of history leading to the last day (2 Pet. 3:1–7). From creation to consummation, we are "worded" all the way down.

Throughout the prophetic writings, scrolls are eaten and burn in bellies; they fly around like a giant parchment with razor-sharp edges, bringing judgment to the ends of the earth. All of this imagery is meant to underscore the point that God's word as covenant canon not only speaks of but actually brings blessings and curses. Its sanctions are always effectively realized. Therefore, not only as word-events, but as an enduring constitution, God's word is living and active. By this canon, the Suzerain constructs a temple-house.[19]

Yet in order for it perpetually to regulate the covenant community, especially its preaching, it must also become a written treaty with all of its canonical elements: historical prologue, stipulations (doctrines and commands), and sanctions (death and life). Only as it conforms to that norm is the church's proclamation genuinely to be regarded as the Word of God. The Word of God spoken by the immediately commissioned prophets and apostles is magisterial in its authority, while the Word of God spoken by and in the church is ministerial. It is obvious from the prophetic writings as well as the gospels that the Word that comes through the prophets and apostles typically disrupts and judges the covenant community and its official ministry.

Consequently, the Word is not made alive, active, or effective by human decision or effort. The Word not only provides an occasion for this covenantal arraignment and absolution, if we can somehow make it present and relevant; but through it, Christ himself—personally, by his Spirit—also arraigns and absolves sinners. The Spirit's dynamic agency *traverses* the gap between revelation then and there and illumination here and now, without making them identical. It *is* God's presence-in-action and therefore establishes its own relevance. It binds and frees, hardens and softens, wounds and heals. Not even faith makes this Word effective; faith itself is created by the Spirit through that evangelical pronouncement. We see this in the event of Pentecost itself, where the first public evidence is Peter's proclamation of the gospel (Acts 2:14–36). Repeatedly in Acts, the growth of the church is attributed to the fact that "the word of God spread" and "prevailed" (6:7; 13:49; 19:20), and "proclaiming the good news" is the central activity described in this history of the early church. The spreading of the Word is even treated as synonymous with the spreading of the kingdom of God. By the Word we are legally adopted and by the Spirit we receive the inner witness that we are the children of God (Rom. 8:12–17). The Word of Christ creates faith in Christ, and where this is present, there is the church.

19. As I have referred to elsewhere, M. G. Kline's treatment of this theme is richly suggestive, in *The Structure of Biblical Authority* (Grand Rapids: Eerdmans, 1975; repr., Eugene, OR: Wipf & Stock, 1989), chap. 3.

What the Reformation reintroduced with respect to the medium is no less rev-
·olutionary than its insight into the message itself. It involved the recovery of the
more Hebraic understanding of the linguistically mediated character of all reality and the effectual character of speech. Furthermore, it eliminates the false
choice between forensic declaration and effective transformation. When God
declares something to be so, the Spirit brings about a corresponding reality within
us. By the same Spirit, this same evangelical Word justifies and renews.[20] Creaturely subjectivity becomes constitutively defined by the Creator's address. There
is not first a self or a community and then a word spoken to it; rather, both exist
as they have been worded to exist by God. This means that speech cannot be
reduced to the externalization of internal thoughts and states of mind; on the
contrary, God's covenantal speech is an external word that redefines us and consequently renews us inwardly, yielding the fruit of the Spirit.[21]

Stephen H. Webb goes so far as to suggest that the Reformation represents "an
event within the history of sound," an event of "revocalizing the Word."[22] Instead
of a chiefly visual event—a theatrical display—that fills the spatial distance
between transcendent Lord and the people separated by a screen, public worship
became a verbal event: even Communion was a vocal pledge which the whole
covenant community received and to which it responded in celebration. "This
follows," notes Webb, "from Calvin's belief that God's Word accomplishes what
it commands. It is covenantal speech, active and full of life. Even in its stutter-
ing, it has the power to give what it asks. God's Word called the world into being,
and it continues to uphold the world through the speech of the Spirit-filled
church."[23] Where medieval worship subordinated speech to sight, the Reformation (capitalizing on humanist concern for history and exegesis in the original
languages) sought to expose the people to God's voice.[24] "This was a verbosity
caused not by the need to explain an image or to make a moral point. Rather, it
was a verbosity intended to convey grace through sound."[25]

Luther led the way in recovering this emphasis on the church as the
creation of the Word. Summarizing the Lutheran confession, Oswald Bayer
explains, "Another person, speaking in the name and on the commission of
God, speaks this promise to me, but this is in fact the speaking and acting of God

20. I develop this point at length, esp. in part 2 of my previous volume in this series *Covenant
and Salvation: Union with Christ* (Louisville, KY: Westminster John Knox Press, 2007).

21. Something of a Luther renaissance on this score has occurred within the so-called New
Hermeneutic in the 1970s (Füchs and Ebeling), with their theology of the "word-event." However,
the tendency was to domesticate this eschatological radicalism by relegating it to the field of the individual's existential encounter rather than the sweep of redemptive history. To that extent, it is significantly different from Luther's concept.

22. Stephen H. Webb, *The Divine Voice: Christian Proclamation and the Theology of Sound* (Grand
Rapids: Brazos, 2004), esp. chaps. 4–5. This is a superb treatment of the principal issues addressed
in this chapter. See also Theo Hobson, *The Rhetorical Word: Protestant Theology and the Rhetoric of
Authority* (Hampshire, UK: Ashgate, 2002).

23. Webb, *The Divine Voice*, 159.

24. Ibid., 104–7.

25. Ibid., 106.

himself."[26] The Holy Spirit gives us faith through the means of preaching and sacrament "when and where he wills, in those who hear the gospel," according to article 5 of the Augsburg Confession.[27] Through preaching, the canon becomes not only a deposit of revelation "then and there" in the past, but also a means of grace in the present. God performs the task of slaying and making alive, casting us as characters in his play. Bayer asks,

> Is the Word to be rated that highly? Should we not inquire into its credibility and authority? Must not a material and tangible history stand behind it? Is it not just a witness to an event, from which it must be differentiated? Do we not have to agree with Goethe's Faust that we should "not value the Word so highly"? Should we not correct the first verse of John's Gospel, as Faust did, and say: "In the beginning was the—deed"?[28]

Not at all, answers Bayer: the word is deed and the deed is word.[29] "Our Western philosophical tradition has given the intellect prominence among our human faculties. Luther, however, says that 'there is no mightier or nobler work of man than *speech.*' We are not rational beings first of all; we are primarily speaking beings."[30] This is not a slight point for Luther.[31] "For Luther everything depends upon the Bible; hearing, using, and preaching it as the living voice of the gospel (*viva vox evangelii*)."[32] This is in contrast to Augustine, for whom "the external Word is a sign [*signum*] that simply points us to the matter [*res*]."[33]

Augustine assumed the realist (i.e., Platonist) view of sign-and-signified that tends to reduce discourse to reference—that is, merely describing rather than also creating states of affairs. Similarly, Webb reminds us, "For Augustine, . . . the Word that God speaks is heard internally before we give it an external voice. . . . Consequently, faith, like thought, begins in the interior recesses of the heart, where it is silent before it makes a sound."[34] We may even detect here an anticipation of modern epistemology and hermeneutics, from Descartes to Schleiermacher.

Yet for the Reformers, the relation is reversed: the Word is God's speech that comes from outside in, not from inside out. This emphasis on the *verbum externum* (external Word) is simply a correlate of salvation by God in Christ *extra nos* (outside of ourselves). In other words, the formal principle (*sola scriptura*) is not

26. Oswald Bayer, *Living by Grace: Justification and Sanctification*, trans. Geoffrey W. Bromiley (Grand Rapids: Eerdmans, 2003), 43.

27. *The Book of Concord*, trans. and ed. Theodore G. Tappert (Philadelphia: Fortress Press, 1959), 31.

28. Oswald Bayer, *Living by Faith: Justification and Sanctification*, Lutheran Quarterly Books (Grand Rapids: Eerdmans, 2003), 45.

29. Ibid.

30. Ibid., 47.

31. See, e.g., Martin Luther, *Luther's Works*, ed. Jaroslav Pelikan (St. Louis: Concordia, 1968), 35:117–24, 254, 359–60.

32. Bayer, *Living by Faith*, 45.

33. Ibid., 48, citing Augustine's *De magistro*, trans. and ed. J. Burleigh under the title *"The Teacher" in Augustine: Early Writings* (Philadelphia: Westminster Press, 1953), 70–71.

34. Webb, *The Divine Voice*, 131

an independent article, but is integrally connected with the material principle (*solo Christo, sola gratia, sola fide*) and the final end of our salvation (*soli Deo gloria*). Whatever becomes visible *within* individuals and the community—repentance, faith, love, and other aspects of moral renewal—is the progressive result of this definitive declaration *outside* of them.

This emphasis on the external Word as the medium of God's saving action is the line that separates the Reformers from what they regarded as the "enthusiasm" common to Rome and the Radical Protestants.[35] Though highly esteemed as divine revelation, Scripture was a dead letter that had to be supplemented by ongoing revelation: the living voice of the Spirit through the church or the contemporary prophet. However, the Reformers emphasized that proclamation of the Word is not simply the preacher's discourse about Christ (much less the myriad other things that preachers are wont to address). Rather, as Bayer summarizes, "the preached Word that comes to us by word of mouth is Jesus Christ himself now present with us."[36] Far from a dead letter awaiting animation, "The gospel *is* the kingdom. It does not simply proclaim it or point to it; it [actually] brings and causes all the hearers, including myself, to enter it." The gospel is God's own utterance. "As Jesus Christ, as God himself, the gospel, when preached by word of mouth, does more than simply offer us the possibility that I can actualize and make it real by my own decision of faith. The Word itself is the power of God, God's kingdom."[37] Luther famously declares,

> For if you ask a Christian what the work is by which he becomes worthy of the name "Christian," he will be able to give absolutely no other answer than that it is the hearing of the Word of God, that is, faith. Therefore, the ears alone are the organs of a Christian man, for he is justified and declared to be a Christian, not because of the works of any member but because of faith.[38]

The choice of preaching as a medium is not incidental. This puts us on the *receiving* end of things; not only does justification come through faith alone, but faith itself also comes through hearing.[39]

We discover the same emphasis on the preached Word in the Reformed confessions. "For Calvin as for Luther," as John H. Leith observes, "the ears alone are the organ of the Christian."[40] Calvin summarizes, "When the Gospel is preached

35. See Willem Balke, *Calvin and the Anabaptist Radicals*, trans. William J. Heynen (Grand Rapids: Eerdmans, 1981).

36. Bayer, *Living by Grace*, 49.

37. Ibid., 50; see Rom. 1:16–17 with 1 Cor. 4:20.

38. Luther, *Luther's Works*, vol. 29, *Lectures on Titus, Philemon, and Hebrews*, ed. Jaroslav Pelikan (St. Louis: Concordia Publishing House, 1968), 224; quoted in Webb, *The Divine Voice*, 144.

39. This comparison between hearing and seeing is not meant to suggest that there is some magical quality to hearing or that God is bound by this medium. Rather, it is to say that God has bound himself to the spoken word as the *ordinary* method of self-communication. Like Augustine, many Christians would refer to their reading of Scripture as a moment of conversion. Furthermore, physical disabilities such as deafness are no obstacle to God's grace. Webb offers a well-informed treatment of this issue in *The Divine Voice*, 51–55.

40. John H. Leith, "Doctrine of the Proclamation of the Word," in *John Calvin and the Church: A Prism of Reform*, ed. Timothy George (Louisville, KY: Westminster John Knox Press, 1990), 212.

in the name of God, it is as if God himself spoke in person."[41] Leith elaborates, "The justification for preaching is not in its effectiveness for education or reform. . . . The preacher, Calvin dared to say, was the mouth of God." It was God's intention and action that made it effective. The minister's words, like the physical elements of the sacraments, were united to the substance: Christ and all of his benefits. Therefore, the Word not only describes salvation, but also conveys it. "Calvin's sacramental doctrine of preaching enabled him both to understand preaching as a very human work and to understand it as the work of God."[42]

Following the Pauline logic in Romans 10, Calvin emphasizes that we must refuse any contrast between the outer and inner Word. "We hear his ministers speaking just as if he himself spoke. . . . God breathes faith into us only by the instrument of his gospel, as Paul points out that 'faith comes by hearing.'"[43] Paul "not only makes himself a co-worker with God, but also assigns himself the function of imparting salvation."[44] Without the work of the Spirit, the Word would fall on deaf ears, but the Spirit opens deaf ears *through* the external Word.[45]

Similarly, the Heidelberg Catechism, after treating justification, asks, "If it is by faith alone that we share in Christ and all his benefits, then where does this faith come from?" It answers, "The Holy Spirit produces it in our hearts by the preaching of the holy gospel [Rom. 10:17; 1 Pet. 1:23–25] and confirms it through our use of the holy sacraments [Matt. 28:19–20; 1 Cor. 10:16]."[46] According to the Second Helvetic Confession,

> The preaching of the Word of God is the Word of God. Wherefore when this Word of God is now preached in the church by preachers lawfully called, we believe that the very Word of God is proclaimed, and received by the faithful; and that neither any other Word of God is to be invented nor is to be expected from heaven: and that now the Word itself which is preached is to be regarded, not the minister that preaches; for even if he be evil and a sinner, nevertheless the Word of God remains still true and good.[47]

Regardless of the subjective piety or intention of the minister, the Word of God is effective.

This should caution us against identifying effectiveness either with the antiquity and prestige of a particular office or with the charisma and communicative gifts of a particular person. The medium is consistent with the message of the cross. The fact that some of the most significant witnesses in the history of redemption are characterized as inferior speakers—Moses (Exod. 4:10), Isaiah

---

41. Quoted by Leith, "Doctrine of the Proclamation," 211.
42. Ibid., 210–11.
43. Calvin, *Institutes* 4.1.5–6.
44. Ibid., 4.1.6.
45. John Calvin, *Commentary on John*, trans. and ed. William Pringle (repr., Grand Rapids: Baker, 1993) on 15:27.
46. The Heidelberg Catechism, Q. 61, in *Ecumenical Creeds and Reformed Confessions* (Grand Rapids: CRC Publications, 1988).
47. The Second Helvetic Confession, chap. 1, in *BC*.

(Isa. 6:5–8), and Paul (1 Cor. 2:4), among others—is surely of some consequence. Yet all of this is "so that your faith might rest not on human wisdom but on the power of God" (cf. 1 Cor. 2:5). The power of the Word lies in the ministry of the Spirit, not in the ministers themselves.

In this conception, God's Word is both a vital energy and a normative constitution. The Spirit is the source of both the original hearing and speaking of the prophets and apostles and of the hearing and speaking of ministers today whose proclamation conforms to that rule. Unlike the constitutions of nation-states, Scripture was not regarded by the Reformers or their heirs as an impersonal legal document or as a social contract, much less as an expression of inner piety or religious experience. Rather, "the supreme judge of all controversies," according to the Westminster Confession, "is the Holy Spirit speaking in the Scripture."[48]

Whenever the Word is proclaimed, the Lord of the covenant assembles his people and the rainbow reappears amid dissipating clouds as God remembers the truce that he has made with us. Through this canon—written, read, sung, and prayed—but especially as it is proclaimed anew, strangers to God and each other become a communion. Only this canon can create this particular community. It is through these Scriptures alone that the Spirit makes Christ's mediatorial headship real in the life of the church, since it is only these texts that are "exhaled" (*theopneustos*) by the Spirit (2 Pet. 1:21; 2 Tim. 3:16).

Challenging the Radical sects for their contrast between the Word that "merely beats the air" and the "inner Word" resident within the individual, the Second Helvetic Confession continues, "Neither do we think that therefore the outward preaching is to be thought as fruitless because the instruction in true religion depends on the inward illumination of the Spirit, or because it is written, 'And no longer shall each one teach his neighbor . . . , for they shall all know me' (Jer. 31:34)."[49] That God *can* illumine inwardly apart from the external preaching is not denied, but this work of the Spirit within is in Scripture connected to the outward preaching of mere mortals (the confession cites Mark 16:15; Acts 16:14; and Rom. 10:17). The Westminster Larger Catechism adds,

> The Spirit of God maketh the reading, *but especially the preaching* of the Word, an effectual means of enlightening, convincing, and humbling sinners, of *driving them out of themselves*, and drawing them unto Christ, of conforming them to his image, and subduing them to his will; of strengthening them against temptations and corruptions; of building them up in grace, and establishing their hearts in holiness and comfort through faith unto salvation. (emphasis added)[50]

It is not only the message but also the method that drives us out of ourselves, which an "inner word" cannot do. We cannot tell ourselves what is most important. We do not already know what is relevant. How can we judge or justify

---

48. The Westminster Confession of Faith, chap. 1, in *BC*.
49. Ibid.
50. The Westminster Larger Catechism, Q. 155, in *BC*.

ourselves when we have so cleverly suppressed and distorted the truth that we do not even know when we are obscuring it? We may even embellish our self-constructions with biblical references and allusions. However, the patient cannot diagnose herself. The law must be proclaimed in all of its force, as God's unmasking of the "spin" with which we have told the story of our lives, and the gospel must be proclaimed in all of its joy, as God's own act of clothing us in Christ's righteousness.

Just as we cannot set the Spirit against the Word, we cannot set the Word against the church. Because the Spirit works through creaturely means, rather than directly and immediately, a creaturely community arises. Faith does not arise spontaneously in one's soul, but in the covenantal gathering of fellow hearers. As Bonhoeffer writes,

> If there were an unmediated work of the Spirit, then the idea of the church would be individualistically dissolved from the outset. But in the word the most profound social nexus is established from the beginning. *The word is social in character, not only in its origin but also in its aim.* Tying the Spirit to the word means that the Spirit aims at *a plurality of hearers* and establishes a visible sign by which the actualization is to take place. The word, however, is qualified by being the very word of Christ; it is effectively brought to the heart of the hearers by the Spirit. (emphasis added)[51]

In public proclamation, distinct even from reading Scripture myself, "it is another who speaks, and this becomes an incomparable assurance for me."

> Total strangers proclaim God's grace and forgiveness to me, not as their own experience, but as God's will. It is in the others that I can grasp in concrete form the church-community and its Lord as the guarantors of my confidence in God's grace. The fact that others assure me of God's grace makes the church-community real for me; it rules out any danger or hope that I might have fallen prey to an illusion. The confidence of faith arises not only out of solitude, but also out of the assembly.[52]

Therefore, the church is the community created by the gospel, not just entrusted with it. Baptism and the Supper are inextricably linked to preaching and catechesis: the church always remains a "creation of the word," Bonhoeffer insists.

> To summarize, the word is the sociological principle by which the entire church is built up, . . . both in numbers and in its faith. Christ is the foundation upon which, and according to which, the building of the church is raised (1 Corinthians 3; Eph. 2:20). And thus it grows into a "holy temple of God" (Eph. 2:21), and "with a growth that is from God" (Col. 2:19), "until all of us come to maturity, to the measure of the full stature of Christ" (Eph. 4:13), and in all this growing "into him who is the head, into Christ." The entire building begins and ends with Christ, and its unifying center is the word.[53]

51. Dietrich Bonhoeffer, *SC*, 158.
52. Ibid., 230.
53. Ibid., 247.

The preaching creates the community, while the Supper, by evoking personal acceptance through faith, makes that community in some sense visible.[54] "We hear the word of God through the word of the church, and this is what constitutes the authority of the church."[55] Only because of this does one owe obedience to the church, submitting private opinions to her tutelage, yet never contrary to the Word itself.[56] Insofar as the church speaks God's Word, its authority is not illusory or an exercise in arbitrary power.

THE HEGEMONY OF VISION: MASTERS OF ALL WE SURVEY

Although contrasts between Hebraic and Hellenistic modes of thought are often overblown, the priority of hearing and seeing in each respectively suggests strong evidence of real differences in these two major tributaries of Western thought. Our opening chapter already drew the contrast between the economy of grace and the ascent of mind, the latter captive to a Platonist theory of vision.

In an important essay, Hans Blumenberg traced the genealogy of the metaphor of vision in Western philosophy back to "a dualistic conception of the world" found, for example, in Parmenides' poem *The Way of Opinion*, but made common coinage by Plato.[57] Despite its transformations and permutations, vision/light becomes the master metaphor for knowledge and experience from antiquity, through the medieval era, on into the modern age, suitably named the Enlightenment. Blumenberg reminds us of the significance of "the closed, medieval chamber in Descartes' portrayal of the turning point in his thinking: 'I remained for a whole day by myself in a small stove-heated room.'"[58] With Descartes especially, modernity turns inward for illumination. Interestingly, Paul Tillich draws attention to the common theme of an "inner light" running throughout both the radical mystical sects and the rationalists in the modern era, though he is not alone in observing that connection.[59]

As Blumenberg points out, the modern appropriation of the metaphorics of light is in many respects indistinguishable from ancient gnosis, identifying "the inner light of the mind" with a primal divine light dispersed and trapped in matter. No longer a metaphor for an ethical, eschatological, covenantal, and historical

---

54. Ibid.

55. Ibid., 250.

56. Ibid., 251.

57. Hans Blumenberg, "Light as a Metaphor for Truth: At the Preliminary Stage of Philosophical Concept Formation," in *Modernity and the Hegemony of Vision*, ed. David Michael Levin (Berkeley: University of California Press, 1993), 32.

58. Ibid.

59. Paul Tillich, *The History of Christian Thought*, ed. Carl E. Braaten (1967; repr., New York: Simon & Schuster, 1967), 317–18. Among the many historians pointing out this relationship, see Peter Gay, *The Enlightenment: An Interpretation* (New York: W. W. Norton, 1966), 62, 291, 326–29, 348, 350.

transition from sin (darkness) to redemption (light), gnosis advocates a return of light to itself, the inner spirit's deliverance from its imprisonment in matter.[60] This description seems to fit the pedagogical ascent of mind in Origen. Yet the flight upward is also a flight inward, and this is no more obvious than in the Enlightenment. Interiorization and rationalization lead inexorably to the captivity of the Word to the inner self, an immanentization that eventually assimilates the alien Word of a transcendent yet personally immanent God to the autonomy of a purely human word. It is significant that an epoch that would no longer *hear* God speak would announce its arrival as "enlightenment."

Yet all of these terms were so fundamentally bound up with metaphors of vision (concepts, ideas, contemplation, comprehending, recognizing, viewing, etc.) in the Western intellectual tradition that it has always been difficult to make the aural analogies primary. For example, intuition comes from the Latin *intueri*, "to gaze upon."[61] As Derrida reminds us, even speech itself can be assimilated to intellectual vision (full presence) when it is conceived primarily as the manifestation of inner thoughts rather than as communication and communion with the other.[62]

Christian theology was bound to recognize dissonance between Hellenistic and biblical interpretations at this point. Already in Genesis, "the light of the first day represents created light," originating "not in a primordial dualism" between light and darkness but in "a divine command." "God Himself is beyond this opposition and has it at His disposal. This requires a reversal of the initial, dualistic cast that late antiquity gave to metaphors of light."[63] The word comes before the light.

It was Irenaeus who first confronted gnostic dualism directly and in the process also challenged Neoplatonism's metaphorics of light.[64] Augustine also trans-

60. Hans Blumenberg, "Light as a Metaphor," 40.

61. Ibid., 54 n. 1.

62. Derrida notes that primacy of *phonē* (speech) assumes the illusion of presence, "the system of 'hearing (understanding) oneself speak' . . . which presents itself as the nonexterior, nonmundane, therefore nonempirical or noncontingent signifier" (Jacques Derrida, *Of Grammatology*, ed. Gayatri Chakrovorty Spivak [Baltimore: Johns Hopkins University Press, 1976], 8; cf. 16). This presence as Parousia is "another name for death, historical metonymy where God's name holds death in check. That is why, if this movement begins its era in the form of Platonism, it ends in infinitist metaphysics. *Only infinite being can reduce the difference in presence.* In that sense, the name of God, at least as it is pronounced within classical rationalism, is the name of indifference itself" (271, emphasis added). The world presents itself in thought: "the Greek domination of the Same and the One, . . . an oppression certainly comparable to none other in the world, an ontological or transcendental oppression" (Jacques Derrida, *Writing and Difference* [Chicago: University of Chicago Press, 1978], 83). See also idem, *Specters of Marx* (New York: Routledge, 1994) (esp. 75). For a fascinating conversation between Marion and Derrida on the so-called "metaphysics of presence" in the Christian Neoplatonic tradition, see the first two chapters in *God, the Gift, and Postmodernism*, ed. John D. Caputo and Michael J. Scanlon (Bloomington: Indiana University Press, 1999), 20–78. However, Derrida's account (and criticism) of *phonē* presupposes a Greek rather than Hebraic (covenantal) conception.

63. Blumenberg, "Light as a Metaphor," 40–41.

64. Paul Ricoeur, *History and Truth*, trans. Charles A. Kelbley (Evanston, IL: Northwestern University Press, 1965), 111: "Let us think about the scope of the revolution in the history of thought that this text [Irenaeus's *Against Heresies*] represents in relation to that Neoplatonism in which reality is a progressive withdrawal, an ineluctable beclouding that increases as we descend from the One,

formed this metaphorics, away from seeing into the light in the direction of see-ing in the light. In other words, light illumines the word.[65] It is an act of grace experienced in conversion.[66] The light by which we see, rather than the object at which we gaze in a blinding and comprehensive vision, governs Augustine's con-ception. Blumenberg actually goes so far as to judge, "Never before and never since has the language of light been handled in such a subtle and richly nuanced way."[67]

In spite of such transformations, the metaphorics of light and vision contin-ued to exercise a dominant epistemological role, notes Blumenberg:

> For Greek thought, all certainty was based on visibility. What *logoi* referred back to was a sight with form . . . , i.e., *eidos*. Even etymologically, "knowl-edge" and "essence" (as *eidos*) are extremely closely related to "seeing." *Logos* is a collection of what has been seen. For Heraclitus, eyes are "more exact witnesses than ears." . . . For the Greeks, "hearing" is of no significance for truth and is initially nonbinding. As an imparting of *doxa* [opinion], it rep-resents an assertion that must always be confirmed visually. For the Old Tes-tament literature, however, and for the consciousness of truth it documents, seeing is always predetermined, put into question, or surpassed by hearing. The created is based on the Word, and in terms of its binding claim, the Word always precedes the created. The real reveals itself within the horizon of its signification, a horizon allocated by hearing.[68]

This clash is seen in Philo's attempt to "translate" hearing into seeing.[69]

By contrast, Blumenberg observes, Luther's *De servo arbitrio* (*On the Bondage of the Will*), "plays metaphors of the ear against those of the eye."

> The eye wanders, selects, approaches things, presses after them, while the ear, for its part, is affected and accosted. The eye can seek, the ear can only wait. Seeing "places" things; hearing is placed. . . . That which demands unconditionally is encountered in "hearing." Conscience has a "voice," not light.[70]

Luther shifted attention back to founding utterances going forth from God's mouth rather than primordial ideas in the divine mind that remain eternally still.

---

which is formless, to the Mind, which is bodiless, to the World Soul, and to souls which are plunged into matter, which itself is absolute darkness." Ricoeur asks, "Are we sensitive to the distance between this text" and Neoplatonic speculations?

65. Hans Blumenberg, "Light as a Metaphor," 43.

66. Ibid., 44.

67. Ibid., 42.

68. Ibid., 46.

69. Ibid., 46–47. Stephen H. Webb offers another example, from Philo's *On the Life of Moses*, which shifts the concentration from the voice to the burning bush and goes so far as to assert that the voice was seen. "Why is God's voice visible?" asks Webb, offering Philo's answer: "'Because whatever God says is not words but deeds, which are judged by the eyes rather than the ears'" (Webb, *The Divine Voice*, 182). Evidently, words were not to be regarded as deeds. This is the danger of the hermeneutics of signification that we find not only in Philo but also in Origen and Augustine. Whereas, according to the biblical outlook, we accomplish things by speaking, in this worldview words "stand for" or "re-present" (visual metaphors) the reality signified.

70. Blumenberg, "Light as a Metaphor," 48.

Oswald Bayer explains concerning Luther's view, "The new creation is a conversion to the world, as a conversion to the Creator, hearing God's voice speaking to us and addressing us through his creatures. Augustine was wrong to say that his voice draws us away from God's creatures into the inner self and then to transcendence."[71] Hearing actually calls us out of our subjectivity and renders us extrinsic, extroverted, and social creatures.

While the Western intellectual tradition (which shares obvious affinities in this respect with Eastern thought) aims at transcending the realm of temporal and changing shadows (i.e., history) in the contemplative ascent toward timeless truth, biblical faith concentrates its attention on God's descent to us in history. The oral/aural is therefore inextricably related to the historical, as Walter Ong also points out in his magisterial study.[72] Something has happened in the datable past (which is itself connected to speech) and must therefore be told; those who tell the story are witnesses to events, and their telling and retelling of the story is itself an event. Unlike other religions, biblical faith was oriented not toward contemplation of eternal truths or natural cycles, but toward the proclamation of happenings.[73]

To historical events corresponds a personal summons:

> God calls to Abraham, "Abraham!" and Abraham answers, "Here I am" (Gen 22:1). A similar thing happens to Jacob . . . (Gen 31:11). Erich Auerbach has made clear in the first chapter of his *Mimesis*, this direct and unexplained confrontation—verbal assault on a given person by God—is not the sort of thing one meets with in Greek or other nonbiblical tradition. God's word impinges on the human person as a two-edged sword. In the prophets, the sense of the word of God reaches particular intensity. . . . The word is not an inert record but a living something, like sound, something going on.[74]

In an oral/aural culture, the past is present, not only in records but also in the living speech and institutions of the people. Homer's epic occurred in a setting of singing and play, and it was always told in such social events. "As events, words are more celebrations and less tools than in literate cultures," Ong suggests, offering examples from the Psalms and Jesus' Beatitudes.[75] In these cultures, truth, like speech, is an event, a happening within one's life situation. Unlike Plato's timeless ideas, "it is never remote."[76] In an oral culture, I am not the dispassion-

71. Bayer, *Living by Faith*, 28.

72. Walter J. Ong, SJ, *The Presence of the Word: Some Prolegomena for Cultural and Religious History* (Minneapolis: University of Minnesota Press, 1981), 4: "Thorlief Boman has brought together massive evidence of the Hebrew-Greek contrast, and, although James Barr has contested some of Boman's interpretations and procedures, the contrast itself remains clear enough." Cf. Thorlief Boman, *Hebrew Thought Compared with Greek*, trans. Jules L. Moreau (Philadelphia: Westminster Press, 1961); and James Barr, *The Semantics of Biblical Language* (London: Oxford University Press, 1961).

73. Ong, *The Presence of the Word*, 10.

74. Ibid., 12.

75. Ibid., 30.

76. Ibid., 33.

ate master of objects in space, but a participant in the middle of happenings. Homeric stories were recited; they were communal events, while Plato's "beatific vision" was a lonely intellectual pursuit.[77]

It is not surprising that in our highly literate cultures, visual metaphors dominate our lexicon for coming to truth. An idea can be stopped, observed, and dissected, while speech cannot.[78] Speech "implies movement and thus implies change."[79] This is what makes hearing and speaking so appropriate within a covenantal context, where history and witness, summons and response, are central. Unlike ideas, concepts, and other static images apprehended by the inner or outer eye, orality is reciprocating communication. As Ong reminds us, as the Word of God the incarnate Son "is God's communication to man, he is also man's response to God."[80]

Ong distinguishes not only between biblical and Hellenistic approaches, but also highlights important differences in Greek culture between the Homeric era and Plato. Where the oral cultures of the Bible and Homer regarded the spoken word as "winged words," Plato made speech subordinate to intellectual contemplation of eternal ideas. Furthermore, modernity increasingly assimilated even the written deposits of these oral cultures to the inert matter that could be dissected, mapped, and controlled in space by mind.[81] "Sight presents surfaces," while hearing presents us with interiors without violating them for inspection.[82] Speech reveals purpose and depth, without allowing us to seize an object by our gaze.

If anything, the Enlightenment intensified this reduction of the senses to vision. Hearing and testimony give us opinion; seeing something for oneself (intellectually, for the rationalist or idealist; physically, for the empiricist) yields knowledge. Ong observes that in Locke's "An Essay concerning Human Understanding" (1690), the entire sensorium is reduced to sight.[83] Thinking and seeing can be private activities, but communication is social. "Inevitably, 'individualism' came into its own as the socializing effects inherent in voice as sound were minimized." This is the "devocalization of the universe," reaching its apex in Newton.[84] Eighteenth-century deists commonly referred to God as an architect more than a communicator and the human person became "a spectator and manipulator in the universe rather than a participator."[85] As Kant pointed out, "phenomena [*phainomenon*]" means "appearance," from *phainein*, "to show."[86] In the modern age, this attempt to "envision" the world is encouraged with the apparatus of maps and globes.[87]

77. Ibid., 34–35.
78. Ibid., 40–41.
79. Ibid., 42.
80. Ibid., 13.
81. Ibid., 93.
82. Ibid., 117–18.
83. Ibid., 66–68.
84. Ibid., 72.
85. Ibid., 73.
86. Ibid., 74.
87. Ibid., 9.

We see ourselves less as indwelling or inhabiting the world that sustains us than as masters of all we survey. It is little wonder that the problem of "noumena" beyond the surfaces of "phenomena" arises, when all of reality is reduced to spatial modes of thinking. And it is no wonder that we also lose the depth of being in the bargain, since temporal events, change, coming into being, and passing away become relegated to the realm of mere appearances even more viciously than in Platonism. "To bring us where we are, the word must have been transplanted from its natural habitat, sound, to a new habitat, space," says Ong.[88]

Even written texts could serve this transformation, especially with the advent of movable type. Words on a page, written and read individually, necessarily lose something of the social, living, present-tense, and eventful character of orality.[89] Although Ong may sometimes overly contrast the spoken and written word, he does point out that the incarnation of the Word occurred just at the historical intersection of oral and written cultures.[90] This is an important observation for my argument in this chapter and the next: the proclamation of Christ that gave and gives the church is also a canon that defines and norms it. While textuality better preserves the record of the past and its originary discourse, sound binds us to each other in the present, in an existential relationship. One may privately read a text that was originally a public, social event, but the dynamics are different. In the latter, we discern personal presences and not simply the words. "It is 'here.' It envelops us."[91] Furthermore, speech "establishes here-and-now personal presence." "Abraham knew God's presence when he heard his 'voice.'"[92] The same could be said of Adam and Eve fleeing the voice of Yahweh. There may be presence without voice, but there is no voice without presence. The voice "simply conveys presence as nothing else does."[93] When we are addressed by someone, we can say yes or no, but we cannot be indifferent or aloof, as is more easily the case with reading.

In our age of mass communications, Ong wonders, "May it not be that God is not dead but that we rather are deaf?"[94] If Ong's analysis captures the differences between sound and mechanical media, his conclusions are even more obviously evident more recently in the assimilation of interpersonal speech to

88. Ibid., 92.

89. Ibid., 96–97.

90. Ibid., 23. Since writing the almost-final draft of this volume, I read Webb's *The Divine Voice* (see note 4 above). Among his tremendous insights is his nuanced analysis of Ong's contribution. Though generally appreciative, he points out some of the reductionisms in Ong's treatment, such as a nostalgia for orality over writing motivating a somewhat facile generalization that "primitive" equals oral-aural and "modern" equals visual (39–40). Furthermore, Webb notes that the torch that Ong carries for oral over written speech is largely driven by his commitment to "the relative autonomy of unwritten tradition" as opposed to *sola scriptura* (37). In spite of these criticisms, I think that the priority that Ong attributes to orality is a view shared by the Magisterial Reformers. As I mention above, as late as the Westminster Confession, it is "the reading, but especially the preaching" of Scripture that God employs as a means of grace.

91. Ong, *The Presence of The Word*, 101.

92. Ibid., 113.

93. Ibid., 114.

94. Ibid., 16.

textual-graphic vision in the Internet age and its false promises of presence and social communion apart from embodied (face-to-face) encounter. Words themselves become assimilated to vision: characters on the screen and on countless pages of advertising copy that we daily encounter. Our sense of time becomes assimilated to the spatial register.

Words—especially spoken words—were regarded as more powerful in oral cultures. Even the messenger was the monarch's representative precisely in the official act of *speaking for* the crown.[95] Orality also invites broad social participation and forms community along different lines than literate cultures. Even reading words on a page can allow withdrawal into oneself, which is why reading silently to oneself was virtually unheard of until quite recent times.[96] Furthermore, because writing has rules and "will not tolerate all that goes on in oral speech," the latter is available to everyone, establishing a sociability that is not ranked according to class or education.[97] "Sound unites groups of living beings as nothing else does."[98] This is not to marginalize the other senses, but our sense of sound requires "a certain distance" while inviting reciprocal communication. Real community comes into being with a common language.[99]

Ong refers to the way sound shapes and mediates space to our bodies. Notice how closely his account of speech is especially appropriate for a covenantal ecclesiology: "Since pure interiors (persons) do communicate with one another so largely by voice, the silencing of words portends in some way withdrawal into oneself."[100] We are reminded once again of Descartes's autobiographical account mentioned above, not to mention the Internet as the bricolage for modernity at least as much as postmodernity. At last, words themselves—in a constant stream that can finally render us immune to their power—become almost entirely assimilated to the iconic and even oral discourse can be reduced to sound bites. As a consequence, despite the advertisements of techno-evangelists, everyone is "connected" at the expense of bodily presence or speech. It is a "real presence" that threatens the reality of being actually present: Gnosticism with a vengeance.

Whereas sound situates us in the middle of things as they are happening, vision puts us in front of things in a sequential order. We can only "fix" our gaze on one part of a given landscape in any given moment. With sound, however, we hear things all around us, simultaneously, which places us in the middle of things rather than in front of them. So although it is more fleeting, sound is more enveloping as well.[101] "Hearing does not of itself dissect as sight does. . . . 'I am *in* his presence,' we say, not 'in front of his presence.' *Being in* is what we experience in a world of sound."[102]

---

95. Ibid., 112.
96. Ibid., 126.
97. Ibid., 116.
98. Ibid., 122.
99. Ibid., 123–24.
100. Ibid., 125–26.
101. Ibid., 129.
102. Ibid., 130.

Although our theology of the word cannot be made subordinate to a general theory of sound, it is worth reminding ourselves why, in God's creation and providence as well as redemptive history, *proclamation* of Christ has been the primary means of grace. "Sound of itself generates a sense of mystery," accenting personal activity, Ong reminds us. A speaker cannot be a thing, a mere object arranged mathematically in space.[103] Acoustic space becomes inhabited space: in other words, a place, situating us in the middle of things, not on the periphery, observing.[104] While communication is a two-way dialogue, vision "is of itself a one-way operation."[105] Touch "can certainly mediate present, but at the risk of loss of reverence," notes Ong, referring to Jesus' warning after his resurrection, "Do not touch me, for I have not yet ascended to my Father" (cf. John 20:17 KJV). "Only the sense of hearing gives us a space which is by direct suggestion peopled and by the same token endowed with sacral qualities."[106]

"In a world dominated by sound impressions, the individual is enveloped in a certain unpredictability. As has been seen, sound itself signals action that is going on. Something is happening, so you had better be alert."[107] In the light of Ong's observations, we gain a better sense of Jesus' comparison of the Spirit's mysterious and unpredictable working with the wind that "blows where it wishes, and you hear the sound of it but cannot tell where it comes from" (John 3:8 NKJV).

"HEAR, O ISRAEL . . .": COVENANTAL SPEECH

The covenantal liturgy of hearing-and-answering is evident already in creation, reminding us that creation itself is covenantally constituted rather than being a relationship added to creation. God prepares a place by speaking, "Let there be!" and even the "response" of inanimate creation can be assimilated metaphorically to this antiphonal liturgy of the covenant (Ps. 19:1–4). Yet it is only humans who, as God's royal image-bearers, reply with specific intentionality and in fulfillment of their specific commission, "Here I am."[108] In this way, they not only testify to God's goodness and glory, but through their own speech also accept the created place that God has assigned them in the cosmos, instead of fleeing to some supposedly autonomous or neutral space. Whatever space anyone occupies, it is always a place spoken into being by God. It is through covenantal discourse as well as their embodiment that human beings are located in a time that becomes history and a space that becomes place.

---

103. Ibid., 163.
104. Ibid., 164.
105. Ibid., 167.
106. Ibid.
107. Ibid., 131.
108. I develop this point in *Lord and Servant: A Covenant Christology* (Louisville, KY: Westminster John Knox Press, 2005), esp. chap. 4.

Idols and Speakers

Significantly, the arraignment of Adam and Eve after the fall reveals the interruption of this covenantal liturgy of summons and response. It occurs first of all with the choice to seize the object of the gaze rather than hear and obey the command, then again in the summons, "Adam, where are you?" which is met no longer with, "Here I am," but first with silence and then the word games between Eve and the serpent, between Adam and Eve, and then finally with Adam's response to God. The fragile cord of truthful discourse is broken and along with it, the covenant itself.

One of the running subplots in these three volumes, as I believe in Scripture itself, is the contrast between idolatry and faith. The former requires its gods to make themselves available, fully present, visible, which means capable of being possessed and, if need be, manipulated to produce whatever the individual's or group's felt needs are determined to be in any moment.

The nihilistic *eros* of the consumer society, which seems to have drawn much of American Christianity into its wake, creates a desire that can never be satisfied. Ads and shop windows offer us a perpetual stream of icons promising to fulfill our ambitions to have the life that they represent: a fully realized eschatology. Handing our credit card to the salesperson can be a sacrament of this transaction between sign and signified. Yet this anonymous space of endless consumption is the parody of the place of promise: true *shalom*. Consuming images, living on the surface of immanence, we refuse to be called out of ourselves by an external word that would truly unite us to God and our neighbor. Silently and alone, we surf channels and Web sites, window-shopping for identities.

Significantly, the prophets often center their protest against the idols on the fact that they do not speak; they are utterly breathless.

> What use is an idol once its maker has shaped it—a cast image, a teacher of lies? For its maker trusts in what has been made, though the product is only an idol *that cannot speak!* Alas for you who say to the wood, "Wake up!" to silent stone, "Rouse yourself!" Can it *teach*? See, it is gold and silver plated, and there is no *breath* in it at all. But the LORD is in his holy temple; let all the earth *keep silence* before him! (Hab. 2:18–20, emphasis added)

It is this contrast that the Heidelberg Catechism emphasizes when it rejects any visible image of God even as "teaching aids for the unlearned." "We should not try to be wiser than God. He wants his people instructed by the living preaching of his Word—not by idols that cannot even talk."[109]

In idolatrous religion, the worshipers do all the talking—they are the creators of their religious poetics, expressing in symbols their own inner experience of what, finally, is simply themselves and their awareness (falsely interpreted) of the immanent creation. One never really meets a stranger but only encounters oneself in the

---

109. The Heidelberg Catechism, Q. 98, in *Ecumenical Creeds and Reformed Confessions*.

mirror (hence, the truth in the account of religion that one finds in Feuerbach, Nietzsche, and Freud). By contrast, *Yahweh* speaks and the *people* are told to be silent, to give ear to their Covenant Lord. Unlike the idols that cannot speak, God created all things by the word of his mouth (Jer. 10:1–5). "When he utters his voice, there is a tumult of waters in the heavens, and he makes the mist rise from the ends of the earth" (vv. 12–13). Not only the worship but even the making of images is strictly forbidden in the Decalogue.[110]

The "god" who is made present for the human gaze and manipulation is never the true God, Yahweh. Hence, the close connection between the first and second commandments: worshiping the right God (i.e., Yahweh) is dependent on worshiping God in the right manner (i.e., giving ear to his word). In fashioning images, the worshiper is the judge; as a hearer of God's voice, the worshiper is judged—and in this judgment, is saved by the Good Shepherd. "The sheep hear his voice. He calls his own sheep by name and leads them out, . . . and the sheep follow him because they know his voice" (John 10:3–4).

Elsewhere I have appealed to Paul Ricoeur's contrast between a hermeneutics of the sacred and a hermeneutics of proclamation, which is exactly right.[111] It also highlights the broader contrast between "overcoming estrangement" (revelation as a new awareness of the sacredness of all things in an ontological unity and harmonious whole through the ascent of mind) and "meeting a stranger," especially as it relates to the consequences for ecclesiology outlined in chapter 1 (above). Drawing on Gerhard von Rad, Ricoeur points out, "The whole of Israel's theology is organized around certain fundamental discourses." Even hymn, wisdom, and other genres "are grafted onto the polarity of tradition" (i.e., narrative), which consists of founding events, and "prophecy," which is criticism of Israel's self-confidence. Torah smashes idols. "A theology of the Name is opposed to any hierophany of an idol. Hearing the word has taken the place of a vision of signs."[112] The idol, as the prophets routinely point out, is the expression of the inner self's felt needs. Idols do not come to us from the outside and address us; rather, they come into existence from our own experience, longings, representations, and delusions.

Although there is still sacred space and time in the biblical traditions, the emphasis is ethical, eschatological, and theological rather than aesthetic and mystical. Furthermore, ritual is "no longer founded on the correlation between myth and ritual as in the sacred universe," since the sacredness of nature "withdraws

---

110. See John Bright, *A History of Israel*, 3rd ed. (1972; repr., Philadelphia: Westminster Press, 1981), 160–61; cf. Walter Brueggeman, *Theology of the Old Testament: Faith, Dispute, Advocacy* (Minneapolis: Fortress Press, 1997), 429–50. On contemporary application of the second commandment, see especially Hughes Oliphant Old, *Worship That Is Reformed according to Scripture* (Atlanta: John Knox Press, 1984), 3.

111. Paul Ricoeur, *Figuring the Sacred*, trans. David Pellauer; ed. Mark I. Wallace (Minneapolis: Fortress Press, 1995), 49–50. I interact at some length with this contrast in *Covenant and Eschatology: The Divine Drama* (Louisville, KY: Westminster John Knox Press, 2002), 143, 154–55, 168–169; and *Lord and Servant*, 109–10.

112. Ricoeur, *Figuring the Sacred*, 56.

before the element of the word, before the ethical element, and before the historical element. In particular, a theology of history could not accommodate a cosmic theology. The battle had to be merciless, without any compassion," as we see in the prophets' sarcasm.[113]

The ascent of mind displayed in Platonic, Neoplatonic, and Hegelian versions of the *totus Christus* considered in chapter 1 celebrate this hermeneutics of the sacred (overcoming estrangement) over against the hermeneutics of proclamation (meeting a stranger). John Milbank's retrieval of Christian Neoplatonism announces a resacralized cosmos.[114] Wherever there is tension between the biblical worldview and that of the pre-Christian West, Milbank sides with the latter. Milbank even goes so far as to wonder, "Is not this supposed Hebraism and nonpaganism after all a very serious kind of idolatry?" There should be room again in our theology, as there was in the early medieval world, even for the pagan deities, with different levels of reality, he insists. We must recover "the full plenitude of the Western mythopoeic, metaphysical, and theological vision. For this alone will save us now."[115]

However, Ricoeur (unlike some, including Barth) does not stop at a simple contrast between the sacred and the word. Rather, he goes on to say that this priority of the word over the sacred does not abolish the sacred; rather, the sacred is now reinterpreted in its light. True, the word breaks away from the numinous, but only to take over its functions.

> There would be no hermeneutic if there were not proclamation. But there would be no proclamation if the word were not powerful; that is, if it did not have the power to set forth the new being it proclaims. A word that is addressed to us rather than our speaking it, a word that constitutes us rather than our articulating it—a word that speaks—does not such a word reaffirm the sacred just as much as abolish it?[116]

In this light, even the sacraments themselves derive their efficacy from the Word that they ratify. Abolishing the idolatrous "sacred" in the name of the Word, the Word reintroduces a genuine sacredness or holiness that permeates the new creation.

Long before the hermeneutical turn, covenant theology has emphasized the linguistic construction of reality. Created by speech, upheld by speech, redeemed by speech, and one day glorified by speech, we are, like the rest of creation, *summoned* beings, not autonomous. We exist because we have been *spoken* into existence, and we persist in time because the Spirit ensures that the Father's speaking, in the Son, will not return void.

---

113. Ibid.

114. John Milbank, "Alternative Protestantism," in *Radical Orthodoxy and the Reformed Tradition: Creation, Covenant, and Participation*, ed. James K. A. Smith (Grand Rapids: Baker Academic, 2005), 40.

115. Ibid., 41.

116. Ibid., 66.

Modernity clearly stands on Babel's side of history. The thesis that a metaphorics of vision over hearing reinforces autonomy rather than covenantal obedience is explicitly argued by Schopenhauer. Schopenhauer even refused to allow reading (much less hearing) to have priority, since it is more passive than sheer rational reflection.[117] The philosopher correctly perceived that submitting to a text disrupts the immediacy and autonomy of the sovereign self, whose "judgments" (he thinks) should, "like the decisions of a monarch, arise directly from his own absolute power."[118]

Nor does postmodern deconstruction really transcend the logic of modernity's sovereign subject. The death of the author is truly no way to treat a stranger. Pentecost, in both its message and method, delivers us from this illusion, so that the other (divine and human) becomes a gift rather than a threat. Through this ministry, we are reconciled not only to the divine stranger but also to the human strangers that we are to each other. This ministry never eliminates the *strangeness* (otherness) of the divine or human other, but breaks down the wall of *hostility* between them. Even those rendered one in Christ by the gospel become brothers and sisters, not a fusion of persons.

The close connection between covenantal thinking and hearing is highlighted more explicitly by Jŏn Levenson. Jewish rabbinical tradition, he says, was committed to "the exposition of the plain sense of scripture."[119] Through this covenantal discourse, "God beckons with one hand and repels with the other."[120] "In its quality of indivisible charm and threat, it is eminently exotic, lying outside the boundaries of what is familiar."[121] We are clearly in the domain of meeting a stranger, who summons us, and what is said takes the form of a narrative, a self and a community that is given and made in the very act of telling and retelling a story.

> In the words of the rabbinic Passover liturgy (Haggadah), "Each man is obligated to see himself as if he came out of Egypt." . . . It is significant for our understanding of the nature of the religion of Israel among the religions of the world that meaning for her is derived not from introspection, but from a consideration of the public testimony to God. The present generation makes history their story, but it is first history. They do not determine who they are by looking within, by plumbing the depths of the individual soul, by seeking a mystical light in the innermost reaches of the self. Rather, the direction is the opposite. What is public is made private. History is not only rendered contemporary; it is internalized. One's people's history becomes one's personal history. One looks out from the self to find out who one is meant to be. One does not discover one's identity, and one certainly

---

117. John Webster, *Holy Scripture* (Cambridge: Cambridge University Press, 2006), 72, citing Arthur Schopenhauer, *Essays and Aphorisms* (New York: Penguin, 1970), 89.

118. Cited by John Webster, *Holy Scripture*, 73.

119. Jŏn D. Levenson, *Sinai and Zion: An Entry into the Jewish Bible* (San Francisco: HarperSanFrancisco, 1985), 7.

120. Ibid.

121. Ibid., 16.

does not forge it oneself. He appropriates an identity that is a matter of public knowledge. Israel affirms the given. The given that is affirmed in the covenant ceremony is not a principle; it is not an idea or an aphorism or an ideal. Instead, it is the consequence of what are presented as the acts of God. . . . Israel began to infer and to affirm her identity by telling a story.[122]

The covenant is a story that has to be *told*, a series of events over which the covenant community does not have control and did not create, but must receive and embrace as its identification in the present. "To be sure, the story has implications that can be stated as propositions. For example, the intended implication of the historical prologue is that YHWH is faithful, that Israel can rely on God as a vassal must rely upon his suzerain. But Israel does not begin with the statement that Yahweh is faithful; she infers it from a story," and one that depends on the particulars of time and place.[123]

Although suspicious of generalizations, Levenson confirms the contrast between idols that are seen and Yahweh's voice that is heard:

> It is sometimes asserted that whereas the Greeks thought with the eye, the Hebrews thought with the ear. To be sure, there is considerable truth in the generalization. The Homeric epics are filled with acute visual description. In the Hebrew Bible, visual description is usually of little account: we do not know, for example, even the color of Abraham's hair or Moses' height. This is because in Israel, the focus is upon the word of God, not the appearance of man and his world (1 Sam 16:7).

To be sure, the other senses are involved. "Still, the dominance of ear over eye does seem to be characteristic of ancient Israelite sensibility."[124] Even when the eye is called upon, it does not fall upon an object to be mastered, but a subject who is guiding history toward redemption—seeing as a way of hearing, rather than vice versa.

Eschatology and the Ear

As the incident of the golden calf reminds us, idolatry is motivated simultaneously by an overrealized eschatology and a demand for autonomy: to be in possession and in control of the divine, to determine their future rather than to receive it as a gift. Having heard Yahweh's terrifying voice, the people sought to domesticate this presence and subjugate the Other to manipulation through sight and touch. They would not wait for the advent of the *eikōn tou theou*—the icon of God—in history, and in the eschatological tension they sought to make the invisible God visible on their own terms. The tree with its fruit that was "pleasing to the eye," the nostalgic craving for the daily provisions in Egypt, the golden

122. Ibid., 39.
123. Ibid.
124. Ibid., 147–48.

calf, the high places with their sacred poles and pillars, and the countless icons of immanence that envelop us in a culture of advertising—all point to this attempt at mastery: a controlled environment of pure presence, immune to any disruption of autonomy.

Hearing and seeing are not set in abstract antithesis in the Hebrew Scriptures, Levenson reminds us. He maintains that at Sinai it is the ear that is central, while for Zion it is the eye.[125] That which they have heard with their ears has now been fulfilled before their eyes.[126] Immediately after affirming the priority of the ear over the eye, Levenson adds, "There is, however, one area in which the relationship is reversed, the Temple."[127] Interpreting this in the light of Christian eschatology, I suggest that this exception is due to the typological relationship that the temple bears to Christ: more than the energetic word that must be heard, the incarnate Word became the object of the other senses as well.

All of these points lead us toward the conclusion that hearing and seeing are conditioned by the particular place that events occupy in the history of redemption. Not only has Israel heard about the promises concerning Zion; through the message of the prophets, Israel also sees their fulfillment, though off in the distance: "As we have heard, so have we seen" (Ps. 48:8a). Hearing and seeing correspond to promise and fulfillment. Blumenberg points out, "In the New Testament, hearing the Word is the source of faithfulness. Not wanting to hear means rejecting an offer of salvation." In fact, "vision comes to represent a mode of eschatological finality." Hence, the emphasis in John on seeing, both in his Gospel (where Christ is bodily present) and in the Apocalypse.[128] Among other things, idolatry is the attempt to take heaven by storm, jumping the eschatological gun, in order to have a full presence on one's own terms. However, when promises are legitimately fulfilled rather than simulated, it is entirely appropriate for an eyewitness to say,

> We declare to you what was from the beginning, what we have *heard*, what we have *seen with our eyes*, what we have *looked at* and *touched with our hands*, concerning the word of life—this life was revealed, and we have seen it and testify to it, and declare to you the eternal life that was with the Father and was revealed to us—we declare to you what we have seen and heard so that you also may have fellowship with us; and truly our fellowship is with the Father and with his Son Jesus Christ. We are witnessing these things so that our joy may be complete. (1 John 1:1–4, emphasis added)

In Paul's appeal to the Sinai/Zion contrast, Sinai must give way to Zion, just as promise surrenders gladly to fulfillment (Gal. 4).

In redemptive-historical perspective, we recognize that the emphatic prohibition of even making, much less worshiping, symbolic representations of Yahweh

125. Ibid.
126. Ibid., 150–51.
127. Levenson, *Sinai and Zion*, 148.
128. Blumenberg, "Light as a Metaphor," 47.

is grounded in the fact that Christ alone is "the image [*eikōn*] of the invisible God" (Col. 1:15). The glory of the old covenant, symbolized in Moses' visage after descending the Mount, pales in comparison to the greater glory of the new covenant. "For it is the God who said, 'Let light shine out of darkness,' who has shone in our hearts to give the light of the knowledge of the glory of God in the face of Jesus Christ" (2 Cor. 3:7–11; 4:6). Yet Levenson's central thesis maintains that Sinai finally prevails over Zion in Judaism. In rabbinic Judaism, the Sinaitic tradition (studying Torah) prevailed over the iconic.[129] Judaism and the New Testament therefore offer two different reasons for the prohibition of images. For the latter, it is precisely because Sinai has surrendered to Zion that God cannot be represented in visible form apart from the incarnate presence of Immanuel.

Yet, reckoning with the ascension, we cannot identify our experience with that of the apostles. We do not behold Christ as did the eyewitnesses, but as those who have heard his Word and have seen him act in baptism and Eucharist, though "through a glass darkly," and will one day see him together "face to face" (1 Cor 13:13 KJV). We too find ourselves in the dialectic of promise and fulfillment. However further along we are in the progress of redemptive history, faith and hope engendered by the promise that we hear have not yet given way to the perfect vision and consummate love that characterize the age to come. As with Israel at the foot of Sinai, it is not sight itself that is the problem, but the premature seizure of the beatific vision that provokes idolatry. Demanding the food they craved rather than embracing the gospel that was preached to them, the wilderness generation was barred from the land of promise. Yet precisely because that gospel is now being proclaimed to us, "the promise of entering his rest is still open" (Heb. 4:1–13).

Seeing for ourselves that the fruit is pleasing to the eye remains, ever since the fall, more friendly to our own autonomy than *hearing from someone else* how things actually are. Descartes's philosophy concerns "*clear* and *distinct* ideas," a pure presence that eschews mystery, avoiding the hiddenness that always comes with speech. Similar to Ong above, Hans Urs von Balthasar refers to the proscription against looking directly at a monarch, which would give the impression of equality, perhaps even the aim at mastery. Seeing denotes possessing, which must be restrained. We do not hear objects, "but their utterances and communications." Balthasar adds,

> Therefore it is not we ourselves who determine on our part what is heard and place it before us as an object in order to turn our attention to it when it please us. That which is heard comes upon us without our being informed of its coming in advance. And it lays hold of us without our being asked. We cannot look out in advance and take up our distance. It is in the highest degree symbolic that only our eyes—and not our ears—have lids. . . . The basic relationship between the one who hears and that which is heard is thus one of defenselessness on the one side and of communication on the

---

129. Levenson, *Sinai and Zion*, 148.

other. . . . The equality of stance between the two is fundamentally removed; even in a dialogue between equals in rank, the one who is at the moment hearing is in the subordinate position of humble receiving.[130]

Although the beatific vision awaits us in the future, the church is a "listening Church" that "stands under the Word of God," writes Balthasar.[131] "If the act of seeing aims . . . at the encounter face to face of the highest, identical mutual gaze, the act of hearing aims upward into an ever more perfect obedience and thus into a creatureliness that distinguishes itself ever more humbly from the Creator."[132]

Unlike the prophets and apostles, we are ear-witnesses, not eyewitnesses. Yet because of the place that we occupy at this stage in redemptive history, through this proclamation we know Christ in a deeper, fuller, and richer way than those who had eyes but did not see and ears but did not understand. In hearing the eyewitnesses, we hear God addressing us. Yet it is striking that even in the testimony of the eyewitnesses, the emphasis still falls on what is heard. Stephen H. Webb reminds us that we have no physical descriptions of Jesus from his disciples. "But they cared about his voice. This is especially true in the Gospel of John, which reports that the temple police said, 'Never has anyone spoken like this!' (7:46)."[133] The New Testament does not give us enough material to make Jesus into an interesting personality for celebrity interviews, but we have the words and deeds of Jesus, to which the apostles "testify," and a gospel which they "declare."

The past is mediated to the present through the word of testimony, engendering here and now the same community that was originally related as "eyewitness" to the events, which themselves do not stand alone but have "more fully confirmed" the message of the prophets (2 Pet. 1:16–21). Yet just as Jesus' ascension makes way for Pentecost, the era of eyewitnesses prepares the way for the preaching of Christ in the power of the Spirit, which brings with it even more convincing and effective testimony. Together with the apostles, we at least share in the same Spirit and the same gospel, and are therefore in a sense their contemporaries as those who are living in "these last days." If the disciples were asked by the two angels, "Why do you stand gazing?" (Acts 1:11 NKJV), surely the same rhetorical question can be put to us. Now is the time to "sit hearing," and to declare what we have heard to others.

In postmodernity, words simply refer to other words: an intertext of pure immanence, or as articulated by Jean Baudrillard, the triumph of the order of simulacra: the representation becomes the reality.[134] In many respects, the trajectory that Ong recounts above is consummated in the theories of Deleuze and

---

130. Hans Urs von Balthasar, *Spouse of the Word: Explorations in Theology* (San Francisco: Ignatius Press, 1991), 2:476–77.

131. Ibid., 480.

132. Ibid.

133. Webb, *The Divine Voice*, 31.

134. Jean Baudrillard, *Simulations*, trans. P. Foss, P. Patton, and P. Beitchman (New York: Semiotext[e], 1983); cf. Ernest Sternberg, "Transformations: The Eight New Ages of Capitalism," *Futures* 25, no. 10 (Oxford: Butterworth-Heinemann, 1993): 1019–40.

Baudrillard and the postmodern condition more generally. After centuries of the metaphorics of light and vision, interiors and depth surrender entirely to surfaces and simulacra. We are no longer hearers enveloped in worldly happenings all around us—participants—but spectators of an endless play of signs generated by a culture of marketing.

If this is so, then this development cannot be treated simply as the consequence of late medieval thought turning away from the Platonist legacy, as Radical Orthodoxy supposes. It has at least as much to do with the metaphorics of vision in Western thought that Platonism helped to create, as well as the sociology of knowledge as orality giving way to visual cultures. Icons attract our gaze to the surface of things, but they cannot tell a community-generating story that places hearers in the middle of the action. The market can create the surface *image* of a community, but only interpersonal communication—the shared stories, practices and customs, histories, goods and services—woven through generations can generate a real community. A church that turns its ear away from proclamation as the primary means of grace will similarly generate ecclesial simulacra: signs without any deeper reality. As the vast literature in their defense demonstrates, icons are employed for mediating between a supposed ontological fracture between the spiritual and the material. However, the Bible is not aware of any such ontic wound, but is concerned with the mediation between a holy God and sinful humanity, the powers of this age and the powers of the age to come. Grace is given not to elevate or supplement nature, but to restore truthful communication—and therefore relationships—in a world fond of lies.

Platonism is the tradition against which Derrida and poststructuralism react in their protest against "full presence." "This metaphor of shadow and light (of self-showing and self-hiding) [is the] founding metaphor of occidental philosophy as metaphysics. . . . *The entire history of our philosophy is a photology.*"[135] Consequently, "presence" means the present as consummation, independent of past and future and, on the epistemological level, presence-to-self, or self-certainty.[136] Following Lévinas, Derrida writes, "The metaphysical domination of the concept of form cannot fail to give rise to a sort of submission to the gaze."[137] The object is assimilated to the knower.

Given the assimilation of powerful speech that overwhelms us to visual metaphors that in some sense make us masters of all that we survey, it is not surprising that words lose their present-tense drama, their mystery, and their ability to constitute genuine community. Even God can become an idol when we bring words under our own mastery of immanent ends and means, as when the Bible becomes

135. Quoted by John McCumber, "Derrida and the Closure of Vision," in *Modernity and the Hegemony of Vision*, ed. David Michael Levin (Berkeley: University of California Press, 1993), 235, emphasis added.

136. Ibid., 236.

137. Jacques Derrida, "Forme et vouloir-dire," in *Marges de philosophie* (Paris: Editions de Minuit, 1967), 188; cf. 158; ET, *Margins of Philosophy*, trans. Alan Bass (Chicago: University of Chicago Press, 1982).

a sourcebook for timeless principles and techniques for morality, spirituality, and doctrine at the expense of its covenantal role in mediating the new creation.

The following chart contrasts these different modes of thinking under the wider contrast I have been pursuing between overcoming estrangement, meeting a stranger, and the stranger we never meet.

Overcoming estrangement	Meeting a stranger	The stranger we never meet
Full presence (already)	Already/not-yet	Pure absence (forever not-yet)
Manifestation	Proclamation	Play of signs
The idol	The word	The trace/silence
Univocity	Analogy	Equivocity
Grasping vision	Receptive hearing	Endless wandering/straying
New awareness	New news	New choices

Hearing Is Believing: The Medium and the Message

The Word written and preached is not a field guide for enthusiastic spiritual tourists, but a means of grace. We do not find God by our own ascent, through "the righteousness that is by works." God finds us and justifies us through "the righteousness that comes from faith," as "the word of Christ" is proclaimed by one whom God has sent (Rom. 10:6, 15–17). Paul's logic is consistent: salvation is by grace because it is through faith; this faith comes through the receiving event of hearing; this event itself is the result of God's having sent someone to declare the gospel to us. It is divine condescension all the way down. All of the manuals of mystical, ethical, or intellectual ascent belong to a message ("the righteousness that comes from the law"; 10:5) that is antithetical to the gospel ("the righteousness that comes from faith"). This is why "the message about the cross is foolishness to those who are perishing, but to us who are being saved it is the power of God. . . . For since, in the wisdom of God, the world did not know God through wisdom, God decided, through the foolishness of our proclamation, to save those who believe" (1 Cor 1:18, 21).

The form in which Christ is "seen"—even "placarded," as on a billboard—in this time between the times is the delivery of the gospel in Word and sacrament. Notice how Paul mixes his metaphors of seeing and hearing, finally assimilating the former to the latter: "It was before your *eyes* that Jesus Christ was *publicly exhibited* as crucified! The only thing I want to learn from you is this: Did you receive the Spirit by *doing* the *works* of the law or by *believing* what you *heard*?" (Gal. 3:1b–2, emphasis added). As Luther pointed out in his Heidelberg Disputation, a theology of glory trusts what is visible. Some people may appear righteous on the surface. The striver is in control. However, faith is a resting in the promise announced, a receiving in the present of the future verdict of the last day, interpreting reality—God, the world, my neighbor, and myself—as it has been "worded" by God, not as I find it or suppose that it might be. Luther's contrast between a theology of glory and a theology of the cross is a distinctly evangelical critique of the fact that, in Derrida's expression above, "the entire history of our philosophy is a photology." Theologies of glory find everything on the surface, obvious to the gaze, while the theology of the cross searches the depths of the heart and draws us out of ourselves to cling to Christ.

There have been erudite attempts to escape such critiques without surrendering the priority of the visible. Unlike the idol, suggests Jean-Luc Marion, "The icon does not result from a vision but provokes one, . . . is not seen, but appears."[138] Marion's icons do not speak but rather envisage. He writes, "Whereas the idol results from the gaze that aims at it, the icon *summons sight* in *letting the visible . . . be saturated little by little with the invisible*" (emphasis added).[139] Yet not even icons can summon faith, nor can they create a community, since they place the worshiper before an object rather than in the middle of an irreducibly public and social action. Even by making the Word subservient to the Eucharist (and the audible promise in the Eucharist subservient to the summons of the icon), Marion surrenders the source of the sacrament's validity and efficacy.[140] Focusing on the disciples' recognition of the risen Christ in the breaking of the bread (Luke 24:30–31), Marion omits the events of his self-proclamation in the surrounding verses, before and after this episode (vv. 1–27, 44–49). In fact, immediately after the breaking of the bread, Jesus said, "'These are the words that I spoke to you while I was still with you—that everything written about me in the law of Moses, the prophets, and the psalms must be fulfilled.' Then he opened their minds to understand the scriptures" (vv. 44–45).

Barth expresses well part of the rationale for the Reformed rejection of all visible representations of deity: "It is almost inevitable that such static works should constantly attract the eye and therefore the conscious or unconscious attention of the listening community, fixing them upon the particular conception of Jesus Christ entertained in all good faith no doubt by the artist." This draws attention away from the proclamation of Christ, directing our gaze to the artist's conception of Christ rather than to "the ongoing proclamation of His history as His history with us, so that it moves from one provisional Amen to another, in the wake of His living self-attestation pressing on from insight to insight."

---

138. Jean-Luc Marion, *God Without Being*, trans. T. A. Carlson (Chicago: University of Chicago Press, 1991), 17.

139. Ibid.

140. Ibid., 23. A valid icon, Marion argues, "is the concept or group of concepts that reinforces the distinction of the visible and the invisible as well as their union, hence that increases the one all the more that it highlights the other." On our account, this rule could be heartily affirmed, but only if we recognize "visible" and "invisible" not as corresponding to static presences but as indexes of that aspect of the new creation that is already present under the form of the cross and suffering (the visible made known in the gospel) and that is yet to be consummated in the future (the *as yet* invisible). I would offer the same objections to Zizioulas's account of Truth as an event of communion (i.e., the Eucharist) apart from communication of truths and human response. Not even the Eucharist circumvents noetic content, since it is linguistically constituted (as a liturgy) and serves to confirm faith, which is knowledge, assent, and trust.

Supremely, however, even the most excellent of plastic arts does not have the means to display Jesus Christ in His truth, i.e., in His unity as the true Son of God and Son of Man. There will necessarily be either on the one side, as in the great Italians, an abstract and docetic over-emphasis on His deity, or on the other, as in Rembrandt, an equally abstract, ebionite over-emphasis on His humanity, so that even with the best of intentions error will be promoted.[141]

It is significant that pictures and images of Christ were not permitted in the church until the sixth century.[142] They arose as part of a general trajectory of looking away from the historical Jesus, as detailed in chapter 1 (above), precisely as the church increasingly lost its sense of precariousness in being lodged between the two ages.

Idols of vision certainly do not have to be material artifacts; they can be intellectual concepts. Edward T. Oakes notes concerning Balthasar's view that "the subordination of sight to hearing automatically closes off certain avenues to human speculation (and how telling is that word: speculation!)."[143] Preaching not only subverts idols of the outer eye, but also idols of the inner eye of speculation, forbidding us from domesticating or mastering the Stranger who has met and claimed us along the way.

We need to move beyond even Augustine's transformation of Platonism's mimesis, which treats truth as recollection (note the spatial-visual metaphor) rather than as advent. "By speaking," he writes, "we merely call something to mind since, in turning over the words stored therein, memory brings to mind the realities themselves which have words for signs."[144] From our Platonic legacy we received the notion that words referred to other worlds; then, in Romanticism, they were objectifying expressions of subjective states of affairs (thoughts and feelings). Roger Lundin reminds us that "by the time of the romantic movement, hermeneutics had come to be associated with the search for ways of making discredited texts relevant to skeptical readers, rather than with the task of explaining an authoritative word or command."[145]

In the face of the various attempts (whether ancient, modern, or postmodern) to domesticate God's transcendent word through an autonomous mastery, the church desperately needs to recover its confidence in the sacramental Word

141. Karl Barth, *CD* IV/3.2:868.

142. Jaroslav Pelikan, *The Christian Tradition: A History of the Development of Doctrine*, vol. 2, *The Spirit of Eastern Christendom (600–1700)* (Chicago: University of Chicago Press, 1974), 99–133; Ernst Kitzinger, *The Cult of Images in the Age before Iconoclasm*, Dumbarton Oaks Papers 7 (Dumbarton Oaks, Washington, DC: Trustees for Harvard University, 1954), 85–150; Peter Brown, *The Rise of Western Christendom: Triumph and Diversity AD 200–1000* (Oxford: Blackwell, 1997), chap. 14.

143. Edward T. Oakes, SJ, *Pattern of Redemption: The Theology of Hans Urs von Balthasar* (New York: Continuum, 1994), 140.

144. Augustine, *De magisto*, trans. Robert Russell (Washington, DC: Catholic University of America Press, 1963), 9.

145. Roger Lundin, *The Culture of Interpretation: Christian Faith and the Postmodern World* (Grand Rapids: Eerdmans, 1993), 39; cf. Christoph Schwöbel, "Human Being and Relational Being," in *Persons Divine and Human*, ed. Christoph Schwöbel and Colin Gunton (Edinburgh: T&T Clark, 1991), 162–70.

that comes to us from outside to make all things new. Yet precisely because the gospel is counterintuitive, its enormous impact is often unrecognized on the surface of things.

After elaborating Calvin's treatment of the preached Word as the living voice of God through a weak messenger, Elizabeth Achtemeier adds,

> No one believes that God speaks through his Word until they hear it. And no argument can convince the unbeliever apart from the work of the Spirit. "Faith comes by what is heard," writes Paul, "and what is heard comes by the preaching of Christ" (Rom. 10:17, RSV). And it is the preaching of Christ—the testimony of faith that there is beyond our human words a transcendent Word—it is that alone which can awaken and renew the church.[146]

However, she concludes, "Because much of the church in this country no longer believes or expects to hear God speaking through its Scriptures, it therefore is not very Christian anymore."[147] Although a generalization, Achtemeier's jarring charge is not to my mind an exaggeration. If so, it presents the greatest threat to ecclesial identity before us. My goal in the next chapter is to substantiate her claim and, more importantly, to offer some suggestions about how the church may become more confident not in itself but in the Word that creates it.

---

146. Elizabeth Achtemeier, "The Canon as the Voice of the Living God," in *Reclaiming the Bible for the Church*, ed. Carl E. Braaten and Robert W. Jenson (Edinburgh: T&T Clark, 1995), 122–23.
147. Ibid., 120.

Chapter Three

A Liberating Captivity

The Word as Canon

John Calvin complained of being assailed by "two sects"—"the Pope and the Anabaptists"—which, though quite different from each other, "boast extravagantly of the Spirit" in order to distort or distract from the Word of God.[1] By "Anabaptists," Calvin no doubt had in mind extreme groups, particularly Thomas Müntzer and his followers. In our day, however, the "two sects" targeted in Reformation polemics are not as neatly identified by tradition or denominational affiliation. Assimilating the external Word that judges and justifies to the inner word of either the self or the church, these tendencies are in evidence across the ecclesiastical landscape, including Reformed and Presbyterian bodies. In William Placher's fine expression, it is the "domestication of transcendence."[2]

Against the claims of either pope *or* Scripture, the Enlightenment lodged sovereign authority in the self more radically than had ever been done by radical mys-

---

1. John Calvin, *Reply by Calvin to Cardinal Sadolet's Letter*, in *Tracts and Treatises on the Reformation of the Church*, ed. Thomas F. Torrance, trans. Henry Beveridge (reprint of Calvin Translation Society edition, Grand Rapids: Baker, 1958), 1:36.
2. William Placher, *The Domestication of Transcendence: How Modern Thinking about God Went Wrong* (Grand Rapids: Eerdmans, 1996).

tics.[3] Following Walter Ong, Stephen H. Webb points out the radical shift that occurred from the Reformation's emphasis on hearing the Word to "the Enlightenment's 'devocalizing of the universe,'" when a God who speaks came to be seen as an offense to the hegemonic voice of reason."[4] Whereas God's Word calls us out of ourselves, to hear the divine summons, the search for enlightenment calls us deeper into ourselves, to see the vision of light and glory that we can autonomously determine and possess.

Captivity of the Word to Inner Reason and Experience

As the creature made in God's image for obedient fellowship, law is our native tongue. Although we suppress its truth in our own unrighteousness, we still know the law and the God who still requires this stipulated love of God and neighbor. As a surprising announcement that in Christ we have passed from death to life and from wrath to grace, however, the gospel is counterintuitive. So if we allow reason and experience—that which is inherent, familiar, and inwardly certain— not only to guide our access but also to determine reality, we will be left with Kant to "the starry heavens above and the moral law within." The good news has to be *told*, and to the extent that it is assimilated to what we think we already know and experience, it will not be good news at all: perhaps pious advice, good instruction, and practical suggestions, but not good news.

One's view of the *source* of ecclesial existence determines one's view of the church's *identity*. Privileging an "inner word," whether reason (as in the Enlightenment) or pious experience (as in radical forms of mysticism and pietism), preserves the individual's presumed autonomy over against either God or the church (or both). An inner word creates an inner church. Without dispensing with appeals to the Bible (often even exhibiting a biblicistic tendency), pietism and revivalism have often displayed unease toward the visible church with its creeds and confessions, liturgies, sacraments, and educated ministry with its processes of ordination. Where Paul emphasized a theology of divine condescension by giving us ministers who are sent to proclaim the gospel (Rom. 10:15), which involves the ordained ministry (1 Tim. 4:14), and this ordination ought never to be done rashly or without testing (1 Tim. 5:22), there have always been groups that have seen this external order as opposed to the internal witness of the Spirit.

The often close relationship between pietism and the Enlightenment has been frequently observed.[5] This is clearly seen in Kant's distinction between "pure

---

3. Parallels have often been noted between the "inner light" of the medieval mystic, Radical Protestants in the sixteenth and seventeenth centuries, and the "Enlightenment" of the Age of Reason. See, e.g., Paul Tillich, *A History of Christian Thought*, ed. Carl E. Broaten (New York: Simon & Schuster, 1968), 315–18.

4. Stephen H. Webb, *The Divine Voice: Christian Proclamation and the Theology of Sound* (Grand Rapids: Brazos, 2004), 118.

5. Tillich, *History of Christian Thought*, 317–18. Among the many historians pointing out this relationship is Peter Gay, *The Enlightenment: An Interpretation* (New York: W. W. Norton, 1966), 62, 291, 326–29, 348, 350.

religion" and "ecclesiastical faith."[6] For Kant and his philosophical heirs, there is *faith* (pure morality, which is universal) and there are *faiths*—it is the latter that are in one sense necessary external vehicles of conveying the inner faith, but also dispensable and dangerous. "So too the so-called religious struggles, which have so often shaken the world and spattered it with blood, have never been anything but squabbles over ecclesiastical faiths."[7] If it comes down to a contest between the right doctrine ("salvation by grace") and right moral conduct, says Kant, "then the pure moral faith must take precedence over the ecclesiastical."[8] It never seems to have occurred to Kant that his own "pure moral faith" was also a historically conditioned, particular, and personally appropriated "ecclesiastical faith." Accordingly, liberal Protestantism became predictable: whatever God did and does belongs to the mythological husk, while whatever we did and do (or experience) belongs to the kernel of eternal, unchanging, pure religion. As Wilhelm Herrmann expressed this outlook, "To fix doctrines . . . into a system is the last thing the Christian Church should undertake. . . . But if, on the other hand, we keep our attention fixed on what God is producing in the Christian's inner life, then the manifoldness of the thoughts which spring from faith will not confuse us, but give us cause for joy."[9]

The quasi-gnostic presupposition of this trajectory is that the spiritual, ethical, private, universal, ideal, inward, and autonomous are divine, while the physical, theological, public, particular, concrete, external, and heteronomous are merely human corruptions of pure religion.[10] Where interpreters like Ireneaus, Augustine, Luther, and Calvin understood Paul's statement "The letter kills, but the Spirit gives life" (2 Cor. 3:6) as referring to the law's command without the promise, gnostics old and new have interpreted it in terms of the external as opposed to the internal word. Not only the visible church, but also the Bible itself, becomes relegated to the "external religion" that threatens individual autonomy.

The doctrine of the church as a creation of the external Word disputes every claim that prioritizes human agency (individual or corporate) over divine agency.

---

6. Immanuel Kant, "Religion within the Boundaries of Mere Reason," in *Religion and Rational Theology*, trans. and ed. Allen W. Wood and George Di Giovanni (Cambridge: Cambridge University Press, 1996), esp. 148–50.

7. Ibid., 140–41. One is reminded of the report some years ago that Prince Charles plans to change one of his inherited titles, "Defender of *the* Faith," to "Defender of Faith." Aside from the fact that there is no divine commission for a secular office defending either, the proposed change reflects a thoroughly modern sensibility, despite the constant refrain that such moves reflect our "postmodern" milieu of religious pluralism.

8. Ibid., 148.

9. Wilhelm Herrmann, *The Communion of the Christian with God* (New York: G. P. Putnam's Sons, 1913), 16.

10. On the quasi-gnostic character particularly of American Protestantism, see Philip E. Lee, *Against the Protestant Gnostics* (New York: Oxford University Press, 1987). Describing himself as a Jewish gnostic, Harold Bloom wrote a magnificent book, *The American Religion: The Emergence of the Post-Christian Nation* (New York: Simon & Schuster, 1992), making many of the same points, although largely in praise rather than criticism. Interestingly, he singles out Karl Barth and J. Gresham Machen as two notable exceptions to the dominance of "gnostic" tendencies in the modern West (212–13, 228–29).

"Deeds, not creeds," amounts to "law, not gospel." The Bible may be a useful source for our activity, but it is not allowed to have its full force as a sovereign Word of judgment and grace. Kantianism is a good indicator of what we are left with apart from an external Word, the surprising evangelical announcement. The law is intuitive and familiar; the gospel is counterintuitive and strange.

Kant's contrast can be discerned not only in the assumptions of the average person in our day (for example, in John Lennon's "Imagine"), but also in Derrida's contrast between a universal "messianic structure" of the endlessly deferred arrival and dangerous attachments to any particular messiah who has arrived, echoing Kant's very arguments.[11] We encounter something like this contrast between ecclesiastical faiths and pure religion whenever polls reveal a lack of concern with church membership, specific beliefs, and rituals on one hand, alongside a high degree of interest in spirituality and the universal moral imperatives on the other.[12] One might describe this phenomenon as "postmodern," but it is actually the old Enlightenment creed and has maintained its parallel course alongside Christianity, often under the pretense of "pure religion," ever since the serpent's enticement to look within for authoritative revelation. However, this "spirituality" and "morality" does not need the Spirit—that is, the third person of the Trinity, any more than it needs a divine redeemer, since "spirit" refers primarily to the inner self.

This legacy has found fertile soil in American religious experience, particularly in the history of revivalism. Writing in the nineteenth century, Alexis de Tocqueville observed that Americans wish "to escape from imposed systems" of any kind, "to seek by themselves and in themselves for the only reason for things, looking to results without getting entangled in the means toward them." They do not need external guidance to discover truth, "having found it in themselves."[13] Placing human experience at the center was a more general trend in European Romanticism, notes Bernard Reardon, with its "intense egoism and emotionalism."[14] The effect of pietism (esp. culminating in the Great Awakening), as William McLoughlin observes, was to shift the emphasis away from "collective belief, adherence to creedal standards and proper observance of traditional forms, to the emphasis on individual religious experience."[15] The effect of the Enlightenment was to shift "the ultimate authority in religion" from the church to "the mind of the individual."[16] Yet Romanticism simply changed the faculty (from mind to heart), not the subject (from the self to an external authority).

11. Jacques Derrida, *Deconstruction in a Nutshell*, ed. John D. Caputo (New York: Fordham University Press, 1997), 22–24, 162–63, 167, 173.

12. See, e.g., Wade Clark Roof, *Spiritual Marketplace: Baby Boomers and the Remaking of American Religion* (Princeton, NJ: Princeton University Press, 1999), 189.

13. Alexis de Tocqueville, *Democracy in America*, ed. J. P. Mayer, trans. George Lawrence (New York: Harper & Row, 1988), 429.

14. Bernard Reardon, *Religion in the Age of Romanticism* (Cambridge: Cambridge University Press, 1985), 9.

15. William McLoughlin, *Revivals, Awakenings, and Reform* (Chicago: University of Chicago Press, 1980), 25. I am grateful to Toby Kurth for providing this and the following reference.

16. Ned Landsman, *From Colonials to Provincials: American Thought and Culture, 1680–1760* (New York: Twayne Publishers, 1997; Ithaca, NY: Cornell University Press, 2000), 66.

Ralph Waldo Emerson, that quintessentially American thinker, captured this fear of meeting a stranger well when he said, "That which shows God in me, fortifies me. That which shows God out of me, makes me a wart and a wen. There is no longer any reason for my being." Already in this Harvard address in 1838, Emerson could announce that "whatever hold the public worship had on men is gone or going," calling us to turn inward.[17] Yet this inner spark, inner light, inner experience, and inner reason that guides mysticism, rationalism, idealism, and pragmatism in all ages—this is precisely that autonomous self which, according to the New Testament, must be crucified and buried with Christ in baptism, so that one can be raised with Christ as a denizen of the new age.

To whatever extent Romanticism, idealism, and existentialism—and now, postmodernism—represent reactions against certain features of the Enlightenment, they all belong to a family quarrel. Curved in on ourselves, we trust what we see rather than what we hear, what we control, manipulate, and assimilate rather than what remains mysterious and different, what we can find within ourselves rather than outside of ourselves. By contrast, the word creates extroverted, evangelically constituted, and ecclesially shaped community.

The root of all "enthusiasm" is hostility to a God outside of us, in whose hands the judgment and redemption of our lives are placed. To barricade ourselves from this assault, we try to make the "divine" an echo of ourselves and our communities: the very sort of motive that the prophets ridiculed in their polemics against the idols—and so did Feuerbach, Marx, Nietzsche, and Freud in their description of religion generally. The idea of being founded by someone else has been treated in modernity as a legacy of a primitive era. In line with Emerson's comment above, we have come to think that what we experience directly within ourselves is more reliable than what we are told by someone else. Thus, we are always ready for new awareness or new advice, but not for new news that can only come to us as a report that is not only told by someone else but that is entirely concerned with the achievement of someone else for us.

Even when preaching is properly submitted to the text as canonical norm, private practices of reading are often abstracted from their wider covenantal ambiance. When we read it primarily to discern, "What does this mean for me? How can I make it relevant for my daily living?" even the Bible becomes a servant of our autonomous self-creation rather than a sovereign Word that opens us up and places us in a disorienting, covenantal ambiance, before God and among his covenant community. As we have seen, the public proclamation of the Word is not only a social event; it also creates a new society. When Luther said, "The church is not a pen-house but a mouth-house,"[18] and when the Westminster divines confessed that the Spirit blesses "the reading but especially the preaching of the Word" as a means of grace,[19] they were asserting that faithful, meditative,

---

17. Ralph Waldo Emerson, "The Divinity School Address," in *Ralph Waldo Emerson: Self-Reliance and Other Essays* (New York: Dover, 1993), 108.

18. Quoted in Webb, *The Divine Voice*, 143; from Martin Luther, *Church Postil* of 1522.

19. Westminster Shorter Catechism, Q. 89, in *BC*.

and prayerful reading of Scripture in private or family devotions was subordinate to the public ministry of the Word in the common life of the church. Just as the Word creates the community, it can only be truly heard, received, and followed in the concrete covenantal exchanges within that community.

Writing as a self-professed Jewish gnostic, Harold Bloom has approvingly characterized American religion generally as gnostic: an *inner* word, spirit, and church set over against an *external* Word, Spirit, and church.[20] This is precisely what the Reformers had in mind when they targeted radical Protestant sectarianism as "enthusiastic" (*en-theos*, God-within). Yet it is a "singular privilege" that God has condescended "to consecrate to himself the mouths and tongues" of fellow sinners so that "his own voice may resound in them," writes Calvin.

> For although God's power is not bound to outward means, he has nonetheless bound us to this ordinary manner of teaching. Fanatics, refusing to hold fast to it, entangle themselves in many deadly snares. Many are led either by pride, dislike, or rivalry to the conviction that they can profit enough from private reading and meditation; hence they despise public assemblies and deem preaching superfluous. But . . . no one escapes the just penalty of this unholy separation without bewitching himself with pestilent errors and foulest delusions.[21]

When hearing is subordinated to reading, a spatializing, visualizing, individualizing, mastering logic of autonomy threatens the sonic, aural, communal, hearing logic of reception.

Not surprisingly, a spate of recent sociological studies has indicated that the operating theology of those reared in evangelical youth groups and churches, as much as the unchurched, can be described, in Christian Smith's formulation, as "moralistic, therapeutic deism."[22] Given the point above, that law is intuitive while gospel is not, is it really any surprise that, according to this study and others, a generation reared in evangelical youth groups is just as inclined to exhibit this basic religious orientation?[23]

Reflecting on the counterintuitive logic of the gospel, William Willimon, a former homiletics professor at Duke Divinity School and now a bishop in the United Methodist Church, points out that it is not the homiletical gap between

---

20. For an intriguing narrative of the ways in which these values characterize American religion generally, see Bloom, *The American Religion*.

21. John Calvin, *Institutes* 4.1.5.

22. Christian Smith with Melinda Lundquist Denton, *Soul Searching: The Religious and Spiritual Lives of American Teenagers* (New York: Oxford University Press, 2005).

23. Wade Clark Roof has also observed that across the board the contemporary attitude toward religion "celebrates experience rather than doctrine; the personal rather than the institutional; the mythic and dreamlike over the cognitive; people's religion over official religion; soft, caring images of Deity over hard, impersonal images; the feminine and the androgynous over the masculine" (*A Generation of Seekers* [San Francisco: HarperCollins, 1993], 195. See also the important, though now somewhat dated, research of sociologist James Davison Hunter in his book *Evangelicalism: The Coming Generation* (Chicago: University of Chicago Press, 1987). Cf. Marsha G. Witten, *All Is Forgiven: The Secular Message in American Protestantism* (Princeton, NJ: Princeton University Press, 1993).

speaker and listener but "the space between *us and the gospel*" that is most deci-sive.[24] The problem is not that the modern (or postmodern) person cannot relate to the gospel apart from our attempts to rescue its relevance, but that the auton-omy lying at the heart of the fallen self in general and modernity in particular simply finds the notion of an authoritative *verbum externum* intolerable. To main-tain its relevance, God's Word must be removed from the category of authority, lodging its appeal in its practical usefulness and meaningfulness. This does not require conversion, but assimilation: overcoming estrangement rather than meet-ing a stranger.

Willimon rightly calls us to recover our recognition that the gospel itself is the main problem of communication: we think people can accept it without con-version.[25] He perceives that much of contemporary preaching, whether mainline or evangelical, assumes that conversion is something that we generate through our own words and sacraments. "In this respect we are heirs of Charles G. Finney," who thought that conversion was not a miracle but a "'purely philo-sophical [i.e., scientific] result of the right use of the constituted means.'"

> We have forgotten that there was once a time when evangelists were forced to defend their "new measures" for revivals, that there was once a time when preachers had to defend their preoccupation with listener response to their Calvinist detractors who thought that the gospel was more important than its listeners. I am here arguing that revivals are miraculous, that the gospel is so odd, so against the grain of our natural inclinations and the infatua-tions of our culture, that nothing less than a miracle is required in order for there to be true hearing. My position is therefore closer to that of the Calvin-ist Jonathan Edwards than to the position of Finney.[26]

Nevertheless, "The homiletical future, alas, lay with Finney rather than Edwards," leading to the evangelical church marketing guru George Barna, who writes, "Jesus Christ was a communications specialist. He communicated His message in diverse ways, and with results that would be a credit to modern adver-tising and marketing agencies."[27] The question that naturally arises in the face of such remarks is whether it is possible to say that Jesus made anything new.

Willimon also reminds us that preaching presupposes that it will "work" not because of its audience analysis but because of its confidence in the Spirit. If our preaching does not require a miracle in order to believe it, then it is not gospel preaching.[28] Finney's legacy is evident also among mainline Protestants. He cites Robin R. Meyers: "We are not using symbolic language to achieve some sort of

24. William H. Willimon, *The Intrusive Word: Preaching to the Unbaptized* (Grand Rapids: Eerd-mans, 1994), 15.

25. Ibid., 18–19.

26. Ibid., 20.

27. Ibid., 21, citing George Barna, *Marketing the Church: What They Never Taught You about Church Growth* (Colorado Springs: NavPress, 1988), 50.

28. Willimon, *The Intrusive Word*, 22.

conceptual precision; rather we are using metaphors to generate insight that comes from recognizing common human experience."[29] Meyers adds,

> Self-persuasion theory rests on one very simple but central premise: the messages we generate for ourselves are more authoritative than those from an outside source. This clear and decisive break with classical rhetoric locates persuasion at the ear of the listener, not at the mouth of the rhetor. And there exists a substantial body of research to back up the claim that when it comes to authority, the holiest of trinities is Me, Myself, and I.[30]

Besides pointing out the idolatrous position of the self in this approach, Willimon properly questions the very notion of such a neutral and uninterpreted "common experience." Offering a fresh definition of what it means for the church to be a creature of the Word, he proposes, "Church is the human experience evoked by the gospel. . . . Preaching means to engender experience we would never have had without the gospel."[31]

> The gospel is an intrusion among us, not something arising out of us. Easter is the ultimate intrusion of God. The gap between our alliance with death and the God of life as revealed on Easter is the ultimate gap with which gospel preaching must contend. Easter is an embarrassment the church can't get around. Yet this embarrassment is the engine that drives our preaching. . . . If God did not triumph over Caesar and all the legions of death on Easter, then God will never triumph on Sunday in my church over *The Wall Street Journal* and Leo Buscaglia.[32]

We do not bring Christ down by our clever efforts at translation and relevance; Christ comes down to us and creates his own atmosphere: confrontative as well as comforting. "Alas," adds Willimon, "most 'evangelistic' preaching I know about is an effort to drag people even deeper into their subjectivity rather than an attempt to rescue them from it."[33] "Our intellectual problem with the gospel is not one of meaning but really is about power. Not the limitedly intellectual problem of 'How can I believe this?' but rather 'In what power configurations am I presently enslaved?'"[34] This is why we need "an external word."[35] "So in a sense, we don't discover the gospel; it discovers us. 'You did not choose me but I chose you' (John 15:16)."[36] We need a word outside of ourselves because we need a salvation from outside of ourselves. Willimon surmises, "Self-salvation is the goal

29. Ibid., citing Robin R. Meyers, *With Ears to Hear: Preaching as Self-Persuasion* (Cleveland, OH: Pilgrim Press, 1993), 79.

30. Willimon, *The Intrusive Word*, 79, citing Meyers, *With Ears to Hear*, 49.

31. Willimon, *The Intrusive Word*, 23.

32. Ibid., 25.

33. Ibid., 38.

34. Ibid., 42.

35. Ibid.

36. Ibid., 43.

of much of our preaching."[37] By contrast, Scripture repeatedly underscores the point that the gospel is new news, not merely a new awareness.

> To be a Christian is to be part of the community, the countercultural community, formed by thinking with a peculiar story. The story is *euangelion*, *good news*, because it is about grace. Yet it is also news because it is not common knowledge, not what nine out of ten average Americans already know. Gospel doesn't come naturally. It comes as Jesus.[38]

This external Word works against all of our attempts to *ascend* ladders of mysticism, moralism, and speculation, to *receive* God's gift that is wrapped in the ignominy of swaddling cloths, lying in a manger.

Without discounting the significance of the ways in which we marginalize human others, the greatest tragedy in our day is that even in our churches *it is God whose voice we are marginalizing*. Our own inner voice, or that of our various communities, may be revealing, but it is not the revelation of God's good news for the whole world. Not only in preaching, but also in the wider service of the Word in catechesis and the liturgy, we have so filled ecclesial space with our own voices that we cannot hear God speak. Where scripture indicates that the purpose even of singing in the church is so that "the word of Christ [may] dwell in you richly" (Col. 3:16; cf. Eph. 5:19), even here the accent seems in many cases to be on self-expression. The accent is on immanence rather than God's transcendent presence, as Stephen Webb observes:

> The soothing rhythms of praise music now set the tone for worship services more than the sermon does. As a result, the spoken word seems to accompany the music, rather than the other way around. How can the Word be preached with authority today if we have lost the ability to listen to it? . . . Ministers frequently respond to this dire situation by supplementing their sermons with visual aids, which only reinforces the idea that the spoken word does not matter.[39]

Many of our services seem to give credence to Marx's charge that religion is "the opiate of the masses." Can anything—or anyone—get to us from outside of this self-enclosed world that we create in order to immunize ourselves against the reality of death?

In bondage to that which it thinks is liberating, the world (and a worldly church) does not really know how to throw a real party; suppressing the law and the gospel, it can neither mourn nor dance (Matt. 11:16–19). Unable to conceive of true *shalom*, we shop. Unaware of the festival of grace, and in perpetual denial of death, sin, and judgment, the world cannot be expected to offer a reliable judgment about what is ultimately useful or relevant in the grand scheme of things.

---

37. Ibid., 53.
38. Ibid., 52.
39. Webb, *The Divine Voice*, 26.

I take this to be Jesus' point when he says that those who strive to save their lives will lose them while those who hand over their lives to Christ for death and burial will get them back in a resurrected condition that they could never have imagined for themselves (Matt. 16:25). It is the way of the cross rather than a way of glory (vv. 24, 26). Through Word and sacrament, the Spirit baptizes us into Christ's death and raises us together with him in newness of life (Rom. 6:1–14). For its own good, which it does not recognize, the sovereign self must not be encouraged, cajoled, entertained, or even enlightened, but summoned to the heavenly tribunal. There the truth will be told, not only about God by other people like us, but also about ourselves by the God who became flesh and still addresses us through sanctified words.

None of us like this, however. The curved-in self will muster every tool in its arsenal against such assaults. However, as Bonhoeffer argues, the attempt to make the church's preaching and practice more relevant to its cultured despisers "assumes that we have in ourselves (whether in reason, or culture, or *Volk*) 'the Archimedean point by which Scripture and proclamation are to be judged.'"[40] However, "That word is not as it were waiting on the fringes of the human present, hoping somehow to be made real; it announces itself in its own proper communicative vigour."[41] According to Bonhoeffer,

> We are uprooted from our own existence and are taken back to the holy history of God on earth. There God has dealt with us, with our needs and our sins, by means of the divine wrath and grace. What is important is not that God is a spectator and participant in our life today, but that we are attentive listeners and participants in God's action in the sacred story, the story of Christ on earth. God is with us today only as long as we are there. Our salvation is "from outside ourselves" [*extra nos*]. I find salvation, not in my life story, but only in the story of Jesus Christ. . . . What we call our life, our troubles, and our guilt is by no means the whole of reality; our life, our need, our guilt, and our deliverance are there in the Scriptures.[42]

Elsewhere, he adds, "Any other place outside the Bible has become too uncertain for me. I fear that I will only encounter some divine double of myself there."[43] Instead of trying to correlate this disrupting Word to our experience and reason, we must correlate it with renunciation (mortification) and discipleship (vivification), as Webster has argued.[44]

As the previous chapter indicated, the Reformers' notion of the church as the creation of the Word affirmed neither the inner eye of rationalism nor the outer eye of idolatrous gaze, but the hearing of God's voice in a covenant assembly.

40. John Webster, *Word and Church* (Edinburgh: T&T Clark, 2001), 81.

41. Ibid., 82.

42. Quoted in ibid., 83, from Dietrich Bonhoeffer, *Life Together* (Minneapolis: Fortress Press, 1996), 62.

43. Quoted in Webster, *Word and Church*, 85, from Dietrich Bonhoeffer, *Meditating on the Word* (Cambridge, MA: Cowley, 1986), 46.

44. Webster, *Word and Church*, 86, 88, 92.

Through the organ of the ear, the whole person—not simply the mind or the emotions—is justified and renewed, since "faith comes by hearing . . . the word of God" (Rom. 10:17 NKJV). The emphasis on the sacramental Word shifts the discussion to the plane of covenantal discourse: a divine speaking and human answering that is dramatic and eventful at its very core.

Captivity to Ecclesial Praxis

Reacting against the chaos of evangelical individualism and liberal attacks on tradition, a growing number of Protestant theologians are attracted to the traditional Roman Catholic contention that the church is the mother of the Word.[45] Highlighting the important role of practices in shaping us as the people we are, many postliberal Protestants argue that we not only hear God's Word together as Christ's body (as the Reformers emphasized), but that the Bible is also the *church's* book.[46] "When *sola scriptura* is used to underwrite the distinction between text and interpretation," writes Stanley Hauerwas, "then it seems clear to me that *sola scriptura* is a heresy rather than a help in the Church."[47] Elaborating George Lindbeck's theory of doctrine, which draws on Wittgenstein's later linguistic theory, Hauerwas is among many postliberals who argue that it is the church—specifically, its virtuous and virtue-shaping practices—that gives the Word its sense.[48]

Helpfully reminding us of the integral relationship of faith and practice and of the social (i.e., ecclesial) context in which preaching makes sense, this approach seems more appealing from the perspective of a covenantal ecclesiology, where the concrete context of the covenant refuses any dualism between form and content. Yet ecclesial pragmatism shares with its more individualistic rival an anthro-

45. Some are influenced by Lindbeck's cultural-linguistic model. For the statement of his rule theory of doctrine, see George Lindbeck, *The Nature of Doctrine* (Louisville, KY: Westminster John Knox Press, 1984). Others who adopt more traditional "Catholic" ways of interpreting this relation of canon and church include Archbishop of Canterbury Rowan Williams. See his chapter on Scripture in his work *On Christian Theology* (Oxford: Blackwell, 2000). See also Robert Jenson, *Systematic Theology* (Oxford: Oxford University Press, 1997), 1:27–30. Stephen Fowl and L. Gregory Jones argue along similar lines in their work *Reading in Communion: Scripture and Ethics in Christian Life* (Grand Rapids: Eerdmans, 1991).

46. David Kelsey, in *The Uses of Scripture in Recent Theology* (Philadelphia: Fortress Press, 1975), evidences the wariness of his former colleagues (Hans W. Frei and George Lindbeck) toward rendering ontic judgments. If I am reading him correctly, Kelsey suggests that Scripture, finally, is authoritative in the church because the church has adopted it as its canon. Thus, its authority is functional and ecclesially derived. Although for Robert Jenson, for example, the canon is ontically authoritative, this authority is as dependent on its mediation through the church as it is on God's act of speaking itself (*Systematic Theology*, 1:25–50). Therefore, mutatis mutandis, the Wittgensteinian postliberalism represented by the Yale school and the evangelical and Catholic circle associated with Jenson offer a functionalist account: how the Bible functions in the church, without wanting to say much about what the Bible is, distinct from the church that its proclamation generates and its text norms.

47. Stanley Hauerwas, *Unleashing the Scripture: Freeing the Bible from Captivity to America* (Nashville: Abingdon, 1993), 27. Cf. Stanley Hauerwas, *A Community of Character: Toward a Constructive Christian Social Ethic* (Notre Dame, IN: University of Notre Dame Press, 1981).

48. See also Reinhard Hütter, *Suffering Divine Things: Theology as Church Practice*, trans. David Scott (Grand Rapids: Eerdmans, 2000), 131–32.

pocentric and immanentistic tendency to embrace self-poiesis rather than the hearing that creates faith. The Word easily becomes a creation of the church rather than the other way around. The heart of the question is whether we call the Bible "Scripture" because of what it is (ontologically) or because of the church's decision and use of it (functionally). Opting for the latter is hardly postliberal or postmodern, however; it was followed by Adolf von Harnack, for example.[49] This actually was an argument that the Reformers and their heirs had regularly encountered and answered with impressive arguments.[50]

John Webster has observed that the notion of a canon standing over against ecclesial tradition is also repudiated by sociocultural, sociopolitical, and ideology criticism, treating Scripture "as a product, not a norm."[51] The "naturalization of the canon" may seem to favor ecclesiastical tradition and authority, but it presses on to deconstruct the authority of the church as well.[52] Such criticism therefore stands in the long shadow cast by the Enlightenment, with the ultimate goal of excluding altogether any final authority external to the self. Alisdair MacIntyre, Stanley Hauerwas, and John Milbank are among the most insightful critics of modernity's flight from authority, but they risk replacing one form of immanent sovereignty (the self) with another (the church). Only *sola scriptura* secures a genuine transcendence that keeps the legitimate ministerial authority of the church from degenerating into magisterial absolutism. This sovereignty of the triune God by his word places the church as much as the world under Christ's scepter.

Webster rightly contends that we properly understand the canon (*sola scriptura*) only when it is closely tied to *sola gratia, solo Christo*, and *sola fide*.[53] If the church's agency and use displace God's, then the gracious character of the gospel itself is at stake. The question is whether we rise up (collectively or individually) to God with our sacred thoughts, experiences, and practices, or whether God descends to create a new world. There is no reason to dispute Wittgenstein's

49. In his *Word and Church*, Webster quotes Adolf von Harnack's *History of Dogma* (New York: Dover, 1961), 2:62 n. 1: "No greater creative act can be mentioned in the whole history of the Church than the formation of the apostolic collection and the assigning to it of a position of equal rank with the Old Testament" (11). "In effect," judges Webster, "the canon shifts from the category of 'Scripture' to that of 'tradition,' precisely because Scripture and tradition are so difficult to distinguish with any clarity. And thereby the dogmatic principle of *sola scriptura* becomes increasingly difficult to operate" (12). In this seminal essay "Canon," Webster includes some crucial citations of Calvin in refutation of this interpretation. It may be added that the Reformed scholastics offered sophisticated arguments on this point, nuanced by the recognition that (1) the church preceded the canon in time and (2) the church agreed upon the canon. However, the Word preceded both church and textual canon, and the church received rather than created the canon. The fact that objective criteria (esp. authenticity of a document as of apostolic origin) were employed demonstrates that the church did not think that it was in a position to authorize but instead merely to accept Scripture.

50. See Richard Muller, *Post-Reformation Reformed Dogmatics*, vol. 2, *Holy Scripture: The Cognitive Foundation of Theology* (Grand Rapids: Baker Book House, 1993), esp. 357–88.

51. Webster, *Word and Church*, 11–46.

52. Ibid., 17.

53. This is the thrust of Webster's own position as cited already in his essay "Canon," in *Word and Church*.

hermeneutical observation that "practice gives the words their sense."[54] Yet the important question is whether the practice that gives the words their sense is first of all God's or ours. Aside from the confusion of the church's *recognition* of the canon with a presumed authority to *create* one, there is a more fundamental challenge posed by this trajectory. The triumph of the canon over the church stands or falls with the triumph of grace over human rebellion and judgment. The church is simply that part of the sinful world that accepts its place under the Word's judgment as well as its grace.

Wherever the *totus Christus* idea conflates Christ as head with his ecclesial body, Christ's external Word (*verbum externum*) to his church can easily become an instance of the church simply talking to itself. And since we are dealing with speech about salvation, can this mean anything other than the church saving itself (and perhaps the world) by its good praxis? This immanentizing of the Word—in other words, domesticating it into a clever, relevant, mysterious, virtuous, or useful human word—is exhibited in different ways across the ecclesiastical spectrum today, and they all feed the interiorization that allows the self or the community to remain comfortably ensconced inside its autonomous shell.

Converging Captivities

Reflecting a convergence of these two versions of "enthusiasm" described by Calvin, some recent evangelical theologies draw simultaneously on a pietistic emphasis that prioritizes individual experience over ecclesial norms and a postliberal emphasis on the church as the mother of the Word. Whether these proposals are successful in integrating these apparently contradictory trajectories remains to be seen.

Evangelical theologian Stanley Grenz, for example, combines the experiential-expressivism of pietist and liberal traditions with a cultural-linguistic pragmatism that finally assimilates the external Word to ecclesial discourse.[55] In *Revisioning Evangelical Theology*, he leads with the first emphasis, arguing that evangelicalism is more a "spirituality" than a "theology," more interested in individual piety than in creeds, confessions, and liturgies.[56] Experience gives rise to—in fact, he says, "determines"—doctrine, rather than the other way around.[57] Evangelicals follow their heart—their converted instincts—"to accept the biblical stories as in some sense true as they are told."[58] However, the main point is how these stories

54. Ludwig Wittgenstein, *Lecture on Ethics, Culture and Value*, ed. G. H. von Wright, trans. P. Winch (Oxford: Blackwell, 1966), 81.

55. I am using George Lindbeck's categories here, from his landmark work *The Nature of Doctrine* (Louisville, KY: Westminster John Knox Press, 1984). Lindbeck contrasts a "cognitive-propositionalist" theory of doctrine of conservative Protestants and Catholics with an "experiential-expressivist" view of liberalism and offers his own alternative to both: the "cultural-linguistic" model.

56. Stanley Grenz, *Revisioning Evangelical Theology: A Fresh Agenda for the 21st Century* (Downers Grove, IL: InterVarsity Press, 1993), 17, 31, and throughout the volume.

57. Ibid., 30, 34.

58. Ibid., 31.

can be used in daily living—hence, the emphasis on daily devotions. This emphasis on the inner life of the individual has ecclesiological implications, Grenz recognizes. "Although some evangelicals belong to ecclesiological traditions that understand the church as in some sense a dispenser of grace, generally we see our congregations foremost as a fellowship of believers."[59] We share our journeys (our "testimonies") of personal transformation.[60]

Thus, "a fundamental shift in self-consciousness may be under way" in evangelicalism, "a move from a creed-based to a spirituality-based identity" that is more like medieval mysticism than Protestant orthodoxy.[61] "Consequently, spirituality is inward and quietistic,"[62] concerned with combating "the lower nature and the world,"[63] in "a personal commitment that becomes the ultimate focus of the believer's affections."[64] Nowhere in this account does Grenz locate the origin of faith in an external gospel; rather, faith arises from an inner experience. "Because spirituality is generated from within the individual, inner motivation is crucial"—actually more important than "grand theological statements."[65]

> The spiritual life is above all the imitation of Christ. . . . In general we eschew religious ritual. Not slavish adherence to rites, but doing what Jesus would do is our concept of true discipleship. Consequently, most evangelicals neither accept the sacramentalism of many mainline churches nor join the Quakers in completely eliminating the sacraments. We practice baptism and the Lord's Supper, but understand the significance of these rites in a guarded manner.[66]

In any case, he says, these rites are practiced as goads to personal experience and out of obedience to divine command.[67] "This view marks a radical shift in the relationship of soteriology and ecclesiology, for it exchanges the priority of the church for the priority of the believer."[68]

> "Get on with the task; get your life in order by practicing the aids to growth and see if you do not mature spiritually," we exhort. In fact, if a believer comes to the point where he or she senses that stagnation has set in, evangelical counsel is to redouble one's efforts in the task of exercising the disciplines. "Check up on yourself," the evangelical spiritual counselor admonishes.[69]

We go to church, he says, not in order to receive "means of grace," but for fellowship, "instruction and encouragement."[70] Grenz acknowledges that his

59. Ibid., 32.
60. Ibid., 33.
61. Ibid., 38, 41.
62. Ibid., 41–42.
63. Ibid., 44.
64. Ibid., 45.
65. Ibid., 46.
66. Ibid., 48.
67. Ibid.
68. Ibid., 51.
69. Ibid., 52.
70. Ibid., 54.

interpretation calls into question the confessional Protestant emphasis on "a material and a formal principle"—in other words, *solo Christo* and *sola scriptura*.[71]

Thus, in Grenz's account (similar to Schleiermacher's) the individual and the community seem to converge at the level of common experience. Consequently, a revisioning of evangelical theology entails viewing "theology as the faith community's reflecting on the faith experience of those who have encountered God through the divine activity in history and therefore now seek to live as the people of God in the contemporary world."[72] Grenz concludes that neither the orthodox nor the neo-orthodox view of Scripture does adequate justice to the view that revelation arises in "the process of community formation." Far from abandoning an experiential-expressivist approach, Grenz simply extends it beyond the individual to the community. Scripture is essentially the church's record of its religious experience.[73] The Word's transcendence is therefore doubly threatened by the convergence of private and communal experience. "Faith is by nature immediate," Grenz astonishingly asserts, and Scripture is the record of the faith-community's encounter with God.[74]

Grenz therefore reverses the word-faith relationship. Rather than faith being created by the Word of God, the Word itself is created by the experiences of the community. Obviously this requires "a revisioned understanding of the *nature* of the Bible's authority."[75] *Sola scriptura* has a noble history in evangelicalism. "The commitment to contextualization, however, entails an implicit rejection of the older evangelical conception of theology as the construction of truth on the basis of the Bible alone." Instead of the sole norm for faith and practice, evangelicals should explicitly embrace what in practice has already characterized the movement: "the well-known method of correlation proposed by Paul Tillich."[76]

Grenz appreciates the growing popularity within evangelical circles of the "Wesleyan quadrangle"—Scripture, reason, experience, and tradition—as shared norms.[77] The Bible, our heritage, and the contemporary cultural context should be reciprocally rather than hierarchically related. And even here, it is "the Bible *as canonized by the church*," as if the church authorized rather than received the canon (emphasis added).[78] As the canon is drawn into the sphere of ecclesial tradition, both are relativized by culture.[79] Grenz explicitly adopts a functionalist view of the canon.[80] Not only our illumination but also Scripture's inspiration depends on the fact that "believers in every age hear in them the voice of the Spirit as they seek to struggle with the issues they face in their unique and ever-changing

71. Ibid., 62.
72. Ibid., 76.
73. Ibid., 77.
74. Ibid., 80.
75. Ibid., 88.
76. Ibid., 90.
77. Ibid., 91.
78. Ibid., 93.
79. Ibid., 101–3.
80. Ibid., 119.

context."[81] "In contrast to the understanding evangelicals often espouse, our Bible is the product of the community of faith that cradled it. . . . This means that our confession of the moving of the Spirit in the Scripture-forming process, commonly known as inspiration, must be extended."[82]

Not surprisingly, Grenz suggests that this will yield greater convergence between Protestants and Roman Catholics on the relation of Scripture and tradition.[83] Yet it also incorporates an important charismatic and Pentecostal perspective on continuing revelation. "In this way, paradigmatic events become a continual source of revelation, as each succeeding generation sees itself in terms of the events of the past history of the community." Such conclusions "chart the way beyond the evangelical tendency to equate in a simple fashion the revelation of God with the Bible—that is, to make a one-to-one correspondence between the words of the Bible and the very Word of God."[84]

Similar arguments are made by John Franke (Grenz's coauthor of *Beyond Foundationalism*) particularly with respect to the reciprocal relation between gospel and culture. "The speaking of the Spirit through Scripture and through culture do not constitute two communicative acts but rather one unified speaking."[85] Franke also appeals to Lindbeck's cultural-linguistic method as he identifies the church as the mother of Scripture, urging "a broader concept of inspiration."[86] On one hand, it provides the constitutive narratives of the church. "On the other hand, it is itself derived from that community and its authority."[87] Neither has final authority over the other; revelation (the Spirit's speaking) occurs as a conversation between God, the church, and culture.[88]

Amos Yong also follows this growing trend among a new generation of evangelical and Pentecostal theologians to treat *sola scriptura* as a product of modern foundationalism. Instead, he argues that we must understand Spirit, Word, and community as mutually definitive.[89] However, by making the written and preached Word a product of the community and its experience as much as the divinely given norm for faith and practice, soteriology as well as ecclesiology can only be understood in synergistic terms. Consequently, the Scriptures "are deemed by the community to be inspired of the Spirit *insofar as the people of God are empowered, healed, and transformed in this encounter*" (emphasis added).[90] What has priority is not the forensic, declarative power of the Word to create the

81. Ibid., 120.
82. Ibid., 121–22.
83. Ibid., 123.
84. Ibid., 130.
85. John Franke, *The Character of Theology* (Grand Rapids: Baker Academic, 2005), 141–42.
86. Ibid., 151.
87. Ibid., 152.
88. Ibid., 153.
89. Amos Yong, *The Spirit Poured Out on All Flesh* (Grand Rapids: Baker Academic, 2005), 156. See also his *Spirit-Word-Community: Theological Hermeneutics in Trinitarian Perspective* (Burlington, VT: Ashgate, 2002).
90. Yong, *The Spirit Poured Out*, 298.

world it describes, but its functional potential for assisting us in our experience and process of transformation. Only insofar as the Word facilitates this human action is it inspired.[91] The Word and the sacraments—as well as "glossolalia, the dance, the shout, and healings"—afford opportunities for "the Spirit's manifestation in the material and embodied experiences" of Christians.[92]

ABOVE ALL EARTHLY POWERS

So far, this chapter has been one-sidedly given to critique, so I must move to construction: first, by suggesting how the Word deconstructs the autonomy of the individual and, second, that of the church.

The Kingdom of the Individual

Not only the message but also the method is correlated with redemption from outside of ourselves. As Stephen H. Webb reminds us, "Sound thus denotes distance and temporality in a way that sight does not. Rather than an inner illumination that emanates outward, hearing proceeds from the external to the internal. . . . Sound draws us out of ourselves by leading us to the source of the noise, while sight brings the image to us. . . . Sound is intimate without being immediate."[93] The Westminster divines pointed out that the preaching of the word is "an effectual means" of salvation by "driving them out of themselves and drawing them unto Christ."[94] It is just this event of being driven out of ourselves that we resist, preferring immediacy precisely because it overcomes the otherness that puts us in question. This is what Merold Westphal has called "ontological xenophobia," "the fear of meeting a stranger, even if the stranger is God."[95]

The priority of the divine speaker over the experiencing, symbolizing, expressive, reasoning, calculating, and legislating self is, as Paul Louis Metzger reminds us, vigorously reasserted by Barth, drawing on Kierkegaard. "Contra paganism old and new, Kierkegaard exhorts his reader to look outside himself, for within himself he only 'discovers his untruth.'" More than a midwife, this sovereign Teacher comes to save and deliver us not only from external oppressors, but also from ourselves. God comes not to give us "an occasion for the discovery of truth, or really untruth," but as "'savior,' 'deliverer,' 'reconciler,' 'judge.' This one is the sole wisdom of God, but foolishness to the Greeks and their descendants."[96] This constitutes the sharpest point of the gospel's offense. That it might help us reach our

---

91. Ibid., 156.
92. Ibid.
93. Webb, *The Divine Voice*, 46.
94. The Westminster Larger Catechism, Q. 155, in *BC*.
95. Merold Westphal, *Overcoming Onto-theology: Toward a Postmodern Christian Faith* (New York: Fordham University Press, 2001), 238.
96. Paul Louis Metzger, *The Word of Christ and the World of Culture: Sacred and Secular through the Theology of Karl Barth* (Grand Rapids: Eerdmans, 2003), 68.

goals, encourage us in our projects, confirm us in our self-esteem, inculcate a community of virtue, and provide useful instruction, no one will dispute. However, the reduction of the Word to therapeutic or moral usefulness invites rather than repels Feuerbach's critique, as Barth clearly recognized.

Robert Jay Lifton, a pioneer in brain research, has characterized the contemporary personality as "the protean self." Always in the process of self-transformation, in the middle of a makeover and on the way to a new identity, the postmodern self craves cataclysmic moments of rebirth.[97] Peter Berger notes, "Modernity creates a new situation in which picking and choosing becomes an imperative."[98] Refusing to receive reality as a gift, radical voluntarism acknowledges only those realities that the self has chosen for itself. The problem with this condition, as Lifton points out, is that the protean self, no matter how many transformations it undertakes, cannot rid itself of "a nagging sense of unworthiness all the more troublesome for its lack of clear origin."[99] It is precisely this naming of Proteus that the word accomplishes. No longer able to elude capture by self-transformation, the protean self is forced to come to terms with the disorienting Stranger and in the process now recognizes not only the origin of its guilt but also the source of its forgiveness.

The protean self should be surprising for an era that is indebted to Nietzsche's assumption that truth is made rather than discovered. "That my life has no aim, is evident from the accidental nature of its origin," he wrote. "*That I can posit an aim for myself* is another matter."[100] In our day, the market promises to give us all the resources necessary for this self-transformation, yet, far from autonomy, this only makes us slaves of the choices that the market gives us. To the extent that the Bible *facilitates* these transformations, it is God's Word, according to a view of inspiration that is essentially Romantic in character. Where modern atheism from Feuerbach to Freud argued that religion is essentially a projection of the self and its felt needs, much of contemporary church practice actually seems implicitly to embrace this perspective instead of recognizing it as a devastating critique.

It is precisely the aim of the sacramental Word to pull us out of ourselves—our pious experience, works, history, solemn pronouncements, hopes, and fears—and to fasten our hearing gaze (the mixed metaphor is intentional) on the Savior who is outside of us (Heb. 12:2). Since the essence of sin is being curved in on ourselves, turning to the familiar "god within," even in the name of pious introspection or spirituality, can only finally lead to the discovery of the God of wrath, not the God of grace.

Luther and Calvin both issued stern warnings to those who thought that they could become faithful Christians by sitting in a corner alone with their Bible, a

---

97. Robert Jay Lifton, "The Protean Self," in *The Truth about the Truth*, ed. Walter Truett Anderson (New York: Putnam, 1995), 130–35.

98. Peter Berger, *The Heretical Imperative* (New York: Doubleday, 1979), 78.

99. Lifton, "The Protean Self," 133.

100. Friedrich Nietzsche, *The Portable Nietzsche*, ed. W. Kaufmann (New York: Viking Press, 1968), 40.

parody rather than an implication of *sola scriptura*.[101] Similarly, William J. Abraham effectively draws our attention to the dangers of a conversionism that uproots Christian experience of the Word from its social-ecclesial context, "making it an orphan, hopelessly starved of moral and theological content."[102] The notion that the Word comes to the self from outside challenges and judges attempts of the autonomous self to make even the Bible captive to its projects, in order to sweep "strangers and aliens" into God's drama. It is neither the pious individual nor the sacred church, but the "living and active" Word of God that creates the communion of which it speaks. Yet God's liberating grace is encountered by the closed-in self as an act of aggression and bondage.

Neither the gospel nor the practices ordained by Christ to deliver it are self-evident. It is a story that must be told, and it is an odd story that continues to surprise us, catching us off guard. Instead of making the Word captive to the intuitions of our reason and experience, the Word takes us captive. The church's praxis will also play a part in this, but it is (thankfully) never the gospel itself, but always points away from itself to "the word of Christ" (Rom 10:17). The church's performance may help or hinder its ability to get a hearing in the world, but its faithfulness is always the effect of the Word, not part of that Word itself. A self or a church that proclaims its own works as part of the gospel has already set itself up for evangelistic failure. Part of the testimony of the church concerning itself is not only that it has faith in Christ, but also that this faith is often weak and its actual praxis often sinful. The church is simply that part of the world that, by God's grace, acknowledges its ungodliness and receives God's justifying and sanctifying work in Jesus Christ. Wherever the Word breaks into our lives and our churches, there is a clash of the two ages. More than affirming the status quo, this Word can be expected to constantly challenge and disturb the church.

The Kingdom of the Community

In the covenant of grace, we are summoned out of our introspective, moralistic, self-absorbed, and self-justifying *eros* and instead find our supreme joy and satisfaction—*eros* truly fulfilled—in the Stranger who has reconciled us. First, we are drawn out of ourselves to God and his grace in Christ. Second, we are drawn out of our isolated experience to the covenant community; and finally, we are liberated from spiritual, moral, and emotional narcissism to love and serve our neighbor in the world. It is the work of the Word to do this. Because God speaks, there is a community that bears his name. However, if we reverse this relation, we lose both Word and church in the bargain.

Through the Word and the sacraments, God is at work. These divine practices make us extroverted creatures: looking up to God in faith and out to our neighbor

101. For a good treatment of this topic, see Keith A. Mathison, *The Shape of Sola Scriptura* (Moscow, ID: Canon Press, 2001).

102. William J. Abraham, *The Logic of Evangelism* (Grand Rapids: Eerdmans, 1989), 95.

in loving service. To avoid the sovereignty and strangeness of this Word, rationalizations abound. Surely the Scriptures are not clear in themselves, the self (or the church) reasons, so that it can remain in charge of the relationship. However, Webster properly counters, "Scripture is self-interpreting and perspicuous by virtue of its relation to God; its clarity is inherent, not made, whether by magisterial authorities, the scholar-prince or the pious reader."[103] The postmodern emphasis on poesis and the interpreter's cocreation of textual meaning reflects "a sort of hermeneutical Pelagianism."[104] "And last: it may suggest that, however genuine they may be, exegetical difficulties are, in the end, not the heart of the difficulty in reading Scripture. The real problems lie elsewhere, in our defiance of grace."[105]

The trend away from modernity's intoxication with the self is closely connected with the neo-Hegelian *totus Christus* ecclesiologies, as well as the cultural-linguistic emphasis on the priority of ecclesial praxis. In the experience of many evangelicals, *sola scriptura* has become transferred from its ecclesial habitat to the domain of private spirituality. Downplaying the sacramental Word, through which God works his own magic, the Bible becomes a resource for "personal growth." In some cases, criticism of *sola scriptura* is fueled by yet one more attempt to escape the clutches (imaginary and real) of "fundamentalism" and "modernity," particularly in what has come to be called the emergent movement.[106]

From a Reformation perspective, however, to say that Scripture is the sole norm for faith and practice is simply to assert the sole lordship of Christ over the church. Christ reigns from heaven by his Spirit through his canon. Only in this way can the church be said truly to be the creation of the gospel rather than the other way around. "God begets and multiplies his Church only by means of his word," Calvin insisted. "It is by the preaching of the grace of God alone that the Church is kept from perishing."[107]

Preaching and sacrament surely are ecclesial practices, and in a covenantal perspective evangelism is understood as incomplete until one is joined publicly to the visible church (Acts 2:47). Since this task of evangelism is to be focused on those who are already in the covenant community—believers and their children—as well as on "all who are far away" (2:39), the church is not only the sum total of *people* who are saved but the *place* where this happens. Paraphrasing Cyprian, Calvin can even say that "for those to whom [God] is Father the church is Mother."[108]

But this does not mean that the church is the effectual agent, much less the founder and authorizer of such practices. Just as an ambassador's speech conveys

103. Ibid., 93.

104. Ibid., 100. See also Reinhard Hütter's excellent point in this regard in *Suffering Divine Things: Theology as Church Practice* (Grand Rapids: Eerdmans, 2000), 61–63.

105. Ibid., 106.

106. See, e.g., Brian McLaren, *A Generous Orthodoxy* (Grand Rapids: Zondervan, 2004), 133–40, 198, 210.

107. John Calvin, *Commentary on the Psalms*, trans. John King (repr., Grand Rapids: Baker, 1998), 1:388–89.

108. Calvin, *Institutes* 4.1.1.

the policy of a nation without initiating or causing it to take effect, the church's ministry is a means rather than a cause of divine action. Also like an ambassador, the church cannot invent its own practices, its own means of grace. God has promised to be truly active in saving mercy, but at the place and through the means of God's own choosing.

Once again, ecclesiologies that confuse the head with the body, the *extra nos* of redemption with the *in nobis* of sanctification, extrinsic justification with intrinsic renewal, cannot do justice to the fact that the church is a recipient of grace. Low-church versions confuse Christ with the believer, while high-church versions collapse Christ into the community. They "give insufficient attention to the free majesty of God," notes Webster. "The gracious or miraculous character of the Church, its sheer difference over against the perfect work of God which brings it into being," he adds, "is often in some measure compromised by the easy, unproblematic way in which the language of participation is often deployed."[109] He adds, "The Hegelian cast of much modern ecclesiology is very much in evidence, and meets little resistance from those who interweave ecclesiology and the doctrine of God," representing "a drift into divine immanence." Emphasizing the agency of the church as in some sense actualizing or continuing Christ's incarnation and redemptive work rather than witnessing to it, such ecclesiologies lead to the conclusion that "the holiness of the Church is no longer sheerly alien, no longer the result of the Word's declaration, but in some sense infused into the Church by the Church's *koinōnia* with God, its perichoretic relation to the Holy Trinity."[110]

If the gospel creates the church, then the gospel alone preserves the church as something other than the world (including a "Christian" agency of some sort). Were it not for the eschatological irruption of pure grace, which comes to us from outside of ourselves and is first of all an extrinsic righteousness, there could be no possibility of any intrinsic holiness in the believer or the church. It is the Word that keeps the church from being assimilated again into the history of this passing age.

Challenging fellow Lutherans like Wolfhart Pannenberg and Robert Jenson, Mark C. Mattes maintains that instead of defining the church according to the gospel, ecclesiology is being allowed to redefine the gospel itself. "Here, justification is no longer primarily seen in forensic terms but rather in ontological terms," with what Jenson himself calls "the 'triumph of community.'"[111] The visible unity of the church under episcopal government, not distinguishing law and gospel, becomes the primary mission.[112] The evangelical view of justification is judged to be too sectarian from an ecumenical perspective and contrary to a participatory ontology.[113] "Similar to Hegel's Platonic assumption of the triumph of

---

109. John Webster, *Holiness* (Grand Rapids: Eerdmans, 2003), 55–56.

110. Ibid.

111. Mark C. Mattes, *The Role of Justification in Contemporary Theologies* (Grand Rapids: Eerdmans, 2004), 118; see Robert W. Jenson, *Systematic Theology*, 2 vols. (New York: Oxford University Press, 1999), 2:126.

112. Ibid., 119.

113. Ibid.

reason over sense is Jenson's idea that participation in God is no longer tantamount to the instantiation of an eternal form in temporal reality, but rather a vehicle of the eternal divine life in its self-development toward its own telos, in which we are graciously permitted to share."[114] However, assimilating the gospel to communal mediation converts the *divine* promise—the *verbum externum*—into the *community's* promise. Jenson rejects "the Protestant supposition that the church is a 'creature of the word'"; rather, they mutually determine each other.[115] However, Mattes responds, "It is the gift of the gospel as a linguistic reality, not its deliverers, that defines the church's life."[116] "The church is to deliver the goods. It is not itself to be conflated with the goods."[117]

> The word as law and gospel creates the communal leadership that can give the social support, wise diplomacy, and healthy community needed for its proclamation. . . . *Sola scriptura* must prevail. Undoubtedly, the gospel is embedded in the creeds and teaching office. However, these latter two receive life from the gospel insofar as they convey the gospel. Jenson fails to understand that both world and church remain ambiguous.[118]

Though usually advertised as a shift away from modern individualism, the drift toward assimilating soteriology to ecclesiology, justification to the church and its virtuous practices, and the word to ecclesial interpretation is more aptly described as a shift away from God's redeeming work to our own.[119] To ask what *constitutes* the unity of the church, then, is to inquire as to what *creates* the church itself. The answer to both is the Word of God, both as means of grace and canonical norm. The gospel does not depend on reason, politics, marketing, or even on the church; it creates its own rationality, polis, publicity, and church. The gospel is self-sufficient, pulling everything else behind it.

This raises the critical issue at the heart of protests new and old against *sola scriptura*: the logical priority of canon and church. The sufficiency of Scripture is not an abstract, predogmatic rule but is intrinsically related to our view of God, the covenant, and redemption. Just as creation is the result of a conversation between the persons of the Trinity, the church is the offspring rather than the origin of the gospel. It is no wonder then that Paul compares the work of the gospel to God's word in creation (Rom. 4:16–17). While the covenant community is temporally prior to the inscripturated canon, the word that creates ex nihilo

---

114. Ibid.

115. Ibid., referring to Jenson, *Systematic Theology*, 1:5. Furthermore, Mattes adds, "The church about which Jenson speculates is one that is largely hypothetical, since it does not seemingly correspond to any actual, present ecclesial community."

116. Ibid., 133.

117. Ibid., 137.

118. Ibid., 141.

119. As I point out in part 1 of my previous volume *Covenant and Salvation: Union with Christ* (Louisville, KY: Westminster John Knox Press, 2007), this tendency is apparent also in the work of James Dunn, N. T. Wright, and other proponents of what has come to be called the New Perspective on Paul.

asserts its temporal and communicative priority over both. Happily, the church of Galatia (or Corinth, Ephesus, or Rome) is not canonical, though the apostolic letters addressed to them are. The script has priority over even its most significant performances.[120] Furthermore, the canon not only judges our poor performances but also liberates us from having to repeat or defend them.

The covenantal context proves its value once more when considering the claim that the church created the canon. God's word *spoken* has now also been committed to *writing*, a canon or constitution. The Bible is the textual deposit of God's unfading Word, whose oral proclamation had all along been creating and sustaining a church in the world since the protevangelium in Genesis 3:15. The church is not purpose-driven, but promise-driven. All of the commands that bind the church are grounded in the word that has first liberated it: "I am the LORD your God, who brought you up out of Egypt, out of the house of bondage." This is the historical prologue that justifies the assertion of Yahweh's sole rights as the sovereign over his people: *Therefore*, "you shall have no other gods before Me" (Exod. 20:2–3 NKJV). Ecclesiastical authority derives from and is qualified and measured by its constituting norm: because we have this covenantal constitution, we are this particular covenant community. Thus, the priority of canon over church is the corollary of the priority of God's grace over "human will or exertion" (Rom. 9:16).

As M. G. Kline and others have pointed out, the Bible parodies the pagan myths of conquest and house-building. According to these myths, after defeating the chaos monster Leviathan, the hero-god then builds a sanctuary for its worship. However, the Bible presents Yahweh as the sole Lord over creation, who, after his work of creation, builds a temple-house to celebrate his triumph.[121] Just as the creation story (historical prologue) leads to the stipulations and sanctions of the covenant that God makes with humanity in Adam, the exodus story of victory over Leviathan leads to the "law of the house" that at Sinai Israel swore to obey. And in exactly the same way that this canon-house, once completed, is not to be altered in any way by human hands (Deut. 4:2; 12:32), the new covenant canon-house carries the same solemn warning (Rev. 22:18–19). Whoever adds to or subtracts from this canon is to be blotted out of the covenantal registry.

As the house is God's, the "law of the house" is God's as well: the constitution or charter unilaterally bestowed by the suzerain on the liberated vassal. Since it is the sacramental source and canonical norm of the covenant community's very existence, the Word must always be given priority over the church. As Gerhard Sauter contends,

> The final court of appeal for Christians on earth is not what Christians think or feel about God, nor their inner voice, which may have direct access to

---

120. Michael S. Horton, *Covenant and Eschatology: The Divine Drama* (Louisville, KY: Westminster John Knox Press, 2002), 271–72; cf. Kevin Vanhoozer, *The Drama of Doctrine: A Canonical-Linguistic Approach* (Louisville, KY: Westminster John Knox Press, 2006), who develops this theme more fully and richly.

121. M. G. Kline, *The Structure of Biblical Authority* (Grand Rapids: Eerdmans, 1975), 27–93.

God. It is also not the church as God's earthly representative, as a spokesperson for Jesus Christ and the embodiment of God's Spirit. Thus *sola scriptura* proves to be an alternative to a final appeal to the church (*sola ecclesia*), or to one's own conscience (*sola conscientia*), or to reason (*sola ratio*), and especially to one's own good feeling (*solus affectus*).[122]

Sauter summarizes, "Searching in Scripture is not just looking up quotes to reinforce opinions and prior knowledge, or using it as a book of oracles. *Whoever really searches in Scripture hopes that, in the process of searching, God will become audible*" (emphasis added).[123]

When the church dares to speak to the world as God's ambassador, it also humbly reminds its hearers that it too stands under that Word's judgment and grace. If Jesus himself appeals to the Father's authority for his speech (John 12:49–50), and the Spirit will only "speak whatever he hears" from the Son (16:13–15), then it would be presumptuous, to say the least, for the church to do otherwise. Germinating around its nucleus of Christ's words and deeds, this canon—at first proclaimed, heard, and recalled—became a completed deposit and was treated as such long before the list of canonical books was officially prescribed in response to spurious texts.[124] The development of the canon was distinct from the process of its creation, and this fact was attested by the ancient church, particularly in the fact that its judgments were guided by historical criticism of the documents and their relation to the apostles rather than by arbitrary fiat.

"Theology is not free speech but holy speech," notes Webster. "Hence the authority of Scripture is a matter for the Church's *acknowledgement*, not its *ascription*."[125] When firmly ensconced in its proper covenantal context, the preaching of the law as well as the gospel contributes to the upbuilding of God's sanctuary. Appealing to the 1541 Geneva Catechism, Webster says that the *solo verbo* [by the Word alone] is the correlate of the *sola fide* [through faith alone].[126] To give priority to the Word is to give priority to the action of God.[127]

> Defined by Word and faith, the church is not a self-realising institution with Scripture as an instrument of its steady identity. Through Scripture the church is constantly exposed to interruption. Being the hearing church is never, therefore, a matter of routine, whether liturgical or doctrinal. It is, rather, the church's readiness "that its whole life should be assailed, convulsed, revolutionised and reshaped."[128]

122. Gerhard Sauter, *Gateway to Dogmatics: Reasoning Theologically for the Life of the Church* (Grand Rapids: Eerdmans, 2003), 217.

123. Ibid., 220.

124. Bruce Metzger, *The Canon of the New Testament* (Oxford: Clarendon, 1987); cf. William Abraham, *Canon and Criterion in Christian Theology* (Oxford: Clarendon, 1998); John Barton, *Holy Writings, Sacred Text: The Canon of Early Christianity* (Louisville, KY: Westminster John Knox Press, 1997); F. F. Bruce, *The Canon of Scripture* (Downers Grove, IL: InterVarsity Press, 1988).

125. John Webster, *Holiness* (Grand Rapids: Eerdmans, 2003), 2, 19.

126. Ibid.

127. Ibid., 45.

128. John Webster, *Holy Scripture* (Cambridge: Cambridge University Press, 2006), 47, citing Karl Barth, *CD* I/2:804.

An individual or a church that simply talks to itself can never be *converted*. The dethroning of all human sovereignties is actually our liberation. The "then and there" of the play itself, now committed to a written script, stands over (and sometimes against) its performances here and now, and this means that even the church can be saved.

As the ecclesial body cannot be equated with its sovereign head, ecclesial speech (tradition) cannot be equated with God's Word. Since Christ's person and work—and apostolic testimony to it—are qualitatively distinguished from the church and its practices, the canon does not simply offer us a good story to complete by imitation (a corollary of an exemplary view of the atonement) or repeat by further acts of atonement and reconciliation, but a completed script that draws us into its story line as performers. The canonical characters are in a qualitatively different class than the postcanonical church that performs the play. Even to speak of intentionally *departing* from the script is to assume that the script is normative.

Hauerwas, Jenson, and others remind us of the degenerate versions of *sola scriptura* in our day: individualistic approaches that abstract interpretation from the faith and practice of the church. However, rebounding from one form of enthusiasm to another is no solution. As in the secular polis, so in the covenant community: the distinction between the constitution (text) and the courts (interpretation) preserves us from reducing ecclesial speech to solipsism: the arbitrary exercise of power based on the church talking to itself. Yet there are still the courts. We read the Bible together, and our communal interpretations—in the form of creeds, confessions, catechisms, and church orders—have a binding, though secondary, authority. Just as the extraordinary vocation of prophets and apostles is qualitatively distinguished from the ordinary calling of ministers today, the magisterial authority of the canon must take precedence over the ministerial authority of the church.

As the church recognized upon receiving it, the canon is authoritative simply because of *what* it is and *whose* it is in the sphere of God's activity, not because of what we make of it individually or corporately. The practice that gives the words their sense is first of all God's, not our own, since not only the speech but also the practices of baptism, the Supper, fellowship, the prayers, outreach, and diaconal care also find their authorization and efficacy in the canonical Word.

The growing popularity of the notion of Scripture as "the church's book" in some Protestant circles, Webster observes, tends to reflect "a broadly immanentist ecclesiology, one which accords great significance to the church's social visibility, which gives prominence to anthropological concepts such as 'practice' and 'virtue,' but which lacks much by way of the instability of a thoroughly eschatological concept of the church." He adds, "Indeed, such accounts can sometimes take the form of a highly sophisticated hermeneutical reworking of Ritschlian social moralism, in which the centre of gravity of a theology of Scripture has shifted away from God's activity towards the uses of the church."[129] Because sal-

---

129. Webster, *Holy Scripture*, 43.

vation is by God's work, not our own, "the definitive act of the church is faithful hearing of the gospel of salvation announced by the risen Christ in the Spirit's power through the service of Holy Scripture."[130] "Accordingly, 'tradition' is best conceived of as a *hearing* of the Word rather than a fresh act of *speaking*."[131] The canon is not being extended or completed by the church, but interpreted and performed in a variety of times and places. Otherwise, church authority, however qualified and hedged about, "lays itself open to critique as an arbitrary exercise of social power."[132] *Tradition as servant*

LOOSENED TONGUES

Whenever humanity has assembled together in a synaxis of autonomy and pride that parodies the public gathering of the nations in the Spirit through Word and sacrament, it is to take heaven by storm. Yet the same Spirit who descended in judgment on Babel, scattering its workers and dividing their languages, descended in grace at Pentecost to unite receivers around the Word of Christ.

Although the Word comes first of all to decenter the self deluded in its claims to autonomy, it is with the goal not of drowning out the voice of the servant but of training the voice to sing the "Amen." It is striking that Scripture records not only the direct "Thus says the Lord," but also the histories, laments, praises, proverbs, and interpretations of God's people as they wrestle with how they will answer back in the historical circumstances of this relationship.

Thus, God has not only given us his Word of judgment and grace, but our own appropriate lines in the script of faith and gratitude. This re-creative Word arrives not to subvert human poesis, but to overthrow the presumption that this is an original (archetypal) poesis rather than a responsive (ectypal) one. Our speaking and making are always analogically related to God's, never identical to the ex nihilo speech that is the heartbeat of reality. Therefore, God's Word does not render us silent; it gives us back our voice—or rather, it gives us back the appropriate lines in the script intended for us. Webb describes the Reformation view of the Word in preaching and liturgy: "Words could spring forth as praise because God had already said the Word that releases us from our sin."[133] Once more we see that the forensic Word generates an effective economy that is as extensive as it is intensive.

The Word that rules is the Word that first of all liberates. Unlike the other words of other sovereigns to which we give our allegiance, this Word brings about a liberating captivity and a captivating liberation. Yet it is always something strange, something to which we must be converted by the Spirit. And this is true as much for the community as for the self, neither of which can be exempt from

130. Ibid.
131. Ibid., 51.
132. Ibid., 53.
133. Webb, *The Divine Voice*, 107.

this sovereign grace that refuses to let us define ourselves, which would be our death. Like Isaiah, we are "undone," yet only to be forgiven, clothed, and sent out with good news on our lips and in our hearts (Isa. 6).

While the church is not the master of the text, it is the amphitheater in which the Word creates the reality of which it speaks, the place where a valley of dry bones becomes a resurrected community (Ezek. 37). "The Church is the place of fruitful and hopeful repentance; and it is nothing else," Barth wrote in connection with Romans 10.

> When the Church crashes up against this point, it is overwhelmed with disgust at its convulsive attempts, at one moment to—*ascend into heaven*, at another to—*descend into the abyss*; it is appalled that it should have tried to be both "height" and "depth," to occupy them, speak of them, point them out, and apportion them. There is a certain horror at all attempts to bring about the work of God, to effect the incarnation of divinity or the resurrection of humanity, by employing the dynamic, demonic power of the Church's own word. The Church may refine its liturgy; popularize its technical language; broaden the basis of the education of its clergy; see that its administration is made more efficient; yield hurriedly to the demands of the laity, however doubtful they may be; encourage theological journalism; approximate more closely to the uncertainties of the "spirit of the age," to romanticism, liberalism, nationalism, and socialism; may, in fact,—"bring Christ into the picture"! But when He is brought into the picture, it is discovered that we cannot introduce Him thus, either by *bringing* Him *down* or by *bringing* Him *up*. For Christ is not the exalted and transformed ideal man. He is the *new man*.[134]

Only when we are silenced can "all moralizings and sentimentalities" give way to the Word of the cross. Yet even this Word must not be transformed into a descent into the abyss: "a gospel of demolition," which would just be another way of moralizing.[135] Barth wonders, "Shall we never permit our hands to be empty, that we may grasp what only empty hands can grasp?"[136] Yet even this emptying of our hands is the judging and liberating work of a God who is too gracious to let us have the last word.

---

134. Karl Barth, *The Epistle to the Romans*, trans. Edwyn C. Hoskyns from the 6th ed. (London: Oxford University Press, 1933), 378.
135. Ibid., 379.
136. Ibid., 380–81.

Chapter Four

Signs and Seals

Ratifying the Treaty

My proposal thus far suggests that there is a great deal to be *heard*, but is there then nothing to *see* in this time between? It was not a suspicion of the visible but a suspicion of idolatry that motivated the Reformed tradition to restrict images to the water, bread, and wine. Phillip Walker Butin observes, "Calvin's concern for 'the visibility of grace' was also expressed in his particular understanding of the sacraments.'" The word creates faith, Calvin insists. "But the sacraments bring the clearest promises."[1] In asking, "Where does faith come from?" the answer of the Heidelberg Catechism works just as well for the origins of the church: "The Spirit creates faith in our hearts by the preaching of the holy gospel and confirms it by the use of the holy sacraments."[2] The goal of this chapter is to provide a covenantal interpretation of the sacraments as signs and seals: first, by offering a broader account of presence; next, by bringing this interpretation to bear specifically on baptism and the Supper.

1. Philip Walker Butin, *Revelation, Redemption and Response: Calvin's Trinitarian Understanding of the Divine-Human Relationship* (New York: Oxford University Press, 1995), 103.
2. The Heidelberg Catechism, Lord's Day 25, Q. 65, in *Ecumenical Creeds and Reformed Confessions* (Grand Rapids: CRC Publications, 1988), 41.

PRESENCE AND ABSENCE WITHIN THE BOUNDS
OF COVENANT (AND ESCHATOLOGY) ALONE

Whatever important metaphysical questions may be asked in any treatment of divine presence, particularly in relation to the sacraments, the categories of presence and absence, near and far away, are spatial metaphors for a covenantal relationship. Roughly speaking, these terms correspond to blessing and curse, respectively. So, for example, Gentile believers are described as those who in the past were "*separate* from Christ, *alienated* from the commonwealth of Israel, and *strangers from the covenants of the promise*, having *no hope* and *without God* in the world. But now in Christ Jesus you who once were "without Christ, being aliens from the commonwealth of Israel, and strangers to the covenants of promise, having no hope and without God in the world" (Eph. 2:12–14).

In addition to its covenantal context, the concept of presence—particularly in relation to creaturely mediation—is always eschatologically conditioned. The same Spirit who brings about in us the filial cry, "Abba! Father!" (Rom. 8:15), also provokes a longing cry for the Parousia that Jesus has promised. "The one who testifies to these things says, 'Surely I am coming soon.' Amen. Come, Lord Jesus!" (Rev. 22:20–21).

Given this covenantal and eschatological context, instead of thinking merely in static ontological terms—*what* a thing is—we should consider *where* a thing is in relation to the covenant Lord and in the unfolding plot of redemptive events. Those who are within the covenant, even as no more than visible members, are within the sphere of the Spirit's activity of separating the waters of this age so that through the penetrating energies of the age to come, a dry place may be prepared for communion (Heb. 6:4–9).

As Derrida contended, the notion of a sign-signified relation (whether conceived in Platonist or nominalist terms) belongs to the history of metaphysics, particularly the metaphysics of presence that is dominated, as we saw in chapter 2 (above), by the metaphorics of vision.[3] Nevertheless, I suggest that covenant theology offers a different account of the sign-signified relation, as exhibited in the history of treaty-making and as eschatologically conditioned. Rather than mediating between the lower (sensible) and higher (intelligible) rungs of the ontological ladder, a covenantal view of God's presence concentrates on communicative action: proclamation rather than manifestation. For the "ontological" legacy (overcoming estrangement), the question of being and presence is already privileged, while for the covenantal paradigm (meeting a stranger), it is a question of sin and redemption.[4] As Richard Kearney para-

---

3. Jacques Derrida, *Of Grammatology*, trans. Gayatri Chakravorty Spivak (Baltimore: Johns Hopkins University Press, 1976), 13.

4. One further point might be mentioned in relation especially to Derrida's criticism. Apart from Jesus Christ, there can be no real connection between signs and the Transcendental Signified. He is the mediator between God and world both in creation and in redemption. And as God and human, Jesus Christ is himself both the signified and the signifier. There is no one or nothing—system, idea, or principle—other than this person in whom the sign and signified are fully united.

phrases Lévinas' challenge to Platonism, "The good *beyond* finds itself inscribed *between* one another."[5]

If this is the case (as this chapter will argue), then a more constructive path may be discerned beyond the metaphysical debates over Christ's true presence in Word and sacrament. In a covenantal context, signs do not merely represent or bring to mind an absent signified. Nor do they become fused in essence. Rather, words and signs together create a covenant. It is significant that the Hebrew idiom for making a covenant is *cutting* a covenant (*kārat bĕrît*). The ritual is inseparable from the treaty itself, establishing and not merely symbolizing a new relationship between two parties. *The question, then, is not the abstract nature of signs-and-signified but whether the agent effectively executes a speech-act through signs (both words and ceremonies).*

SIGNS AND SEALS OF THE COVENANT: PRESENCE-AS-ACTION

As in the treaty-making rituals of the ancient Near East, the covenant of grace is publicly proclaimed (as well as deposited in written form) and ratified by a ceremony. The covenant provides the legal and relational context within which certain authorized human words and actions count as God's own means of grace, thereby constituting and certifying a new state of affairs. Borrowing on the distinction between essence and energies employed especially in the Christian East, I suggest that God's acts of speaking belong to his energies rather than to his essence, and in a covenantal economy, the signs and seals of the treaty are part of that speech. Wherever Jesus Christ was present in the flesh among his contemporaries, God was *bodily present* (essence/manifestation); wherever the Word is now proclaimed and the sacraments are administered on the earth today, God is *present in action* (energies/proclamation).

Sacraments as Treaty Ratification

God's call begins the migration of God's people to their homeland. To Abram, Yahweh declares, "Leave your country and your father's house" (Gen. 12:1). "In these words is already contained the entire destiny of the Jewish people," notes Vincenzo Vitiello.[6] No allegorical interpretation will do here.

> The *migration of Abraham* is to be understood in the most literal and concrete way: the Judaic God is a jealous God who will share his people with nothing and no one. . . . Accompanying the command is a promise that will, when he senses his people's faith in him waver, become a pact. Of this pact,

5. Richard Kearney, "Desire of God," in *God, the Gift, and Postmodernism*, ed. John D. Caputo and Michael J. Scanlon (Bloomington: Indiana University Press, 1999), 117.

6. Vincenzo Vitiello, "Desert, Ethos, Abandonment: Towards a Topology of the Religious," in *Religion*, ed. J. Derrida and V. Vattimo (Palo Alto, CA: Stanford University Press, 1998), 137.

this *alliance*, which in the course of time will be renewed on several occasions, his male protégés must carry an indelible sign on their very bodies. A jealous God, and one who estranges his people.[7]

When considering God's presence, it was this fundamental concern for God's covenantal judgment that most concerned Israel: was God *with* the people in the sense that despite their missteps Yahweh was still committed to his promises? How could they know?

In the covenantal economy, the function of signs is not primarily to express an inner experience or wish. Nor is it primarily to refer symbolically to a state of affairs that transcends it. Rather, it is an obligation-creating act in the present that can only obtain in a relationship of persons. A classic example of this function can be found in the covenant with Noah, although there Yahweh assumes the role of the oath-taker, which turns the tables on the usual relationship between suzerains and vassals. "I set my rainbow in the cloud as a sign of the covenant between me and the earth" (cf. Gen. 9:12–13 NKJV). The bow of judgment—once drawn toward human beings and the arrow released in the deluge—is now drawn and pointing toward God himself in a self-maledictory oath similar to the one that God took before Abraham in Genesis 15. In Revelation 4:3 (cf. 10:1), the bow of judgment hangs behind the throne as a gesture of peace.

The sign does not stand for something else. It is not a question of something that is present representing something that is absent or of somehow making the beloved present in one's mind (like looking at a picture). It is not an object lesson or illustration. On the other hand, it does not overwhelm or replace ordinary natural phenomena but sanctifies them for an extraordinary communicative event. Not because it undergoes ontological metamorphosis, therefore, but because of God's practical use of it, the rainbow can be called "the covenant." A common meteorological phenomenon becomes holy. If the meaning of language is its use, then the meaning of water, bread, and wine in the context of a covenantal ceremony between God and human beings must be determined in terms of their relation to the covenant treaty that they ratify.

The rainbow is a pledge of peace in the most vivid terms possible: by this sign God unilaterally assumes his own judgment should this promise be broken. "When I bring a cloud over the earth," Yahweh adds, "that the rainbow shall be seen in the cloud; and I will remember My covenant which is between Me and you and every living creature of all flesh. . . . The rainbow shall be in the cloud, and I will look on it to remember the everlasting covenant" (Gen. 9:14–17 NKJV). "Remembering" here is not simply a mimetic activity. The rainbow sign is not established in order to trigger a memory of a past event. Rather, to remember the covenant on the basis of the sign is to acknowledge once again one's pledge. Furthermore, since this is a unilateral covenant of pure mercy, it is Yahweh who will "remember" his oath whenever he sees the sign. For God, *remembering* is synonymous with *acting* here and now in accordance with a prior pledge.

7. Ibid.

The promise to Abraham is confirmed and ratified first by the vision of the theophany passing through the severed animal halves, and then by circumcision (Gen. 15–17). Only two verses after we read that Abram "believed the LORD; and the LORD reckoned it to him as righteousness" (Gen. 15:6), Abram asks, "O Lord GOD, how am I to know that I shall possess it?" (v. 8), and God accedes to the request by ratifying the spoken promise in the vision of Yahweh passing through the halves (vv. 9–21).

In the previous two volumes of this series, I explored the significance of Abram's vision in Genesis 15, where a theophanic smoking torch passes through the severed halves of animals, a treaty-making practice well-known in the ancient Near East. In this vision we not only recognize the familiar verbal parallels; we also see the close association of the ratification ceremonies themselves. McCarthy's *Treaty and Covenant* provides an example of an eighth-century treaty of Ashurnirari V and Mati'ilu:

> This ram is not brought from his herd for sacrifice, nor is he brought out for a *garitu*-festival, nor is he brought out for a *kinitu*-festival, nor is he brought out for (a rite for) a sick man, nor is he brought out for slaughter a[s . . .]. It is to make the treaty of Ashurnirari, King of Assyria, with Mati'ilu that he is brought out. If Mati'ilu [sins] against the treaty sworn by the gods, just as this ram is broug[ht here] from his herd and to his herd will not return [*and stand*] at its head, so may Mati'ilu with his sons, [his nobles,] the people of his land [be brought] far from his land and to his land not return [to stand] at the head of his land. This head is not the head of a ram; it is the head of Mati'ilu, the head of his sons, his nobles, the people of his land. If those named [sin] against this treaty, as the head of this ram is c[ut] off, his leg put in his mouth [. . .], so may the head of those named be cut off [. . .]. (col. 1.10ff.)[8]

In Abram's vision, Yahweh himself takes a solitary self-maledictory oath, calling down upon his own head the sanctions that he himself has imposed even in the case of the human partner's malfeasance. Not only employed in treaty-making, such animal sacrifices were also involved in repairing the relationship in the case of breach, as in the atoning sacrifices for which an elaborate cultus was prescribed for Israel.

The feasts solemnized a perpetual, present participation in the redemptive events of the past and their fulfillment in the future. The Israelites who left Egypt "were baptized into Moses in the cloud and in the sea," and drank of the rock in the wilderness, which "was Christ" (1 Cor. 10:1–4). Furthermore, each generation celebrating the Passover was to recognize its participation in this "baptism." It is not surprising that this reference begins an extended discourse on public worship, with specific focus on the practice of the Supper. Even as they looked back to what God had done (such as the Passover, the exodus, the tabernacles, and so

---

8. Quoted by Dennis J. McCarthy, SJ, *Treaty and Covenant: A Study in the Ancient Oriental Documents and in the Old Testament* (Rome: Biblical Institute Press, 1963), 195.

forth), they anticipated a far greater fulfillment in Christ, which John's Gospel especially elaborates. As part of the same covenant community, those who were removed from the original events by epochs could nevertheless be included federally in the founding generation. Unlike its neighbors, Israel's feasts do not celebrate the cycle of nature, but the historical events of covenant deliverance in the past in anticipation of still greater fulfillment in the future. It is not surprising, then, that the Gospels (esp. John) follow the sequence of Israel's feasts in narrating the story of Jesus.

What does it mean then for signs to "participate" in the reality they signify? Instead of beginning with the usual philosophical solutions, there is the ancient Near Eastern answer: "This is the head of Mati'ilu and his sons." The biblical sacraments closely parallel the sign-signified relation that was presupposed in such treaties as the one referred to above. So close was the representative identification of the forswearer with the ritual animal and the sign with the thing signified that circumcision was called simply "the covenant," just as Jesus designated the cup he raised in the upper room as "my blood of the new covenant" (Matt. 26:26–28 NKJV). In these actions, we encounter neither mere illustrations (bare signs representing an absent signified) nor magic, but performative communication that actually places Jesus under the sword of judgment. He offers them the "cup of salvation" because he will drink the "cup of wrath" to its dregs, a cup that he will dread in Gethsemane but will accept for us. It is no wonder, then, that Paul called the cross "the circumcision of Christ" (Col. 2:11).[9] It was he of whom Isaiah prophesied, "that he was *cut off* out of the land of the living, *stricken* for the transgression of my people. . . . He bore the sin of many, and made intercession for the transgressors" (Isa. 53:8–12, emphasis added).

United to Christ in his circumcision-death, the baptized too come under God's sword of judgment. "It is a judicial death as the penalty for sin," says Kline. "Yet to be united with Christ in his death is also to be raised with him whom death could not hold in his resurrection unto justification."[10] And as Peter affirms, baptism, foreshadowed by the salvation of Noah and his family in the flood-ordeal, "now saves," not by cleansing the body but "as an appeal to God for a good conscience, through the resurrection of Jesus Christ, who has gone into heaven and is at the right hand of God" (1 Pet. 3:21–22). "Now conscience has to do with accusing and excusing; it is forensic," Kline emphasizes. "Baptism, then, is concerned with man in the presence of God's judgment throne."[11] Here, as in the exodus, we are reminded of the eschatological nature of both the water

9. M. G. Kline reminds us that like Isaac, Jesus was circumcised as an infant, "that partial and symbolic cutting off"—the "moment, prophetically chosen, to name him 'Jesus.'" But it was the circumcision of Christ in crucifixion that answered to the burnt-offering of Genesis 22 as a perfecting of circumcision, a 'putting off' not merely of a token part but 'of the [whole] body of the flesh' (Col. 2:11, ARV), not simply a symbolic oath-cursing but [actually] a cutting off of 'the body of his flesh through death' (Col. 1:22) in accursed darkness and dereliction" (*By Oath Consigned* [Grand Rapids: Eerdmans, 1968], 45).

10. Ibid., 47.

11. Ibid., 66–67.

and fire ordeals: Now when the people pass through the waters, they will not be drowned, because God is with them as he was in the exodus (Isa. 43:1–3).

Just as circumcision could be called "the covenant" because of the close union of the sign and the thing signified, the Passover ritual was itself called "the LORD's passing over," with successive generations called upon to regard themselves as representatively (i.e., covenantally) present with the founding generation, dressed for the road in anticipation of their redemption (Exod. 13:14–16). So too, in the Supper's words of institution, Jesus simply calls the cup and the bread "the new covenant in my blood." "This is my body. . . . This is my blood of the new covenant, shed for many for the remission of sins" (Matt. 26:26–28 NKJV).

The invocation of Yahweh has its parallel in the secular treaties, where the vassal could call upon the name of the suzerain to deliver his people from invading armies. It is in this context of treaty-invocation that Israel took up its Passover cup: "I will life up the cup of salvation, and will call on the name of the LORD" (Ps. 116:13). The same cup that was filled with judgment for the Messiah (Matt. 26:39) is now drunk by those who, united to his death and resurrection, receive from it only forgiveness and life. The sacraments correspond to the Word (law and gospel) as the ratification of covenantal sanctions: "The cup of blessing that we bless, is it not a participation [*koinōnia*] in the blood of Christ? The bread that we break, is it not a participation in the body of Christ? Because there is one bread, we who are many are one body, for we all partake of the one bread" (1 Cor. 10:16–17). Thus the union is covenantal and centers on legal and relational mediation between erstwhile enemies.

So the focus is not upon divine *presence* per se but on divine *action*. Just as the covenantal word is, as Westphal notes, "a voice of law and of grace, a voice that decenters the would-be autonomous self,"[12] so also the sacraments are God's means of effecting what Rowan Williams has called "dislocation":

> While theologians have sometimes rather loosely talked about the sacramental "principle" in Christianity as an affirmation of some inherent capacity in material things to bear divine meanings, the actual shape and rhetoric of sacramental actions says more about how such meanings emerge from a process of estrangement, surrender and re-creation than we might expect if we begin only from the rather bland appeal to the natural sacredness of things that occasionally underpins sacramental theology. . . . Baptismal identity is given, not chosen.[13]

Williams's contrast of the "sacramental 'principle'" and "dislocation" bears unmistakable similarities to the larger contrast between overcoming estrangement and meeting a stranger. The infant presented for baptism is not in a neutral condition, but is in baptism "redescribed as one of danger or unfreedom, liability to divine

12. Merold Westphal, *Overcoming Onto-Theology: Toward a Postmodern Christian Faith* (New York: Fordham University Press, 2001), xx.

13. Rowan Williams, "Sacraments of the New Society," in *Christ: The Sacramental Word*, ed. David Brown and Ann Loades, Incarnation, Sacrament and Poetry (London: SPCK, 1996), 90.

'wrath.'" The Supper follows the same pattern: "The 'pre-sacramental' state is one in which God's commitment is not assured, or not perceptible to us as certain." God's presence is ambivalent: should it evoke fear or delight?

> It seems that until we have actually received the tokens of the covenant we remain locked in sin, in the hostility to God and each other that flows from lack of assurance in God. When we physically receive the pledge of that assurance, we become "covenanted" ourselves to God and each other (the [1662] Book of Common Prayer speaks of our being thus made "living members" of a "holy fellowship"). The divine initiative of promise creates a *bonded* community, a "faithful people" (to quote 1662 again).[14]

Alongside preaching, the Word that is delivered in baptism and the Supper creates the world of which it speaks. Preaching does not simply *refer to* an extralinguistic reality, but is indeed the linguistic means through which the Spirit *brings it about* (Ezek. 37; John 6:63; Acts 10:44; 12:24; Phil. 2:16; 2 Tim. 2:9; Heb. 4:12; 1 Pet. 1:23).

Even the sacraments, then, obtain their efficacy from the word that they ratify. As Stephen H. Webb notes, "For the Reformers, the sacraments are more than verbal, but they are never less than verbal."[15] At the same time, they are also visual—indeed, tactile and edible, words. Since the Word creates community beyond individual consumerism, it guarantees the efficacy of the sacraments not only as means of grace but also as a means of grace-enabled communion with human strangers. God does what he says. Because his word is no mere sign, but powerful ("living and active"), in the hands of the Spirit the sacraments also truly communicate God's saving grace.

Means of Grace: Infusion or Ratification?

According to Aquinas, unlike just any sign of a sacred thing, a sacrament "makes people holy."[16] Thus, "only those are called sacraments which signify the perfection of holiness in man."[17] The sacraments accomplish this by causing grace to be infused into the recipient, and this is where the different understandings of grace underlying the sacraments emerge.[18] While for Thomas grace is an infused

---

14. Ibid., 95. This threat to every earthly security, to every autonomous reason or experience, to intention and intuition, is what Scripture calls being "born again to a living hope through the resurrection of Jesus Christ from the dead, to an inheritance that is imperishable, undefiled, and unfading, kept in heaven for you, who by God's power are being guarded through faith for a salvation ready to be revealed in the last time" (1 Pet. 1:3–5 ESV).

15. Stephen H. Webb, *The Divine Voice: Christian Proclamation and the Theology of Sound* (Grand Rapids: Brazos, 2004), 43.

16. Thomas Aquinas, *Summa theologia*, Q. 60, Art. 2, Part III; trans. Fathers of the English Dominican Province (repr., Westminster, MD: Christian Classics, 1948), 4:2340.

17. Ibid.

18. Ibid., Q. 69, Art. 9, Pt. III, Ninth Art., 2409: While infants, all being equal in capacity, receive the same effect in baptism, "adults, who approach Baptism in their own faith, are not equally disposed to Baptism; for some approach thereto with greater, some with less, devotion. And therefore

substance—*a potency for overcoming estrangement*, for the Reformers grace is *the favorable event of meeting a stranger*. Although Lutheran and Reformed traditions affirm with Rome and Orthodoxy that the sacraments are means of grace, the deepest differences lie in quite different understandings of grace. For the Reformed, there is no such thing as a nature-grace problem, but only a sin-grace one. Consequently, their understanding of sacraments as means of grace is striving to overcome an ontological concept of grace and a causal understanding of sacraments in favor of a covenantal, relational, promissory, and proclamatory function that is thoroughly eschatological and therefore pneumatological.

It is key to recognize what the term "means of grace" may sometimes obscure: nothing happens *in nobis* that is impersonal. There is no substance, even grace, that is poured into us or at work in us; rather, it is Christ himself, by his Spirit, who "works in you, both to will and to work for his good pleasure" (Phil. 2:13 ESV). As John Webster puts it, grace "is a movement of relation and not a mere handing over of a commodity."[19] This personal work of the Spirit can be identified with grace because it is a gift: the gift of participation in the realities of the age to come. This close connection of the Spirit with eschatology is crucial in the Reformed understanding.[20]

The presence of the triune God among his people in this age truly is an *adventus*, yet tastes rather than fully realizes the Parousia itself. *Parousia* is the Greek translation of the Hebrew word *pānîm* (face/visible presence). The *adventus* of Christ in our midst during this age anticipates but cannot be identified with the bodily return of Christ at the end of the age. "For now we see in a mirror, dimly, but then we will see face to face" (1 Cor. 13:12).

At the same time that the Supper communicates to believers Christ and his benefits, ratifying the covenant, there is a real sense in which we will not eat and drink together with Christ until the eschaton. In instituting the Supper, Jesus says, "I tell you, I will never again drink of this fruit of the vine *until that day* when I drink it new with you in my Father's kingdom" (Matt. 26:29, emphasis added). "For as often as you eat this bread and drink the cup, you proclaim the Lord's death *until he comes*" (1 Cor. 11:26, emphasis added).

It is neither the action of the *signs* themselves nor of the *people* but the action of *God* that makes the sacraments, in the words of the Westminster Shorter Catechism, "the outward and ordinary means whereby Christ communicates to us

---

some receive a greater, some a smaller share of the grace of newness," just as those who come closer to the fire receive more of its heat. Grace is obviously a power (*potentia*) and a substance (*substantia*) with which one must cooperate in order to receive its fullest effect: "Consequently in order that a man be justified by Baptism, his will must needs embrace both Baptism and the baptismal effect. . . . Wherefore it is manifest that insincerity hinders the effect of baptism."

19. John Webster, *Word and Church* (Edinburgh: T&T Clark, 2001), 63.

20. Geerhardus Vos, "Paul's Eschatological Concept of the Spirit," in *Redemptive History and Biblical Interpretation: The Shorter Writings of Geerhardus Vos*, ed. Richard B. Gaffin Jr. (Phillipsburg, NJ: Presbyteran & Reformed Publishing Co., 1980), 125: "For Paul," writes Geerhardus Vos, "the Spirit was regularly associated with the world to come, and from the Spirit thus conceived in all His supernatural and redemptive potency the Christian life receives throughout its specific character."

the benefits of redemption."[21] The covenant community gathers around the table with Abraham and Moses for the same reason that God gave them signs: to receive the ratification and assurance of God's favor toward us. The sacraments are God's answer to Abram's query (above), "How can I know that this will happen?" (Gen. 15:8). Since God's presence is not always felicitous (since he also frequently comes in judgment), we need the assurance that he comes to us now in peace. This, it seems to me, is the crux of the Reformed understanding of sacramental presence. The parties to the ancient Near Eastern treaty cited above did not imagine that Mati'ilu and his people were present substantially in the ram's head. Nor did they think that the sacrifice merely represented the people. Rather, they believed that in this ceremonial action they were making (lit., "cutting") a covenant with all of its attendant threats and blessings.

Aquinas spends eight articles in his *Summa theologia* providing a series of philosophical arguments for "the way in which Christ is in this sacrament."[22] Yet again, this is consistent with his treatment of grace as a metaphysical substance whose infusion is caused by baptism and subsequent sacraments. In a scheme dominated by the analogy of physical causes and infused substances, anxiety over the question of how Christ is present makes sense—and the logic of his arguments will seem perfectly valid. The covenantal paradigm we have been exploring, by contrast, emphasizes the interpersonal agency involved in the economy of giving and receiving a promise. It is not a matter of infusing new qualities in order to make humans divine, but of exchanging vows to make enemies friends—more than friends, a family. The declaration issues in transformation, not vice versa. Therefore, as I have argued at length elsewhere, infusion is the wrong category for God's gracious action.[23]

Nicholas Wolterstorff presents a good case for understanding the contrast between Thomas and Calvin in terms of *presence* versus *action*.[24] Calvin and the Reformed confessions are strongly "inclined to use the language of God-agency rather than the language of sign-agency in their discussions of the sacraments."[25] In other words, the issue is not the efficacy of signs, but the efficacy of divine

21. The Westminster Shorter Catechism, Q. 88, in *Trinity Hymnal* (Atlanta and Philadelphia: Great Commission Publications, 1990), 867.

22. Thomas Aquinas, *Summa theologia*, Q. 76, Pt. III. Thomas does not deny the reality of the ascension, and he carefully distinguishes his understanding of presence from natural and local concepts (involving movement from one place to another, for example). Yet for all that, "the whole substance of the bread is changed into the whole substance of Christ's body, and the whole substance of the wine into the whole substance of Christ's blood. Hence this is not a formal, but a substantial conversion; nor is it a kind of natural movement: but, with a name of its own, it can be called *transubstantiation*" (Q. 75, Art. 5, Pt. III, 2444). I am inclined to believe that such an account (and rival accounts that remain in this circle) could only evolve within the onto-theological discourse. Even when Thomas engages in proof texts from Scripture, in the treatment of the sacraments Aristotle is everywhere the dominant voice.

23. I develop this point at some length throughout part 2 of my previous volume in this series, *Covenant and Salvation: Union with Christ* (Louisville, KY: Westminster John Knox Press, 2007).

24. Nicholas Wolterstorff, "Sacrament as Action, not Presence," in Brown and Loades, *Christ: The Sacramental Word*, 124–25.

25. Ibid., 106.

action. He suggests that the contrast is between a "symbol system" and a "discourse system."[26] Even the visible signs are events of discourse.

Could this be the hermeneutical corollary to the contrast we have been exploring? Within a covenantal model, the sacraments do not convey anything different from that which is given through the preaching but rather confirm what has been given in the gospel.[27] Their office is to confirm, pledge, assure, certify, ratify. In the discourse system, in other words, it is not *signs* that refer but *persons*. It is not the metaphysical relation of sign and signified in the abstract, but the personal action of agents in discourse—a particular (covenantal) discourse—that determines the efficacy and validity of these sacraments. The question, in other words, is not what God does *to* the signs to make them participate ontologically in the signified, but what God is doing *with* the signs to ratify and communicate the promised reality. It is apparently not a stretch to see convergences between Reformed conceptions of Word and sacrament and communicative theory. B. A. Gerrish even observes, "One might perhaps equally well appropriate a term from J. L. Austin and call the Calvinistic sacraments 'performative' signs, because their efficacy resides wholly in the divine promise."[28]

According to speech-act theory, notes Wolterstorff, "my illocutionary act is the act of promising you that I will buy new tires for the car this afternoon; my act of inscribing those words *counts* as my act of making that promise. And my perlocutionary act is my act of relieving your anxiety by making that promise to you."[29]

> To enter the liturgy, as Calvin understands it, is to enter the sphere not just of divine presence but [also] of divine action. God, in Calvin's way of thinking, is less a presence to be apprehended in the liturgy than an agent to be engaged. What strikes me, in the second place, is the extraordinary significance that Calvin assigns to God's offering us these material elements of bread and wine and our eating and drinking them. . . . Never, to my knowledge, has ordinary material stuff been freighted with such momentous significance.[30]

The question is not where God is present (by itself relatively uninteresting when we are talking about an omnipresent deity), but where God is present for us, in peace and safety rather than condemnation and destruction.

So the concern of the sacraments is not to make God present in majesty, but to be God's means of action: ratifying, assuring, attesting, confirming, and sealing the covenant promise not only to all people in general (as in the general offer of the gospel in preaching), but to each recipient in particular. "First," according to the Heidelberg Catechism, "as surely as I see with my eyes the bread of the Lord broken for me and the cup given to me, so surely his body was offered and

26. Ibid., 108.
27. Ibid., 109.
28. B. A. Gerrish, *Grace and Gratitude: The Eucharistic Theology of John Calvin* (Minneapolis: Augsburg Fortress Press, 1993), 140 n. 50.
29. Ibid., 110.
30. Ibid., 119–20.

broken for me and his blood poured out for me on the cross." But this is not only past tense: "Second, as surely as I receive from the hand of the one who serves, and taste with my mouth the bread and cup of the Lord, given me as sure signs of Christ's body and blood, so surely he nourishes and refreshes my soul for eternal life with his crucified body and poured-out blood."[31] Similarly, according to the Belgic Confession, "the sacrament of Christ's body and blood" was instituted "to testify to us that just as truly as we take and hold the sacraments in our hands and eat and drink them with our mouths, by which our life is then sustained, so truly we receive into our souls, for our spiritual life, the true body and true blood of Christ, our only Savior."[32]

In contrast both to Zwinglian and Roman Catholic liturgies, Calvin's service (modeled in part on Bucer's) was a liturgy of Word *and* sacrament. His covenantal understanding presupposed the equal importance and inextricable connection between God's verbal and visual pledge. Therefore, as Gerrish claims, "it called also for reconstruing the sacraments as operative, like words, through the communication of meaning, even if, again like the word, they must effect nothing less than the mysterious union with Christ."[33] Again this underscores the point that the sacraments belong to the economy of performative speech-acts rather than the metaphysics of manifestation and presence per se. Calvin writes, "Nor does he feed our eyes with only a bare show but leads us to the reality [*rem praesentem*], and what he depicts [*figurat*] he effectively accomplishes at the same time. . . . God works through external means."[34] God's fatherly goodness in Christ is uppermost in Calvin's interpretation of the sacraments: through baptism he adopts us into his family, and through the Supper he continually feeds us.[35]

Means of Grace or Act of Obedience?

God has publicly promulgated his treaty of grace through the proclamation of the gospel and the administration of baptism and the Supper. If we want to know—and want others to know—where to locate a merciful God, we must find him where he finds us, at the place where he has promised to come in peace.

The Reformers observed that by the addition of sacraments in the medieval church, the force and significance of the dominically sanctioned ceremonies of baptism and Eucharist were undermined. The addition of sacraments could only come about, the Reformers argued, because the criteria for a sacrament was no longer that it was dominically sanctioned and had the express intention of conveying the gift of Christ and all of his benefits. Instead, sacraments had become conduits for infused grace rather than pledges of divine favor. The Mass itself has

31. The Heidelberg Catechism, Lord's Day 28, Q. 75, in *Ecumenical Creeds and Reformed Confessions* (Grand Rapids: CRC Publications, 1988), 45.
32. The Belgic Confession, Art. 35 in *Ecumenical Creeds and Reformed Confessions*, 115.
33. B. A. Gerrish, *Grace and Gratitude*, 108; see Calvin, *Institutes* 4.14.7.
34. Calvin, *Institutes* 4.15.14–15.
35. Gerrish, *Grace and Gratitude*, 122–23, from Calvin, *Institutes* 4.15.1 and 4.17.1.

become, in the words of Vatican II, "the work of the people," with the worshipers' offering of the sacrificial victim at its center.

In our day, we see a similar tendency, ironically, among evangelicals. As the nature of sacraments is understood largely as the work of the believer, it is no wonder that the list of sacraments or "ordinances" can be open-ended. Emergent leader Brian McLaren praises Roman Catholicism's seven sacraments, suggesting that once there are seven, eventually "everything becomes potentially sacramental . . . ," including "the kind smile of a Down's syndrome child, the bouncy jubilation of a puppy, the graceful arch of a dancer's back, the camera work in a fine film, good coffee, good wine, good friends, good conversation."[36] However, this is actually a long-standing view in evangelical circles and can be found today among conservative evangelicals such as Wayne Grudem and Charles Ryrie.

Ryrie says that unlike a sacrament, an ordinance "does not incorporate the idea of conveying grace but only the idea of a symbol."[37] Do we need "actual baptism" in order to symbolize "leaving the old life and entering into the new"? Ryrie asks, "Why not erect a little closet on the church platform, have the candidate enter it in old clothes, change his clothes inside the closet, and then emerge in new clothes? Would that not illustrate the same truth as baptism does? And is it not a scriptural illustration? (Col. 3:9–12)." Therefore, Ryrie concludes, we should have "more flexibility" in our practices.[38] Interestingly, more radical theories of contemporary worship have appeared employing the same logic, such as even abandoning sermons—something that conservative evangelicals would challenge. This points up the fact that in the heritage of American evangelicalism, the categories of conservative/traditionalist and progressive/liberal are difficult to define.

Grudem criticizes Louis Berkhof's restriction of the sacraments to baptism and the Supper, administered by ordained ministers, as carrying "overtones of 'sacerdotalism.'"[39] "But is it wise to make such a short list of 'means of grace'? If we wish to list and discuss all the means of receiving the Holy Spirit's blessing that come to believers specifically through the fellowship of the church, then it does not seem wise to limit the 'means of grace' to three activities whose administration is restricted to the ordained clergy or officers of the church." He recognizes that "such a list may become quite long."[40] However, the consequence is that "baptism is not a 'major' doctrine" that should remain church-dividing, although it is "a matter of importance for ordinary church life." He challenges the argument for infant baptism from the continuity of the covenant of grace for failing to realize that the old covenant "had a physical, external means of entrance

36. Brian McLaren, *Generous Orthodoxy* (Grand Rapids: Zondervan, 2004), 225–26.
37. Charles Ryrie, *Basic Theology: A Popular Systematic Guide to Understanding Biblical Truth* (1986; repr., Chicago: Moody Press, 1999), 487.
38. Ibid., 467.
39. Wayne Grudem, *Systematic Theology: An Introduction to Bible Doctrine* (Grand Rapids: Zondervan, 1994), 950.
40. Ibid., 951.

into the 'covenant community,'" while "the means of entrance into the church is voluntary, spiritual, and internal."[41]

According to Stanley Grenz, "the ordinances symbolize the gospel,"[42] and the chapter that directly treats baptism and the Supper is titled "Community Acts of Commitment." Grenz explains that from the perspective of the Radical Reformers and their Baptist heirs, baptism and the Supper "are basically human, and not divine acts." "At the heart of this theology was a focus on obedience. Believers participate in the ordinances out of a desire to be obedient to the one who ordained these acts for the church. The ordinances, therefore, are signs of obedience."[43]

Viewing the sacraments as our own acts of obedience rather than as God's means of grace has enormous implications for ecclesiology more generally, as we will see, but also for soteriology. Millard Erickson recognizes that the Reformed/Presbyterian view, which "is tied closely to the concept of the covenant," emphasizes "the objective aspect of the sacrament."[44] In opposition to this view, Erickson argues, "The act of baptism conveys no direct spiritual benefit or blessing." "It is, then, a testimony that one has already been regenerated," and is only performed after candidates "have exhibited credible evidence of regeneration" and have therefore "met the conditions for salvation (i.e., repentance and active faith)."[45] "It is a public indication of one's commitment to Christ."[46] Concerning the Supper, Erickson notes that in the Reformed view, "There is, then, a genuine objective benefit of the sacrament. It is not generated by the participant; rather, it is brought to the sacrament by Christ himself," but according to Erickson the Supper is "basically commemorative."[47] "The Lord's Supper has the effect of bringing preconscious beliefs into consciousness."[48]

Although Radical Protestantism reminds us of the importance of personal faith, it must be said that the differences between this perspective and the Reformed position are as great as those that separate the Reformed from the Roman Catholic view. The positions of both Rome and the Anabaptist/Baptist traditions actually agree on a fundamental point, that the sacraments (or ordinances) are first of all an offering (however differently conceived) that we bring to God to testify to our faith and love rather than a gift of God that ratifies his promise. From a Reformed (as well as Lutheran) perspective, once that move is made, disagreements over symbolic and realistic theories are comparatively insignificant.

Regardless of whether its basis is the personal performance of all the stipulations ("All this we will do") or a royal grant (an inheritance bestowed on one's heirs because of the personal performance of a covenant head), a covenant is a relationship between two parties. Therefore, Reformed theology has always

41. Ibid., 976–77.
42. Stanley Grenz, *Theology for the Community of God* (Nashville: Broadman & Holman, 1997), 644.
43. Ibid., 670.
44. Millard Erickson, *Christian Theology* (Grand Rapids: Baker, 1985), 3:1093–1094.
45. Ibid., 1096.
46. Ibid., 1101.
47. Ibid., 1120, 1122.
48. Ibid., 1126.

affirmed that the sacraments, though primarily a divine pledge, also call for the appropriate response of the covenant partner. Yet it is the pledge and its ratification that create and confirm that appropriate human response. In the covenant of grace, this response is faith and repentance. In this way, the indicative (gospel) always comes before the imperative (command), God's action before human response, yet both are involved in the ratification of the covenant. This becomes clearer as we focus on each sacrament.

BAPTISM: DISLOCATION AND RELOCATION

Before Yahweh institutes circumcision (Gen. 17), he appears in a vision to Abraham in which he passes through the carcasses that have been cut in order to ratify his self-maledictory oath (Gen. 15). The Sinai treaty also has its blood-ratification rite, although it differs in a crucial respect. Since it ratifies Israel's oath to abide by all that God has commanded as a condition for preserving its status in the land, the rite is a sign and seal of Israel's judgment rather than Yahweh's self-maledictory oath. In Exodus 24, Moses splashes the blood on the people, with the words of institution, "See the blood of the covenant that the LORD has made with you *in accordance with all these words*" (v. 8, emphasis added). In accordance with *which* words? We are told in the previous verse: the words of the Israelites when they swore, "All that the LORD has spoken we will do" (v. 7).

Not only in the Bible but also in the secular politics of ancient Near Eastern treaties, the words and the signs were inextricably bound in the covenant. Different "words" (i.e., covenants) require different ratification ceremonies, but they always involve "cutting"—the forswearer's life is being put on the line.

On this basis, Jeremiah could paint a picture that contrasts with that vision in Genesis 15; the prophet declares, in God's name, "Those who transgressed my covenant and did not keep the terms of the covenant that they made before me, I will make like the calf when they cut it in two and passed between its parts" (Jer. 34:18–20). "Cutting off" is the covenantal language for the judgment of the covenant community and individuals within it.

Circumcision-Baptism with Christ

Circumcision was a partial "cutting off" that kept one from being wholly cut off (excommunicated) from the people of God. So one was either devoted to the blessings of the covenant (through circumcision) or to its curses (without circumcision). It was this sort of thorough "cutting off" that was symbolized in the offering of Isaac, but prevented by the Lord's provision of a substitute, a ram caught in the thicket (Gen. 22).

At his own circumcision on the eighth day, Abraham's greater heir was prophetically named "Jesus" (Luke 2:21), identifying him in the history of redemption with the ram caught in the thicket, John's "Lamb of God" (John

1:29). "But it was the circumcision of Christ in crucifixion that answered to the burnt-offering of Genesis 22 as a perfecting of circumcision," Kline notes, "a 'putting off' not merely of a token part but 'of the [whole] body of the flesh' (Col 2:11 ARV), not simply a symbolic oath-cursing but a cutting off of 'the body of his flesh through death' (Col 1:22) in accursed darkness and dereliction."[49] Just as circumcision was a knife drawn in judgment yet "passed over" the recipient by cutting away merely the foreskin, in baptism too we come under the sword of divine judgment. In this event, however, we are entirely dedicated to judgment in order to be entirely raised in newness of life (Rom. 6:1–11).

What is signified and sealed in baptism is nothing less than the eschatological judgment of the last day: our curse in Adam swallowed by our blessing in Christ. In Colossians 2:9–12, as Vos reminds us,

> The "circumcision" of the Christian is not to be understood as following his baptism. Instead, the two actions are to be regarded as simultaneous. The rite of cleansing found in the old covenant finds its fulfillment in the rite of cleansing ordered in the new. . . . The meaning of the passage would be communicated best by a rendering such as "when you were buried with him in baptism, you were circumcised"; or "by being buried with him in baptism you were circumcised." . . . In the fullest possible sense, baptism under the new covenant accomplishes all that was represented in circumcision under the old. By being baptized, the Christian believer has experienced the equivalent of the cleansing rite of circumcision.[50]

Paul also appeals to the analogy of the "baptism" of the children of Israel into Moses through the Red Sea for this union (1 Cor. 10:2), and Peter refers to the Noahic deluge ordeal as a baptism foreshadowing the baptism which now saves us (1 Pet. 3:21). Over against the theologians of glory at his own side, Jesus emphasized that none but he could bear the "baptism" of the cross (Luke 12:50; cf. Mark 10:38), yet we now are included in the benefits of his circumcision-death and resurrection-life. As the promises are greater in the new covenant, so also are the curses for refusing to receive the substance that it promises (Matt. 8:12; John 15:1–8; Rom. 11:17–21; Heb. 4:2; 6:4–8; 12:25). Earthly exile from the geopolitical theocracy is merely typological of being cut off from the heavenly rest.

The sign and thing signified are treated in the New Testament as in the Old as intimately connected. Christ has "cleansed [the church] by *the washing of water with the word [katharisas tō loutrō tou hydatos en hrēmati]*" (Eph. 5:26 NASB) and "saved us, not because of works of righteousness that we had done, but according to his mercy, through the water of rebirth and renewal by the Holy Spirit" (Titus 3:5). Therefore, God's gracious work cannot be set in opposition to creaturely means.[51]

---

49. M. G. Kline, *The Structure of Biblical Authority* (Grand Rapids: Eerdmans, 1975), 45.
50. Geerhardus Vos, *Redemptive History and Biblical Interpretation*, 165–66.
51. So, for example, Karl Barth, *CD* IV/4:113–14. Despite considerable technical skill and knowledge of a wide variety of classical and contemporary interpretations of each passage (acknowledging in the preface the debt to his son, Markus Barth, in this regard), Karl Barth's exegesis from the outset presupposes that these passages cannot be interpreted in a sacramental manner.

Believers have been "buried with [Christ] in baptism" and raised with him "in new-ness of life." Baptism is now the true circumcision (Col. 2:11–12; Rom. 6:4).

The earliest apostolic preaching enjoins hearers to "'be baptized in the name of Jesus Christ for the forgiveness of your sins; and you will receive the gift of the Holy Spirit. For the promise is for you and your children and for all who are far off, as many as the Lord our God will call to himself.' . . . So then, those who had received his word were baptized, and that day there were added about three thou-sand souls" (Acts 2:38–41 NASB). Since the ritual baptisms of Second Temple Judaism, as well as John's, had been performed in water, it would seem apparent that those who received his word were baptized *in water*. Indeed, this was the understanding when, for example, Philip proclaimed Christ to the treasurer of the Ethiopian court. Arriving at some water, the official said, "Look, here is water! What is to prevent me from being baptized?" (Acts 8:36). Returning then to Acts 2, it would seem arbitrary to suggest that references to people being baptized is to be understood in terms of water baptism *unless* forgiveness of sins and renewal in the Spirit are said to be embraced through it.

Nevertheless, although baptism (like circumcision) signifies and seals our par-ticipation in the visible covenant of grace, the reality that it communicates must be embraced by faith.

CIRCUMCISION-BAPTISM APART FROM CHRIST

We know from covenantal history that while circumcision in the flesh was the *sign and seal* of the circumcision in the heart, the former did not *cause* the latter. The two are distinguished in the old covenant (Deut. 10:16; 30:6; Jer. 4:4; 31:32–34), even before we reach the Pauline contrast between outward and inward circumcision (Rom. 2:28–29; 3:30; 4:10; 1 Cor. 7:19; Gal. 5:2–6; Phil. 3:3; Col. 2:11). Apart from faith in Christ, one stands (either in Adam or in Israel) under a covenant of law, requiring complete personal obedience—fulfill-ing all righteousness. Their circumcision-baptism will be borne by themselves alone, apart from Christ, the mediator of the covenant of grace.

Thus, the writer to the Hebrews can compare the wilderness generation to covenant members in the last days. "For indeed the good news came to us just as to them; but the message they heard did not benefit them, because they were not united by faith with those who listened. For we who have believed enter that rest"—in fact, a greater rest than Joshua pioneered (Heb. 4:2–11). Hebrews 6 offers a bracing warning to those who have "once been enlightened"—ancient Christian writers used this term to refer to baptism—"and have tasted the heav-enly gift, and have shared in the Holy Spirit, and have tasted the goodness of the word of God and the powers of the age to come," who nevertheless leave the faith, having fallen short of "things that belong to salvation" (vv. 4–9). If God has bro-ken off unfruitful branches of the natural tree to engraft wild branches, how much less will he tolerate wild branches that are only connected externally to the tree but are not united vitally to Christ through faith (Rom. 11:19–24)? "For if the firstfruit is holy, the lump is also holy; and if the root is holy, so are the branches" (v. 16 NKJV). Nevertheless, it is one thing to be related to the covenant externally and another to be actually united to Christ through faith. One believing parent sanctifies the covenant children (1 Cor. 7:14), and as Hebrews 6 confirms, the covenant is the sphere in which the Spirit is at work visibly even among those who are not (yet) believers, but as the visible means of bringing about a life-giving participation in the Vine.

So, according to the traditional Reformed understanding, the relationship of election and the covenant of grace is that of the invisible and visible church. Not all who are visible members of the covenant and therefore in some sense beneficiaries of the Spirit's sanctifying action are living branches of the vine. Only by turning from ourselves to Christ, placing our confidence in his work, are we actually united to Christ and made living members of his elect body.[52] Therefore, faith is neither separated from the sacraments (since faith embraces the reality promised in baptism) nor rendered superfluous by them.

It is not that there are two covenants of grace or two churches, but that the one covenant of grace and church of Christ exists for now as a "mixed assembly." But this is not a new problem for the new covenant people; it has been part and parcel of God's electing prerogative since the beginning, as Paul insists (Rom. 9:6–18). The sacraments then are, as Paul defines them, signs and seals of the righteousness that we have *by faith* (Rom. 4:11). Only covenant members can be "cut off"—excommunicated from the promises that have been given to them and have had ratified toward them but that they have not actually embraced. That is why Paul warns that those who are now circumcised or require circumcision as a sign and seal of the Sinaitic law-covenant are actually cutting themselves off of the Abrahamic inheritance (Gal. 3:5–25; 5:1–6).

BAPTISM AS GOD'S WORK

In this light, preaching and sacrament are neither mere *witnesses* to grace nor are they *causes* of grace, but they are *means* of grace inasmuch as they ratify the promise and thereby strengthen our faith in the one who promises. Taken up by Word and Spirit, baptism itself as "visible word" is not merely representative or symbolic but is "living and active." Like preaching, it is the lively action of God's energies. In the administration of a sacrament, the Father ratifies his pledge toward us in the Son by the Spirit. Through it, the Spirit brings about, when and where he will, the perlocutionary effect of the gospel promise. As a sign, it objectively witnesses to our inclusion in the covenant of grace; as a seal, it is the means by which the Spirit brings about within us the "Amen" to God's promise and command, not

52. Ibid., 288.

only once but throughout our pilgrimage.[53] Baptism itself does not effect this in an ex opere operato fashion, but when and where the Spirit chooses.

For all of these reasons, as the Belgic Confession argues, children in the new covenant, as in the old, should be baptized, since "Christ has shed his blood no less for washing the little children of believers than he did for adults. . . . Furthermore, baptism does for our children what circumcision did for the Jewish people. That is why Paul calls baptism the 'circumcision of Christ'" (Col. 2:11).[54]

Therefore, a covenantal view of the sacraments serves rather than undermines the crucial point that this is a covenant of *grace*. The Reformers and their heirs emphasized that baptism was, first of all, an action of the whole Trinity. Calvin writes,

> For he [Christ] dedicated and sanctified baptism in his own body in order that he might have it in common with us as the firmest possible bond of the union and fellowship which he has deigned to form with us. . . . All the gifts of God displayed in baptism are found in Christ alone. Yet this cannot take place unless he who baptizes in Christ invokes also the names of the Father and the Spirit. . . . For this reason we obtain and, so to speak, clearly discern in the Father the cause [*causa*], in the Son the matter [*materia*], and in the Spirit the effect [*effectio*] of our purgation and our regeneration.[55]

Note that in the place of the mechanical operations between God and the self (habits, dispositions, and so forth) are the perichoretic relations of the Trinity, so that honor is ascribed to God alone and yet in the distinct operations of each divine person. Just as Calvin had earlier insisted that through the Scriptures, believers hear God as if he were standing before them, they also in baptism "see with their very eyes the covenant of the Lord engraved upon the bodies of their children."[56] As with all of God's works, the Father speaks in the Son and by the perfecting agency of the Spirit.

With the Reformation more generally, Calvin and the Reformed confessions insisted that the sacraments, like the preaching of the gospel, are divine gifts and not human works: God's pledge of goodwill, God's testimony to dispense the inheritance of all riches in Christ to believers and their children. It also calls for faith and repentance on our part, but it is God's promise that comes first. God first serves us; the church comes into existence (not just in the beginning but also throughout the life of the individual Christian and the corporate body) as a recipient of grace. So God is at work here and now among us, as charismatic and pentecostal Christians rightly insist, but when and where he has promised to meet us in peace—in the ordinary ministry of Word and sacrament. Through these signs, God performs wonders. We are already beginning to see how crucial our conception of the sign-signified relation is for broader questions in ecclesiology.

53. The Belgic Confession, Art. 34, in *Ecumenical Creeds and Reformed Confessions*.
54. Ibid.
55. Calvin, *Institutes* 4.15.6.
56. Ibid., 4.16.9.

The same tendency to view creaturely reality as overwhelmed by or absorbed into divine reality with regard to the sacraments appears in the conflation of Christ with his church, while the tendency to separate the sacraments from their reality carries over into a division between divine work (in the invisible church) and human work (in the visible church). In the covenantal interpretation offered here, creaturely reality is not divinized but consecrated by God for the purpose of performing his reconciling activity.

While strenuously avoiding synergism in any form, Karl Barth nevertheless makes baptism a purely human act of response. It is not surprising, therefore, that he came to reject the baptism of covenant children. Not only our response comes first; it is *the* meaning of the sacrament. Baptism witnesses to a grace already bestowed apart from it. "It is not itself, however, the bearer, means, or instrument of grace. Baptism *responds to* a mystery, the sacrament of the history of Jesus Christ, of His resurrection, of the outpouring of the Holy Spirit. *It is not itself, however, a mystery or sacrament*" (emphasis added).[57] However, the price for this dualistic approach is a view of baptism as entirely the work of human beings, with no place at all given to the sacrament as a divine pledge. In this respect (as in his rejection of infant baptism), Barth's position is even more radical (or perhaps more consistent) than Zwingli's. Reflecting on this fact, Barth wrote, "The Reformed Church and Reformed theology (even in Zurich) could not continue to hold" to Zwingli's teaching, and took a "backward step" toward Calvin's "sacramentalism." "We for our part cannot deny that both negatively and positively Zwingli was basically right."[58]

However, in my view at least, Barth does not offer a persuasive exegesis of the overwhelming New Testament testimony to baptism as God's action of pledging forgiveness and the gift of the Spirit. Even as sympathetic an interpreter as John Webster concludes concerning Barth's treatment of baptism in the final fragment of the *Church Dogmatics*,

> The exegesis is sometimes surprisingly shoddy, dominated by special pleading, as well as by what seems at times an almost Platonic distinction between water baptism (an exclusively human act) and baptism with the Spirit (an exclusively divine act). . . . Clearly the Reformed tradition on sacraments had lost its appeal for him, though what replaced it lacked the nuance and weightiness of earlier discussion.[59]

Nor does Barth adequately explain why children would be excluded from the same covenant that included believers and their children all along, especially when Peter (Acts 2:38–39) and Paul (1 Cor. 4:17) reassert their inclusion, and there are examples in Acts of household baptisms (Lydia and her family in 16:15, the jailer and his family in 16:31–34; cf. Stephanas and his family in 1 Cor. 1:16).

---

57. Karl Barth, *CD*, IV/4:73, 102.
58. Ibid., 130.
59. John Webster, *Barth* (New York: Continuum, 2000), 157.

Covenant theology must therefore be distinguished from both an ex opere operato (by doing it, it is done) view of baptism and an Anabaptist perspective, which makes baptism a means of obedience rather than a means of grace.

What I am suggesting here is that we dispense altogether with any notion of infusion and allow baptism to occupy its native (covenantal) habitat. While there are no passages in Scripture that speak of baptism as infusing new habits, there are clear statements that attribute the new birth to the Word (Luke 8:11; Heb. 4:12; Jas. 1:21; 1 Pet. 1:23). Even in the case of Ephesians 5:26, where the church is said to be sanctified and cleansed "with the washing of water by the word," the preposition *dia* makes the Word the instrument. Far from diminishing the significance of baptism as a means of grace, this view indicates why it is such: because it is the sign and seal that confirms the word of promise to the baptized.

Circumcision did not cause Abraham's justification, but was, as Paul explicitly says, the sign and seal of the righteousness that he had by faith (Rom. 4:9–12). Nevertheless, God commanded the circumcision of every male infant (Gen. 17), so in their case it could not have signified and sealed a response that they had already made. Whether administered before or after the act of faith, baptism remains a sign and seal of the righteousness that one has by faith alone (Col. 2:11–12).

Similarly, the blood on the doorpost did not *cause* God to pass over Israelite houses in Egypt, but it both *signified and sealed* the redemption of those households from the judgment of the avenging angel. Like the rainbow, it was a sign and seal not only to the Israelites but also to the God of judgment. Just as the signs and seals of a law-covenant ratify the obligation of the oath-takers to fulfill God's commands as the condition for blessing, the signs and seals of a promise-covenant ratify God's oath and hang his "rainbow" over recipients who, through it, embrace the promise. That is to say, baptism is properly situated in a forensic, communicative, and covenantal rather than a causal framework. Thus, baptism is the pledge of our participation in this age to come, not the cause of regeneration.

THE SUPPER: EUCHARISTIC *KOINŌNIA*

Although the priority lies with God's gracious action, baptism also involves the responsive pledge of the whole church, the family, and eventually the children who will profess faith later in life. I have already indicated that covenant meals were part and parcel of the treaty-making events in the ancient Near East, and in Israel particularly. As with baptism, then, I will begin with the covenantal context.

THE CUP OF SALVATION: THE SUPPER
IN ITS COVENANTAL CONTEXT

Covenant meals both celebrated and ratified the treaty, as when the mysterious king of Salem, "priest of God Most High," "brought out bread and wine" and then pronounced Yahweh's blessing on Abraham (Gen. 14:17–20). The Passover meal is the participation of the generations to come in their night of safely passing under God's sword because of the blood on the doorpost (Exod. 12). Analogous to the above-cited secular treaty sworn by Mati'ilu, the blood-oath is a communicative event. The head of the ram becomes the head of Mati'ilu and his sons federally and representatively (i.e., covenantally), not substantially. In other words, those who participate in the ceremony are *by means of these words and other actions* assuming certain responsibilities as they represent their respective peoples.

Similarly, the prophets frequently speak of God's judgment as a "cup of wrath." Are we not to assume the same covenantal background in Jesus' announcement, "This is my body" and "This is the blood of the new covenant," especially when he speaks of his own crucifixion as the drinking of the "cup of wrath" to its dregs in the place of those he represents (Mark 10:38; Luke 22:42)? That night he truly sealed his fate as the one upon whose head the covenant curses would fall. For those who embrace the reality signified and sealed in the sacraments, the ordeal is liberation, but those who do not embrace the reality but only the signs must personally bear their own guilt. Thus those who in the Supper do not discern the Lord's body and blood (the reality) "eat and drink judgment to themselves" (1 Cor. 11:29).

Covenantal meals are not simply state dinners that follow a treaty-making ceremony; they are part of it. We recall Moses, Aaron, and the elders at the top of Sinai eating with Yahweh, the Great King. The motif of "eating and drinking in the presence of the LORD" that is especially prominent in the patriarchal narratives is explicitly carried over in Luke's Gospel.[60] Unlike the covenant-*breaking* meal enjoyed in God's absence by Adam and Eve, through which their eyes were "opened" to recognize their guilt, the two disciples along the Emmaus road hear the resurrected Christ proclaim himself from all the Scriptures, and "their eyes were opened" to recognize him in the breaking of the bread.[61]

In the Passover meal, "remembering" was an intellectual recollection not merely of past events but also of a contemporary act of deliverance. Invoking the name of the Suzerain for rescue, the participants in the meal took up the Passover cup: "I will lift up the cup of salvation and call on the name of the LORD" (Ps. 116:13). The close bond between sign and signified in Passover is carried over into the New Testament celebration of the Lord's Supper.

If we allow ourselves to be distracted at the outset by metaphysical questions alien to these sorts of actions in their original context, we will miss crucial points. In Luke's account (22:14–23; cf. Matt. 26:26–30; Mark 14:22–25), Jesus emphasizes twice that he will not share this meal with his disciples "until the kingdom of God comes" in all of its fullness (vv. 16 and 18). Even in the physical presence

---

60. For the significance of meal-fellowship, see esp. David P. Mossner, *The Lord of the Banquet: The Literary and Theological Significance of the Lukan Travel Narrative* (Minneapolis: Fortress Press, 1989).

61. Douglas Farrow, *Ascension and Ecclesia: On the Significance of the Ascension for Ecclesiology and Christian Cosmology* (Edinburgh: T&T Clark, 1999), 7 n. 23, drawing on the insights of E. Earle Ellis.

of Jesus at this unique table, there is the expectation of absence, "till he come again." This will keep the celebration tethered not only to the past (the fulfillment of Passover) and the present (Christ's sacrifice), but also to the future, as Paul will include in his words of institution (1 Cor. 11:26).

In this connection between the expiatory death and the eschatological feast yet future, I have found Herman Ridderbos particularly insightful. While Markus Barth, for example, does not maintain (with Schweitzer) that Christ's expectation of the kingdom was an illusion, he nevertheless adopts a realized eschatology according to which the institution of the Supper should not concentrate on the cross.[62] In this Supper, Christ's kingship, not priesthood, should be central, according to Markus Barth, relegating the celebration of Christ's expiatory death to the background of the Supper.[63] Yet, according to Ridderbos, this upsets the already/not-yet tension highlighted by the text itself.[64] "The relation between the Eucharist and eating and drinking in the coming kingdom of God is *not merely that between symbol and reality, but that between commencement and fulfillment.* . . . In a word, it is the meal in which 'the powers of the world to come' have been released in Christ's coming, and in which the 'heavenly gift' and the Holy Spirit have been given and tasted' [Heb. 6:4–6]" (emphasis added).[65]

An overrealized eschatology misses the connection *and temporal gap* between the expiatory death (to which the Supper refers) and the fullness of the kingdom (which it anticipates in the marriage feast still future). Jesus' statement that he will no longer eat and drink with them until he returns constitutes "parting words," says Ridderbos, "a farewell pointing to the future."[66] "When he speaks of the 'fulfillment of the Passover' and of 'the new wine' in the kingdom of God, he has in view the great future to be inaugurated by the *parousia* of the Son of Man," not simply an immanently realized kingdom.[67]

Ridderbos's exegesis thus far fits well also with the interpretation I offered in chapter 1 of Jesus' discourse in John 14–16. This eschatological feast to which Jesus refers in the future, then, is something even greater than the postresurrection meals Jesus shared with his disciples, since it occurs in the wake of his ascension and Pentecost. In our contemporary celebration of the Supper, we are participating in a foretaste of that greater meal, but not in a fully realized sense.[68] (Hence, the significance of Paul's line in 1 Corinthians 11:26: "For as often as you eat this bread and drink the cup, you proclaim the Lord's death until he comes.") For now, the disciples must regularly eat the bread and drink the wine that Jesus allows to pass by him. "Only, they must do so realizing that what they

---

62. Cited by Herman Ridderbos, *The Coming of the Kingdom*, trans. H. de Jongste, ed. Raymond O. Zorn (Philadelphia: Presbyterian & Reformed Publishing Co., 1962), 405.
63. Ibid., 406.
64. See ibid., 406–11, for a text-critical argument in favor of the authenticity of Luke 22:19b and 20, which emphasize the expiatory death along with the Synoptic parallels and 1 Cor. 11.
65. Ibid., 412–13.
66. Ibid., 414.
67. Ibid., 415.
68. Ibid., 416.

in this way will henceforth eat and drink is *the body and the blood of the Lord.*"[69] So in this age, Christ is the food and drink; in the age to come, he will eat and drink together with us. For now, it is a sacrificial meal, although it will be fully realized as the eschatological feast with Christ when he returns.[70] The Supper is not the Passover meal, but is inaugurated after they have celebrated the old covenant feast. Yet it is not the marriage supper of the Lamb.[71] The Lord's Supper occurs between the old age and the new age, locating the church in this precarious intersection of the two ages. In this sense, notes Ridderbos, "that which is received in bread and cup is the sacrificial food and drink of the new covenant, the fruits of the New Testament sacrificial blood. . . . In one supreme concentration, as it were, in one turn of the hand, the Lord's Supper focuses the whole preaching of the gospel upon Christ's sacrifice and sets the table with it."[72] Therefore, we are invited to a table, and not an altar. "The Supper is not the sacrifice itself, but its application, its celebration." Like the paschal meal, the Supper is not a sacrifice, but it is a sacrificial meal: receiving the benefits of Christ's death.[73] Wherever "Christ's body and blood are eaten and drunk at the Communion table, the cross becomes an actual and living reality in the midst of the congregation" and a witness to the world.[74] Thus, it is not the action of the individual or the church, but God's action through these creaturely means, that traverses the temporal gap between the "then and there" of Golgotha and the "here and now" of our existence. It is Christ who gives his body and blood for our food and drink and we who receive. "The connection between bread and body, wine and blood, rests in Christ's words, in his command, in the fact that he is the dispenser and the host. So everything here depends on the reliability of his promise, on the efficacy and the authority of his words."[75]

Instead of the blood dashed on the people at Sinai, confirming their oath to do everything prescribed in the law, Jesus inaugurates the new covenant by saying, "This is my body, which is *given for you.* . . . This cup that is *poured out for you* is the new covenant in my blood" (Luke 22:19–20, emphasis added). Fulfilling the oath to Abraham that was confirmed by the vision of the smoking torch (Gen. 15), this action in the upper room is an unmistakably legal, covenantal event. In the case of the new covenant, we have a treaty between Yahweh and his people in which the Covenant Lord becomes the Servant and bears the sanctions on behalf of transgressors. As the writer to the Hebrews explains, even appealing to the role of sprinkling blood in old covenant worship, Christ's death is both a sacrifice for sin and an inauguration of a new covenant in the sense of "last will and testament." The death of the testator puts the will into effect (Heb. 9:17–22).

69. Ibid.
70. Ibid., 417.
71. Ibid., 431.
72. Ibid., 427.
73. Ibid., 428.
74. Ibid., 432.
75. Ibid., 438.

The writer then goes on to declare the superiority, finality, and unrepeatable character of Christ's sacrifice.

In this light, Paul develops his sacramental theology in 1 Corinthians 10 and 11. Baptized into Christ just as they were "baptized into Moses in the cloud and in the sea" (1 Cor. 10:1), the exodus generation only enters the true promised land together with us, foreshadowed when they "all ate the same spiritual food, and all drank the same spiritual drink. For they drank of that spiritual Rock that followed them, and that Rock was Christ" (vv. 4–5 NKJV).

It is not Greek metaphysics or Roman mystery cults but biblical covenantalism that provided Paul with his conceptual fund for this view of participation. Then when we come to his treatment of the Supper, Paul represents the sign and signified as distinct yet united (1 Cor. 10:16–17; 11:26–32). In this covenantal conception, the Supper can never be reduced to an individualistic encounter with Jesus. Paul's discussion of the Supper in 1 Corinthians is actually occasioned by the divisiveness of the community. Christ's existence as the head of his body makes us coheirs of his last will and testament. Therefore, the horizontal vector is immediately linked to the vertical: "Because there is one bread, we who are many are one body, for we all partake of the one bread" (1 Cor. 10:17). By contrast, those who share in idol feasts are "partners [participants] in the altar" of false gods (v. 18). This is part of an argument already begun in chapter 6 in relation to participation in the common civic practice of cultic prostitution (1 Cor 6:15–17).

To put it somewhat crudely, the church *is* what it *eats*. The point at issue is covenantal identification: with which Lord and under which constitution and therefore to which communion does one belong? The sacred meal in which one shares not only reflects but also constitutes the kind of society of which one is a member. The answer to widespread immorality, schism, and socioeconomic division is a proper recognition of our union with Christ, which is *simultaneously* a union with each other as his body (1 Cor. 11:28–29). In this sense, the Reformed tradition can concur with the position that the *eucharistic* body, appended to the Word, gives the *ecclesial* body because it truly communicates the energies of the *historical* body of Christ, its life-giving head.

Chapter Five

"This Is My Body"

Reformed Eucharistic Theology

In the previous chapter, I proposed a more biblical-theological outline of a covenantal view of sacraments as signs and seals. Looking back to the opening chapter, this chapter interprets Reformed teaching on the Supper in relation to the economy of grace (ascension, Pentecost, Parousia) in an effort to demonstrate the significance of this view for informing the tradition's wider ecclesiological commitments that I will take up in part 2 (below).

Owen F. Cummings suggests that humanity, for Calvin, is "eucharistic man."[1] And according to B. A. Gerrish, "the entire oeuvre of John Calvin may be described as a Eucharistic theology, shot through with the themes of grace and gratitude."[2] "The holy banquet is simply the liturgical enactment of the theme of grace and gratitude that lies at the heart of Calvin's entire theology, whether one chooses to call it a system or not. . . . It is this focal image of the banquet that made Calvin's doctrine (in his own estimate) simple, edifying, and irenic."[3] As

---

1. Owen F. Cummings, "The Reformers and Eucharistic Ecclesiology," *One in Christ* 33, no. 1 (1997): 47–54.
2. B. A. Gerrish, *Grace and Gratitude: The Eucharistic Theology of John Calvin* (Minneapolis: Augsburg Fortress Press, 1993), 52.
3. Ibid., 20, 13.

this "system" was refined with the categories of covenant theology, Calvin's emphasis was not lost, as we can observe in the divisions of the Heidelberg Catechism: guilt, grace, and gratitude.

WHAT IS RECEIVED?

In chapter 1, I noted Douglas Farrow's appeal to Calvin as a critical figure for bringing our attention back to the historical economy of Christ's descent, ascent, and return in the flesh. Reckoning more resolutely with the bodily ascension of Jesus Christ in the flesh than Rome or Luther, Calvin nevertheless affirmed, against Zwingli, a true feeding on the very body and blood of Christ in the sacrament. As strongly as Calvin rejected the Lutheran doctrine of ubiquity, he and his Reformed colleagues (other than those in Zurich) were convinced that they did not disagree with Wittenberg over the question of *what* was received in the Supper.[4]

For Zwingli (like Augustine), it did not seem to matter as much that Christ had bodily ascended since he is omnipresent in his divinity. Crucial in Zwingli's conception was a dualistic view of spirit and matter. "For faith springs not from things accessible to sense nor are they objects of faith," he insists.[5] If followed consistently (which, happily, he did not do), this would render not only preaching ineffectual as a means but the incarnate Christ inappropriate as an object of faith. Zwingli considered it ludicrous to suggest that in the sacrament one fed on the true body of Christ but in a spiritual manner (which became the confessional Reformed position).[6] Zwingli thus concludes, faith "draws us to the invisible and fixes all our hopes on that. For it dwelleth not amidst the sensible and bodily, and hath nothing in common therewith."[7] Yet this dualistic ontology underwrites a not-so-subtle Nestorianizing Christology, as in Zwingli's remark, "We must note in passing that Christ is our salvation by virtue of that part of his nature by which he came down from heaven, not of that by which he was born of an immaculate virgin, though he had to suffer and die by this part."[8] Luther and Zwingli realized

---

4. Ibid., 8. "Later, after Marburg," as Gerrish points out, "it was repeatedly argued that the point at issue between the Lutherans and the Reformed was no longer whether, but only how, the body and blood of Christ were present in the Sacrament. Calvin himself so argued." Since even Bullinger (Zwingli's successor) came to embrace the sacramental union of sign and signified, the focus was on *what* is received (Christ and all of his benefits) in the Supper, rather than on the *manner* of eating—in other words, presence as such.

5. Zwingli, *Commentary on True and False Religion*, ed. Samuel Macauley Jackson and Clarence Nevin Heller, trans. Samuel Macauley Jackson (Durham, NC: The Labyrinth Press, 1981), 214.

6. Ibid.

7. Ibid.

8. Ibid., 204. Besides Gerrish's work, a growing number of helpful studies have appeared, including Ronald S. Wallace, *Calvin's Doctrine of Word and Sacrament* (Grand Rapids: Baker, 1988); Jill Rait, *The Eucharistic Theology of Theodore Beza: Development of the Reformed Doctrine*, AAR Studies in Religion (Chambersburg, PA: American Academy of Religion, 1972); Keith Matheson, *Given for You: Reclaiming Calvin's Doctrine of the Lord's Supper* (Phillipsburg, NJ: Presbyterian & Reformed Publishing Co., 2002); and Leonard J. Vander Zee, *Christ, Baptism and the Lord's Supper: Recovering the*

that they were not only working with different conceptions of the Supper, but also of Christology and even cosmology.

Although Bucer and other Reformed leaders had already reached a certain agreement with Luther (esp. in the Wittenberg Concord), Calvin filled in the arguments for a Reformed consensus. Affirming with Luther the maxim *distinctio sed non separatio*, Calvin refused to separate the sign (bread and wine) from the signified (body and blood of Christ). Yet with Zwingli he held that the doctrine of ubiquity led to a "monstrous phantasm" rather than an actual human person. Calvin recognized that the question *Where* is Christ? was decisive for *who* Christ is in his postresurrection existence, but it was the latter that most concerned him. Consequently, he kept his focus on the economy of grace: descent, ascent, and Parousia *in the flesh*.[9] Insisting on the continuity of the glorified Christ with his natural existence as a human person while equally affirming a communication of the whole Christ in the sacrament, Calvin played a decisive role in shaping Reformed eucharistic teaching. He firmly rejected any rationalizing of the Eucharist, insisting that Christ is not received "only by understanding and imagination."[10] The Supper, according to Calvin, is the assurance of our own participation in what Luther described as the *mirifica commutatio* (marvelous exchange).[11]

Even Zwingli's successor, Heinrich Bullinger, distanced himself from the view of the sacraments as "bare and naked signs," both in the Second Helvetic Confession and in his consensus statement with Calvin.[12] Calvin could assert regarding their consensus, "Although we distinguish, as is proper, between the signs and the things signified, yet we do not sever the reality from the signs."[13] After affirming the sacramental union of sign and signified, the Second Helvetic Confession rejects "the doctrine of those who speak of the sacraments just as common signs, not sanctified and effectual. Nor do we approve of those who despise the visible aspect of the sacraments because of the invisible, and so believe the signs to be superfluous because they think they already enjoy the things themselves, as the Messalians are said to have held."[14] It is difficult to imagine that Bullinger did not know that he was rejecting a prominent line of his predecessor's argument.

"From the very first," notes Gerrish, Calvin "was convinced that Zwingli was wrong about the principal agent in both Baptism and the Lord's Supper. A sacra-

---

Sacraments for Evangelical Worship (Downers Grove, IL: InterVarsity Press, 2004). Where Reformed theology has attracted a growing following among evangelicals, the Reformed understanding of the church and sacraments has been often treated as nonessential to the system, or a Zwinglian interpretation is regarded as an adequate Reformed option.

9. Douglas Farrow, *Ascension and Ecclesia* (Edinburgh: T&T Clark, 1999), 204.

10. Calvin, *Institutes* 4.17.9.

11. Ibid., 4.17.2.

12. The Consensus Tigurinus can be found in *CO* 35:733, and in English translation in John Calvin, *Tracts and Treatises*, trans. Henry Beveridge (Grand Rapids: Eerdmans, 1958), 2:212–20. See Timothy George, "John Calvin and the Agreement of Zurich (1549)," in *John Calvin and the Church: A Prism of Reform*, ed. Timothy George (Louisville, KY: Westminster John Knox Press, 1990), 42–58.

13. Consensus Tigurinus, in *OS* 2:249.

14. The Second Helvetic Confession, in *BC*, 5.180–81.

ment is first and foremost an act of God or Christ rather than of the candidate, the communicant, or the church."[15] Where Zwingli can only force a choice between God's action and creaturely action, Calvin says, "Whatever implements God employs, they detract nothing from his primary operation."[16]

First of all, "*The Lord's Supper is a gift.* This is fundamental to the whole orientation of Calvin's thinking on the Sacrament" and signals a decisive departure from a Zwinglian conception, which Calvin found to be "scarcely less defective than the Roman Catholic." Especially in the *Institutes* 4.17.6, Calvin underscores this point that "the Supper is a gift; it does not merely remind us of a gift." As with receiving the gospel through the preached Word, in the sacrament we are receivers: it is "an *actio mere passiva* (a 'purely passive action')."[17] The human response to a gift is thanksgiving, says Calvin, which is why it is called the Eucharist, in opposition to the Mass, which instead is an atoning sacrifice that the people pay. "The sacrifice differs from the Sacrament of the Supper as widely as giving differs from receiving."[18] Second, "The gift is Jesus Christ himself," not only his divinity but the whole Christ.[19] Third, "*The gift is given with the signs.* Once again a criticism of both Zwingli and Rome is implied."[20] Fourth, "*The gift is given by the Holy Spirit,*" which Calvin goes on to detail in 4.14.9 and 12.[21] Fifth, "*The gift is given to all who communicate, pious and impious, believers and unbelievers.*"[22] One may refuse the gift, but this does not negate the sacrament any more than the preaching of the gospel is invalidated by unbelief. Calvin asks,

> Do the food and drink lose their nature because some reject them? . . . Nothing is taken away from the Sacrament: on the contrary, its truth and efficacy remain unimpaired even if the wicked [*impii*] go away empty from outward participation in it. . . . The integrity of the Sacrament, which the whole world cannot violate, lies in this: that the flesh and blood of Christ are no less truly given to the unworthy than to God's elect believers.[23]

At the same time, the reality is embraced only through faith. "The sacramental word is not an incantation, but a promise. The eucharistic gift therefore benefits those only who respond with the faith that the proclamation itself generates."[24]

When we receive the bread and the wine, says Calvin, "let us no less surely trust that the body itself is also given to us."[25] Rather than transform the sign

---

15. Gerrish, *Grace and Gratitude,* 204.
16. Calvin, *Institutes* 4.14.17.
17. Gerrish, *Grace and Gratitude,* 150, from Calvin, *Institutes* 4.14.26.
18. Calvin, *Institutes* 4.18.7.
19. Gerrish, *Grace and Gratitude,* 136, citing Calvin, *Petit tracté de la sancta Cene* (1541), in *OS* 1:508; cf. *Confessio fidei de eucharistia* (1537), in *OS* 1:435–36, Library of Christian Classics 22:168–69; Calvin, *Institutes* 4.17.7, 9.
20. Gerrish, *Grace and Gratitude,* 137.
21. Ibid.
22. Ibid., 138.
23. Calvin, *Institutes* 4.17.33.
24. Gerrish, *Grace and Gratitude,* 139; see Calvin, *Institutes* 4.14.4; 4.17.15.
25. Calvin, *Institutes* 4.17.10.

into the signified (Rome), confuse the sign and the signified (Luther), or separate the sign and the signified (Zwingli), Calvin affirmed that signs were "guarantees of a present reality: the believer's feeding on the body and blood of Christ."[26] In explicit contrast with Zwingli, Calvin held that the reality—Christ and his benefits—could be truly communicated to believers through earthly means. Otherwise, he says (appealing to Chrysostom), faith becomes a "mere imagining" of Christ's presence.[27]

Although Calvin's formative influence cannot be denied, it is important to recognize that he was articulating a view that was also taught by his Reformed peers (like Bucer, Vermigli, Musculus, and Knox) and their confessional successors. Therefore, with respect to *what* is received in the sacrament, the Reformed position rejected Zwingli's reply and gave the same answer as Wittenberg and Rome: in the words of the Belgic Confession, nothing less than "the proper and natural body and the proper blood of Christ." Reflecting Calvin's contention that there is no communication of Christ's benefits apart from his person, the Confession adds that "Christ communicates *himself* to us *with all his benefits*. At that table he makes us enjoy *himself as much as the merits of his suffering and death*, as he nourishes, strengthens, and comforts our poor, desolate souls by the eating of his flesh, and relieves and renews them by the drinking of his blood."[28]

HOW IS IT RECEIVED?

If, unlike Zwingli, we affirm that the substance of the sacrament is Christ's true and natural body, Calvin wondered, "what could be more ridiculous than to split the churches and stir up frightful commotions" over how this happens?[29] The only pious conclusion, he says, is "to break forth in wonder at this mystery, which plainly neither the mind is able to conceive nor the tongue to express."[30] Typical of Reformed confessions, the Westminster Larger Catechism points out that the mode, not the substance, was spiritual.[31] Furthermore, it is crucial to bear in mind that "spiritual" here refers to a person—the Holy Spirit—and not to a merely intellectual or imaginary mode of feeding. Christ is not spiritually present as opposed to being bodily present in the sacrament, but gives himself as our food and drink by the agency of the Spirit.

26. Gerrish, *Grace and Gratitude*, 165.
27. Calvin, *Institutes* 4.17.5–6.
28. The [Belgic] Confession of Faith, art. 35, *Psalter Hymnal, Doctrinal Standards, and Liturgy of the Christian Reformed Church* (Grand Rapids: CRC Publications, 1976), 87–88.
29. John Calvin, *Defensio doctrinae de sacramentis*, in *OS* 2:287.
30. Ibid.
31. See, for example, the Westminster Larger Catechism, Q. 170, in *BC* 7.280. The Westminster Larger Catechism underscores this point by confessing that believers truly "feed upon the body and blood of Christ" (the substance of the sacrament), "not after a corporeal but in a spiritual manner; yet truly and really, while by faith they receive and apply to themselves Christ crucified and all the benefits of his death."

Beyond this, Reformed theology has been wary of investing too much in arguments over the mechanics, since the Supper is a medium of divine action rather than manifestation per se. The invisible working of the Spirit is mysterious and inaccessible to our senses. Yet when the Father truly gives, the Son is truly given, and the Spirit is truly giving, who are we to dispute his generosity? Calvin writes, "Inquisitive persons have wanted to define how the body of Christ is present in the bread." After summarizing the rival theories, he urges, "But the primary question to be put was how the body of Christ, as it was given for us, became ours; and how the blood, as it was shed for us, became ours. What matters is how we possess the whole Christ crucified, to become partakers of all his blessings."[32] The point is to assure trembling consciences that it is "not a bare figure, but is joined with the reality and substance."[33] Because of the agency of the Spirit, who unites us to Christ in the first place, there can be a real communication of Christ's person and work to the church (*pace* Zwingli), yet without bringing Christ down to an earthly altar (*pace* Rome and Luther). It is not simply Christ's divinity but also the Spirit who makes Christ's reign universally present, so that even Christ's true and natural body and blood can be communicated to believers.

"When this perichoretically trinitarian framework is recognized," Philip Butin observes, "Christ's ascension is no longer a 'problem' for Calvin."

> To the contrary, it contributes a distinctively positive and "upward" emphasis to his entire theology of the eucharist. Calvin's approach at this point thus complements and completes the "downward" Lutheran emphasis on incarnation with an equal "upward" emphasis on resurrection and ascension. There is "a manner of descent by which he lifts us up to himself." Not only does Christ (in the Spirit) condescend to manifest himself to believers by means of visible, tangible, created elements; at the same time by the Spirit, the worshiping church is drawn into the heavenly worship of the Father through the mediation of the ascended Christ, who is seated with the Father in the heavenlies. For Calvin, this accentuates, rather than diminishes, the true humanity of Christ.

Hence comes the emphasis in the eucharistic liturgy on the *sursum corda* and *epiclēsis*.[34]

By the effective working of the Spirit, says Calvin, "the flesh of Christ is like a rich and inexhaustible fountain that pours into us the life springing forth from the Godhead into itself."[35] We are not only related to Christ generically as fellow humans, but also eschatologically, pneumatologically, mystically, and soteriologically: "For we are not bone of his bone and flesh of his flesh because he is a man like ourselves. Rather, it is because by the power of his Spirit he engrafts us into

32. John Calvin, 1536 *Institutes*, in *OS* 1:139.
33. Ibid., 508–9.
34. Philip Walker Butin, *Revelation, Redemption, and Response: Calvin's Trinitarian Understanding of the Divine-Human Relationship* (New York: Oxford University Press, 1995), 118.
35. Calvin, *Institutes* 4.17.8.

his body, so that from him we derive life."[36] Thus, "The Spirit makes things which are widely separated by space to be united with each other, and accordingly causes life from the flesh of Christ to reach us from heaven."[37]

So the question for Calvin is not how to relate spirit and matter, but how Christ, being glorified in heaven, can be related to us in our present condition. As the work of the Spirit, the precise mode of this feeding remains mysterious—something to be marveled at and enjoyed rather than explained. Similarly the Belgic Confession declares that while the mode "cannot be comprehended by us, as the operations of the Holy Spirit are hidden and incomprehensible, . . . we nevertheless do not err when we say that what is eaten and drunk by us is the proper and natural body and the proper blood of Christ."[38]

The Spirit, in this view, is not a substitute for Christ, but is the agent who unites us to Christ and therefore communicates Christ and his benefits to believers. In more recent times, the Princeton theologian A. A. Hodge raised this issue of sacramental presence, with an implicit criticism of those within the tradition who understand "spiritual presence" in a Zwinglian manner:

> If he is not present really and truly, then the sacrament can have no interest or real value to us. It does not do to say that this presence is only spiritual, because that phrase is ambiguous. If it means that the presence of Christ is not something objective to us, but simply a mental apprehension or idea of him subjectively present to our consciousness, then the phrase is false. Christ as an objective fact is as really present and active in the sacrament as are the bread and wine, or the minister or our fellow-communicants by our side. If it means that Christ is present only as he is represented by the Holy Ghost, it is not wholly true, because Christ is one Person and the Holy Ghost another, and it is Christ who is personally present. . . . It does not do to say that the divinity of Christ is present while his humanity is absent, because it is the entire indivisible divine-human Person of Christ which is present.[39]

Christ promised his enduring presence to his church. "But what do we mean by 'presence'?" asks Hodge. "It is a great mistake to confuse the idea of 'presence' with that of nearness in space. . . . 'Presence,' therefore, is not a question of space; it is a relation" (emphasis added).[40] With respect to the Supper, Hodge's point is exactly right, although we should be careful not to lose sight once again of the spatial absence (and therefore reality) of Christ's natural body until he returns.

36. John Calvin, *Commentary on Paul's Epistle to the Ephesians* (Grand Rapids: Baker, 1979), commenting on Eph. 5:30–31.

37. John Calvin, "The Best Method of Obtaining Concord," in *Selected Works of John Calvin: Tracts and Letters*, vol. 2, trans. Henry Beveridge, ed. Henry Beveridge and Jules Bonnet (repr., Grand Rapids: Baker, 1983), 578.

38. The [Belgic] Confession of Faith, *Psalter Hymnal, Doctrinal Standards, and Liturgy*, 87–88.

39. A. A. Hodge, *Evangelical Theology: Lectures on Doctrine* (Edinburgh: Banner of Truth, 1976), 355.

40. Ibid., 356.

WHERE IS IT RECEIVED?

While Calvin can be faulted for focusing too much on the Spirit's mediation of Christ's *spatial* absence, one also discerns more eschatological coordinates that offer some qualification. Calvin's talk of the spatial distance at least faced the issue of the ascension directly, allowing more recognition of the coming-and-going pattern of the economy that Jesus highlighted in the discourse reported in John 14–16. Even Robert Jenson remarks, "But if there is no place for Jesus' risen body, how is it a body at all? For John Calvin was surely right: '. . . This is the eternal truth of any body, that it is contained in its place.'"[41]

Following this emphasis that we find in Calvin and his colleagues, Reformed orthodoxy reiterated the patristic view that the sacrament consists of earthly signs and heavenly realities, without separation or confusion. The rival positions forced one either to locate Christ's true presence in (or as) the elements or deny such presence altogether. Yet in the Reformed view, a sacrament encompasses the earthly signs *and* the heavenly reality. "It is one thing to say that Christ is present in the bread, another to assert the presence in the Holy Supper," says Wollebius.[42] Believers receive the whole Christ in the Supper, even through the reception of the bread and wine. Nevertheless, Christ need not be bodily enclosed in the *elements* in order to be bodily present in the *sacrament*. His bodily presence in the elements would actually disrupt the realism of his coming-going-returning. Zwingli's argument seemed to stop at the ascension, whereas Calvin's equally emphatic affirmation of a true feeding on Christ drew his attention to the activity of the Spirit in this time between the two advents.

Calvin found ample evidence for this eschatological, heavenly feeding not only in Scripture but also in the church fathers. His positive statement of his view of this true feeding (*Institutes* 4.17.8–39) is basically a gloss on a host of passages drawn from Scripture and the church fathers. Integrating comments from Cyril, Chrysostom, and Augustine, Calvin concludes that although Christ has been bodily raised to the right hand of God, "This Kingdom is neither bounded by location in space nor circumscribed by any limits. Thus Christ is not prevented from exerting his power wherever he pleases, in heaven and on earth." But right where one might have expected him to correlate this unbounded extension of Christ's reign with his omnipresent *deity* (as in Augustine and Zwingli), Calvin says, "In short, he feeds his people with his own body, the communion of which he bestows upon them *by the power of his Spirit*" (emphasis added).[43] We need not transform Christ's natural substance into a divine substance in order to affirm that his personal agency is omnipresent.

---

41. Robert W. Jenson, *Systematic Theology* (New York: Oxford University Press, 1997), 1:202, citing Calvin's 1536 *Institutes* 4.122. See Jenson's excellent treatment on 1:202–5.

42. Cited in Heinrich Heppe, *Reformed Dogmatics*, rev. and ed. Ernst Bizer, trans. G. T. Thomson (London: Allen & Unwin, 1950), 642.

43. Calvin, *Institutes* 4.17.18.

Calvin complains that his critics seem to think that "Christ does not seem present unless he comes down to us." But how is Christ less present "if he should lift us to himself"? Why must he be present in the bread and the wine in order to be present in the sacrament? Is this not the point of the Holy Spirit's work of uniting us to Christ in heaven?[44] "Shall we therefore, someone will say, assign to Christ a definite region of heaven?" Again Calvin eschews speculation: "But I reply with Augustine that this is a very prying and superfluous question; for us it is enough to believe that he is in heaven."[45]

I have hinted at how Calvin's spatial emphasis (heaven and earth) might be chastened by a more eschatological interpretation. The paradox of the already and not-yet is not something that we impose on the eucharistic texts: it is already present in the very institution of the Supper itself: "As often as you do this, you proclaim the death of Christ until he comes again." As Calvin and the Reformed tradition emphasized, the prospective aspect, "until he comes again," is meaningless if Christ actually returns bodily to earth in order to be present at every altar or table. Calvin thus interprets the copula (*is*) in the words of institution ("This *is* my body") in the light of Paul's elaboration: the bread that we break and the cup that we drink *is* a *participation in* the body and blood of Christ (1 Cor. 10:16).[46]

Many of the elements of an eschatological understanding of the Supper are present in Calvin's formulations, yet when they are more explicitly drawn together, and heaven and earth are recognized as eschatological more than spatial coordinates, the heavenly feeding can be no less real though mysterious than our being seated with Christ in heavenly places by virtue of our union with him (Col. 3:1–4). When "heavenly" and "earthly" are understood in more eschatological than spatial terms, the location of this meal no longer becomes a matter of speculation about transportation: either Christ's or our own.

This eschatological tension is *accentuated* rather than *resolved* by the Supper, which is why the memory of his redeeming work (anamnesis) and its effects in the present (epiclesis) necessarily engenders a longing for his appearing in the future (*epektasis*). The eucharistic event occurs here—and places us here—in this nexus where the powers of the age to come penetrate this present age. A qualitatively different presence will occur in the Parousia: "When Christ who is our life appears, then you also will appear with Him in glory" (Col. 3:4 NKJV). Nevertheless, even now, he "is our life."

When we think in more eschatological terms, time becomes a more critical category than space. While the Supper is still celebrated on this side of the eschaton itself, and therefore cannot be identical to the marriage feast that awaits us, we "have tasted the heavenly gift, and have become partakers of the Holy Spirit, and have tasted the good word of God and the powers of the age to come" (Heb. 6:4–5 NKJV).

44. Ibid., 4.17.31.
45. Ibid., 4.17.26.
46. Ibid., 4.17.22.

Instead of thinking in terms of our being literally transported (spatially) to a heavenly table prior to the Parousia, then, it is more appropriate to think of the Supper as a fissure in this present age that has been opened up by the Spirit for our semirealized participation in the consummation. So it is true that the Eucharist gives the church, as John Zizioulas, Jean-Luc Marion, and so many others have pointed out. However, at least from a Reformed point of view, this means that the church given is not a fully realized but a semirealized community generated in the collision of the two ages. At the same time, we must not eliminate the importance of spatial distance altogether, since this would once again open the door to a docetic interpretation of the ascension and therefore of the consummation.

Attention to eschatology was undermined by debates over the metaphysics of presence as such. Despite the spatial map he sometimes assumes (often for good reasons, I have argued), Calvin faced the eschatological issues more directly. The Reformed tradition has been concerned that the tendency of Luther and Rome is toward an overrealized eschatology that makes Christ bodily present prior to the Parousia at the cost of turning him into someone other than the same person who ascended. Yet Zwingli tended toward an underrealized eschatology, where Christ's bodily absence admitted no communication or mediation of his whole person until the eschaton.

Nor did the mediation of the Spirit seem so acutely necessary for the alternative Western views (Lutheran, Roman Catholic, Zwinglian). According to Calvin, the Spirit communicates the energies of Christ's life-giving flesh. "If the sun sheds its beams upon the earth and casts its substance in some measure upon it in order to beget, nourish, and give growth to its offspring—why should the radiance of Christ's Spirit be less in order to impart to us the communion of his flesh and blood?"[47]

Here, I suggest, we detect the East's essence-energies distinction, including the usual analogy of the sun and rays. Such statements have sometimes been regarded (esp. in American Presbyterian circles) as an odd inconsistency in Calvin's sacramental teaching. Yet I am convinced that it has to do in part with the fact that Western theology, lacking this distinction, recognizes only two categories: uncreated being and created works. I treated this connection at some length in *Covenant and Salvation* (chap. 12), but for our purposes here it will be sufficient to say that while Western theology only recognizes the categories of Creator (essence) and creature (effect), the East speaks of the working of God's grace (energies) that cannot be identified with either. Athanasius affirmed, "[God] is outside all things according to his essence, but he is in all things through his acts of power."[48] Like many of the ancient Eastern writers, Calvin speaks of Christ's "energies" being communicated to us by the Spirit in the sacrament.

47. Ibid., 4.17.12.
48. Athanasius, *On the Incarnation* 17, trans. R. W. Thomson, in *Athanasius: Contra Gentes and De Incarnatione* (Oxford: Clarendon, 1971), 174.

Recognizing that such references are too explicit to be dismissed as a slip of the pen, Charles Hodge, for example, chalks it up to Calvin's zeal for reconciling Lutheran and Reformed churches, although Lutheranism did not make this patristic motif part of its argument.[49] Recently, Bruce McCormack has argued that there is a tension in Calvin's teaching on imputation on the one hand "and the more nearly patristic understanding of those themes which are suggested by a good bit of rhetoric that Calvin employs in speaking of the eucharist."[50] The latter seems at odds with rejection of communication of attributes, but Calvin does not recognize the ontological perils of Cyril's rhetoric, McCormack surmises.[51]

> Had he done so, he might have realized that he could not reasonably affirm Cyril's rhetoric of the life-giving character of Christ's "body" without accepting Cyril's soteriology of divinization, as well as the (largely) Platonic ontology of "participation" which made that soteriology possible in the first place. He might also have seen that he was creating serious problems for his doctrine of justification.[52]

If union with Christ were, like justification, exclusively forensic, then surely McCormack is correct. However, Calvin and the tradition generally held that forensic justification was the legal ground for a union that is organic, vital, mystical, and real. Although T. F. Torrance is wrong to suggest that we read Calvin's "Cyrillian" eucharistic thinking into his doctrine of justification, it is also unnecessary to conclude that such thinking contradicts it. Justification and mystical union are distinct aspects of salvation for Calvin. A forensic justification brings everything else in its wake, but is not the only gift.[53]

If we have trouble with this aspect of Calvin's eucharistic teaching, then we will have difficulty with his entire doctrine of union.[54] Furthermore, if we interpret the "energies" as "the powers of the age to come" (Heb 6:5), which Christ

---

49. Charles Hodge, "Doctrine of the Reformed Church on the Lord's Supper," selected from *The Princeton Review*, in Charles Hodge, *Essays and Reviews* (New York: Robert Carter & Brothers, 1957). With John Williamson Nevin in his sights, Hodge characterizes even Calvin's understanding of Christ's whole vivifying person being communicated in the Supper (which he acknowledges to be taught in some of the Reformed confessions) as "an uncongenial foreign element" drawn from patristic sources, a too-literal reading of John 6, and a desire to placate the Lutherans (363–66). Even sharper views were expressed by James Henley Thornwell, R. L. Dabney, and William G. T. Shedd, the last of whom attempted to assimilate Calvin's view to his own Zwinglian conception (*Dogmatic Theology*, 3rd ed., ed. Alan W. Gomes [Phillipsburg, NJ: Presbyterian & Reformed Publishing Co., 2003], 814–15). Otto Ritschl expresses the same frustration with Calvin's Cyrillian interpretation of the sacrament in *Die reformierte Theologie* (Göttingen: Vandenhoeck & Ruprecht, 1926).

50. Bruce McCormack, "What's at Stake in Current Debates over Justification?" in *Justification: What's at Stake in the Current Debates?* ed. Mark Husbands and Daniel J. Treier (Downers Grove, IL: InterVarsity Press, 2004), 104–5; cf. Calvin, *Institutes* 4.17.9.

51. McCormack, "What's at Stake?" 104–5.

52. Ibid.

53. On this point, including a defense of a certain kind of "divinization" that avoids any ontological fusion, see my *Covenant and Salvation: Union with Christ* (Louisville, KY: Westminster John Knox Press, 2007), esp. chap. 12.

54. Calvin explicitly connects his view of union with Christ to the Supper. For example, in a letter to Peter Martyr Vermigli (August 8, 1555), Calvin writes,

fully possesses as the firstfruits of the whole harvest, then the same pneumatological mediation that is the hallmark of a Reformed doctrine of mystical union
is at work in its sacramental theology. Recent scholarship has confirmed that
Calvin's formulations at this point reflect his reading of patristic sources, especially Ireneaus and Chrysostom, but also Cyril of Alexandria.[55] Yet Calvin was
hardly alone: his theological contemporaries and heirs reflect similar views,
including the essence (sun) and energies (rays) analogy.[56]

Interpreted eschatologically, this does not mean a fusion of substances, as if
our personal identity is assimilated to Jesus' or vice versa. Nevertheless, it does
mean that the efficacy (energy) of the sun is communicated to us, so that even
now Christ's exalted flesh as well as divine power reach us and renew us with their
vigor. The branches share in the life, not simply the effects, of the vine; the relation of Christ to his body is that of the firstfruits to the harvest.

THE EFFICACY OF THE SACRAMENT

Calvin could affirm the efficacy of the Supper in no less realistic terms than his
critics. First, with respect to his person, Calvin's Christology was free of Zwingli's

---

What I say is that the moment we receive Christ by faith as he offers himself in the
gospel, we become truly members of his body, and life flows into us from him as from
the head. . . . That is how I interpret the passage in which Paul says that believers are
called into the *koinōnia* of Christ (1 Cor. 1:9). The words "company" or "fellowship"
do not seem adequate to convey his thought: it suggests to me the sacred unity by
which the Son of God engrafts us into his body, so as to communicate to us all that
is his. Thus we draw life from his flesh and blood, so that they are not undeservedly
called our "food." How it happens, I confess, is far above the measure of my intelli-
gence. Hence I adore the mystery rather than labor to understand it. (*CO* 15:722–23)

55. See Irena Backus, "Calvin and the Greek Fathers," in *Continuity and Change: The Harvest of
Later Medieval and Reformation History*, ed. Robert J. Bast and Andrew C. Gow (Leiden: Brill, 2000),
253–76; cf. Johannes Van Oort, "John Calvin and the Church Fathers," in *The Reception of the Church
Fathers in the West: From the Carolingians to the Maurists*, ed. Irena Backus (Leiden: Brill, 1997). See
also Anthony N.S. Lane, *John Calvin: Student of the Church Fathers* (Grand Rapids: Baker Books,
1999), 41–42. Especially in Oort, Calvin is cited as estimating that Cyril is next to Chrysostom in
depth of insight ("Calvin and the Church Fathers," 693).

56. Heppe, *Reformed Dogmatics*, 641, offers a number of citations that are pertinent. Like many
early Reformed theologians, Wollebius explicitly appeals to the category of energies in discussing the
Supper, including the usual analogy of the sun and its rays, so that "what is remote spatially is present in efficacy." He adds, "The presence is opposed not to distance but to absence." The eating and
drinking of Christ's body and blood in John 6:51 cannot be reduced to believing or "simple cognition," adds Bucannus; rather, it teaches that "by true participation in himself we should be quick-
ened." His whole life becomes the food that quenches our starvation, according to Olevianus. "Is our
soul merely without the body, united to Christ's soul only, or our flesh also with Christ's flesh?" asks
Bucannus. "Indeed the whole person of each believer, in soul and body, is truly joined to the whole
person of Christ." As he assumed our mortal flesh, so we participate in his immortal flesh. How else,
he asks, could we be assured of our own glorification and resurrection? Martin Bucer, Peter Martyr
Vermigli, Wolfgang Musculus, and other prominent Reformed leaders (seniors and contemporaries
of Calvin) occupied essentially the same eucharistic terrain. The fact that Reformed and Presbyterian confessions (as Charles Hodge concedes) reflect these views further challenges the notion that
Calvin introduced an "uncongenial foreign element" into the tradition's eucharistic teaching.

nearly Nestorian emphasis on the distinction between the two natures. Where Zwingli seems to assume that Christ's deity does all the work of redemption, Calvin writes,

> The situation would surely have been hopeless had the very majesty of God not descended to us, since it was not in our power to ascend to him. Hence, it was necessary for the Son of God to become for us "Immanuel, that is, God with us," and in such a way that his divinity and human nature might by mutual conjunction coalesce with each other [*ut mutual coniunctione eius divinitatas et hominum natura inter se coalescerent*]. Otherwise, the nearness would not have been enough, nor the affinity sufficiently firm, for us to hope that God might dwell with us [*Deum nobiscum habitare*].[57]

If the whole Christ—as human no less than as divine—secured our redemption, then our communion must be with the whole Christ. Second, if we cannot receive the benefits of Christ apart from his person, then the Supper must communicate Christ's person as well as his work.

In the light of this retrieval of Eastern patristic emphases, especially the role of the Spirit and the implicit essence-energies distinction, this eucharistic doctrine shares affinities with the view expressed in our own day by Orthodox theologian Alexander Schmemann: "Like the entire eucharist, the remembrance is not a repetition. It is the manifestation, gift and experience, in 'this world' and therefore again and again, of the eucharist offered by Christ once and for all, and of our ascension to it." The Supper does not complete or extend Christ's redemptive work, adds Schmemann. "No—in Christ all is already accomplished, all is real, all is granted. In him we have obtained access to the Father and communion in the Holy Spirit and anticipation of the new life in his kingdom."

> The purpose of the eucharist lies not in the change of the bread and wine, but in our partaking of Christ, who has become our food, our life, the manifestation of the Church as the body of Christ. This is why the holy gifts themselves never became in the Orthodox East an object of special reverence, contemplation and adoration, and likewise an object of special theological "problematics": how, when, in what manner their change is accomplished. . . . Nothing is explained, nothing is defined, nothing has changed in "this world." But then whence comes this light, this joy that overflows the heart, this feeling of fullness and of touching the "other world"? We find the answer to these questions in the epiclesis. But the answer is not "rational," built upon the laws of our "one-storied" logic; it is disclosed to us by the Holy Spirit.[58]

Like the Eastern view, Calvin's eucharistic theology is natural thread in the larger tapestry of his theology of union with Christ by the Spirit.

Without the essence-energies distinction, the frequent analogy of sun-and-rays could easily collapse into pantheism, which was a constant threat for West-

57. Calvin, *Institutes* 2.12.1.
58. Alexander Schmemann, *The Eucharist: Sacraments of the Kingdom* (New York: St. Vladimir's Seminary Press, 1988), 224–27.

ern mysticism. The only alternative is to reduce God's active working to its crea-turely effect. In my view, this problem lurks beneath the Western debates: either there is a fusion of essences (as in transubstantiation) or merely creaturely signs (the Zwinglian tendency).[59] I am suggesting that the tertium quid that we need (and that Calvin implicitly seems to follow) is the East's category of energies, but translated in the covenantal idiom as the *workings* of God: specifically, the redemptive speech-act of the Father in the Son by the Spirit. The essence of Christ's unique historical existence as the incarnate Word cannot be communi-cated to creatures (even his humanity, since it is determined by the union). Nev-ertheless, the *workings* of Christ—indistinguishable from his whole person—are what render him the head of a body, the vine with its branches, the firstfruits of the whole harvest. It is through the working of God through Word and sacra-ment, received in faith, that the Spirit clothes us with Christ inwardly in this age and outwardly adorns us with righteousness, beauty, glory, and immortality in the age to come. Once more we recognize the point underscored in the previous chapter: the emphasis on the sacraments as mediating God's presence-in-action rather than naked manifestation.

Thus, when Calvin speaks of Christ's flesh as an exhaustible life-giving foun-tain communicated in the Supper (4.17.9), he is not suggesting any more than Cyril that the essence of Christ—either divinity or humanity—was poured into creatures. After all, he added a section to the 1559 *Institutes* in refutation of Osiander's formulation of that view. Rather, Christ's energies are communicated. Therefore, Calvin has a strong doctrine of analogical participation, but it is understood in terms of a communion of persons (*koinōnia*) rather than a fusion of essences (*methexis*). Given the preceding arguments, the emphasis in Reformed eucharistic theology falls not on what the church or the sacraments accomplish, but on what God accomplishes as Father, Son, and Spirit, through covenant-making words and actions.

One's view of the efficacy of Communion largely determines one's views con-cerning frequency. It is not surprising that a more Zwinglian approach, which emphasizes the subjectivity of the believer and the community, will yield a more introspective eucharistic practice. To the extent that the Supper is considered a divine gift, its frequent celebration is likely to be affirmed. Zwingli insisted that genuine faith did not require earthly props, while Calvin, like Luther, not only stated but emphasized the contrary view. Zwingli directed faith to ascend beyond everything earthly, while Calvin—again, like Luther—emphasized God's conde-scension to the weakness of our condition. Hence, against the traditional medieval practice of infrequent Communion (alas, too typical today of Reformed churches), Calvin offered a sustained plea that the Supper should be celebrated whenever the Word is preached "or at least once a week."[60] "The Eucharist is the communion of the body and blood of the Lord," so infrequent Communion is

---

59. I develop this argument in *Covenant and Salvation*, 211–15, 268–69.
60. Calvin, *Institutes* 4.17.44–46.

in effect, says Calvin, a withholding of Christ and his benefits from the covenant assembly.[61] Only a year after the city of Geneva officially embraced the Reformation, Calvin's *Articles for Organization of the Church and Worship at Geneva* (1537) thus stated, "It is certain that a Church cannot be said to be well ordered and regulated unless in it the Holy Supper of our Lord is always being celebrated and frequented."[62]

Considering that the people communicated only once a year (and even then receiving only the bread) and could not hear, much less understand, much of the ceremony, it is not an exaggeration to suggest that the Reformation actually restored the Supper to a place of practical prominence in the life of the church. Appealing to the practice of the ancient church in refutation of medieval infrequency, Calvin said, "All, like hungry men, should flock to such a bounteous repast," again drawing on Chrysostom's support.[63] "Calvin articulated a new conceptualization of 'liturgy' itself," according to Lee Palmer Wandel. "For him, certainly, the Supper was a drama, but the source of that drama was God. No human movement could add to that meaning in any way, no crafted object could draw greater attention to those earthly elements." She adds,

> Perhaps most important of all, however, was Calvin's insistence on frequency. Most evangelicals condemned the medieval requirement of annual communion as nonscriptural. . . . But no other evangelical so explicitly situated the Eucharist within a dialogic process not simply of deepening faith, but [also] of the increasing capacity to read the signs of the Supper itself, and by extension, of God, in the world.[64]

In both Roman Catholic and Zwinglian conceptions, the Eucharist was chiefly a human work, either of offering Christ again for sacrifice, or of remembering and pledging. However, says Wandel, "The Supper, for Calvin, was not 'external'—a ceremony, . . . nor even 'worship' in the sense that other evangelicals, such as Zwingli and Luther, used: a mode of honoring God." Rather, it is a means of binding us together more and more with Christ in an ongoing relationship in which "Christ 'is made completely one with us and we with him.'"[65]

The close connection between the nature and efficacy of the Supper and its frequency was recognized by Bucer, Vermigli, Knox, and others among the Reformed who pointed out, as in the Tetrapolitan Confession, "the Most Holy Supper of Christ" is "administered and received among us very religiously and with singular reverence," not to mention "more frequently and devoutly than

61. Mary Beaty and Benjamin W. Farley, eds., *Calvin's Ecclesiastical Advice* (Louisville, KY: Westminster John Knox Press, 1991), 165.

62. John Calvin, "Articles concerning the Organization of the Church and of Worship at Geneva Proposed by the Ministers at the Council, January 16, 1537," in *Calvin: Theological Treatises*, Library of Christian Classics, ed. and trans. J. K. L. Reid (Philadelphia: Westminster Press, 1954), 48.

63. Calvin, *Institutes* 4.17.46.

64. Lee Palmer Wandel, *The Eucharist in the Reformation: Incarnation and Liturgy* (Cambridge: Cambridge University Press, 2006), 171.

65. Ibid.

heretofore."[66] Archbishop Cranmer moved from a Zwinglian conception to a Calvinian understanding, which obtained doctrinal status in the Thirty-Nine Articles.[67] Nor can Puritanism be understood as Zwinglian, since the Calvinian view is clearly expressed in the Westminster Standards and was shared by Conformists and Nonconformists alike. The Westminster Directory for Public Worship called for frequent celebration of the Supper. Conformists and Non-conformists "shared a common theology of the Lord's Supper," Hywell Roberts observes. "Both parties accepted Calvin's interpretation."[68]

Calvin's logic was covenantal: If we regularly receive the covenantal promise in the Word, it should be ratified in the sacrament.[69] In the Supper, we are not testifying to the strength of our faith or maturity, but are receiving the Gift that strengthens the weak. The sixteenth-century Reformed theologian Johannes Wollebius put it this way: "The true purpose of the holy supper, above all others, is to confirm spiritual nourishment or preservation to eternal life by the merit of the death and obedience of Christ. On this the union of the faithful with Christ and with one another depends. *Consequently*, the holy supper ought to be observed often" (emphasis added).[70] The same position can be found in the Reformed confessions, as in the Westminster Larger Catechism, where believers who lack assurance are especially urged to come to the Supper, "because promises are made, and this sacrament is appointed for the relief even of weak and doubting Christians."[71]

When the Supper is no longer for the weak, but also for the strong, and so much attention is given to introspective preparation in order to partake worthily, the meal becomes a sacrifice that we offer just as surely in Protestant as in Roman Catholic celebrations. Calvin rather sharply scolded those who, when they "would prepare people to eat worthily, have tortured and harassed pitiable consciences in dire ways," as if being in "'in a state of grace'" meant "to be pure and purged from all sin." "Such dogma would debar all the people who are or who ever were on the earth from the use of this Sacrament. For if it is a question of our seeking our worthiness by ourselves, we are undone; only ruin and confusion remain to us."[72]

In addition to the legacy of pietism and revivalism, American Protestantism has been especially on guard against "sacerdotalism," while the threat of a gnosticizing

66. The Tetrapolitan Confession, chap. 18, excerpted by Heppe, *Reformed Dogmatics*, 641–42.

67. The Thirty-Nine Articles of Religion, art. 25–31 in Philip Schaff, *The Creeds of Christendom*, vol. 3, *The Evangelical Protestant Creeds.*, ed. Philip Schaff, revised by David S. Schaff (Harper & Row, 1931; repr., Grand Rapids: Baker, 1990), 502–7.

68. Hywell Roberts, "Union and Communion," in *The Westminster Conference Papers* (London: 1979), 55.

69. Calvin, *Institutes* 4.17.44, 46.

70. Johannes Wollebius, "Compendium Theologiae Christianae," in *Reformed Dogmatics: Seventeenth-Century Reformed Theology through the Writings of Wollebius, Voetius, and Turretin*, ed. and trans. John W. Beardslee III (1965; repr., Grand Rapids: Baker Book House, 1977), 15, 17.

71. Westminster Larger Catechism, Q. 172, in *The Confession of Faith and Larger and Shorter Catechisms* (Glasgow: Free Presbyterian Publications, 1973), 262.

72. Calvin, *Institutes* (1536), trans. Ford Lewis Battles (Atlanta: John Knox Press, 1975), 151.

individualism and inwardness is at least as evident.[73] In all sorts of ways, as Gerrish reminds us,

> Calvin's eucharistic piety has repeatedly been lost, or at least curtailed, in the churches that officially claim him as their Reformer but in fact have moved closer in their sacramental theology to the Zwinglian view, which Calvin rejected as "profane." It has even become commonplace to make a sharp distinction between "evangelical" and "sacramental" piety. The distinction, as such, could hardly find support in Calvin, for whom the Supper attested a communion with Christ's body and blood that is given precisely by the gospel.[74]

Although Reformed theology emphasizes the priority of God's action in the Supper, it also recognizes a broader efficacy, which underscores the importance of its frequent celebration. The forensic yields the effective; the vertical, disrupting, objective work of God *extra nos* issues in a new system of horizontal, ordered, and subjective relationships between human beings. It is a banquet, not a drive-through meal. Here we are coheirs at the family table, not consumers of exotic or "meaningful" religious experiences. As the Lord truly communicates his body to us, writes Calvin, he makes us also "one body by such participation."[75] Like the word, the sacraments draw us out of our private rooms into the dining room and the living room of covenantal fellowship with Christ and each other. Thus, communion with Christ is simultaneously communion with the whole body. So the natural, eucharistic, and ecclesial bodies of Christ are each given their due, while being inextricably connected.

No part of the body can be injured without pain to the whole body; the Supper not only illustrates or represents this point but also is a means through which Christ actually effects ecclesial unity. "Accordingly, Augustine with good reason frequently calls this Sacrament 'the bond of love.'"[76] In this sacrament, Christ makes himself the common property of all believers, Calvin insists, no believer possessing any greater or lesser participation in Christ or any of his benefits than the others.[77] Again, Calvin is not alone but in many ways is simply echoing Bucer, among others.[78]

Much has been written on the remarkable social impact of eucharistic teaching and practice in Reformed churches of the sixteenth century. As the sacra-

---

73. Southern Presbyterian R. L. Dabney explains that Protestants give relatively little space to a treatment of the sacraments (he could not have had the Reformers or their successors in mind), and he adds that in his own work "much of the length assigned it will arise from our attempts to rebut these formal and superstitious tendencies." He even judges that Calvin's view was too "mystical" and "irrational." See R. L. Dabney, *Systematic Theology* (1879; repr., Edinburgh: Banner of Truth, 1985), 727.

74. B. A. Gerrish, "Calvin's Eucharistic Piety," in *Calvin Studies Society Papers (1995, 1997): Calvin and Spirituality / Calvin and His Contemporaries* (Grand Rapids: CRC Publications, 1988), 64.

75. Calvin, *Institutes* 4.17.38.

76. Ibid.

77. Ibid.

78. See Martin Bucer, "The Reign of Christ," in *Melanchthon and Bucer*, ed. Wilhelm Pauck, Library of Christian Classics (Philadelphia: Westminster Press, 1969), 182, 236–59.

ments, like the preached Word, drive us outside of ourselves to become receivers of God's gift, they also direct us outward to our brothers and sisters. In this vein, Dutch pastor Karl Deddens has recently remarked,

> Here we have the very root of diaconal work. The festive spirit in which we celebrate the Lord's Supper is also an occasion for us, in accordance with Lord's Day [sec.] 38 of the Heidelberg Catechism, to show compassion for the poor. . . . And this ideal would become reality if the festive character of the Lord's Supper came to full expression in our services.[79]

Deddens points to important synods in the Netherlands judging that there should be "more frequent celebration of the Lord's Supper . . . , pointing to 1 Corinthians 11:17 by way of support."[80] It is indisputable that its celebration was a critical catalyst for Paul's challenge to greater unity and charity among the Corinthian believers. They were not to come to the Supper when they were sufficiently strong, pious, or loving toward each other, but as weak and sinful believers who, precisely through such a wonderful means of grace, were strengthened in faith and mutual love.

"REAL PRESENCE" IN CONTEMPORARY DISCUSSIONS

Although important differences remain, recent ecumenical conversations have yielded impressive areas of consensus.[81] Anticipating the contrasting ecclesiological paradigms to be explored in part 2 (below), the remainder of this chapter will be restricted to more recent criticisms of Reformed eucharistic teaching from a neo-Zwinglian perspective (diastasis between Christology and ecclesiology) on one side and from Radical Orthodoxy (synthesis) on the other.

79. Karl Deddens, *Where Everything Points to Him*, trans. Theodore Plantinga (Neerlandia, Alberta: Inheritance Publications, 1993), 93.

80. Ibid., 91.

81. On the Lutheran-Reformed consensus, see Keith F. Nickle and Timothy F. Lull, *A Common Calling: The Witness of Our Reformation Churches in North America Today; The Report of the Lutheran-Reformed Committee for Theological Conversations, 1988–1992* (Minneapolis: Augsburg Fortress Press, 1993), 37–49. See also "XI. Lutheran-Reformed Dialogue," in *Growth in Agreement II: Reports and Agreed Statements of Ecumenical Conversations on a World Level, 1982–1998*, ed. Jeffrey Gros (FSC), Harding Meyer, William G. Rusch (Geneva: World Council of Churches; Grand Rapids: Eerdmans, 2000), 230–47, esp. 242. It is important to point out, however, that significant branches of Lutheran and Reformed families have not participated in these discussions and would not endorse their conclusions or consensus. On the Reformed-Roman Catholic discussions, see *Growth in Agreement II: Reports and Agreed Statements of Ecumenical Conversations on a World Level, 1982–1998*, ed. Jeffrey Gros (FSC), Harding Meyer, William G. Rusch (Geneva: World Council of Churches; Grand Rapids: Eerdmans, 2000), "Reformed-Roman Catholic Dialogue," 815. For a general consensus among member bodies of the World Council of Churches, see *Baptism, Eucharist and Ministry 1982–1990: Report on the Process and Responses*, Faith and Order Paper No. 149 (Geneva: World Council of Churches, 1990), 115–16.

Separating the Sign from the Signified

If Lutherans have historically returned to Zwingli's position at Marburg as the "Reformed" view of the Supper, contemporary interpretations of the latter have often been read through the lens of Karl Barth's theology. Hans Urs von Balthasar, for example, chalks up Barth's comparative lack of interest in the church and sacraments to "his affinity for Calvin," suggesting that dialogue with Calvinism will turn on the doctrine of God and Christology rather than on church and sacraments.[82] Whatever one might say for or against Calvin's positions, I hope that the summary thus far is sufficient to reveal this as a caricature.

With respect to the sacraments, the appropriate association is with Zwingli rather than Calvin. As I pointed out in the previous chapter concerning baptism, Barth himself conceded this point, eschewing the "sacramentalism" that, lamentably in his view, the entire Reformed tradition embraced.[83] In volume 4 of the *Church Dogmatics*, under a discussion of how the Spirit works in the life of the believer and the community to direct them to Christ, baptism and the Supper do not even receive mention.[84] This is consistent, however, with his view that these are strictly human acts of obedience rather than God's means of grace.

We have already observed that the notion that God uses material means to convey spiritual blessings was, for Zwingli, a category mistake: the Spirit does not need "a channel or vehicle."[85] For Barth as well, divine and creaturely agency seem to run on parallel tracks, never truly intersecting on an extended horizontal plane. Throughout the last fragment of the *Church Dogmatics* that he was able to complete, Barth repeats his sharp distinction between God's work of salvation and water baptism and the Supper as the purely human work of liturgical obedience.[86] "He is He, and His work is His work, *standing over against all Christian action*, including Christian faith and Christian baptism" (emphasis added).[87] In spite of his recognition that he is departing from the Reformed consensus, Barth elsewhere offers the unusual claim that the Reformation substituted preaching alone for the Mass. "The *verbum visibile*, the objectively clarified preaching of the Word, is the only sacrament left to us. The Reformers sternly took from us everything but the Bible."[88] However, all of the Reformers—even Zwingli—distinguished the sacraments from the written and preached Word as

---

82. Hans Urs von Balthasar, *The Theology of Karl Barth: Exposition and Interpretation*, trans. Edward T. Oakes, SJ (San Francisco: Ignatius Press, 1992), 44.

83. Karl Barth, *CD* IV/4:128–30.

84. Barth, *CD*, IV/2:360–77.

85. Quoted from "An Account of the Faith," in W. P. Stephens, *The Theology of Huldrych Zwingli* (Oxford: Clarendon, 1986), 186. Cf. Ulrich Zwingli, *Commentary on True and False Religion*, ed. Samuel Macauley Jackson and Clarence Nevin Heller (Durham, NC: The Labyrinth Press, 1981), 214–15, 204–5, 239.

86. Barth, *CD* IV/4. Titled *The Christian Life*, this volume is a fragment that Barth developed and published as part of his unfinished dogmatics. Cf. *CD* 4/3:2, 756, 783, 790, 843–901.

87. Ibid., 88.

88. Karl Barth, *The Word of God and the Word of Man*, trans. Douglas Horton (New York: Harper Torchbooks, 1957), 114.

a *verbum visibile*, following Augustine. Here Barth's understandable wariness of Roman Catholic and Neo-Protestant tendencies to "enclose" Christ and his saving work, bringing them under the auspices of human control, motivates an overreaction.[89] For neither Zwingli nor Barth was *preaching* regarded as similarly incapable of mediating grace. George Hunsinger thus points out Barth's inconsistency at this point.[90] Creaturely action can point to but cannot be means of God's grace.

The Supper, for Barth, is concerned with "the action of *the community*, and indeed with the action by which *it* establishes fellowship" (emphasis added).[91] The entire "Zwinglian" trajectory leading all the way not only to Barth's view of the sacraments but also to the working presupposition in many Reformed and Presbyterian churches often exhibits a weak pneumatology together with a corresponding reticence to embrace a genuine union between the sign (heavenly grace) and the thing signified (creaturely elements and action).[92] As that which Barth calls "the subjective side in the event of revelation," the Spirit's work consists entirely of awakening people to what is already true, not actually communicating Christ to the believer.[93] The dominant view of the Supper in contemporary evangelical theology, as observed in the previous chapter, may even go beyond a Zwinglian conception, with the efficacy of the sacraments lodged entirely in their symbolic role of testifying to the believer's "act of commitment."

Confusing Sign and Signified

John Milbank, Graham Ward, and others within the circle of Radical Orthodoxy have applied their genealogy of nihilism (via Scotism) to Reformed sacramental teaching. Corrupted by nominalism, both Trent and the Reformers rejected an analogical participation in being that earlier theology had appropriated from theurgic Neoplatonism. "Concomitantly, sacramental participation and mediation were now downplayed" by Calvin's followers. At least for Calvin, real grace was mediated through the sacraments, but baptism became for these later covenant thinkers a "sign of membership of the covenant community," while "the

---

89. See David Allen, "A Tale of Two Roads: Homiletics and Biblical Authority," *Journal of the Evangelical Theological Society* 43, no. 3 (September 2000), esp. 492. Cf. Barth, *CD* I/1:127.

90. George Hunsinger, *Disruptive Grace: Studies in the Theology of Karl Barth* (Grand Rapids: Eerdmans, 2002), 275–76. However, Reinhard Hütter goes further, citing the firsthand account of Walter Kreck concerning statements that Barth made toward the end of his life, apparently revising his view (in the *CD* I/1) of proclamation as announcing rather than executing divine action. According to Hütter, "This draws the ultimate conclusion of the basic idea by making the gospel proclamation itself, in addition to baptism and Lord's Supper, into the responsive witness to the *testimonium Spiritus internum*." Reinhard Hütter, *Suffering Divine Things: Theology as Church Practice* (Grand Rapids: Eerdmans, 2000), 110.

91. Barth, *CD*, IV/3.2:901.

92. Among the many criticisms of Barth in this connection, see especially Robert Jenson, "You Wonder Where the Spirit Went," in *Pro Ecclesia* 2 (1993): 296–304; Wolfhart Pannenberg, *Systematic Theology*, trans. G. W. Bromiley, vol. 3 (Grand Rapids: Eerdmans, 1998), 1–27.

93. Barth, *CD*, I/1:449.

imputation of grace lies elsewhere, within a direct transaction between God and the individual."[94]

Milbank's nominalist genealogy has priority over the actual history of the tradition. The perspective that Milbank imputes to Calvin's theological heirs (baptism as no more than a "sign of membership within the covenant community") is actually the view that they themselves reject as "Anabaptist."[95]

Continuing with his narrative, Milbank says that this alleged reduction of the sacraments to a badge of visible membership could only lead to a secularization of the church, "as occurred in New England."[96] As a result of these degenerations, says Milbank, "the sense that the Eucharist allows a direct participation in Christ tends to be lost in the seventeenth century in favor of the view that it is simply a sign of the new covenant."[97] Ironically, it is Jonathan Edwards whom Milbank singles out with appreciation as a Calvinistic "Platonist," although Edwards exhibits some of the very declensions from sacramental mediation that Milbank erroneously attributed to the tradition generally.[98]

Milbank's appraisal of late medieval Roman Catholic theology fares little better than Protestantism. All sides in the sixteenth-century debates, basically indebted to nominalism, were trapped in a discourse about "real presence" foreign to the earlier medieval tradition, according to Milbank. Instead of analogically mediating reality, signs became immanentized—surrendering to univocity. Trent located the "real presence" in the "now" of the eucharistic celebration, while Protestants located it in the Bible. Therefore, we are faced with a choice: Time will therefore be understood as defined by the Eucharist, or the Eucharist will be defined by "the metaphysical idolatry of the *here and now*." If the latter, then "real

94. John Milbank, "Alternative Protestantism," in *Radical Orthodoxy and the Reformed Tradition: Creation, Covenant, and Participation*, ed. J. K. A. Smith and James H. Olthuis (Grand Rapids: Baker Academic, 2005), 31.

95. For instance, as late as 1699—the twilight of Protestant scholasticism—Peter Van Mastricht criticized the Anabaptist position on baptism for allowing "no use or efficacy of baptism but *that of signifying the church covenant*, and distinguishing those who are in that covenant from those who are outside of it" (emphasis added). Peter Van Mastricht, *Regeneration*, excerpted from his *Theologia theoretica-practica* (1699), anonymous English translation revised by Brandon Withrow (Morgan, PA: Soli Deo Gloria Publications, 2002), 52.

96. Milbank, "Alternative Protestantism," 31. All of his references here are to E. Brooks Holifield's *Theology in America*, specifically the New England (Independent) theology, which considerably modified the ecclesiology of the Reformed and Presbyterian confessions.

97. Ibid.

98. Following the French Catholic philosopher Nicholas Malebranche, Edwards held that every event in the world is the result of God's immediate power, a fresh ex nihilo act of creation. Thus, he in effect denied instrumental causality. Nicholas Malebranche, *Dialogues on Metaphysics and on Religion*, ed. Nicholas Jolley, trans. David Scott (Cambridge: Cambridge University Press, 1997); cf. Steven Nadler, "Occasionalism and Arnauld's Cartesianism," in *Descartes and His Contemporaries: Meditations, Objections, and Replies*, ed. Roger Ariews and Marjorie Greene (Chicago: University of Chicago Press, 1995), 115–16. On Edwards's appropriation of occasionalism, see Jonathan Edwards, "The Great Christian Doctrine of Original Sin Defended," in *The Works of Jonathan Edwards*, revised by Edward Hickman, vol. 6 (Edinburgh: Banner of Truth, 1990), 223. Cf. Michael Gibson, "The Integrative Biblical Philosophy of Jonathan Edwards," *Westminster Theological Journal* 64 (Spring 2002): 154–55.

presence" can only be the manifestation of an idol: the gaze that seizes the divine and absolutizes immanence (the present as full presence).[99]

When Milbank and Ward (following de Lubac and Marion) point up the dangers of the late medieval tendency to reduce the eucharistic event to a theatrical spectacle of pure presence, Reformation theology can only concur. Marion even goes so far as to judge, that "the substantial presence therefore fixes and freezes the person in an available, permanent, handy, and delimited thing."

> Hence the imposture of an idolatry that imagines itself to honor "God" when it heaps praises on his pathetic "canned" substitute (the reservation of the Eucharist), exhibited as an attraction (display of the Holy Sacrament), brandished like a banner (processions), and so on. . . . Real presence: "God" made thing, a hostage without significance, powerful because mute, tutelary because without titularity, a thing "denuded of all signification except that of presence" (Mallarmé).[100]

Marion's criticisms of recent alternatives to transubstantiation (remarkably similar to Zwinglian approaches) can also be received sympathetically by Reformed interpreters.[101] Marion properly insists that Christ's presence in the Supper cannot be reduced either to an objective thing or to a subjective community-consciousness.[102]

Graham Ward has particularly drawn out the implications with vigor and insight in his *Cities of God* (2000), as contemporary culture offers "a secular eschatology" that "idolizes the present."[103] As I have suggested throughout this project, univocity reflects a realized eschatology, while the postmodern equivocity is endless deferral. Ward offers what he calls an analogical view: our present participates in but is not itself eternity.[104] Augustine and Aquinas do not talk about "presence" in relation to the Eucharist, much less *real* presence, Ward observes.

Yet just at this point, Ward asserts, "It is the collapse of analogy and the movement towards univocity, the transparency of 'clear and distinct' ideas, that can be traced in the difference between Aquinas' and Calvin's notions of 'presence.'"[105] Despite their different views, Calvin and Trent were both simply following the spatializing logic of Ockham, according to Ward. By contrast, Augustine held that nothing can be fully realized in the present for us: that would make us God.[106] "The language of *praesens/prasentia* is, therefore, I suggest, the language of idolatry (reifying that which cannot be plucked out of time and fully present

---

99. Ibid., 176.

100. Jean-Luc Marion, *God Without Being*, trans. Thomas A. Carlson (Chicago: University of Chicago Press, 1991), 164–65.

101. For the most thorough development and defense of transsignification, see Edward Schillebeeckx, *The Eucharist* (London: Sheed & Ward, 1968), 108–19.

102. Ibid., 166–67.

103. Graham Ward, *Cities of God* (New York and London: Routledge, 2000), 154.

104. Ibid., 155.

105. Ibid., 157.

106. Ibid.

to itself) for Aquinas." While Aquinas spoke of a true presence (*vere praesens*), the nominalism at work in the Tridentine (and allegedly Protestant) conception began to speak of a real presence (*realis praesens*).[107] "The present is now a commodity to be abstracted, a property to be grasped."[108]

Not only does this misrepresent Calvin's position; it also is not even consistent with Ward's own recognition that "Calvin does not employ the terms *realitas* or *realis*—only *vere/vrai*"—the very thing that distinguishes Augustine and Aquinas from nominalism. Nevertheless, *somehow* Calvin must be a carrier of the nominalist virus.[109] Although it makes for a good story, the following conclusion will strike those who have read Calvin closely as implausible:

> A sense of haunting, an ectoplasmic aura behind or beyond the material will lead to an emphasis on "spirituality" at the expense of the body—and eventually the emphasis upon solitary religious experience as the authentic mark of sanctity. The pacification of the natural prepares the metaphysical ground for the secular, demystified world-view (and later the scientific world-view of the capitalist cult of worldly goods). . . . We are entering the society of the spectacle.[110]

At this point, Ward seems to entirely miss the thrust of Calvin's objection to both transubstantiation and ubiquity: the significance of Christ's natural body *against* all attempts at its "spiritualization."

Ward recognizes that Calvin frequently appealed to Augustine in developing his eucharistic theology, but asserts that the latter "understands the participation of the sign in the signified," in contrast to Calvin.[111] Yet once again, this gravely distorts Calvin's explicit defense of this view, with abundant citations of Augustine, not to mention the equally explicit affirmation in the Reformed confessions of the sign-signified union. Yet just as Christ's presence-in-action through the Word is not a transubstantiated presence but a union of signs with the promised reality, so too in the sacraments, says Calvin. "It is therefore with good reason" that we call the bread and wine the body and blood of Christ." And at this point Calvin reiterates the Chalcedonian formula: "Distinction is proper, but never division."[112]

---

107. Ibid., 159–60.
108. Ibid., 161.
109. Ibid., repeated on 163.
110. Ibid., 162.
111. Ibid., 164.
112. Ibid., 172. To be sure, the bread and wine are signs—and always remain so. Even in the hypostatic union, the transcendent deity of the Son cannot be contained within or confused with the human nature. In this light, the so-called *extracalvinisticum* might be more appropriately attributed to Augustine (and Chalcedon). It is this *extracalvinisticum* that guarantees that even in the incarnation, God transcends his advent while nevertheless appearing. The integrity of each nature, and of sign and signified, must be retained. "But," Calvin is quick to say, "we likewise add, that the sacraments of the Lord should not and cannot be at all separated from their reality and substance." Is it too much to suggest that ontological approaches (esp. strongly Neoplatonic versions) turn to ontology and metaphysical accounts of presence, while the obvious resource for "meeting a stranger" is Christology?

In spite of all of this, Ward asserts that for Calvin,

> Dualistic thinking substitutes for mediation. It cannot itself mediate, but it establishes a logic that gives definition to one thing (the objective, the natural, the public) only with respect to its diametrical opposite (the subjective, the cultural, the private). Calvin's analogical reasoning is not analogical at all (where analogy defines the mediation between similarity and difference, univocity and equivocity).[113]

Yet nowhere in this discussion (nor in others that I have examined) does Ward even seem to be aware of the role of pneumatology for this very mediation that he thinks Calvin lacks.[114] Nor is there any evidence that Ward has encountered Calvin's repeated polemics against Manichean dualism and his strong affirmation of material creation, the incarnation, and as we have seen, the ascension and return of Christ in the flesh. Nevertheless, Ward continues, "This spatialising produces an economy of desire based upon lack, as not-having, not-attaining, not-reaching."[115] Ward sees abstract categories of static metaphysics where Calvin sees a dynamic economy of salvation. "Not Aristotle," wrote Calvin, "but the Holy Spirit teaches that the body of Christ from the time of his resurrection was finite, and is contained in heaven even to the Last Day."[116] Ward interprets Calvin as advocating a sort of proto-Derridean ontology of endless deferral, while Calvin is simply trying to think through the exegetical trajectories concerning both the real absence of Christ's natural body and the *availability* of that body, mediated by the Spirit, *to* his church—in a way that does not simply *replace* that natural body *with* the church.

Since Calvin (and the rest of the tradition) explicitly rejected the notion that the Supper consisted of "mere naked signs" without communicating the reality signified, it is difficult to know what to do with Ward's repetition of Simon Oliver's charge that the Eucharist for Calvin is "mere theatre," a "virtual reality."[117] This is charged despite Calvin's own comment above that "the Lord does not mock us with empty signs but accomplishes inwardly what he sets before our eyes, and that the effect is therefore joined with the signs." Yet Calvin writes elsewhere, "Christ's Supper is not a theatrical display of spiritual food but gives in reality what it depicts, since in it devout souls feed on the flesh and blood of

---

113. Ibid., 165.

114. Ward does say in a note, "Calvin, as it is well known, relates eucharistic presence to a trinitarian operation. The Spirit spans the distance between Christ in heaven above and the believer below. Calvin's trinitarianism, which expresses to my mind a modalism, has been well documented, as indeed, has Calvin's doctrine of the eucharist" (ibid, 274 n. 11). Evidently, "as it is well known" and "has been well documented," these comments are to be taken on faith, since there are no references; however, I am not aware of any serious work, Catholic, Protestant, or otherwise, that would identify Calvin's Trinitarianism as modalistic. If he is simply suggesting that Calvin's Trinitarianism and view of the Eucharist have been well-documented, surely that is as accurate as it is obvious.

115. Ibid., 167.

116. Calvin, *Institutes* 4.17.26.

117. Ibid.

Christ."[118] Turning Communion into a "theatrical display" was actually the Reformation's characteristic criticism of the medieval Mass.

What then is Ward's own proposal? Instead of treating the ascension as *absence*, we should view it as a *displacement*. In its displacement, the natural body of Jesus of Nazareth is not really absent but infinitely expands to include all other bodies. This keeps us from becoming fixated on the body of the "gendered Jew," in Ward's repeated identification, and to become incorporated into a crossing of transcorporeal bodies, bodies that defy natural stereotypes (such as gender and sexual orientation). However different Ward's treatment is from the doctrine of ubiquity, the problems are similar: What exactly is a *transcorporeal* body, and how does this affirm embodiment as we understand it (and as Platonism criticizes it)? Ward insists that his view is not docetic because it affirms the body of the "gendered Jew," even though this body is "expanded" until it is no longer recognizable as the subject who said he would leave and come again. According to Ward, "housing" God—which represents "the greatest commodification of them all"— is "evident in the '*reali praesentia*' of the Council of Trent," but also in Calvin's "housing" of the body in heaven.[119]

Like Ward, Milbank redefines the nature of bodies in order to defend the logic of a transubstantiation not determined by Tridentine nominalism. "In consuming this food, we do not assimilate the Christ—to our person or to our 'social body,' or whatever—like the food that finds in us its end and sole justification. On the contrary, we become assimilated through the sacramental body of the Christ to his ecclesiastical body."[120] So far, I would agree. However, this spiritual body is "a body infinitely more united, more coherent, more consistent—*in a word, more real—than any physical body*" (emphasis added).[121] The categories of sign and signified are therefore mapped onto a Platonist ontology, with gradations of reality where the spiritual is more real than the corporeal. The corporeal body is a condescension of Christ to the materiality of the here and now, aiming at "the spiritual incorporation par excellence."[122] Corporeality is at last transcended. The body and blood of Christ are the sign (*sacramentum*); the church is the reality (*res*)—"*only this ecclesiastical Body should be called purely* res" (emphasis added), according to Milbank.[123]

A more complete substitution of the church for Christ is difficult to conceive. In the Supper the order between the real (bread and wine) and the sign (body and blood) is reversed. "The real is exclusively that which seems 'mystical' to the ordinary gaze—the Body of the Christ and his ecclesiastical body."[124] There is therefore nothing left for the Spirit to mediate, since the church itself *is* the

---

118. Cited in Gerrish, *Grace and Gratitude*, 140, from *CO* 15:212–13.
119. Gerrish, *Grace and Gratitude*, 180.
120. John Milbank, in *Radical Orthodoxy: A New Theology*, ed. John Milbank, Catherine Pickstock, and Graham Ward (London: Routledge, 1999), 179.
121. Ibid.
122. Ibid.
123. Ibid., 180.
124. Ibid., 180–81.

expanded Christ. Ironically, what gets lost in the process, it seems to me, is the one who has died, is risen, and will come again just as the disciples saw him leave.

More recently, in conversation with Reformed theology, Milbank writes that "Calvin's sacramental theology is not really coherent. In relation to the Eucharist he is indeed to be thoroughly commended for his strong pneumatological emphasis—reminiscent of Greek views and perhaps superior to some Catholic treatments. . . . But the idea of the spiritual participation in a body that is in heaven makes very little sense." Better is the doctrine of transubstantiation, which avoids a local presence of Christ's body and blood either in heaven or in the bread and the wine by suggesting instead "that participation in a physical— albeit mysteriously physical—reality is itself mysteriously physical."[125]

If one discerns in the phrase "mysteriously physical" the equivalent of "not really a human body," it is simply evidence, for Milbank and Ward, that one has adopted a nominalist ontology that idolizes the here and now and embraces a theory of space and matter that has not been determined by the Eucharist.

At first, Milbank's argument might sound like a critique of dualism, yet seems more like a Dionysian dualism with a Hegelian accent. In other words, the physical (thesis) and spiritual (antithesis) provide the stuff out of which a higher synthesis like transcorporeal bodies and mysteriously physical reality (or Hegel's matter transmuted by Spirit) can emerge. It thus is the ecclesial body—the church—that becomes the subject of that higher synthesis. What troubles Milbank and Ward about Calvin's formulations is the refusal to allow such *assimilations*, which, again like Hegel, are treated erroneously as *mediations*. Milbank concludes, "For reasons I have tried to hint at, Calvin's humanist and practical theology is one that is implicitly in search of a metaphysics," and because he did not adopt a Platonist metaphysics of participation, his program finally fails.[126]

These interpretations of Calvin have not gone unchallenged. As a sympathetic scholar of medieval thought (including Christian Neoplatonism), Laura Smit notes that Ward mischaracterizes Calvin's sacramental theology in Zwinglian terms, failing to recognize his strong affirmation of analogy and participation.[127] She cites Calvin's direct appeals to patristic sources in developing an unmistakably analogical view of participation.[128] Ward misses Calvin's richly nuanced integration of Christ's downward movement and upward movement, all mediated by

125. Milbank, "Alternative Protestantism," 35.

126. Ibid. In critique of Calvin, Milbank adds (on 36) that his "practical" orientation "is one ingredient in the American pragmatist legacy." We are better to follow the more Platonic interpreters of the tradition, then. "To speak of aesthetic discernment—and I think I am pretty close to Jonathan Edwards here—is then to appeal to the divine reason and vision as much as to the divine will and command," which eschews the univocal and voluntarist dimensions of a nominalist program.

127. Laura Smit, "'The Depth behind Things': Towards a Calvinist Sacramental Theology," in Smith and Olthuis, *Radical Orthodoxy and the Reformed Tradition*, 206. In addition to her own research, Smit's survey of Calvin's eucharistic doctrine is informed by Keith Mathison's excellent study, *Given for You: Calvin's Doctrine of the Lord's Supper* (Phillipsburg, NJ: Presbyterian & Reformed Publishing Co., 2002).

128. Ibid., 207–8.

the Spirit.[129] We have already observed Philip Walker Butin's explanation of this point (above). Calvin is interested in Christ's whereabouts not for speculative reasons, but only insofar as the fully human (and therefore nonubiquitous) nature of Christ's ascended body is maintained.[130] Furthermore, Smit points out that Ward's own account offers "an even more radical understanding of absence than Calvin." The Jesus who is somehow "present" is such "in only the most equivocal way, *"since 'Jesus' has now been redefined as no longer the incarnate person who lived and died on the cross;* this clearly is not the same Jesus of whom Calvin is speaking."[131] In Ward's view, "The particular humanity of Jesus of Nazareth has been lost, so that the only presently existent body of Christ is the church invisible." It is precisely Calvin's antidocetic emphasis on the local presence of Christ's natural body at the Father's right hand that guards against such evaporation.[132]

Given his understanding of "transcorporeality," Smit observes, it is ironic that Ward "accuses Calvin of reducing Christ's bodily presence to 'a sense of haunting, an ectoplasmic aura behind or beyond the material' (*CG* [*Cities of God*] 162), which suggests to me that Ward himself has no categories for thinking about a genuinely resurrected body or of materiality that is not confined to our present experience."[133] Although Ward says that the ascension means "not the erasure but the expansion of the body" (*CG* 112), Smit is not convinced that there is really a practical difference, since according to Ward, "We have no access to the body of the gendered Jew" (*CG* 113). "This, I suspect, is why Ward has no theology of the second coming," Smit judges. "How can Jesus Christ return when he now exists only in the body of the church?"[134]

Douglas Farrow's point is similar: "Graham Ward's thesis, of course, stripped of its obfuscations and its postmodern flare, reduces to a familiar refrain: the ascension as the sublation of the all-too-definite humanity of that 'gendered Jew,' as he likes to call him, for the sake of an advancing divinization in which absence becomes the dialectical ground for presence, and ecclesiology smothers eschatology."[135] Ward seems impatient with any suggestion that "there is another kingdom for which we wait."[136] "Precisely because Calvin is not a materialist," Smit adds, "a spiritual communion is a real communion; a spiritual feeding is a true feeding; the communion is nonetheless with Christ's human *body*."[137] Again, as we have seen above, this is because our salvation is no less found in his human life of active and passive obedience, resurrection, and ascension, than in his divine power. "Through the sacrament we participate in the ascension of Christ."[138]

129. Ibid.
130. Smit, "'The Depth behind Things,'" 213.
131. Ibid., 210.
132. Ibid., 211.
133. Ibid.
134. Ibid., 212.
135. Farrow, *Ascension and Ecclesia*, 260.
136. Ibid., 215.
137. Ibid.
138. Ibid., 217.

With Smit, I wonder if Ward's dismissal of such an account as "virtual" rather than "real" reveals his own "lack of apparent interest in the work of the third person of the Trinity."[139] Further, in Calvin's view, a sign actually "presents the reality to us."[140] Ward's interpretation, far from analogical, is actually allegorical.[141] A major impetus of Calvinist iconoclasm has been its insistence that in this "dialogic circle of word and sacrament," we are not creators but receivers, "swept up in God's action."[142]

"Finally," writes Smit, answering Ward's charge that Calvin privatized spirituality, "the celebration of the Lord's Supper must always involve the entire community."[143] This point is elaborated by Nathan R. Kerr, also in criticism of Ward's interpretation of Calvin's eucharistic theology as nominalist.[144] Calvin "refuses to reduce the question of eucharistic presence to the binary structure of Christ's local [natural] and sacramental [eucharistic] bodies."

> Rather, the eucharistic *totus Christus* requires a tertiary structure that includes the affirmation of the ecclesial body as the true body of Christ (the *corpus verum* of the church fathers). Examining the way in which Christ is spiritually present to us in the Eucharist through the Holy Spirit, Calvin goes on to suggest that this Spirit properly unites us with the flesh of Christ by embodying Christ in the church, through the flesh of its members (*ICR* [*Institutes*] 4.17.8–10).[145]

The Spirit after all is the Spirit of Christ, not requiring an additional incarnation or enhypostasization alongside the Son's.[146] Therefore, the sacramental and ecclesial bodies are not binaries, but coefficients.[147]

Only the communication of Christ himself with all his benefits is sufficient to generate an ecclesial body. In all of these ways, Calvin is able to hold together the ascension (and therefore the real "distance" of the true flesh of Christ), which provokes our longing for his bodily return (and therefore, the eschatological dimension), as well as the current communion with his body, in his body, as his body. In its expansion as well as its deepening maturity and unity, the church is *becoming* this body, and this ecclesial reality binds in close harmony the sacramental and historical bodies.[148] Through the Supper, the believer who "apprehends Christ's

---

139. Ibid., 220.
140. Ibid., quoting Calvin, *Commentary on Corinthians*, trans. John King (repr., Grand Rapids: Baker Book House, 1998), 1:234.
141. Farrow, *Ascension and Ecclesia*, 220.
142. Ibid.
143. Ibid., 223.
144. Nathan R. Kerr, "Corpus Verum: On the Ecclesial Recovery of Real Presence in John Calvin's Doctrine of the Eucharist," in Smith and Olthuis, *Radical Orthodoxy and the Reformed Tradition*, 232.
145. Ibid., 235.
146. As we saw in chap. 1 (above), this is exactly where Milbank takes the logic of this argument: the incarnation of the Spirit in and as the church. Remarkably, the Spirit shares the same fate as Jesus: transubstantiated into the church.
147. See esp. Calvin's *Institutes* 4.17.39.
148. Nathan R. Kerr, "Corpus Verum," 232.

body through the reception of faith participates by actively *becoming* what she receives," which creates a community on earth that, as the *corpus verum*, "offers us a real foretaste of that glorious heavenly body that we all shall share together with Christ on that final eschatological morning."[149]

Radical Orthodoxy, as Catherine Pickstock explains, seeks to overcome "'a literalist concern with what the Eucharist "is," as an isolated phenomenon,' by way of reemphasizing the Eucharist as 'an ecclesial event,' in which the question of presence is subordinated to that of 'sacred action.'"[150] Yet this is precisely what Calvin articulated, as we have seen.[151] However, for Calvin this event required genuine participation in the concrete person of "the gendered Jew," while for Radical Orthodoxy this person is less real than the church. Given the correlation of head and members, is it any wonder that in the displacement-as-expansion of Jesus' natural body, the eschatological hope according to these writers is not the resurrection of the body but a transcorporeal existence?[152] This is the logical consummation of Origen's ascent of mind.

Recent emphasis on the centrality of the Eucharist for ecclesial identity is salutary, but only as long as it is connected to the Word and baptism, and only if one's eucharistic doctrine locates the church in that precarious crevice between this age of sin and death and the age of righteousness and life, in constant dependence on the Spirit. When it forgets to take its cues from what Christ has done apart from us in history (anamnesis) and to wait for his return in the flesh to do what he has left to accomplish for the renewal of creation (*epektasis*), with the Spirit as the *arrabōn* (deposit) of things to come (epiclesis), the church easily imagines itself as the substitute for its absent Lord.

Taking its coordinates from the redemptive economy of Christ's descent, ascent, and Parousia—concretely manifested and truly constituted by the Spirit through Word and sacrament, the covenantal ecclesiology developed in part 2 (below) locates the church's identity at this unsettling, strange, even dangerous yet wonderful intersection between the two ages.

---

149. Ibid., 242.

150. Catherine Pickstock, *After Writing: On the Liturgical Consummation of Philosophy* (Malden, MA: Blackwell, 1998), 163.

151. Kerr, "Corpus Verum," 239.

152. John Milbank and Catherine Pickstock, *Truth in Aquinas* (London: Routledge, 2001), 37. I am grateful to James K. A. Smith for pointing to this reference in his carefully nuanced interpretation in "Will the Real Plato Please Stand Up?" in Smith and Olthuis, *Radical Orthodoxy and the Reformed Tradition*, 70.

PART TWO
IDENTITY
Figuring the Body

Chapter Six

Totus Christus

One and Many

After addressing the *where* question in the first chapter, chapters 2–5 have taken up the *how* question: the source, basis, and origin of the church in the means of grace. This section concentrates on the *what* question: the identity and mission of the church as a result of the circumstances of its location and origin.

Using the creedal adjectives as a general rubric ("one holy, catholic, and apostolic church"), this chapter will take up the unity of the church (one and many). On this basis, the following chapters will explore catholicity and holiness (local and universal), then apostolicity (historical institution and eschatological event), in an effort to reintegrate the marks and the mission of the church.

PRIVILEGING THE ONE: CONFLATING CHRIST AND THE CHURCH

Despite his affirmation of Christ's ascension in the flesh, the identity between Christ and his church is so complete in Augustine's concept of the *totus Christus* that it is made not only one with and in Christ, but is actually made "Christ."[1] Kingdom and church, head and members, eschatology and history began to merge. As chapter 1 elaborated, the assimilation of Christology to ecclesiology was accelerated in the medieval era, especially through Dionysian mysticism, yet only with late medieval nominalism was the mystical body identified with the Eucharist rather than the church. Consequently, as Henri de Lubac, Karl Rahner, and others have observed, the concept of the church that came to dominate the late medieval period was that of a legal, juridical institution under "the one vicar of Christ on earth, the Roman pontiff."[2] There was nothing questionable, ambiguous, or precarious about the church's location or identity in this age. It is simply the kingdom of God—the historical replacement for the natural body of Christ.

Roman Catholic Ecclesiologies of the *Totus Christus*

Karl Adam, a disciple of Johann Möhler at Tübingen, furthered the transition from a Tridentine legalism to a more organic ecclesiology, now known as "reform Catholicism."[3] Organic analogies were in the air in the springtime of romanticism and had already been put to extensive use in political and social as well as ecclesiological discourse. Adam discerns no ambiguity between the church as a historical institution and the eschatological kingdom: there is simply a progressive unfolding from seed to full flower.[4] As an extension of the incarnation, the church is the actual occurrence of the Absolute Idea in history. Only now are we at the place, according to Adam, where we can envision a return of alienated children to Rome, so that "the great and urgent task of the West is to close at long last the unwholesome breach that has divided us for centuries, to create a new spiritual unity, a religious centre, and so to prepare *the only possible foundation for a rebuilding and rebirth of Western civilization*" (emphasis added).[5] The Roman Catholic Church is "the realisation on earth of the Kingdom of God."[6] "Christ the Lord is the real self of the Church," and the church and Christ are "one and the same person, one Christ, the whole Christ."[7]

Here we discover the outline of a Hegelian version of Augustine's notion of *totus Christus* that has come to dominate not only Roman Catholic but also many Protestant ecclesiologies of late. Drawing on Fichte's assimilation of the finite ego to the Infinite Ego, Hegel regarded particulars as necessary for the concrete actualization of the universal in time and space, but "the finite must perish," as it is

---

1. Augustine, *Confessions* 13.28.
2. Robert Bellarmine, *De controversies*, tom. 2, liber 3, *De ecclesia militante*, cap. 2, "De definitione Ecclesiae" (Naples: Giuliano, 1857), 2:75.
3. Robert A. Krieg, CSC, introduction, in Karl Adam, *The Spirit of Catholicism* (New York: Crossroad, 1997), xi.
4. Ibid., 2.
5. Ibid., 6.
6. Ibid., 14.
7. Ibid., 15.

absorbed into the ascending syntheses.[8] "It is the particular which exhausts itself in the struggle and part of which is destroyed. But the universal results precisely from this struggle, from the destruction of the particular."[9] Like Spinoza, Hegel maintains that only the whole is real; the finite, as partial, is the source of evil.[10] Thus, Hegel never really mediated Platonism's binaries, much less transcended them. His view of the relation between finite and infinite is actually more nearly Manichean.[11] The synthesis simply *assimilated* the weaker to the stronger in each antithesis. For example, "matter is transmuted in spirit."[12] The many are assimilated to the one, and the parts to the whole. The antithesis of self and other is finally overcome by this synthesis.

Conceived by Hegel as Absolute Spirit (i.e., the unfolding process of history from acorn to oak tree), even "God" belongs to this order. Although the finite life of Jesus of Nazareth is important for the actualization of the absolute idea in history, it too is sublated by Spirit, as the *Dasein* of Jesus is taken up into community. Cyril O'Regan observes that interest in the Jesus of history, according to Hegel, "is completely wrongheaded, for it fails to recognize that the vanishing of Jesus is a condition of the presence of the Spirit." Therefore, "the Pentecostal experience is at once the pneumatic substitute for the concrete existence of Jesus Christ and the term of Jesus' vocation which was to make persons free and children of God."[13] Echoing Meister Eckhart, Hegel argues that God needs the world for self-realization and completion just as the world needs God for the same.[14]

Although the Tübingen school did not simply repeat Hegel's phenomenology of Spirit, it is this Hegelian twist on an Augustinian maxim that yields the conclusion for Adam that the church is "the incarnation of Christ in the faithful."[15] Yet the *totus Christus* is hierarchically constituted according to Rome, descending from the pope as its visible head. Therefore, "the whole constitution of the Church is completely aristocratic, and not democratic, her authority coming from above, from Christ, and not from below, from the community."[16] Platonism's ladder of being is in evidence in Adam's treatment, with the highest rungs accorded to the spiritual, yet with divinity flowing down to the lowest rungs to

8. G. W. F. Hegel, *Reason in History*, trans. Robert S. Hartman (New York: Macmillan, 1953), 20–45.

9. Ibid., 43; cf. G. W. F. Hegel, *The Christian Religion: Lectures on the Philosophy of Religion, part 3, The Revelatory, Consummate, Absolute Religion*, ed. and trans. Peter C. Hodgson (Atlanta: American Academy of Religion, 1979). This entire work is critical for understanding the gist of the Hegelian system as it touches especially on Christian faith and practice. However, pages 142–312 are especially important.

10. See Cyril O'Regan, *The Heterodox Hegel*, SUNY Series in Hegelian Studies (Albany: State University of New York Press, 1994), 316 (esp. note 56).

11. Ibid., 175, 177.

12. Hegel, *Reason in History*, 43.

13. O'Regan, *The Heterodox Hegel*, 240.

14. G. W. F. Hegel, *Lectures on the Philosophy of Religion*, ed. Peter Hodgson (Berkeley: University of California Press, 1984), 1:347–48.

15. Adam, *The Spirit of Catholicism*, 20.

16. Ibid., 21.

incorporate all of humanity. "The Church is ordinated towards the invisible, spiritual and eternal. . . . But the Church is not only invisible. Because she is the Kingdom of God, she is not a haphazard collection of individuals, but an ordered system of regularly subordinated parts." Through this hierarchy, "*the divine is objectivised, is incarnated in the community*, and precisely and only in so far as it is a community. . . . So the Church possesses the Spirit of Christ, not as a many of single individuals, nor as a sum of spiritual personalities, but as the compact unity of the faithful, as a community that transcends the individual personalities, . . . *the many as one*." Christ's mission is "to reunite to God mankind as a unity, as a whole, *and not this or that individual man*" (emphasis added).[17]

So although "reforming Catholicism" adopted a more dynamic and organic model, this model itself was no less susceptible to stressing the one over the many than the older legal paradigm. Adam asserts that "the community and not the individual is the bearer of the Spirit of Jesus," which entails a visible head, the pope, the symbol of numerical unicity.[18]

In a somewhat chilling illustration of his time and place, Adam passionately asserts, "One God, one faith, one love, one single man: that is the stirring thought which inspires the Church's pageantry and gives it artistic form."[19] Echoing Hegel, he declares, "For only in the whole can the divine realise itself, only in the totality of men and not in the individual."[20] As a consequence, "the structural organs of the Body of Christ, as that is realised in space and time, are pope and bishops."[21] This empirical polity—the observable structure of the ecclesiastical hierarchy—*constitutes* the visibility of the church in the world. For all of these reasons, says Adam, "the Catholic Church as the Body of Christ, as the realisation in the world of the Kingdom of God, is the Church of Humanity." So the church is simultaneously exclusive (there is no other ladder of grace) and inclusive (since God's grace flows through her down to the lowest rungs).[22] This grace operates "not only in the Christian communions, but also in the non-Christian world, in Jews and in Turks and in Japanese"—at least to "all those who hold themselves ready for it, *who do what in them lies*, who perform what their conscience bids them" (emphasis added).[23]

Although this ecclesiology was refined and balanced with other images, such as the people of God, it has remained the dominant interpretation of Karl Rahner, Vatican II, and the pontificates of John Paul II (esp. his encyclical *Dominus Iesus*) and Pope Benedict XVI.

17. Ibid., 31–32.
18. Ibid., 38.
19. Ibid., 41. Like many Catholic and Protestant theologians of his generation, Adam at first welcomed Hitler's ascendancy. According to Krieg, after declaring for Hitler, six months later Adam criticized the regime (xii).
20. Ibid., 53.
21. Ibid., 97.
22. Ibid., 159–65.
23. Ibid., 168. The italicized clause is the nominalist maxim, "To those who do what lies within them, God will not deny his grace [*facientibus quod in se est deus non denigat gratiam*]," which the Reformation especially targeted in its criticisms.

Also significant, especially in postconciliar ecclesiologies (and recent Protestant variations), is Henri de Lubac, to whom I have already made reference. According to de Lubac, "if Christ is the sacrament of God, the Church is for us the sacrament of Christ; she represents him, in the full and ancient meaning of the term, *she really makes him present. She not only carries on his work, but she is his very continuation,* in a sense far more real than that in which it can be said that any human institution is its founder's continuation" (emphasis added).[24] Transubstantiation was now applied not only to the eucharistic body but also to the ecclesial body in the notion of the church as the "primordial sacrament," with Christ as a "corporate personality" together with his church.[25] "Expressions of grace not historically linked with Christ will be . . . more ambiguous," but not nonexistent.[26]

Another important contribution to contemporary Roman Catholic ecclesiology has come from Hans Urs von Balthasar, especially in his *Church and World* (1967), where we discern a more explicitly christological norm.[27] Nevertheless, this norm is defined according to the neo-Hegelian version of the *totus Christus* maxim, assimilating Christology to ecclesiology, as when he writes, "In fact, this violent, this often *'crucifying' sacrifice of the pious subject to the ecclesial object* (that is what Schleiermacher and Hegel call 'community-consciousness') is ultimately one of the conditions for the presence of the Eucharistic Lord" (emphasis added).[28] The acorn-and-oak analogy is not far from von Balthasar's mind when he writes, "The Church is, at one and the same time, the redeemed world in course of becoming and Christ's instrument for the full redemption of the world. Consequently, the individual member of the Church in time is not, actually, functional as regards the Church, as if it were the executive bearer of this function. He is, rather, functional in and with the Church as a whole."[29]

To be sure, the Second Vatican Council opened up new and even rich vistas to the broader range of biblical images: the church as the pilgrim people of God, covenant community, with a slightly more eschatological reserve (a new emphasis on the church as sign of the kingdom rather than the kingdom unfolding). However, the basic features remain intact: hierarchical unicity, the true church as the Church of Rome, although all people are already members in varying degrees, and the church is still regarded as an extension of Christ's person and work. Even with the salutary effects of a more pneumatological perspective, Yves Congar

24. Henri de Lubac, *Catholicism* (London: Burns, Oates, & Washbourne, 1950), 29.

25. Rahner developed this model further, along with Otto Semmelroth (*Die Kirche als Ursakrament* [The Church as Primordial Sacrament], Frankfurt am Main: Knecht, 1953), reaching perhaps its fullest expression in Schillebeeckx, Congar, and the conclusions of Vatican II. See Avery Dulles, SJ, *Models of the Church* (New York: Doubleday, 1974), 59.

26. Ibid., 66. The World Council of Churches at its Uppsala Assembly in 1968 echoed Vatican II: the church is "the sign of the coming unity of mankind" (quoted in ibid., 70).

27. Hans Urs von Balthasar, *Church and World*, trans. A. V. Littledale with Alexander Dru (Montreal: Palm Publishers, 1967), 20–23.

28. Ibid., 32.

29. Ibid., 107–8.

repeats the traditional view of the Spirit as the "soul of the Church."[30] However, this not only deepens the mind-body dualism that makes the church the visible substitute for Christ's ascended body; it also easily reduces the Spirit to the immanent "spirit of the community." As a consequence, the Spirit's agency in mediating the difference and affinity of Christ with his ecclesial body is reduced to the church as the phenomenal/concrete form of the Spirit's existence and work in history.

Prior to becoming Pope Benedict XVI, Cardinal Ratzinger, in his book *Called to Communion: Understanding the Church Today* (1996), elaborated this understanding: the union of head and members is a "fusion of existences."[31] The sacrifice of the individual to the whole (*totus Christus*) in Ratzinger's account is especially evident in his reiteration of the traditional view that faith itself is "a gift of the church." "Believing in a personal fashion means essentially 'coming to participate in the already existing decision of the believing community.'"[32] "Accordingly," as Miroslav Volf points out, "the self of the creed, according to the studies of Henri de Lubac, whom Ratzinger follows, is a collective rather than an individual self, the self of the believing *Mater Ecclesiae* 'to which the individual self belongs insofar as it believes.' Ratzinger even elucidates this notion of cobelief with the church with the expression 'surrender one's act [of faith] to it [the church].'"[33] Volf also underscores the debt to German idealism.[34]

Once again we see the consequences of looking away from the particular person, Jesus of Nazareth. Instead of longing for his return and invoking the Spirit to mediate difference, the church steps in to fill the void. The existence of the church allays any anxiety about Christ's bodily absence. The ontological dualism of invisible and visible displaces the eschatological dualism of the now and not-yet. As Volf judges,

> Ratzinger has a tendency to search for something more profound or real behind the historical, and to view concrete reality merely as a sign for spiritual, transcendent content. Hence the earthly Jesus is portrayed less as a concrete human being than as "merely an *exemplum* of human beings." . . . This is the result of Ratzinger's Platonizing "commitment to the primacy of the invisible as that which is genuinely real" (Ratzinger, *Einführung*, 48).[35]

Ratzinger can go so far as to assert that the pope is "placed in direct responsibility to the Lord . . . to embody and secure the unity of Christ's word and work."[36]

30. Yves Congar, *I Believe in the Holy Spirit*, trans. David Smith, 3 vols. (New York: Seabury Press, 1983), 2:19–20.

31. Joseph Cardinal Ratzinger, *Called to Communion: Understanding the Church Today*, trans. Adrian Walker (San Francisco: Ignatius Press, 1996), 37.

32. Joseph Cardinal Ratzinger, *Principles of Catholic Theology: Building Stones for a Fundamental Theology*, trans. Mary Frances McCarthy (San Francisco: Ignatius Press, 1987), 38.

33. Miroslav Volf, *After Our Likeness: The Church as the Image of the Trinity* (Grand Rapids: Eerdmans, 1998), 35, 37.

34. Ibid.; quoting Joseph Ratzinger, *Introduction to Christianity* (London: Burns & Oates, 1969), 178.

35. Volf, *After Our Likeness*, 49.

36. Ibid., 58, quoting Joseph Ratzinger, *Das neue Volk Gottes: Entwürfe zur Ekklesiologie*, 2nd ed. (Düsseldorf: Patmos-Verlag, 1977), 169.

As a consequence, "loss of this element of unity with the successors of Peter wounds the church 'in the essence of its being as church.'"[37]

At this point a crucial question, as Volf notes, is whether there really are ecclesial subjects that constitute this one body.[38] Ratzinger's view of the persons of the Trinity as "pure relations" moves logically from the unity of God in the one substance—and that conceived in idealist terms—to a "monistic structure for the church."[39]

As an abstraction, the number one is vastly overrated. Yet at the heart of biblical faith is the mystery of the Trinity, where the one God who is the ontological source of all being is just as essentially three persons. Where unity means unicity, however, difference must finally be sacrificed to sameness: what I (borrowing on Tillich's typology) have been referring to as the metaphysics of overcoming estrangement, fearful of meeting a stranger (Westphal's diagnosis of "ontological xenophobia"). All that is real must flow down this hierarchically arranged ladder from its unitary source.[40] As William James finely observed, monism is "totality," which aims at "neither variety nor unity taken singly."[41] Without the abstract antitheses, there can be no synthesis. However, the latter is neither a single particular nor a communion of various particulars but the conflation of opposites in an exalted whole.

As in Adam's ecclesiology, the Spirit indwells the community rather than believers; the church as a whole is Christ's ongoing incarnation in the world. It is this concept of unity that seems to be the fundamental presupposition of the approach represented by Ratzinger, and we will meet it again (below) in other proposals.

Augustine's *totus Christus* reappears with a vengeance in Radical Orthodoxy, as I have already indicated, moving well beyond the original formulation. "Indeed, via the resurrected body of the Lamb in the heart of the eternal city," writes Milbank, drawing on Nicholas of Cusa, "the Bride Jerusalem is equalized with God and drawn through deification entirely into the life of the Trinity. . . . Even hierarchical structures are erected by fashioned consensus, beginning with God himself."[42] Through such retrievals, Milbank suggests, we can transcend both the

---

37. Volf, *After Our Likeness*, 59, quoting Joseph Cardinal Ratzinger, *Gemeinschaft gerufen: Kirche heute verstehen*, 2nd ed. (Freiburg, 1992), 88. On the same page, quoting Ratzinger's "Die Kirche *in die Welt*," 178–79, Volf notes Ratzinger's claim, albeit before Vatican II, "The *sedes apostolica* as such is Rome, so that one can say that *communio catholica* = *communio Romana*; only those who commune with Rome are standing in the true, that is, catholic *communio*; whomever Rome excommunicates is no longer in the *communio catholica*, that is, in the unity of the church."

38. Volf, *After Our Likeness*, 67: "As in Nietzsche's anthropology, so also here: the agent is nothing; the activity is everything. Nor does Ratzinger shy away from expressly drawing this conclusion; there is no 'I' remaining behind the deeds and actions of the divine persons; their actions *are* their 'I.'"

39. Ibid., 69–71.

40. See Colin Gunton, *The One, the Three, and the Many: God, Creation and the Culture of Modernity*, The 1992 Bampton Lectures (Cambridge: Cambridge University Press, 1993).

41. William James, *Pragmatism: A New Name for Some Old Ways of Thinking* (New York: Longmans, Green, & Co., 1912), 130.

42. Ibid., 132.

Reformation and Trent, since "Protestantism privileged the historical body of Christ, Trent the sacramental body. Equally, this meant a preference either for Scripture or Tradition, respectively."[43] Milbank revives Origen's ascent of mind, including ecclesiological universalism, a cosmic Christology, and an exemplarist atonement doctrine—all subservient to the notion of the church as the extension of the incarnation—indeed, even of Christ's atoning work. Through the Holy Spirit, "the Bride" is "enhypostasized by the descent of the Spirit (in her full eschatological plenitude of commencement and ending) and so as *equal* with the Bridegroom."[44]

Far from mediating the presence of Christ, the Spirit merges with the church to fill the vacuum left by Christ's absence with pure presence. Milbank even adds, "For atonement to be ontologically actual, Christ's appeal must still after all work within history: there must really in some sense exist the *ecclesia*. His example must somewhere and somehow be followed, and this mimesis must clearly involve further acts of mutual atoning which realize the hypostatic presence of the Holy Spirit."[45] Once again, the foil for Milbank's account is Luther's alleged "nominalist univocalism," with its "extrinsicist, imputational account of grace," at odds with the view that "everything, for Aquinas, not just humanity, is already as itself more than itself, and *this more is in some sense a portion of divinity*" (emphasis added).[46]

We are far from the world of ancient treaties, where grace refers to a merciful pardon and a restored relationship with the suzerain. Instead, there is the ontic hierarchy of theurgic Neoplatonism, which was appropriated especially in Dionysian mysticism.[47] In ecclesiastical terms, this means that "the Bishop is above the laity, but the whole Church is above the Bishop."[48]

The neo-Hegelian *totus Christus* eclipses both the natural body of the ascended Christ, which is sublated by the ecclesial body, as well as the natural bodies of individual believers, who together form that ecclesial body. Hegel himself was indebted to Dionysian mysticism, especially through Eckhart and Boehme, and we discern echoes of the "spiritual hierarchy" in the ever-ascending syntheses that assimilate the particular and finite to the unity of Absolute Spirit.[49] Even in Milbank's appeal to this Dionysian tradition, we are reminded that sublation, not mediation, is the upshot of Hegelian logic. Merold Westphal points to this in

43. Ibid., 133–34.
44. Ibid., 208.
45. John Milbank, *Being Reconciled: Ontology and Pardon* (London and New York: Routledge, 2003), 42.
46. Ibid., 110–11, 115.
47. Ibid., 130. Discovered in the late Renaissance to have been written probably in the fifth or sixth centuries (perhaps by a Syrian monk), the texts can be found in translation in *Pseudo-Dionysius: The Complete Works*, trans. Colm Luibheid and Paul Rorem (New York: Paulist Press, 1987).
48. Ibid., 131.
49. Dionysian mysticism, mediated by Meister Eckhart and Jacob Boehme, is closely explored by Ernst Benz, *The Mystical Sources of German Romantic Philosophy*, trans. Blair R. Reynolds and Eunice M. Paul (Allison Park, PA: Pickwick, 1983); and O'Regan, *The Heterodox Hegel*, 249–70.

connection with Hegel's view of freedom: although one finds oneself in the other, both are finally assimilated to the whole, "and *only the Whole is free.*"[50]

In Graham Ward's *Cities of God,* as with the Origenist tradition generally, the absence of Jesus is only apparent.[51] It is not a loss, but merely a "displacement," "dissemination," and "expansion."[52] Christianity stands "opposed also to the endless deferral and unquenchable grief for a lost body," especially since the kingdom is now being realized "*through our labourings*" (emphasis added).[53] "Matter itself is rendered metaphorical within the construal of such logic."[54] Once the historical body of Jesus has been rendered transcorporeal ("sexed and not sexed," for example), Ward can understandably write, "Not-having the body of Christ is not a lack, not a negative: because Christ's withdrawal of his body makes possible a greater identification with that body. In fact, the Church in its identification becomes the body of Christ."[55] Not surprisingly, Milbank, Pickstock, and Ward conclude that in the consummation we finally will be "freed from our bodily carapace."[56]

So once again we return to Origen's and Schleiermacher's thesis: the disappearance of Jesus is not a problem because he did not really disappear after all, but is just as present—or rather, more fully present—today in and as the church. "The body of Christ keeps absenting itself from the text," says Ward. "Where does it go? What the body is *replaced by* is the witness of the Church" (emphasis added).[57] "The Ascension is the final displacement of the body of the gendered Jew. Again, let me emphasise, that displacement is not the *erasure* but the *expansion* of the body" (emphasis added).[58] Yet if Jesus of Nazareth is everywhere, is he anywhere, and would not this constitute erasure? And what could the *replacement* of Christ's natural body mean other than *erasure*? Despite his disclaimer that his "interpretation of the ascension is not in accord with Origen's 'ascension of the mind rather than of the body,'"[59] Ward's arguments do little to allay the contrary judgment. According to this rather extreme version of the notion of Christ's ubiquity, "We have no access to the body of the gendered Jew. . . . It is pointless because the Church is now the body of Christ, so to understand the body of Jesus we can only examine what the Church is and what it has to say concerning the nature of that body as scripture attests it" (emphasis added).[60]

Ward's proposal is, if anything, more complete than the related versions of *totus Christus* thus far explored in its substitution of the natural and eucharistic

---

50. Merold Westphal, *Overcoming Onto-theology: Toward a Postmodern Christian Faith* (New York: Fordham University Press, 2001), 200–205.

51. Graham Ward, *Cities of God* (London and New York: Routledge, 2000), 93.

52. Ibid., 93–94.

53. Ibid., 94.

54. Ibid., 98–99.

55. Ibid., 102, 108.

56. John Milbank and Catherine Pickstock, *Truth in Aquinas* (New York: Routledge, 2001), 37.

57. Ibid., 109.

58. Ibid., 112.

59. Ibid.

60. Ibid.

bodies for the ecclesial. "As Gregory of Nyssa points out, in his thirteenth sermon on Song of Songs," Ward quotes, "'he who sees the Church looks directly at Christ.'"[61]

Contemporary Eastern Orthodox Ecclesiologies: John Zizioulas

The East and West share many of the same patristic resources and even similar trajectories of Christian Neoplatonism in Byzantine and medieval theologies. Maximus and Dionysius represent a legacy common to both traditions. Nevertheless, by concentrating on the person of the Father as the source of the Trinity rather than the divine substance that they share, the East has been more wary of sacrificing the many to the one.

Especially in *Being as Communion*, John Zizioulas has translated this heritage in a somewhat Western idiom. Throughout his work, Zizioulas points up the distinct contributions of each divine person to the economy of grace. The Father and the Son work *within* history, but the Son *becomes* flesh. Yet precisely because the Spirit is *beyond* history, he can raise the Son from death and "bring into history the last days, the *eschaton*. Hence the first fundamental particularity of Pneumatology is its eschatological character. The Spirit makes of Christ an eschatological being, the 'last Adam.'"[62] This pneumatological grounding accounts for the "corporate personality": Christ as not only an individual "one," but "many."[63] The Spirit not only *brings about* this communion (*koinōnia*), but *is* or *constitutes* this communion. Because of the Spirit, Christ has a body—the church.[64]

If this is so, then we cannot say (as Rahner and Roman Catholic ecclesiology typically do) "that the 'essence' of the Church lies in the universal Church." Rather, "the one Christ event takes the form of *events* (plural), which *are as primary ontologically as the one Christ event itself*. The local Churches are as primary in ecclesiology as the universal Church. No priority of the universal over the local Church is conceivable in such an ecclesiology."[65] Further, eschatology keeps ecclesiology from becoming a mere affirmation of a historical institution.[66] Christ *in-stitutes* the church; the Spirit *con-stitutes* it.[67]

There is much here that I find not only consistent with but also useful for elaborating a covenantal ecclesiology. At the same time, Zizioulas's account suffers from some of the same weaknesses as Ratzinger's, particularly as both are deeply indebted to idealist notions of the "corporate personality" that finally sur-

---

61. Ibid., 116.

62. John Zizioulas, *Being as Communion: Studies in Personhood and the Church* (Crestwood, NY: St. Vladimir's Seminary Press, 2002), 130.

63. Ibid.

64. Ibid., 131.

65. Ibid., 132–33.

66. Ibid., 140.

67. Ibid. "The fact that Orthodoxy has not experienced situations similar to those of the Western churches, such as the problem of clericalism, anti-institutionalism, Pentecostalism, etc. may be taken as an indication that *for the most part* Pneumatology has saved the life of Orthodoxy up to now" (140).

renders the many to the one after all. A covenantal head is a fundamentally different concept than a corporate personality. Where the former affirms the representative character of the head, the latter assimilates the many to the one: *totus Christus* now understood as a single (corporate) person more than as a communion of saints. To be sure, his version is different from Ratzinger's in that each believer "is the whole Christ." But what about the passages (esp. Eph. 4; Rom. 12; and 1 Cor. 12) where we are reminded that each member has its role *in* the body, not that each member *is* the whole body?

Zizioulas draws a sharp contrast between biological individuals (inherently autonomous and nonrelational) and ecclesial persons, so once again the focus shifts from the covenantal domain of faithfulness, transgression, and forgiveness to the sphere of ontological binaries. Consequently, Zizioulas (like Ratzinger) moves from the ontological to the forensic rather than vice versa. According to a covenantal view, even the ontological fact of death is the sanction for violation of this office (Gen. 2:17; 3:3–5, 14–19; Rom. 3:23; 1 Cor. 15:56). However, for Zizioulas, there is first of all an ontic fissure in nature itself as created by God that must be healed by baptism, transforming us from biological individuals to ecclesial persons. According to Zizioulas, we can even speak of Christ as both an individual and as a person; according to the latter, he is a "corporate personality," the one subject that is the church.[68] Yet, according to Zizioulas's definition of *individual*, this places the biological subject, Jesus of Nazareth, under a category of ontological fault, making his historical identity at the very least ambiguous in its saving efficacy before or since his ascension. "To eat the body of Christ and to drink his blood," according to Zizioulas, "means to participate in him who took upon himself the 'multitude' . . . in order to make of them a single body, his body."[69] Yet in his view, this means that in Christ the multitude constituted biologically as fallen *individuals* becomes ontologically constituted as one *ecclesial person*, even if each person is a microcosm of the whole. Does plurality therefore belong to the negative side of the ontological ledger after all? Again, the Hegelian shadow appears, with the finite individual representing an ontological deficit that must be overcome by sublation in the whole.

In contrast to the "corporate personality," the covenantal headship of Christ does not save us from biological (i.e., ontological) individuality, but redeems us from the condemnation and tyranny of being individuals *who are turned in on ourselves*. Thus, from a covenantal perspective, there are no "biological individuals" as described by Zizioulas, but only persons created in God's image who nevertheless deny and suppress their covenantal relationship with God and fellow creatures. The contrast drawn by the New Testament between "in Adam" and "in Christ" does not correspond to any map of ontological binaries. Even the Pauline "flesh" and "Spirit" contrast is eschatological, identifying one as either dead in

68. Ibid., esp. 130–49.
69. Cited by Miroslav Volf, *After Our Likeness*, 98, from John Zizioulas in John Zizioulas, J. M. R. Tillard, and J. J. von Allmen, *L'eucharistie* (Paris: Mame, 1970), 55.

Adam or alive in Christ.[70] Consequently, instead of Zizioulas's heavily freighted distinction between individual and person, we can distinguish between Christ as covenant-head of his *ecclesial* body (which can be expanded in the event of communion) and his *natural* body (which cannot).

In its eucharistic assembly, then, the "multitude" remain as ontologically diverse and distinct as they are covenantally united as one body. It is precisely in the diversity of gifts bestowed by the *head* on "*each one individually*" that the *whole body* receives what it needs (1 Cor. 12:4–31; cf. Eph. 4:7–13). Even Christ is one of the "many" who constitute this body, though he constitutes it as *head*.

Totus Christus and Recent Protestant Ecclesiologies

As we will see below, even Calvin could appropriate Augustine's notion of *totus Christus*, though within the wider scope of a doctrine of union with Christ that is more Pauline than Platonic. However, a radical (more Origenist and Neoplatonic) version runs through Schleiermacher and Hegel all the way to Cardinal Newman and Teilhard de Chardin; it can also be discerned in the recent systems of Robert Jenson and Radical Orthodoxy.

Exhibiting this danger of confusing the hypostatic union of God and humanity in Jesus Christ with the mystical union of the saints with God in Christ, Charles Gore wrote at the end of the nineteenth century,

> The Church embodies the same principle as the "Word made flesh," that is, the expression and communication of the spiritual and the divine through what is material and human. . . . But this visible, material society exists to receive, to embody and to communicate spiritual life. And this life is none other than the life of the Incarnate.[71]

As John Webster points out, this emphasis on the church as an extension of Christ's person and work, which owes "as much to Hegelian theory of history as to theology, . . . has become something of a commonplace in some now dominant styles of modern theology and theological ethics." God's work of reconciling the world in Christ merges with the church's moral action.[72]

Interpreted within a more cultural-linguistic paradigm, Stanley Hauerwas, Timothy Gorringe, and others join this trajectory. As I observed in chapter 1, "incarnational" is becoming a dominant adjective in evangelical circles, often losing the specificity and uniqueness of Christ's person and work. As Webster acknowledges, these approaches often appeal to the Trinity and grace. "Never-

---

70. This point is explored in chapter 1 of my first volume in this series, *Covenant and Eschatology: The Divine Drama* (Louisville, KY: Westminster John Knox Press, 2002).

71. Charles Gore, *The Incarnation of the Son of God* (London: Murray, 1892), 219. Cf. Lewis Smedes, "The Incarnation: Trends in Modern Anglican Thought" (PhD diss., Free University of Amsterdam, 1953). I am grateful to Michelle Elizabeth Hahne for pointing out this reference in a student paper.

72. John Webster, *Word and Church* (Edinburgh: T&T Clark, 2001), 226.

theless, they are characteristically less drawn to expansive depiction of the sheer gratuity of God's act of reconciliation, and more commonly offer lengthy accounts of the acts of the church, sacramental and moral, often through the idiom of virtues, habits and practices."[73] According to Timothy Gorringe, "the community of reconciliation" is "the means through which atonement is effected, which is the reason, presumably, Christ bequeathed to us not a set of doctrines or truths, but a community founded on betrayal and the survival of betrayal."[74] The force of Christ's completed work, Webster judges, "is simply lost" in this inflated talk of the church's redemptive activity.[75] Christ's person and work easily becomes a "model" or "vision" for ecclesial action (*imitatio Christi*), rather than a completed event to which the church offers its witness.

Following in this trajectory, Robert Jenson denies that the church is "an *opus ad extra* as is the creation, even when it is perfected in God"; rather, "the *totus Christus* is Christ with the church."[76] While we do not place our faith in the world, "we do place our faith in the church," says Jenson, recognizing that this "takes the Catholic side" in the ecumenical debate in favor of the church as the instrument as well as the fruit of salvation.[77] Jenson goes so far as to say that the modernist Catholic Alfred Loisy's infamous quip, "Jesus announced the Kingdom, but it was the church that came," despite his sarcastic intent, "states the exact truth."[78] Jenson will not allow that the "body of Christ" is an analogy. "In the complex of these [Pauline] passages, there is no way to construe 'body' as a simile or other trope that does not make mush of Paul's arguments."[79] Bodies are simply a person's availability to others, he argues. "For the proposition that the church is a human body of the risen Jesus to be ontically and straightforwardly true, all that is required is that Jesus indeed be the Logos of God, so that his self-understanding determines what is real."[80]

Radicalizing the Lutheran interpretation of the *communicatio idiomatum*, Jenson seems to be saying that in his ascended state, even Jesus' human body need not have the properties that render it genuinely human. Besides erasing the distinction between Christ and the church, this interpretation loses the Reformation's insistence that grace redeems and restores nature rather than adding something to it or elevating it to a supernatural status. Humanity is absorbed into deity, and the church is the site of this new being.

73. Ibid.

74. Cited by Webster, "Christ, Church and Reconciliation," in *Word and Church*, 217, from Timothy Gorringe, *God's Just Vengeance* (London: Verso, 1991), 268.

75. Ibid. Webster (*Word and Church*, 218–20) evaluates Miroslav Volf's *Exclusion and Embrace* (Nashville: Abingdon, 1996) along similar lines.

76. Robert Jenson, *Systematic Theology*, vol. 2, *The Works of God* (New York: Oxford University Press, 1999), 167.

77. Ibid.

78. Ibid., 170.

79. Robert Jenson, *Systematic Theology*, vol. 1, *The Triune God* (New York: Oxford University Press, 1997), 205.

80. Ibid., 206.

Like Milbank and Ward, Jenson's ontology renders natural bodies unstable, questionable, indefinite, and infinitely expandable. He quotes Geoffrey Preston: "The relation of the Church to Christ is not 'like' that of a man's body to the man himself. It *is* that of Christ's body to the Lord himself."[81] Recognizing that the identity must leave room for referring distinctly "to the one and then to the other," Jenson nevertheless appeals explicitly to Hegel and Fichte in developing his constructive proposal.[82] "The church with her sacraments," Jenson summarizes, "is the object as which we may intend Christ because she is the object as which he intends himself." Therefore, "the relation between Christ as a subject and the church with her sacraments is precisely that between transcendental subjectivity and the objective self; . . . the church is the risen Christ's Ego."[83]

Fellow Lutheran Mark C. Mattes points out that Jenson represents the growing tendency to prioritize ecclesiology over soteriology, the church over the gospel, and the inner word over the external Word. Jenson and his circle are oriented toward a theology of "'supernaturalizing the natural,' as John Milbank has interpreted Blondel's and de Lubac's work."[84] The problem with this view is not its refusal of autonomy to creation; rather, it is that its conception of participation is "configured within a transcendence dominated by the metaphor of 'ascent.' This implies that our agency has bearing *coram deo*."

> It ignores the truth that before God, we are fundamentally passive—solely receivers. . . . The moral life that accords with such passivity is active service to the neighbor, and the appropriate metaphor for the Christian life is "descent" in charity toward others. . . . In a radical departure from the Lutheran affirmation that the church is an assembly of people shaped by the gospel's message and sacraments, Jenson believes that God expresses his identity to the world as a creature, the body of the church.[85]

According to Jenson, the church as "the body of the *totus Christus*" is "that creature that makes sense of the rest."[86]

Often overlooked in contemporary ecclesiologies is Dietrich Bonhoeffer's doctoral thesis.[87] Painfully aware of the triumph of Hegelian monism in both church and state, Bonhoeffer was especially critical of the fusion of Christ and his church, and he already identified this tendency with philosophical idealism. Like Platonism, idealist philosophy transforms ethical categories (like sin and

---

81. Jenson, *Systematic Theology*, 2:212, quoting Goeffrey Preston, *Faces of the Church* (Grand Rapids: Eerdmans, 1997), 89.

82. Ibid., 213–15.

83. Ibid., 215; cf. George Hunsinger's "Robert Jenson's *Systematic Theology*: A Review Essay," *Scottish Journal of Theology* 55 (2002): 196.

84. Mark C. Mattes, *The Role of Justification in Contemporary Theologies* (Grand Rapids: Eerdmans, 2004), 125.

85. Ibid.

86. Ibid., citing Jenson, *Systematic Theology*, 2:159.

87. Dietrich Bonhoeffer, *Communio: A Theological Study of the Sociology of the Church*, in *Dietrich Bonhoeffer Works*, German original ed. Joachim von Soosten, English edition ed. Clifford J. Green and trans. Reinhard Krauss and Nancy Lukens (Minneapolis: Fortress Press, 1998).

grace) into ontological ones (like time and eternity), assimilating eschatology to the plane of immanence, and reducing the many to the one. Thus the state is the highest form of collectivity.[88]

The price of this total immanence is high: the particular and corporeal are assimilated to the universal and ideal. Idealism's concept of "the spirit as immanent" means that "the I is person insofar as it is spirit," and ever since Kant the idealists argued that "the universal and spirit become identical, and the individual loses value," Bonhoeffer explains. Accordingly, "*It is the destiny of the human species to be absorbed into the realm of reason, to form a realm of completely similar and harmonious persons, defined by universal reason or by one spirit and separated only by their different activities.* Most importantly, however, this union of like beings never leads *to the concept of community, but only to the concept of sameness, of unity.*"[89] In this view, there is no concept of voluntary choice or of sin.[90] The price of idealism is not only the fusion of persons, but also "involves the attributing to the human spirit absolute value that can only be ascribed to divine spirit."[91]

By contrast, biblical faith takes its bearings from the Creator-creature rather than the spirit-matter or one-and-many dilemma. Only before the God of Scripture—who is absolutely other than humanity—do we come truly to recognize that we are ethically responsible for our fellow human persons.[92] Once more the close connection between "meeting a stranger" as a discourse on ethical more than ontological questions is recognized in Bonhoeffer's treatment. "*Social relations must be understood, then, as purely interpersonal and building on the uniqueness and separateness of persons.* The person cannot be overcome by apersonal spirit; no 'unity' can negate the plurality of persons."[93]

This does not lead Bonhoeffer to embrace individualism, but rather to a view that I am calling covenantal *koinōnia*: a community of persons. "God does not desire a history of individual human beings, but the history of the human *community.* However, God does not want a community that absorbs the individual into itself, but a community of *human beings.* In God's eyes, community and individual exist in the same moment and rest in one another," yet without any "sense of fusion."[94]

We can see again how different ecclesiology looks when we fix our attention again on the economy of Jesus' coming and going and coming back, when Bonhoeffer counters the idealist interpretation of "body": "But Paul does not want to make the complete identification, because for him also Christ is with God. He has ascended into heaven (Eph. 4:8ff.; 1 Thess. 4:16; 1 Cor. 15:23). We await his coming (Phil. 3:20)," and this gives rise to the pneumatologically determined

88. Ibid., 37.
89. Ibid., 43, emphasis original.
90. Ibid., 48.
91. Ibid., 49.
92. Ibid., 49–50.
93. Ibid., 56.
94. Ibid., 80, 84.

character of this in-between status of the church.[95] Although the organic and biological metaphors employed in Scripture remain critically important, Bonhoeffer reminds us that "as the 'body of Christ,'" the church is "invisible as an eschatological entity." Furthermore, "Paul takes the idea of organism from Greek tradition, but reworks it. . . . The theory of organism in Roman Catholicism, biology, or the philosophy of the state ranks the collective above the individual. For Paul, only Christ exists 'before' and 'above' individuals."[96]

In view of this survey, Farrow seems quite justified in concluding, "Looking away from Jesus has become a natural reflex."

> Ancients and moderns are allied in misconstruing the alienation between God and humanity in terms of epistemological or ontological distance. Consequently they are allied also in constructing systems of mediation which, even where Christological, operate by denying Christ's particularity. For the only way to overcome alienation, thus understood, is to eradicate distance and otherness: to unite, to homogenize, to divinize; in effect, to universalize the incarnation. And there is no way to do that without turning away from the human Jesus, or indeed from what makes *us* human.[97]

PRIVILEGING THE MANY: CONTRASTING CHRIST WITH THE CHURCH

If, according to Roman Catholic ecclesiology, the faith of the believer tends to be absorbed into the faith of the church, the obverse is evident in free-church ecclesiologies. In evangelical contexts, the church is often regarded chiefly as a resource for fellowship. For the uniquely individualized personal relationship with Jesus, the church is not only dispensable but perhaps also a hindrance to personal growth, according to recent works by evangelical leaders considered below.[98] At least in more popular forms (viz., Anglo-American revivalism), evangelicalism has frequently adopted a contractual more than covenantal view both of union (soteriology) and communion (ecclesiology). Especially when wedded to an Arminian soteriology, a voluntaristic emphasis emerges, with human decision as the

---

95. Ibid., 137.
96. Ibid., 141.
97. Douglas Farrow, *Ascension and Ecclesia* (Edinburgh: T&T Clark, 1999), 255.
98. At least in the history of pietism, the individual or circle of believers thought to be more truly earnest about the Christian life remained members of the wider church. In many forms of non-denominational evangelicalism, especially since the "Jesus movement" of the 1970s, church membership is optional or even eliminated. Seeking to replicate the worship of the first Christians (with dubious historical interpretations), the house-church movement is one of many examples of the "triumph of the laity," as it is sometimes called. As George Barna observes (and celebrates), the coming generation that he identifies as the "Revolutionaries" insists on finding forms of spiritual edification and community alternative to the organized church (in George Barna and Thom Black, *The Revolutionaries' Handbook* [Carol Stream, IL: Tyndale House Publishers, 2005]). Just how revolutionary this is may be open to debate, since pietism and revivalism have a long history of such experimentation.

contractual basis for both conversion and ecclesial existence.[99] We have seen how evangelical theologians often separate the sacraments from their reality, so that instead of being means of grace, they are means of commitment. Once again, human choice and agency take precedence over divine election and redemption, although in individualistic terms.

Where the first trajectory (unity over plurality) seems more consistent in its development, this second trajectory can be recognized in two quite distinct trends: evangelical pietism/revivalism and the loose affiliation of "dialectical" theologians: Friedrich Gogarten, Rudolph Bultmann, Emil Brunner, and Karl Barth. Bultmann and Brunner did not get far beyond their mentors' reduction of the kingdom of God to the individual's inner relation to God, and weakened ecclesiologies (including sacramental theologies) are evident in neo-orthodoxy generally.[100] I will interact first with Barth and then with the ecclesiological tendencies of a more pietistic form of evangelical Protestantism.

Karl Barth

The sources of Barth's ecclesiological reflections are far from contractual, individualistic, and synergistic. His sometimes sharp criticism of pietism is actually well-known in this regard.[101] "The 'pillar and ground of truth' (1 Tim. 3:15), the salt of the earth, the light of the world, the city set on a hill," he wrote, "is the community of God and not the individual Christian as such, although the latter has within it his assured place, his indispensable function, and his unshakable personal promise. It is not he but the *ecclesia una sancta catholica et apostolica* that stands (in close connexion with the Holy Spirit) in the third article of the Creed."[102] The title of his project, *Church Dogmatics*, his subordination of theology to proclamation, and his role in the confessing church movement exhibit his commitment to the visible church. However, his attraction to an independent ecclesiology and, finally, his explicit rejection of infant baptism in IV/4 point up what seems to me to be the dominant tendency of his thought from the *Römerbrief* onward, with respect to the visible church.

Barth's sharp distinction (sometimes even contrast) between Christ and the church is motivated by a variety of factors. We have already encountered his neo-Zwinglian view of the sacraments, underscoring once again the close relationship

99. See, for example, Stanley Grenz, *Theology for the Community of God* (Nashville: Broadman & Holman 1997), 611.

100. Dulles, *Models of the Church*, 44, observes, "Rudolph Sohm, for instance, taught that the essential nature of the Church stands in antithesis to all law. Emil Brunner, in *The Misunderstanding of the Church*, argued that the Church in the biblical sense (the *Ecclesia*) is not an institution but a brotherhood (*Brüderschaft*); it is 'a pure communion of persons [*Personengemeinschaft*].' On this ground Brunner rejected all law, sacrament, and priestly office as incompatible with the true being of the Church."

101. These differences are recounted and interpreted in fascinating detail in Eberhard Busch, *Karl Barth and the Pietists*, trans. Daniel W. Bloesch (Downers Grove, IL: InterVarsity Press, 2004).

102. Karl Barth, *CD* IV/1:150.

of one's sacramental theology to one's ecclesiology. Negatively, Barth's ecclesiological reflections were shaped in antithesis to the widespread assimilation of Christology to ecclesiology. The true church belongs to the "submarine island of the 'Now' of divine revelation" that lies beneath observable reality.[103] In *Romans*, he speaks explicitly of "the *contrast* between the Gospel and the Church" (emphasis added).[104] Christ is the only sacrament. In fact, not only is there a difference between the sign and its eschatological fullness; the "invisible church" also is taken to extreme limits when Barth writes, "In the heavenly Jerusalem of Revelation nothing is more finally significant than *the church's complete absence*: 'And I saw no temple therein'" (emphasis added).[105] Totalizing ecclesiologies may be faulted for having an overrealized eschatology. However, Barth's dualistic ecclesiology is not underrealized; he simply does not have any place for the church in the consummation. Therefore, "the activity of the community is related to the Gospel only in so far as it is no more than a crater formed by the explosion of a shell and seeks to be no more than a void in which the Gospel reveals itself."[106]

One of Barth's great achievements was to turn attention back to Jesus. He is properly concerned to see that Christ's reconciling work is in need of no further supplementation, no historical development, thus countering liberal historicism and synergism. The church is not an extension of Christ's person and work.[107] The church simply acknowledges and witnesses to what has been accomplished in this redemptive event. Barth recognizes the difference between covenantal *koinōnia* that leads to communion of the many and a Neoplatonic *methexis* or Hegelian synthesis that generates an ontic fusion. "What constitutes the being of man in this [covenantal] sphere is not a oneness of being but a genuine togetherness of being with God."[108]

However, Barth's Christology also exhibits a monistic tendency: one electing object and one elected subject, a single event with dialectically related facets rather than an unfolding history of redemption through successive events and covenants. History (what Barth calls "history so-called") tends to be sublated into the eternal present. It is "not history but truth" that is at issue in revelation.[109] Unlike the monistic trend of neo-Hegelian thought, which sacrifices the particular to the universal, Barth's "one" is driven by his particularism: the one individual, Jesus Christ, and his history. There does not seem to be any temporal sequence in God's redemptive acts. These events become, as Barth himself says,

103. Karl Barth, *The Epistle to the Romans*, trans. Edwyn C. Hoskyns from the 6th ed. (London: Oxford University Press, 1933), 304; cf. 396 for the same analogy.

104. Ibid., 340.

105. Ibid. That this is the expression of 1920 should perhaps be taken into account here.

106. Barth, *Epistle to the Romans*, 36.

107. Barth, *CD* IV/3:7, 327; IV/2:132.

108. Barth, *CD* III/2:141.

109. Karl Barth, *The Word of God and the Word of Man*, trans. Douglas Horton (New York: Harper & Bros., 1957), 66, 72.

"the same thing."[110] This has tremendous consequences for Barth's treatment of the economy within which ecclesiology is situated.

As critical as it is to maintain with Barth the "once and for all" of Christ's atoning work and the uniqueness of his incarnation, the question arises as to the significance of the subsequent events in the economy of grace. Where the neo-Hegelian trend emphasized continuity between Jesus-history and church history, Barth underscored discontinuity—at least on the human, visible side. Even Jesus' resurrection and ascension, as well as Pentecost, serve merely to persuade us subjectively of what is already objectively true. They are not new events in the history of Jesus Christ and therefore of the elect community, which includes all people. The simultaneous humiliation-exaltation of Christ in his incarnation and atonement "does not need to be transcended or augmented by new qualities or further developments." His existence as the end of the old form of the world and the beginning of the new is already true "even without His resurrection and ascension."[111] The resurrection simply *reveals* "God's decision concerning the *cross*" (emphasis added).[112] It ensures that this event of Golgotha becomes "eternal history . . . and [is] therefore taking place here and now as it did then."[113] Even his return in glory "will still be the same revelation."[114]

Just as Barth does not seem to recognize any successive movement in the Jesus history from humiliation to exaltation, so also he sees no temporal movement from wrath to grace, death to life, condemnation to justification in personal experience.[115] Sanctification is not "a second divine action which either takes place simultaneously with [justification], or precedes or follows it in time. The action of God in His reconciliation of the world with Himself in Jesus Christ is unitary."[116] In the humiliation and exaltation of Christ, humanity is both justified and sanctified.[117]

Barth is understandably wary of pietistic schemes that psychologize salvation. However, it is not only pietism that is threatened by the marginalization of the Spirit's application of redemption, but any notion of creaturely "means of grace."[118] If the resurrection, the ascension, Pentecost, and the Parousia lie on the

---

110. Ibid., 90; cf. Barth, *CD* IV/2:107–9; cf. IV/2:118, 133, 140–41.

111. Barth *CD* IV/2:133.

112. Barth, *CD* IV/1:309.

113. Ibid., 313.

114. Ibid., 142.

115. This is a prominent criticism offered by G. C. Berkouwer: The "*transition* from wrath to grace *in history* is excluded and wrath is no more than 'the form of grace'" (*The Triumph of Grace in the Theology of Karl Barth*, trans. H. R. Boer [Grand Rapids: Eerdmans, 1956], esp. 253).

116. Barth, *CD* IV/1:501.

117. Ibid., 502.

118. There is no such thing as "means of grace" (IV/4:106, 129–30, etc. Cf. IV/3.2:756, 783, 790, 843–901). The sacraments (oddly, unlike preaching) stand on the side of the church's work and witness and not on the divine side of saving events. "The confession of Christians, their suffering, their repentance, their prayer, their humility, their works, baptism, too, and the Lord's Supper can and should attest this event but only attest it." Jesus Christ is the one sacrament (IV/1:296). "He is

"attestation" rather than "redemption" side of the line, it only follows that pneumatology, preaching, and sacraments can only fall on the "witness" side of human answering.

In traditional Reformed systems, the work of applying redemption (i.e., the *ordo salutis*) is treated under the work of the Spirit, albeit through the ordinary ministry of the church. In the neo-Hegelian perspective, this work tends to be identified with the church as the extension of Christ's person and work. For Barth, however, in the single event of Jesus Christ, everything of saving value has already happened, is happening, and will happen for everyone. We are contemporaries of Jesus of Nazareth in the eternal history of the covenant. Conversion, justification, sanctification, and calling have already occurred for every person, even if one is not subjectively aware of it.[119] If every person has already been united to Christ, then not only ecclesial agency but also the work of the Spirit is reduced to the noetic sphere.

However, with respect both to the *historia salutis* and the *ordo salutis*, the New Testament witnesses to genuine transitions. Jesus scolds his followers not for failing to recognize the simultaneity of his humiliation and exaltation, but for failing to realize that he first had to suffer *and then* enter into his glory (Luke 9:28–45; 24:26; Phil. 2; Heb. 1:3–4; 2:9–10; 1 Pet. 1:11). In the same way, there is a transition in the lives of individuals from wrath to grace (viz., John 1:12–13; 5:24; Rom. 4:22–25; 5:1; 6:2–11, 17–22; 7:6; 8:1, 9–17; 8:29–30; Eph. 2:1–5; 1 Pet. 2:9–10; 1 John 3:14). In both cases, the transition is historical, not merely noetic.[120]

Barth's tendency to assimilate the human to the divine evidences what von Balthasar referred to as "a dynamic and actualist theopanism, which we define as a monism of beginning and end (protology and eschatology)."[121] It seems to me that von Balthasar is justified in concluding, "Too much in Barth gives the impression that nothing much really happens in his theology of event and history, because everything has already happened in eternity."[122] Furthermore, a

---

He, and His work is His work, standing over against all Christian action, including Christian faith and Christian baptism" (IV/4:88, emphasis added). Not even the humanity of Christ is a direct revelation of God, despite its union with the Logos. Nevertheless, insofar as his deity is unveiled through the veil of his humanity, this alone attains the status of a sacrament (II/1:53). The whole of the final fragment of the *Church Dogmatics* follows a contrast between the Spirit's work and the purely human response of water baptism.

119. Barth, *CD* IV/1:148.

120. By organizing his Trinitarian theology around the motif of revelation (Revealer, Revelation, and Revealedness) in *CD* I/1, Barth already makes it difficult to see the work of the Spirit as involving anything more than bringing about an awareness of what is already true (one's election, reconciliation, justification, and sanctification) regardless.

121. Hans Urs von Balthasar, *The Theology of Karl Barth*, trans. Edward T. Oakes, SJ (San Francisco: Ignatius Press, 1992), 94.

122. Ibid., 371. Yet the same tendency is evident in Balthasar as well: history is so thoroughly recapitulated in Christ's death on the cross that, as Steffen Lösel puts it, "there is nothing essentially new to be expected in the future." See Steffen Lösel, "Murder in the Cathedral: Hans Urs von Balthasar's New Dramatization of the Doctrine of the Trinity," *Pro Ecclesia* V, no. 4 (Fall 1996): 432. Cf. von Balthsar, *Theo-Drama: Theological Dramatic Theory*, vol. 3, *The Dramatis Personae: The Person of Christ*, trans. Graham Harrison (San Francisco: Ignatius Press, 1992), 46–47, 74, 326.

purely actualistic understanding does not give place to creaturely agency. "Actualism, with its constant, relentless reduction of all activity to God the *actus purus*, leaves no room for any other center of activity outside of God." What the church says "cannot lay claim to divine authority," even a divine authority subordinate to the Word.[123] Thus, even in these later essays, von Balthasar concludes, "everything collapses back into that unholy dualism of *Romans*."[124]

Giving greater space to the postatonement history of Jesus, including the work of the Spirit in uniting us to Christ, is far from undermining and actually reinforces Barth's concern to protect the objectivity and particularity of Christology. For this subsequent work too is the work of God the Father, in Christ, by the Spirit. But added to this we will also need a robust affirmation of God's sovereign activity through creaturely means, actions that not only descend vertically but also extend horizontally through history.

In spite of the similar conflations of Christ and the church in the medieval era, Calvin's language for the church (explicitly rejecting Erasmus's *societas* and *communio* as translations of *koinōnia* in favor of stronger participationist language) is less reactionary than Barth's. Closer to Erasmus and Zwingli, it would seem, Barth characteristically refers to the church as the "community [*Gemeinde*]," society, and fellowship.[125] Any relation between God and humanity must be indirect, whether scripture, preaching, sacraments, or the church. For Barth, signs are really only signs insofar as they are themselves "bare and naked signs," to borrow the language rejected by the Reformed confessions. In terms of ecclesiology, the parallel and never-intersecting lines of divine and creaturely action mean an absolute duality between the visible and invisible church. Barth offers important warnings about collapsing Jesus Christ into the church.[126] However, in my view, it represents an overcorrection of the neo-Hegelian trajectory.

In contrast to the *univocal* tendencies of neo-Hegelian ecclesiologies and the *equivocal* tendencies of dialectical theology, an *analogical* relation between the sign and signified once again displays its potential for avoiding false alternatives. If the head must be distinguished from the members, a covenantal ecclesiology must nevertheless recognize the union mediated by the Spirit. It is the distinction between Christ and his church that makes pneumatological mediation both possible and necessary, but pneumatological mediation, as well as God's self-binding pledge, keeps the distinction from devolving into contrast or opposition.

---

123. Ibid., 105.

124. Ibid.

125. To be sure, Barth affirms the New Testament motif of *koinōnia*, founded on Trinitarian presuppositions: the persons (modes of being) in communion with each other, the communion between God and human beings, the communion of believers with each other and indeed with all creatures. Each communion is a different kind of *koinōnia*, but all are ultimately grounded in this Trinitarian perichoresis (ibid., 256–60). There are more recent historical reasons for preferring *Gemeinde* to *Kirche,* such as the way these are distinguished in German Protestantism.

126. Even better than Barth, in my estimation, is Webster's treatment in *Word and Church*, 227–40.

Again, the critical question is whether an event of revelation and redemption can be fully attributed *to God* yet *through creaturely mediation.*

Evangelical and Pentecostal Ecclesiologies

Quite different sources will have to be sought for the individualistic trend in more recent Christian movements. As I indicated above, much of evangelical and Pentecostal revivalism assumes a basically contractual view both of conversion and ecclesiality. This, no doubt, accounts in part for the global success of these movements, as the traditional bonds of community (natural and ecclesial) are increasingly replaced with the self-chosen affinities of personal choice in the marketplace. In his defense of free-church ecclesiology, Miroslav Volf is not uncritical:

> Whether they want to or not, Free Churches often function as "homogeneous units" specializing in the specific needs of specific social classes and cultural circles, and then in mutual competition try to sell their commodity at dumping prices to the religious consumer in the supermarket of life projects; the customer is king and the one best suited to evaluate his or her own religious needs and from whom nothing more is required than a bit of loyalty and as much money as possible. If the Free Churches want to contribute to the salvation of Christendom, they themselves must first be healed.[127]

Volf also points out that the privatization of faith that warps ecclesiology also makes free-church ecclesiologies more effective in contemporary cultures. He recognizes that when decisions have been privatized, "the transmission of faith" is threatened.[128] Yet he also judges that this adaptability to a culture of personal choice renders such ecclesiologies especially effective in our day.[129]

Stanley Grenz observes, "The post-Reformation discussion of the *vera ecclesia* formed the historical context for the emergence of the covenant idea as the focal understanding of the nature of the church."[130] With its insistence on the marks of the church, "the Reformers shifted the focus to Word and Sacrament," but the Anabaptists and Baptists "took yet a further step," advocating a congregational ecclesiology. "This view asserts that the true church is essentially people standing in voluntary covenant with God."[131] Free-church traditions remind us that the church is not a department of religious affairs under an empire, nation-state, or city council. Grenz properly reminds us that the church is "a spiritual people gathered out from the wider society," even when that society is nominally "Christian."[132] The Reformers often spoke in similar terms, insisting that the Word alone and not secular power should be allowed to persuade people of the

127. Volf, *After Our Likeness*, 18.
128. Ibid., 16.
129. Ibid., 17.
130. Grenz, *Theology for the Community of God*, 609.
131. Ibid., 610–11.
132. Ibid., 611.

gospel. Nevertheless, in actual practice, persecuted Anabaptists and Baptists seem to have had a better sense of the difference between church and society.

However, the Reformed confessions defined the visible church as believers *together with their children*. Yet even this violates the rule that is basic to congregational polity: a *voluntary* covenant, which not only entails the independence of local churches but also the independence of individuals within them until they mutually agree on the terms of that relationship. "No longer did the corporate whole take precedence over the individual as in the medieval model," notes Grenz. Rather, individuals formed the church rather than vice versa. "As a result, in the order of salvation the believer—and not the church—stands first in priority."[133] "Because the coming together of believers in mutual covenant constitutes the church, it is the covenant community of individuals," although it has a history as well.[134]

Taken to its extreme, contractual thinking easily leads to the view expressed by George Barna, an evangelical pioneer of church marketing: "Think of your church not as a religious meeting place, but as a service agency—an entity that exists to satisfy people's needs."[135] Not surprisingly, Barna has recently suggested that the institutional church is no longer relevant and should be replaced by informal gatherings for fellowship and Internet communities. He has even introduced a new demographic: the "Revolutionaries," the "millions of believers" who "have moved beyond the established church and chosen to be the church instead."[136] Barna explains his use of "church" (small *c*) to refer to "the congregation-based faith experience, which involves a formal structure, a hierarchy of leadership, and a specific group of believers" and "Church" (capital *C*) to denote "all believers in Jesus Christ, comprising the population of heaven-bound individuals who are connected by faith in Christ, regardless of their local church connections or involvement."[137] The Revolutionaries have found that in order to pursue an authentic faith, they had to abandon the church.[138]

However, Barna is hardly a dispassionate pollster; he takes his stand with the Revolutionaries, who will have an "unprecedented" effect on the institutional church.[139] Intimate worship, says Barna, does "not require a 'worship service,'" just a personal commitment to the Bible, prayer, and discipleship.[140] Offering a gloss on Acts 2:42–47, Barna suggests that preaching is simply "faith-based conversation," with the means of grace being merely "intentional spiritual growth," "love," "resource investment," "spiritual friendships," and "family faith."[141]

---

133. Ibid.
134. Ibid., 614.
135. George Barna, *Marketing the Church* (Colorado Springs: NavPress, 1988), 37
136. George Barna, *Revolution: Finding Vibrant Faith beyond the Walls of the Sanctuary* (Carol Stream, IL: Tyndale House Publishers, 2005), back-cover copy.
137. Ibid., x.
138. Ibid., 17.
139. Ibid.
140. Ibid., 22.
141. Ibid., 24–25.

Notice how all of the emphasis falls on what individuals do. There is no suggestion in this book that the church might be defined by God's work for us. "What
matters is not whom you associate with (i.e., a local church), but who you are,"
says Barna.[142] Given the statistics, churched Christians do not live any differently
from the rest of the population, so the usefulness of ecclesiastical involvement is
put in question.[143] "Scripture teaches us that devoting your life to loving God
with all your heart, mind, strength, and soul is what honors Him. Being part of
a local church may facilitate that. Or it might not."[144]

While, according to Barna, the Bible does not establish the idea of the local
church, much less its "corporate practices, rituals, or structures, it does, however,
offer direction regarding the importance and integration of fundamental spiritual disciplines into one's life."[145] He recognizes that the shift from the institutional church to "alternative faith communities" is largely due to market forces:

> Whether you examine the changes in broadcasting, clothing, music, invest-
> ing, or automobiles, producers of such consumables realize that Americans
> want control over their lives. The result has been the "niching" of Amer-
> ica—creating highly refined categories that serve smaller numbers of peo-
> ple, but can command greater loyalty (and profits). During the past three
> decades, even the local church has undergone such a niching process, with
> the advent of churches designed for different generations, those offering
> divergent styles of worship music, congregations that emphasize ministries
> of interest to specialized populations, and so forth. The church landscape
> now offers these boutique churches alongside the something-for-everybody
> megachurches. In the religious marketplace, the churches that have suffered
> most are those who stuck with the one-size-fits-all approach, typically prov-
> ing that one-size-fits-nobody.[146]

Furthermore, American consumers are demanding "practical faith experiences" over
doctrine, with "novelty and creativity, rather than predictability in religious experiences; and the need for time-shifting, rather than inflexible scheduling of religious
events."[147] Instead, the Revolutionaries are turning to house churches, family
churches (i.e., devotions with the immediate family), and what he calls "cyber-
church": "the range of spiritual experiences delivered through the Internet."[148]

However thin, there is a theology behind Barna's interpretation of Jesus as the
paradigmatic "Revolutionary," and it is basically that of the nineteenth-century
revivalist Charles Finney. According to Finney, conversion does not depend on a
miracle of divine grace, but is the result of individual decision, as any other
choice. Nor is it mediated by the regular ministry of Word and sacrament, but is

142. Ibid., 29.
143. Ibid., 30–31.
144. Ibid., 37.
145. Ibid.
146. Ibid., 62–63.
147. Ibid., 63.
148. Ibid., 65.

produced through "excitements sufficient to induce repentance," whatever the methods.[149] Just as rational methods produce results in industry (for Finney), market principles apply equally to the growth of believers, churches, and fast-food chains. The Pelagian tendency of his contractual approach is clearly evident in Barna's exhortation: "So if you are a Revolutionary, it is because you have sensed and responded to God's calling to be such an imitator of Christ. It is not a church's responsibility to make you into this mold. . . . The choice to become a Revolutionary—and it is a choice—is a covenant you make with God alone."[150]

A similar perspective can be found in numerous representative books by evangelical leaders in recent years. For the most committed members, a recent Willow Creek study concluded, the church is less important for continued growth. "These people have fully surrendered their lives to Christ."[151] For them, the "church's primary role is to provide serving opportunities."[152] The study found that a large number of these highly active members were dissatisfied with Willow Creek. "Why is there this disconnect?" the authors ask. "The quick answer: Because God 'wired' us first and foremost to be in growing relationship with him—not with the church."[153] Their conclusion is that God meant for his people to move from dependence on the ministry of the church to "personal spiritual practices," which include "prayer, journaling, solitude, studying Scripture—things that individuals do on their own to grow in their relationship with Christ." As believers mature, they should shift their interest from the church to their own private activities.[154] "The research strongly suggests that the church declines in influence as people grow spiritually."[155] Those who are "fully surrendered" are likened to young adults

---

149. In his *Lectures on Systematic Theology* (repr., Minneapolis: Bethany House Publishers, 1976), Charles Finney called the doctrine of original sin "anti-scriptural and nonsensical dogma" and rejected any notion of substitutionary atonement or justification by the imputation of Christ's righteousness to the believer. Besides being "legally impossible," such theories can only undermine "our own return to personal obedience . . . as a sine qua non of our salvation" (206). Justification depends moment-by-moment entirely on the "present, full, and perfect obedience" of the individual (46–57; cf. 320–22). As Finney put it, "The evangelist must produce excitements sufficient to induce sinners to repentance" (31). As a result, Finney conceived of the church not as a community of forgiven sinners but as a moral-reform society. In a letter on revival, Finney issued the following: "Now the great business of the church is to reform the world—to put away every kind of sin. The church of Christ was originally organized to be a body of reformers, . . . to reform individuals, communities, and governments." If the churches will not follow, they will simply have to be left behind, Finney contended:

> Law, rewards, and punishments—these things and such as these are the very heart and soul of moral suasion. . . . My brethren, if ecclesiastical bodies, colleges, and seminaries will only go forward—who will not bid them God speed? But if they will not go forward—if we hear nothing from them but complaint, denunciation, and rebuke in respect to almost every branch of reform, what can be done? (*Lectures on Revival*, 2nd ed. [New York, 1835], 184–204)

150. Barna, *Revolution*, 70.
151. Ibid., 39.
152. Ibid., 42.
153. Ibid., 39.
154. Ibid., 42–43.
155. Ibid., 44.

who no longer need the "parenting" of the church and can now fend for themselves.[156] "Our people need to learn to feed themselves through personal spiritual practices that allow them to deepen their relationship with Christ. . . . We want to transition the role of the church from spiritual parent to spiritual coach." The authors suggest the analogy of a trainer at the gym who provides a "personalized workout plan."[157]

Although a leader of the emerging church movement (often critical of the megachurch model), Dan Kimball advocates the same ecclesiological assumptions.[158] Across the spectrum of evangelicalism, the presupposition is widely shared that the individual believer's personal relationship with Jesus is immediate, inward, and direct, based on one's decision to accept Christ, and that membership in the church is also an individual decision that may (or in some cases may not) serve that basic contract. Sociologist Marsha Witten observes that secularization combines privatization, pluralization, and rationalization. Yet where the older theory (esp. of Max Weber) thought that this would inevitably destroy religion, evangelicalism has thrived precisely because it is already disposed to making faith a private matter, emphasizing its subjective (therapeutic) benefit more than its objective truth, and offers a variety of procedures, formulas, rules, and steps for personal transformation.[159]

Barna's message is hardly innovative. It is simply a radical version of a tendency throughout the history of religious enthusiasm to contrast the inner, moral, spiritual, individual, personal, and immediate with the external, theological, visible, corporate, and mediated gifts of God through the covenant community. Once direct, internal, and unmediated divine action is opposed to authorized, external, and mediated creaturely action in principle, both the magisterial authority of Scripture and the ministerial authority of the church are undermined. And when this quasi-gnostic presupposition is combined with an extreme theological voluntarism, the church becomes a demographic profile of consumers rather than a communion of saints. Contract, in effect, replaces covenant. No longer the creation of the Word, the church becomes a creation of the market.

Nevertheless this version of independent ecclesiology (indeed, independence from *ecclesia*) occupies a different orbit than traditional free-church thinking, whether in Puritan congregationalism or in Barth. In fact, Barth noted that this withdrawal into a "private Christianity" can be found in "all forms of mysticism and pietism" as well as in Kierkegaard. "As Calvin puts it (*Instit*[*utes*]. IV, I, 10), to try to be a Christian in and for oneself is to be a *transfuga et desertor religionis* and therefore not a Christian." Such a person "may even risk and forfeit his sal-

156. Ibid., 45.

157. Ibid., 65.

158. Dan Kimball, *The Emerging Church: Vintage Christianity for New Generations* (Grand Rapids: Zondervan, 2003), esp. 91.

159. Marsha Witten, *All Is Forgiven: The Secular Message in American Protestantism* (Princeton, NJ: Princeton University Press, 1998), 1–90.

vation, . . . his participation in the reconciliation of the world with God. It may be something akin to the sin against the Holy Ghost of which he is guilty. For the Holy Ghost leads him directly into the community and not into a private relationship with Christ."[160]

Among contemporary evangelical and Pentecostal theologians is a growing appreciation of the need for a more robust ecclesiology. Nevertheless, there is a broad tendency among many to skip over the Reformation resources in an effort to blend the best of free-church and Roman Catholic ecclesiologies.[161] As in the "converging captivities" discussed in chapter 3 (above), the ironic convergence of pietistic and neo-Hegelian interpretations threatens to repeat the heritage of Schleiermacher, Ritschl, Herrmann, and Harnack. My principal goal in this volume is to offer a covenantal account as a "third way."

Before turning to that account of unity and plurality, however, there is one more articulation of a free-church ecclesiology worth mentioning: Miroslav Volf's remarkable study *After Our Likeness* (Eerdmans, 1993). Engaging with Ratzinger (Pope Benedict) and Zizioulas, Volf's work begins with careful analysis and critique. Pointing out their common debt to idealism and existentialism, Volf argues (with Moltmann) that both Ratzinger and Zizioulas finally assimilate the many to the one: either to the one substance or to the one person of the Father, respectively. Hierarchy is for both the natural outworking of the ontological priority of the one over the many.[162] As plurality is folded into a hierarchical unity, "Creation and Fall coalesce into a single entity in Zizioulas's thinking. . . . The Fall consists merely in the revelation and actualization of the limitations and potential dangers inherent in creaturely existence."[163] "Hence salvation must *consist in an ontological deindividualization that actualizes their personhood*."[164] Volf judges, "In that case, however, the result would be precisely what Zizioulas is trying to avoid: Persons would disappear in 'one vast ocean of being,' namely, in the divine person."[165] As persons (rather than individuals), each believer "is the whole Christ."[166] Yet this is an eschatological reality that the Spirit performs in a fully realized manner at the Eucharist: a "retroactive causality."[167]

Consequently, according to Zizioulas, truth cannot involve the mediation of propositions (which would return the person to being an individual), but an event of communion.[168] "This is why God's word does not stand over against the church, nor even over against the world," says Volf. For Zizioulas, the Word refers

---

160. Barth, *CD* IV/1:689.

161. See, e.g., Amos Yong, *The Spirit Poured Out on All Flesh* (Grand Rapids: Baker Academic, 2005), esp. 121–25; and Veli-Matti Kärkkäinen, *An Introduction to Ecclesiology: Ecumenical, Historical, and Global Perspectives* (Downers Grove, IL: InterVarsity Press, 2002).

162. Volf, *After Our Likeness*, 78–79, emphasis in original.

163. Ibid., 81–82.

164. Ibid., 83, emphasis in original.

165. Ibid., 87.

166. Ibid., 89.

167. Ibid., 90.

168. Ibid., 94.

exclusively to a person, not to the preached or written Word. "Deindividualization demands direct or immediate relationships, and these in their turn demand the replacement of language by sacrament. This is why the Eucharist is *the* place where truth occurs. As a communal event *par excellence*, the Eucharist incarnates and actualizes our communion with the life and communion of the Trinity itself."[169] However, Volf declares that there could be no genuine faith without knowledge and assent as well as trust, requiring "verbal proclamation" of the gospel.[170]

Not only does such a saving deindividualization eliminate linguistic mediation; faith itself plays no role in Zizioulas's soteriology or ecclesiology, since even divinely given faith would include cognition. "Zizioulas's soteriology brings the notion of *sola gratia* fully to bear, but in such a way that not only human origination of faith remains excluded (as with the Reformers), but also human experience of faith."[171] Again, the problem is Zizioulas's ontological contrast (biological individual versus baptized person) as opposed to an ethical one (unbelief versus faith). Not *bad* choices, but choice itself belongs to the inherently flawed individuality of biological creation.[172]

Only in the Eucharist can there be this direct and immediate communion in Zizioulas's interpretation, which leads to the conclusion that "the church is a strictly eschatological reality realized fully in history in every Eucharist."[173] Yet, as Volf points out, "if the local church is identical with Christ, then the eschaton itself must become fully realized in the eucharistic gathering."[174]

In contrast to Zizioulas and Ratzinger, Volf stresses that the universal church is an essentially *eschatological* reality. "The local church is not a concrete realization of the existing universal church, but rather the real anticipation or proleptic realization of the eschatological gathering of the entire people of God." Thus, a necessary mark of the church, Volf argues, is "the openness of every church toward all other churches."[175] "Within history, the one church exists only as the *communion* of churches."[176]

When an overrealized eschatology is combined with the *totus Christus* emphasis, "not only is Christ the subject of the church—of the universal church—but the *church itself [also] becomes a subject*, that is, the subjectivity of Christ is transferred to the church."[177] In contrast with the proposals of Ratzinger and Zizioulas, "one must insist that the church is not the [acting] subject of salvific activity with Christ; rather, Christ is the only subject of such salvific activity. This is the soteriological reason why one must reject the notion

---

169. Ibid.
170. Ibid., 170.
171. Ibid., 95–96.
172. Ibid., 97.
173. Ibid., 101.
174. Ibid., 101, 140.
175. Ibid., 156.
176. Ibid., 158.
177. Ibid., 141, emphasis in original.

of *Christus totus, caput et membra; Christus totus* is incompatible with *solus Christus*."[178] The church can lead a person to faith, but *fiducia* "is exclusively a gift of the Spirit of God."[179]

On the basis of 1 Corinthians 12:12 and the analogy of the "one flesh" formed by husband and wife, drawn in Ephesians 5:31–32, Volf argues that the "body of Christ" must be conceived "not organically as the body of the one person, but rather communally as the *body*, a totality conceived in whatever fashion, *of several persons.*"[180] Zizioulas and Ratzinger have failed adequately to appreciate the *metaphorical* character of the body of Christ. "Precisely this metaphorical usage makes it possible for every local church to be called the 'body of Christ' in an original sense."[181] Thus, the church is "not a collective subject, but rather a communion of persons," for which he also appeals to social Trinitarianism as the archetypal model.[182] In this way, the christological conditioning of the church works not simply from the top down (drawing plurality into a higher unity), but from the "multiple relations" between persons.

So for Volf a church exists wherever there is a faithful confession of Christ (Acts 2:42; 1 Cor. 15:11; 2 Cor. 11:4).[183] The "being of the church" is "constituted by the assembled people confessing Christ."[184] "That which the church *is*, namely, believing and confessing human beings, is precisely that which (as a rule) also constitutes it."[185] Not only the particular form of church government, but also the very notion of ordained office is represented as belonging to the *bene esse* (well-being) rather than the *esse* (existence) of the church.[186] Not even the sacraments are ultimately constitutive; instead, they "are a public representation of such confession."[187]

I will draw on Volf's insights in the next chapter as we broaden our discussion to the catholicity (local and universal aspect) of ecclesial existence. At this point, however, a few points can be made by way of analysis.

Volf offers both decisive criticisms of the idealistic philosophy of personhood that underlies both Ratzinger's and Zizioulas's interpretations of the *totus Christus* motif, while challenging some extremes to which independent ecclesiologies may be prone. For example, in contrast with some of the arguments for independency above, Volf does not believe that the church is simply a collection of individual believers. "While several 'I's' together do constitute a grammatical plural, they do not yet constitute an ecclesial 'we.'"[188] However, the specter of

178. Ibid., 164.
179. Ibid., 163.
180. Ibid., 142.
181. Ibid.
182. Ibid., 145.
183. Ibid., 147–49.
184. Ibid., 150 n. 93.
185. Ibid., 151.
186. Ibid., 152.
187. Ibid., 153.
188. Ibid., 10.

subjectivism appears, especially when the faith and confession of the local assembly is regarded as constituting the church. This means that the church is not chiefly understood as the place where God is at work, creating faith, but as the place where individuals are responding. The visibility of the church necessarily shifts from preaching and sacrament to their effects within individuals and the community. Volf criticizes John Smyth's "unfortunate decision to baptize himself" because the Separatist leader judged that there was no "true church" to perform it, yet it is not clear that Volf's own view offers a sufficient rebuttal apart from the insistence that openness to other churches is an essential mark of ecclesial identity.[189]

Surely the Word is necessary for there to be a faithful confession of Christ, and later Volf does seem to allow that the sacraments belong to the *esse* of the church when he writes, "There is no church without sacraments." However, he immediately adds, "But there are no sacraments without the confession of faith and without faith itself."[190] At this point, Reformed theology would insist with other traditions that faith does not *constitute* a sacrament, but *receives* the reality a sacrament communicates. The Word and the sacraments retain their validity regardless of personal response, although one cannot receive their benefits apart from faith. Free churches are only consistent, therefore, when they identify the church with any local gathering of truly regenerate believers, given the presupposition that it is the response of individuals that constitutes the church.[191]

Affirming greater proximity to the Reformers' view of the church as "mother," Volf distances himself from John Smyth's counsel that those who are "born again . . . should no longer need means of grace," since the persons of the Godhead "are better than all scriptures, or creatures whatsoever."[192] While I would affirm his critique of an "over-realized eschatology" in Ratzinger and Zizioulas, Volf's insistence that only the *local* church is "the real anticipation or proleptic realization of the eschatological gathering of the entire people of God" seems implausible. In what way is such a universal gathering realized even proleptically if the visible form that it takes in the present is reduced to "openness to other [local] churches"?

Wary of the conflation of head and members as well as the free-church tendency to regard the visible church as extrinsic to the believer's salvation and communion with Christ, Volf's model offers tremendous insight. However, although plurality is more relationally oriented in his account, for the reasons I have mentioned (not least of which is the social-Trinitarian model), the unity of the body—and the connection between local churches—remains less decisive.

189. Ibid., 153 n. 108.
190. Ibid., 154.
191. On this point, Barth quite properly directs us away from either corporate or individual faith as church-constituting. Rather, the Word to which faith responds constitutes the church (Barth, *CD* IV/1:151). I would only add that is just as true for the sacraments.
192. Volf, *After Our Likeness*, 161–62.

IDENTIFYING "THE BODY": ONE AND MANY

In 1877, Frederick Tönnies distinguished between two types of political organization in the modern world: *Gesellschaft*, based on the social contract and mutual self-interest; and *Gemeinschaft*: informal communities such as family, village, neighborhood, and friendship.[193] As most fully evident in Thomas Hobbes's political philosophy, the sovereign self surrenders a certain degree of autonomy to the prince (or state) in exchange for security in "the war of all against all." The triumph of this version of community-as-gesellschaft is apparent in the myriad forms of modern life: political, economic, and even spiritual.

The covenant community does not exactly fit either of these categories as described by Tönnies, but it sharply contrasts with the social contract. For all of their differences, some of the modern versions of *totus Christus* we have encountered share with Protestant individualism a contractual rather than covenantal outlook. Reflecting his heritage in pietism, Schleiermacher wrote, "The Christian Church is formed through regenerate individuals coming together for mutual interaction and cooperation in an orderly way."[194]

So, ironically, he could simultaneously view the church as a voluntary society among others (though of *regenerate* individuals) and speak of the sacrificing of the individual to the community.

In contrast to both, a covenantal approach insists that there are no sovereign selves in the first place, either to invest with autonomy or to sacrifice to the whole. In Christ, the many remain, yet now in a communion of life rather than in a state of perpetual war. In Christ, there is no scarcity to be overcome by an ecclesiastical rationing of grace; it is an economy of sheer abundance: the grace that exceeds the guilt and power of sin (Rom. 5:20), "the riches of his grace that he lavished on us" (Eph. 1:7–8), and "the grace of our Lord [that] overflowed for me with the faith and love that are in Christ Jesus" (1 Tim. 1:14). It is the grace that elects, redeems, calls, justifies, sanctifies, and glorifies rather than obliterates the biological individual, placing the self in a nexus of relationships identified as the new creation. We are one because we have all received the same Gift.

Although Reformed theology also appeals to the *totus Christus* motif without scruple, it is always connected with the historical economy: sharing in Christ's death and resurrection, so that what has happened to Jesus will also happen to us. Christ is the representative head in a covenant, not the "corporate personality" in whom his own identity as well as ours is surrendered to the whole.

The ascension keeps this version from substituting either a pyramidal church or a cosmic body for Christ, and directs us to the work of the Spirit in uniting us to Christ so that there is real affinity despite real difference. In Calvin's words,

193. Frederick Tönnies, *Community and Society*, trans. C. Loomis (New York: Harper & Row, 1963).
194. Friedrich Schleiermacher, *The Christian Faith*, § 115, ed. H. R. Mackintosh and J. S. Stewart (Edinburgh: T&T Clark, 1928), 532.

> This is the highest honour of the Church, that, until He is united to us, the Son of God reckons himself in some measure imperfect. What consolation is it for us to learn, that, not until we are along with him, does he possess all his parts, or wish to be regarded as complete! Hence, in the First Epistle to the Corinthians, when the apostle discusses largely the metaphor of a human body, he includes under the single name of Christ the whole Church.[195]

It is no wonder, then, that Calvin insisted upon stronger language for *koinōnia* than Erasmus's *societas*, and this also measures the reformer's distance from Barth on this point. Nevertheless, for Calvin and his heirs, this version of *totus Christus* is eschatologically oriented: "the Son of God reckons himself in some measure imperfect" or incomplete only because he is the firstfruits of the harvest, the head of a body. What he possesses perfectly and completely in himself is at present only imperfectly and incompletely realized in his body. Though chosen and redeemed, the whole body has not yet been gathered and justified. Even those who are justified only begin that progress in sanctification that will be fully realized in their glorification.

Yet the visible church does participate proleptically in the eschatological reality: the whole communion of the elect in all times and places. One cannot help but observe at this point how crucial the practice of infant baptism is to a covenantal view of the communion of saints more generally. While eschewing an ex opere operato view of baptism, which tends to make the church the effectual cause of union and communion, a covenantal view of baptism keeps us from conceiving of the church simply as a voluntary society. "What is the point of admitting infants into an association?" asks Bonhoeffer. "No chess player, no matter how passionate, would enroll a small child in a chess club. . . . Only a community [*Gemeinschaft*], not a society [*Gesellschaft*], is able to carry children. Infant baptism within an association [*Gesellschaft*] is an internal contradiction."[196] Infant baptism, therefore, is not incidental but essential for a covenantal ecclesiology. It is integral not only to the continuity of the covenant through Old and New Testaments but also to a conception of the church as the *place* where faith is born and fed as well as the *people* who exhibit it. The inclusion of believers' children underscores the priority of God's sovereign grace in ecclesiology as well as soteriology, challenging all voluntaristic and contractual interpretations that contribute to an individualistic faith and practice. When construed in the context of a covenantal theology, the baptism of believers together with their children underscores (1) the priority of divine activity in creating the church (i.e., covenant over contract); (2) the "mixed" character of the body of Christ at present, which subverts overrealized eschatologies; (3) the importance of personal faith as well as communal mediation in the nurture of faith and repentance.

---

195. John Calvin on Eph. 1:23, in *Commentaries on the Epistles of Paul to the Galatians and Ephesians*, trans. William Pringle (Grand Rapids: Eerdmans, 1957), 218.
196. Bonhoeffer, *SC* 254, 257.

In a covenantal model, the *hypostatic* union of deity and humanity in Christ is distinguished from the *mystical* union of the church with its head.[197] Christ is the federal head of his body, rather than the corporate personality. The person and work of Christ then and there, completed once and for all, is in no way extended or completed by the church; nevertheless, the Spirit's work here and now is just as crucial if there is to be an actual union with Christ and his benefits.

Whether by overly inflated or deflated ecclesiologies of head-and-members, we lose much of the eschatological tension and pneumatological richness required for a sound ecclesiology. As an analogy, body of Christ is neither a univocal description nor an equivocal figure of speech. Taken univocally, the theory of the church "as 'the extension of the Incarnation,'" as Newbigin observes, "springs from a confusion of *sarx* with *soma*." "Christ's risen body"—that is, his ecclesial distinguished from his natural body—"is not fleshly but spiritual." "He did not come to incorporate us in His body according to the flesh but according to the Spirit." Hence comes his promise that when he ascends, he will send the Spirit.[198] Newbigin's point reminds us of the importance of both the ascension of Christ in the flesh and the descent of the Spirit. Our union with Christ does not occur at the level of fused natures, but as a common participation of different members in the same realities of the age to come by the same Spirit.

Far from spiritualizing the metaphor, this view underscores the specific, corporeal, and irreducible particularity of the head and members. Volf properly argues, "A *theological interpretation* going beyond Paul himself is needed to transform the Pauline 'one *in* Christ' into Ratzinger's 'a single subject *with* Christ,' or certainly into 'a single . . . Jesus Christ.'"[199] To be sure, Ratzinger says that "through the Holy Spirit, the Lord who 'departed' on the cross has 'returned' and is now engaged in affectionate dialogue with his 'bride,' the church." "Yet even recourse to the representational work of the Holy Spirit," says Volf, "cannot free the idea of dialogue within the *one, single* subject of the suspicion of being mere conversation with oneself. It does not seem possible to conceive the juxtaposition of church and Christ without giving up the notion of the one subject that includes both bridegroom and bride."[200]

Furthermore, wherever it occurs, the Pauline phrase is deployed to affirm plurality as much as unity, as in 1 Corinthians 12:12: "For just as the body is one and has many members, and all the members of the body, though many, are one body, so it is with Christ." Not only are the many and the one treated with the same ontological weight, but the formula itself also expresses a simile: "just as . . . , so it is with Christ." Analogies are not rhetorical flourishes, but the communication of truth in a way that accommodates to our capacities.

197. I am grateful to George Hunsinger for giving me this handy way of putting the matter in recent conversations.

198. Lesslie Newbigin, *The Household of God: Lectures on the Nature of the Church* (London: SCM Press, 1957), 80.

199. Volf, *After Our Likeness*, 34. Since Volf's references are to Ratzinger before he became pope, I will use this identification throughout this chapter.

200. Ibid.

As Avery Cardinal Dulles properly reminds us, the variety and richness of biblical analogies must be taken into account.[201] The key is not to objectivize one model to the exclusion of others. For example, organic models are richly illuminating but "fail to account for the distinctively interpersonal and historical phenomena characteristic of the Church as a human community that perdures through the generations. Thus societal models, such as that of God's People on pilgrimage, are used to supplement the organic metaphors."[202]

> The New Testament, for example, combines the images of Temple and Body of Christ in logically incoherent but theologically apposite ways. In 1 Pet. 2:5 we are told that Christians are a Temple built of living stones, whereas Paul in Eph. 4:16 says that the Body of Christ is still under construction. This "profuse mixing of metaphors," Paul Minear reminds us, "reflects not logical confusion but theological vitality."[203]

Dulles goes so far as to point out that the body-of-Christ analogy is itself dependent on the more basic motif of covenant. "The root of the metaphor," he says, "is the kind of treaty relationship into which a suzerain state entered with a vassal state in the ancient Near East." In addition to providing the background for the body-of-Christ analogy, "that kind of military and political treaty afforded the raw material out of which the concept of 'People of God' was fashioned."[204]

This suggests the possibility that rather than assimilating the covenantal context of biblical ecclesiology to a single Pauline metaphor (esp. as interpreted within an idealist framework), we should understand "body of Christ" as an analogy for a covenantal ecclesiology. Dulles himself recognizes that "body of Christ" by itself may lead "to an unhealthy divinization of the Church," as if the union "is therefore a biological and hypostatic one" and all actions of the church are ipso facto actions of Christ and the Spirit.[205]

In a covenantal context, there is both affinity and difference. The vassal is so identified with the suzerain that a threat or injury to the one is a threat or injury to the other. Yet this is not due to a biological unity of a single subject consisting of suzerain and vassal, but is based on the responsibility that the suzerain has freely assumed as the head of the imperial body. Nevertheless, the suzerain always stands over against the vassal by means of the treaty. There is union without fusion, communion without absorption, with the covenant people (*ecclesia*) always in the position of receiving rather than extending the personal existence and gracious reign of its ascended Lord.

There is a lot of talk these days about the Eucharist as the site of ecclesiology and the church as the sacrament of the kingdom of God, but this is salutary only

---

201. Avery Dulles, *Models of the Church*, 17, 21–30. Paul Minear's *Images of the Church in the New Testament* (Philadelphia: Westminster Press, 1960), lists 96 images.
202. Ibid., 22–23.
203. Ibid., 29–30.
204. Ibid.
205. Ibid., 51.

if we allow this event to situate us precariously between the two ages. The Eucharist, properly understood, preserves us from any fusion of head and members or of members with each other, just as it challenges any private relationship with the head abstracted from the whole body. Again Farrow helpfully underscores this point of "eucharistic ambiguity":

> The one around whose table we are said to gather is "in a manner present and in a manner absent," to borrow Calvin's way of putting it. . . . For it is in its eucharistic ambiguity that the church is marked off from the world ontologically and not merely ideologically. It is in confessing that ambiguity that its appeal to the Holy Spirit is spared the banality, or rather the blasphemy, of reducing to self-reference. It is in knowing the provisionality of its own existence that the church is able to speak with some integrity of a reality that lies beyond itself and beyond the world in which it lives. To put the matter more positively, there is something more to the church than meets the eye, and that "something more" belongs to the christological enigma which the eucharist introduces.[206]

Not without reason do the eucharistic liturgies include remembering what has happened once and for all without the possibility of repetition, imitation, or extension (anamnesis), the invocation of the Spirit (epiclesis) in the present, and the confession that he will come again (*epektasis*). In this way, the church and the individual believer both recognize that their identity exists ecstatically—that is, outside of themselves. This identity is never autonomous, in the free will of the magisterium or of the individual, but *extra nos*.

Christ is not now present on earth in his natural body, and his ecclesial body cannot serve as his substitute. Yet the church is not orphaned by its ascended Lord, since the Spirit unites us to Christ and therefore to each other in a communion of faith, hope, and love. Thus, even now there is a society spread throughout the kingdoms of this age that, however ambiguous to our empirical observation, is not only a community but also a communion; not only a sign but also a proleptic realization of that difference-in-union and unity-in-difference that will characterize the Sabbath feast.

---

206. Farrow, *Ascension and Ecclesia*, 3.

Chapter Seven

Catholicity and Holiness

"Sanctify Them in the Truth;
Your Word Is Truth" (John 17:17)

The previous chapter highlighted the ontological equality of unity and plurality and affinity and difference, by defining the relationship of head and members in terms of distinction without separation: an analogical and covenantal account that is sensitive to the eschatological tension between the already and the not-yet. Building on that discussion, this chapter extends this conception to our understanding of the catholicity and holiness of the church.

ECCLESIAL HOLINESS

Sanctification has already been introduced as a critical category for ecclesiology, allowing us to navigate between the Scylla of confusing and the Charybdis of separating head and body. God takes creation as it is, both in its essential goodness and covenantal fallenness, claims it for special purposes, and in the case of human beings, redefines and refashions it by his grace and glory so that it is a reflection of his own character. Without undergoing any substantial change, such staples of everyday life as water, bread, and wine have been recruited as an essential part of an event of covenantal pledging. Nature is not elevated or divinized, but claimed by God and freed to serve his communicative ends. It is God's promise that makes ordinary water, bread, and wine holy elements. Analogously, Jesus prays in Gethsemane concerning his followers, not that they would be taken out of the world but that they may be sanctified in it: "Sanctify them in the truth; your word is truth" (John 17:17).

Before sanctification is a process of inner renewal, it is a definitive claim made by the triune God: a forensic act that, like justification, initiates reverberations through every nook and cranny of personal and ecclesial existence. Furthermore, it is not an immediate activity of the Spirit, nor an infusion of sanctifying grace, but a matter of being reworded. No longer "*Lo-ammi*," "Not my people" (Hos. 1:9), we are proclaimed to be the very people of God. Even while the church remains sullied both internally and externally, it calls on the name of the Lord in assurance, knowing that Christ "became for us wisdom from God, and righteousness and sanctification and redemption, in order that, as it is written, 'Let the one who boasts, boast in the Lord'" (1 Cor. 1:30).

Although its arrival brings blessing to every aspect of our existence and experience, holiness comes to the church corporately as to members individually, *extra nos*. In Isaiah 60, for example, the land lies in darkness. There are no immanent resources for recovery, but the promise arrives with its declarative force: "Arise, shine; for your light has come, and the glory of the LORD has risen *upon* you. For darkness shall cover the earth, and thick darkness the peoples; but the LORD will arise *upon* you, and his glory will appear *over* you" (Isa. 60:1–2). The church is never the sun, but always the moon; never creating, but only reflecting the Light of the world. And as a result, a remnant from all the nations streams to Zion (vv. 4–22). In Isaiah 62, Salvation arrives swiftly from conquest with his reward, to maintain his presence again among his people. "They shall be called, 'The Holy People, The Redeemed of the LORD'; and you shall be called, 'Sought Out, A City Not Forsaken'" (vv. 11–12).

As the parlay between Yahweh and Moses in Exodus 34:12–16 makes clear, God's presence—which is to say, his electing, redeeming, and preserving action— is the only thing that keeps Israel from being assimilated back into the *tōhû wā-bōhû*—darkness and void (Gen. 1:2)—of the nations. As a prophet to the returning exiles, Zechariah relates a vision of Joshua the high priest being accused by Satan in the divine courtroom, but Joshua's guilt and his filthy garments are removed, and he is clothed "with festal apparel" (Zech. 3:4). There is the forensic word and deed. All of these things are "an omen of things to come: I am going to bring my servant the Branch. For on the stone that I have set before Joshua, on a single stone with seven facets, I will engrave its inscription, says the LORD of hosts, and I will remove the guilt of this land in a single day. On that day, says the LORD of hosts, you shall invite each other to come under your vine and fig tree" (vv. 8–10). The rest in the holy land is secured by the removal of guilt from the land and the clothing of the people in royal apparel. The Branch will be "a priest by his throne," mediating peace (Zech. 6:13). "On that day there shall be inscribed on the bells of the horses, 'Holy to the LORD.' And the cooking pots in the house of the LORD shall be as holy as the bowls in front of the altar. . . . And there shall no longer be traders in the house of the LORD of hosts on that day" (Zech. 14:20–21). In other words, the holy/unholy or clean/unclean distinction will be lifted. Israel's separation from the nations, symbolized in the detailed ceremonial legislation of the old covenant, will no longer be in force.

The revelation of this promise's fulfillment staggered and scandalized Peter, yet it resulted in the mission to the Gentiles (Acts 10:1–11:18). In Christ, even the "unclean" are holy; no-people (*Lo-ammi*) can become children of Abraham (Luke 3:8; John 1:12; Gal. 3:13–18; 4:21–5:1; 1 Pet. 2:10) and their children can be holy to the Lord (1 Cor. 7:14). As the gospel claims and renames strangers to the covenant, the kingdom of God spreads in holiness. Yet in this time between the times, there is still the conflict between the holy and the common, the heirs of promise and a world that prefers the darkness to light. The divine claim that makes us holy also makes us aliens and strangers in this age.

The external word of the gospel not only definitively creates but progressively disrupts, reorients, and renews the church. Jesus' petition on the eve of his crucifixion was fulfilled: the church is holy because it has his word. The holiness that renews is first of all the decisive divine act of consecration. A "new name" is this definitive holiness, a new identity that is an immediate transfer from condemnation to justification, death to life, no-people to the people of God (Isa. 62:2 with Rev. 2:17). Not because of any inherent holiness, but by covenantal union with our head, we are made beneficiaries, personally and corporately, of that perfect righteousness. We are holy because of our election, redemption, and calling *in Christ* (Eph. 1:4-15).

By contrast, a corollary of conflating the head and its members in a single subject, whether understood in juridical, organic, or even pneumatic terms, is the loss of the necessary distinction between the holiness of Christ and that of his body. Instead of ecclesial justification deriving from the perfect righteousness of its head, Christ himself is assimilated to the inherent holiness of his body. According to Vatican I, "the Church itself, with its marvelous extension, its eminent holiness, and its inexhaustible fruitfulness in every good thing, with its Catholic unity and its invincible stability, is a great and perpetual motive of credibility and an irrefutable witness of its own divine mission."[1] Even according to the more recent encyclical *Humani generis*, "The Mystical Body of Christ and the Roman Catholic Church are one and the same thing,"[2] although other churches have "*vestigia ecclesiae.*"[3] Thus, holiness and catholicity flow from the unicity of the *totus Christus*: the single subject that is Christ and his church. As a consequence,

---

1. Quoted by Avery Dulles, SJ, *Models of the Church* (New York: Doubleday, 1974), 123.
2. Cited in ibid., 132.
3. Ibid., 133. Dulles reminds us (ibid., 140) that the way one reads these magisterial decisions depends to a large extent on the ecclesiological model that one favors. If Vatican II had accepted a purely institutional ecclesiology, Protestant churches could not be considered true churches, but by widening its ecclesiology, the door is left open to that possibility in the future. Adopting a "church-as-sacrament" model over a merely institutional one allows, Dulles suggests, treating Protestant churches as "imperfect realizations of the sacrament of the Church." Despite the challenges (such as

the church is always holy, never simultaneously justified and sinful. The holiness of the church is in no way compromised by the sins of its members, not because of an *alien* righteousness but because of an *inherent* righteousness that is infused into the church and flows from it.

On the institutional model of Trent, the magisterium is the judicial dispenser of this sanctifying grace from the treasury of merits; on the more organic model (esp. retrieving the Dionysian emphasis), grace simply emanates from the One (*totus Christus*) to the many (all of humanity). Instead of thinking in terms of true and false, elect and nonelect, von Balthasar encourages us to think again of a descending scale. He commends the Dionysian mysticism of the Middle Ages, "which sees in the Church all gradations of holiness from the highest, most unsullied sanctity of Mary to the very brink of damnation, in fact even beyond it, in the case of the gravely sinful who are not yet, in some way, members of the Church."[4] Especially with Rahner's formulations, what is needed is not so much a new creation, incorporating strangers and aliens into Christ, but a new awareness that they already belong to the church at least implicitly. In either case, the holiness is inherent, infused, and hierarchical. Rahner summarizes, "As the great theologians of the Middle Ages used to say (St. Thomas, *Summa Theologia*, I, IIae, q. 106, a.1), what principally constitutes the Church is the Holy Spirit in men's hearts; all the rest (hierarchy, papacy, Eucharist, sacraments) are in the service of this inner transformation."[5]

Drawing on the doctrine of dispensations developed by John Fletcher (Wesley's successor), Pentecostal theologian Amos Yong reaches the same goal, but by way of the immediacy of the Spirit apart from any necessary connection to the word of Christ or the church.[6] However, from a covenantal perspective, all ways of locating holiness in someone or something other than Jesus Christ overlook the inseparable connection between Christology and pneumatology, as already highlighted.

God certainly may meet strangers wherever he chooses, but he has *promised* to meet us in the covenant of grace, through the invocation of Christ's name (Acts 4:12; Phil. 2:9–11). Lesslie Newbigin nicely expresses a perennial Reformed objection to the notion of the "anonymous Christian":

> Nor can we attempt to preserve some remnants of consistency by the use of the conception of uncovenanted mercies, by suggesting that we can

---

agreeing on the nature of a sacrament), this seems to me to not only be a more fruitful ecclesiological model for ecumenism, but also for understanding the reality of the church more generally. Throughout this volume, I employ the sign-signified analogy as a way of navigating between "Zwinglianism" and "transubstantiation."

4. Ibid., 152.

5. Ibid., 319.

6. Amos Yong, *The Spirit Poured Out on All Flesh* (Grand Rapids: Baker Academic, 2005), 130. This allows him also to affirm that "the mystical and universal body of Christ would include the entire spectrum from all those who explicitly confess his name to all who may not be knowledgeable about Jesus but are spiritually united with him by the power of the Holy Spirit."

> acknowledge fully the works of grace outside the visible Church and yet
> retain intact our conviction that the Church only exists where visible con-
> tinuity has been preserved. This attempt lands us into an impossible situa-
> tion. If God can and does bestow His redeeming grace with indiscriminate
> bounty within and without the confines of His Church, then the Church is
> no essential part of the whole scheme of salvation, and its order and sacra-
> ments, its preaching and ministering have no inherent and essential relation
> to God's saving work in Christ, but are merely arbitrary constructions which
> God Himself ignores.[7]

Though the visible church is indeed a "mixed assembly," according to Reformation theologies, it is the exclusive site of God's covenanted blessings in Christ. It
is this affirmation that fuels the missionary spirit intrinsic to Christian identity.

In contrast to Rome, many evangelical Protestants and Pentecostals locate the
visibility of the church in the personal holiness and activity of individual believers. While Rome identifies this inherent holiness with the historical institution
as such, independent ecclesiologies tend to identify it with the piety and actions
of the individual, ranging from identifiable conversion experiences to speaking
in tongues.[8]

In both Roman Catholic and free-church ecclesiologies, then, the church's visible holiness is inherent, although for the former it flows from the one to the
many and for the latter from the many to the one. To the extent that free churches
treat as central the inner experience of conversion and renewal, there is substantial agreement with Rahner's description of the Roman Catholic position cited
above, that "what principally constitutes the Church is the Holy Spirit in men's
hearts, all the rest . . . are in the service of this inner transformation." In both paradigms, then, the means of grace employed (whether conceived as sacraments,
ordinances, or methods) are oriented first of all toward an infused, inherent, and
inward holiness. Where Rome has typically emphasized the church as the *place*,
evangelicals and Pentecostals ordinarily think of the church as the *people*.[9] In both
ways, however, the emphasis is placed on the church as actor more than receiver.
Roman Catholic theology refers to the Mass as "the work of the people," and
Protestant evangelicals typically regard the church primarily as the platform for
their service to God and neighbor more than as the place where God serves them.

Covenant theology has taken a different route than either of these paradigms.
Regardless of the personal holiness of its members, the church (understood in

---

7. Ibid., 79.

8. Ibid., 84. Yong provides a helpful survey of the differences that emerged within the Wesleyan-
Holiness/Pentecostal traditions, including debates over "whether there are one, two, or even three
'works of grace'" (cf. 98p.). Throughout this discussion, Yong defends the importance of successive
"crisis experiences" throughout the Christian life. This contrasts with a covenantal orientation in
which such experiences may or may not occur, yet life in the Spirit is seen as the common property
of all believers.

9. I recognize that the documents of Vatican II explicitly embrace a "people of God" model alongside the others, yet this characterization (of church as place) still seems valid in terms of traditional
emphases.

terms not only of its local but also its broader assemblies) is holy because it is the field of divine activity, in which the wheat is growing up into the likeness of its firstfruits, even though weeds are sown among the wheat. Reformed (as well as Lutheran) ecclesiologies emphasize that the holiness of the church that sets it apart from the world does not arise from within the corporate body (hierarchically) or its members (democratically), but from the ministry of the Son and the Spirit, sent from the Father, working through the Word and sacraments. This ministry remains holy in spite of the unholiness and even unbelief of those who participate outwardly in its covenantal life. Not even the personal holiness of its ministers is a condition of the church's holiness, but the holy action of God working through the ministry. The forensic word generates, sustains, and permeates every transformative moment in life of the believer and the history of the church. Only as the field of God's covenantal action is the church something other than another worldly institution or society.

Furthermore, Reformed theology has maintained that the church, as the covenant community in both testaments, consists of *professing* believers *and their children*. Even if only one parent is a believer, the children are holy (1 Cor. 7:14). This is due not to any inner transformation or infused grace, but simply to God's promise. In covenantal thinking, the tree is holy even if some of its branches will finally fail to yield fruit and be broken off to make room for others (Rom. 11:16–24). The tree is holy neither because it is collectively identical to Christ, nor because it is the sum total of the regenerate, but because of the eschatological connection of the covenant people to their living root (vv. 16, 18–20). At any given moment, in any local expression, the church will be a "mixed assembly" and yet the field of God's action where faith is created and sustained.

Once we realize this priority of the speaking of salvation over that which is spoken into being because of it, the church takes its proper place as a recipient rather than master of grace; the amphitheater in which God converts, instead of being either the reservoir of grace or the sum total of converted individuals. This means that conversion is an inherently ecclesial experience, although God remains the effectual agent.

Once the forensic word of absolution and justification is pronounced, the new creation dawns, bringing with it all of its own unique potentialities. Definitively sanctified vessels are put to sanctified use. Therefore, covenant membership gives rise to obligations and, when necessary, to the admonitions and discipline of the body through its elders.

The very people to whom Paul "could not speak . . . as spiritual people, but rather as people of the flesh, as infants in Christ," are nevertheless infants *in Christ* (1 Cor. 3:1, emphasis added). The letter is even addressed "To the *church of God that is in Corinth*, to those who *are sanctified* in Christ Jesus, *called to be saints*, together with all those who in every place *call on the name of our Lord Jesus Christ*, both their Lord and ours: Grace to you and peace from God our Father and the Lord Jesus Christ" (1 Cor. 1:2–3, emphasis added). A church that is not sinful and does not sin is not a church at all, but a religious society that stands in defiance of grace and forgiveness. "The purest churches under heaven," accord-ing to the Westminster Confession, "are subject both to mixture and error; and some have so degenerated, so as to become no churches of Christ, but synagogues of Satan. Nevertheless, there shall be always a church on earth, to worship God according to his will."[10]

While Christ has instituted church government and discipline to guard the peace and purity of his body, the success of the church's mission does not lie in its own experience or piety but in its witness to Christ. In the words of Dietrich Bonhoeffer, "The intention of the preacher is not to improve the world, but to summon it to belief in Jesus Christ and to bear witness to the reconciliation which has been accomplished through Him and His dominion."[11] In addressing this point, Bonhoeffer speaks for Reformed as well as Lutheran churches:

> For the Lutheran concept of the church it is crucial that the *sanctorum com-munio* always has been a community of sinners and remains so. This fact is ultimately the reason why the Hegelian theory is untenable. Absolute spirit does not simply enter into the subjective spirits, gathering them up into the objective spirit; rather, the Christian church is the church of the word, that is, of faith. Real sanctification is only a precursor of the last things. . . . The "word" is the rock upon which the idealist spirit-monism founders; for the word implies that sin still exists, that the absolute spirit has to fight for its rule, that the church remains a church of sinners.[12]

It is this word that "breaks up" the church into "the community-of-the cross," to be "built up" into "the Easter community."[13]

> If one were to say that sin must be ascribed to the individual but not to the objective spirit of the church, then this would be correct to the extent that the sum total of all wills in the church now has a new direction. But this does not mean that wherever the empirical church-community acts as "a whole," its action would be an action of the Holy Spirit. This would amount to the Hegelian position.[14]

Despite the visible lack of holiness in the church, the Spirit nevertheless sets the church apart to receive and minister the Word and the sacraments.[15] "Even the institutions sanctified by God can therefore never be the path to salvation," Oswald Bayer wisely reminds us, "and even though they are and remain holy, in them we may either be lost or we may find deliverance—by faith alone."[16]

---

10. The Westminster Confession, chap. 25.5, in *Trinity Hymnal*, rev. ed. (Atlanta and Philadel-phia: Great Commission Publications, 1990), 863.

11. Dietrich Bonhoeffer, *Ethics* (New York: Macmillan, 1965), 350.

12. Dietrich Bonhoeffer, *SC*, 212.

13. Ibid., 212–13.

14. Ibid., 214.

15. Ibid., 216.

16. Oswald Bayer, *Living by Grace: Justification and Sanctification*, trans. Geoffrey W. Bromiley (Grand Rapids: Eerdmans, 2003), 62; cf. Martin Luther, *LW* 37:365.

Based on the logic of Romans 9, Lesslie Newbigin similarly concluded:

> There is a covenant and a covenant people, and God is faithful to His covenant. But the substance of that covenant is all pure mercy and grace. If men presume to claim for themselves upon the basis of the covenant some relationship with God other than that of the sinner needing God's grace, the covenant has been perverted. And where that has happened God, in the sovereign freedom of His grace, destroys these pretensions, calls "No people" to be the people, breaks off natural branches and grafts in wild slips, filling them with the life which is His own life imparted to men. . . . She who is essentially one is divided; she who is essentially holy is unclean; she who is essentially apostolic forgets her missionary task.[17]

No ecclesiology is adequate that fails to acknowledge the mystery and reality of ongoing sin in the believer and also in the church.[18] The grace of God does not flow down a cosmic ladder by gradations and degrees; rather, every believer is a coheir with Christ and each other. Everything that is in Christ is as holy as he is, because he *is* their sanctification (1 Cor. 1:30–31). This being the case, the objective holiness of the whole body in its head is also *at work* throughout the body, so that each member will realize more and more the fruit of that definitive identity, which can be neither improved nor diminished.

In the light of the priority of the word in sanctifying a people and a place, Bonhoeffer properly concludes, "No empirical body 'in itself' can claim to have authority over the church-community. Every claim derives from the Word."[19] This view also refuses to lodge ecclesial holiness in what Bonhoeffer called a "community romanticism" that glories in its distinctiveness from the world and the institutional church.[20] He quotes Calvin: "Only the *opera* [works] are perceptible but not the *persona, quae in manu Dei est* [the person, who is in the hand of God], since 'the Lord knows those who are his.'"[21] Thus, our confession of "one holy, catholic, and apostolic church" remains significantly an article of faith that, like our justification, is not always experienced. "Our age is not short on experiences, but on *faith*. But only faith creates a genuine experience of the church."[22]

Even the church's unregenerate members are in some sense beneficiaries of the Spirit's activity in the covenant community, which, according to Hebrews (esp. chaps. 4, 6, 10), makes them all the more responsible for embracing the promises signified and sealed to them in baptism. The church is never the effectual agent; instead, it is the recipient and field of God's sanctifying work in the world: the theater in which the Spirit is casting and staging dress rehearsals of the age to come.

17. Ibid., 84.
18. Ibid.
19. Ibid., 266.
20. Ibid., 278.
21. Ibid., 279.
22. Ibid., 282.

COVENANT AND *KOINŌNIA*

The covenantal motif has tremendous potential to orient ecclesiology toward an integration of the one and many, local and broader assemblies, the invisibility of the church in election, and the visibility of the church in the covenant community. To the extent that more recent Roman Catholic ecclesiologies have appealed to this motif, for example, there has been a deeper understanding of plurality in *koinōnia*.[23] On the free-church side, Stanley Grenz notes that a covenantal perspective challenges the individualism to which congregationalism may be prone.[24]

Yet another crucial decision must be made at this juncture: Is the church a merely passive recipient, or is it an active agent of redemption? Affirming the former in no uncertain terms today is Eberhard Jüngel, while the latter is defended by a growing chorus, ranging from Radical Orthodoxy to the evangelical Protestant heirs of Charles Finney.

Although evangelicals would be disinclined to view the institutional church as an extension of the incarnation, they are quite familiar with a more individualistic version of Teresa of Avila's statement, "Christ has no body now on earth but yours; no hands but yours, no feet but yours; yours are the eyes through which his love looks out to the world; yours are the feet with which he goes about doing good; yours are the hands with which he blesses men now."[25] Even Geoffrey Wainwright asks whether, in light of the incorporative language of the New Testament, "How far may, and indeed must, the church be viewed as the continuing body of Christ in which the Holy Spirit dwells transformatively in such a way that in its very being, as well as in its words and its gestures, the church becomes an active bearer of the gospel by which it is itself constituted?"[26] Indeed, this question practically summarizes the others we are considering.

Must we choose between a view of the church as a purely passive recipient of grace and as an active bearer of grace? In volume 3 of this series, *Covenant and Salvation*, I defended a traditional Reformed account of the covenant of grace as absolute and unconditional in its basis, yet giving rise to a genuine covenantal partnership. This is not a way of beginning with monergism only to be perfected by synergism (a move that is reproved in Gal. 3:3). Rather, we are always passive recipients of grace from God and active agents of love to our neighbor. A forensic economy yields effective transformation: the Word does what it declares; the believer and the church become what they already are in Christ. *In this light, the*

23. See, e.g., Kilian McDonnell, SJ, "Vatican II (1962–1964), Puebla (1979), Synod (1985): *Koinōnia/Communio* as an Integral Ecclesiology," *Journal of Ecumenical Studies* 25, no. 3 (Summer 1988): 414.

24. Stanley Grenz, *Theology for the Community of God* (Nashville: Broadman & Holman, 1994), 614.

25. Quoted by David Brown and Ann Loades, "Introduction: The Divine Poet," in *Christ: The Sacramental Word*, ed. David Brown and Ann Loades, Incarnation, Sacrament and Poetry (London: SPCK, 1996), 8.

26. Geoffrey Wainwright, "Church and Sacrament(s)," in *The Possibilities of Theology*, ed. John Webster (Edinburgh: T&T Clark, 1994), 103.

church is always a recipient of grace in relation to God yet also active in witness, love, and service toward the neighbor. When in its ministry the church brings the gospel to human beings, it is neither merely a passive recipient nor an active bearer of grace, but the ordained instrument through which *Christ* actively draws people to himself, expanding his ecclesial body.

Only the free Spirit who is Lord guarantees our unity, catholicity, holiness, and apostolicity. These attributes cannot be defined by the immanent virtues of the church itself: its inherent orthodoxy, orthopraxy, or orthopathy. The Father is the source of our unity, catholicity, holiness, and apostolicity because of his electing and redeeming grace. The Son is the content, material cause, and ground of our reconciliation with God, which is why the gospel is the sine qua non of ecclesial existence. The Spirit brings about within us a genuinely human answering that corresponds analogically to the unity and catholicity of the Trinity: a lively, vocal, and eucharistic fellowship of the one in many and the many in one. We cannot therefore harness the Spirit by our individual enthusiasm or corporate agency (ex opere operato), whether by the purity of our lives and experiences or the church's doctrine, history, and polity. Rather, it is in view of and "because of the mercies of God" that we can yield our "reasonable service," no longer being "conformed to this world [age]" but being "transformed by the renewing of your minds" through the Word of God (Rom. 12:1–2).

Holiness and Catholicity in the Word

Lutheran and Reformed ecclesiologies share many common themes and emphases, especially on the church as the creature of the Word and as simultaneously justified and sinful, but Veli-Matti Kärkkäinen aptly captures the essence of Reformed ecclesiology in terms of "The Church as Covenant."[27] As the covenant is made visible and accessible through Word and sacrament, there is an objectivity to ecclesial existence that resists tendencies to simply reduce the church to a people rather than a place. It is not the people who create the covenant by their pious experience, discipleship, or social agendas, but the covenant that defines this otherwise heterogeneous community as the body of Christ. The visible church is always put in the position of having to receive its identity from outside of itself.

Weary of its ambiguous location between the two ages, a church that preaches another gospel or corrupts the sacraments is no longer holy, but is assimilated into the world—the age that is passing away—despite its outward forms (1 Cor. 3:10–17; Gal. 1:6–9). We cannot deny that there will be those who finally hear these chilling words of Jesus Christ: "I never knew you; go away from me," although they protest that they performed wonders in his name (Matt. 7:22–23). The candlestick of any particular church or group of churches can be removed

---

27. Veli-Matti Kärkkäinen, *An Introduction to Ecclesiology: Ecumenical, Historical and Global Perspectives* (Downers Grove, IL: InterVarsity Press, 2002), 50–58.

when it ceases to bear illuminating witness to Christ in the world (Rev. 2:5). This tragic end may come upon a church not only for abandoning the doctrine of the gospel itself, but also for failing to bear witness to it.

In spite of this danger, in and through this ministry, the church as it is in this age already participates in the eschatological kingdom. Despite the church's compromised, ambiguous, schismatic, and sinful character, the covenant of redemption ensures that our unfaithfulness will not have the last word. Christ's life is now so bound up with ours that Calvin can even say, "For it is an immutable fact that His life would be nothing if his members were dead." Otherwise, his body would be "mutilated."[28] In the resurrection of the dead, the so-called invisible church—the communion known only to God—will become fully visible. The *totus Christus* is affirmed, therefore, but in covenantal rather than Platonic terms. Its frame of reference is treaties of peace rather than ladders of being.

Holy in Christ: Catholicity and Election

According to the Heidelberg Catechism, to affirm "one holy catholic church" means, "I believe that the Son of God, through his Spirit and Word, out of the entire human race, from the beginning of the world to its end, gathers, protects, and preserves for himself a community chosen for eternal life and united in true faith. And of this community I am and always will be a living member."[29]

Taking the catholicity of the church entirely out of our hands, election proscribes all overrealized eschatologies, whether they identify the pure church with a universal institution or with the sum total of the regenerate. Only in the eschaton will the visible church be identical with the catholic church. The union of Christ and his body—the one, holy, catholic, and apostolic church—is the eschatological communion of the elect, chosen "in Christ before the foundation of the world to be holy and blameless before him in love" (Eph. 1:4).

With the Augustinian heritage generally, Calvin locates the catholicity of the church in election. "Now this society is catholic, that is, universal, because there could not be two or three churches. But all God's elect are so united and conjoined in Christ that, as they are dependent upon one Head, they also grow together into one body." It is *this* church that is indefectible. It must always have its visible expression in every era, but this visibility is always ambiguous because the church is a mixed assembly and even the elect are simultaneously justified and sinful.[30]

Catholicity is therefore lodged ultimately in God's electing grace, not in individual choice or the vicissitudes of ecclesial faithfulness or unfaithfulness in history, but it becomes visible in history through Christ's work (2 Tim. 1:9–10). In

---

28. John Calvin, *Commentary on 1 Corinthians*, on 12:12.
29. The Heidelberg Catechism, Lord's Day 21, q. 54, in *The Psalter Hymnal: Doctrinal Standards and Liturgy of the Christian Reformed Church* (Grand Rapids: CRC Publications, 1976), 27.
30. John Calvin, *Institutes* 4.1.2–3.

short, the covenant of grace is the visible, already/not-yet, semirealized form of the glorified communion of the elect in the eschaton.

Besides preserving the eschatological tension between the ecclesial already and not-yet, election upholds both unity and plurality in Christ. In contrast both to totalizing models of the *totus Christus* and social models of plurality that downplay an essential unity, a covenantal model affirms both unity and difference as essential to the being of the church, because it is rooted in election. We are not one Christ (*methexis*), but one in Christ (*koinōnia*), and this is ultimately the result of God's choice rather than our own. It is not only the *church* that has been elected, Bonhoeffer reminds us, but *each member*.[31] "God therefore really sees the individual, and God's election really applies to the individual." Nevertheless, it is only part of the story. The communion that Christ creates by his Spirit is unique not because it overcomes ontological barriers in a miraculous fusion of persons, but because it justifies the ungodly and consequently, liberates them for each other in Christ. Yet this work of the Spirit is not only individual; it is also social—or, as I would put it, covenantal. The Spirit is at work in each of the elect, says Bonhoeffer, but precisely because this is so, "it follows that in moving the elect who are part of the church-community established in Christ, the Holy Spirit simultaneously leads them into the actualized church-community."[32] Hegelian monism, in contrast, "destroys the concrete person, and thus prevents any concrete concept of community."[33] Thus, the community always remains an idea, never an actual reality.

Far from legitimizing a spiritual elitism, the doctrine of election is meant to ensure that in spite of the failures of the visible church, God will preserve a remnant, not just from one nation but "from every tribe and language and people and nation" (Rev. 5:9). And yet, this ransomed plurality constitutes "*a* kingdom" (v. 10, emphasis added). Like its unity and holiness, the church's catholicity is affirmed in faith, not by sight. Its security lies in God's election, not in determinations that can be made by empirical inspection of its historical continuity and structure or the piety and enthusiasm of its membership.

Covenantal catholicity is grounded neither in a hierarchical unicity that derives from ecclesial agency nor in an egalitarian plurality that derives from individual choice, but in the intra-Trinitarian covenant of redemption. Jesus reminds us, "You did not choose me but I chose you. And I appointed you to go and bear fruit, fruit that will last" (John 15:16). Consequently, we are commanded to "love one another" (v. 17). I did not choose these people for my sisters and brothers; God did. If I am to be God's child, I must accept these others as my siblings, coheirs in Christ. A local church (or wider body of churches) is not free to develop its identity in continuity simply with the givens of racial, ethnic, socioeconomic, generational, or consumer affinities. Each particular expression of the church

---

31. Bonhoeffer, *SC*, 162.
32. Ibid., 158–59.
33. Ibid., 194–95.

must seek to exhibit the catholicity that is grounded in God's electing choice rather than in our own.

Election simultaneously keeps us from making catholicity depend on visible, institutional unicity while motivating a desire to see the churches reflect here and now in some sense the catholicity that is fully realized in God's electing purposes. In that light, local churches have an imperative set before them to pursue visibly, however imperfectly, the catholicity that awaits them in the consummation.

Philip Walker Butin observes of Calvin's view,

> If believers' sense of membership in Christ and the church were based primarily on the faithfulness of their own Christian commitment (or visible holiness, works, or even faith, subjectively understood), it would always be subject to doubt in the face of their human sin and failures. Calvin was well aware of how debilitating this subjectivistic understanding of church membership could be to the church's stability. On the other hand, when the "invisible" conception of the church was properly understood to aim at establishing the Trinitarian basis and stability of the church's necessarily corporeal, contextualized existence, the two perspectives could be seen as inseparably aspects of a single reality.[34]

Calvin says that Scripture speaks of the church sometimes as "that which is actually in God's presence," but also as "the whole multitude of people spread over the earth who profess to worship of God and Christ. . . . Just as we must believe, therefore, that the former church, invisible to us, is visible to the eyes of God alone, so we are commanded to revere and keep communion with the latter, which is called 'church' in respect to human beings."[35]

Thus, "invisible" and "visible" refer not to two different churches (much less do they correspond to "true" and "false"), but to the body of Christ as known to God in eternity and as known to us now as a "mixed assembly." The catholic church of God's elect is the reality of which the catholic church spread through all times and places in this age is a sign. So, for example, the Westminster Confession first defines the catholic church as "*invisible*," which "consists of the whole number of the elect, that have been, are, or shall be gathered into one, under Christ the Head thereof; and is the spouse, the body, the fullness of him that filleth all in all" (emphasis added). Yet in the next article, "The *visible* church, which is *also catholic* or universal under the gospel (not confined to one nation, as before, under the law), consists of all those throughout the world that profess the true religion; and of their children: and is the kingdom of the Lord Jesus Christ, the house and family of God, out of which there is no ordinary possibility of salvation" (emphasis added).[36] As such, it truly participates in the signified, but is not yet identical with it as one day it will be. "For the creation waits with eager longing for the

---

34. Philip Walker Butin, *Revelation, Redemption, and Response: Calvin's Trinitarian Understanding of the Divine-Human Relationship* (New York: Oxford University Press, 1995), 100.

35. Calvin, *Institutes* 4.1.7.

36. The Westminster Confession, chap. 25, in *Trinity Hymnal*, 863.

revealing of the children of God" (Rom. 8:19). Despite the confusion, error, and dissension that has always plagued the church, "God's firm foundation stands, bearing this inscription: 'The Lord knows those who are his'" (2 Tim. 2:19).

Reformed treatments of the invisible/visible church distinction do not therefore reflect, as Stanley Grenz suggests, "more platonic conceptions which regard the church in the world as the manifestation of some pure Form or Idea."[37] I will not dispute similarities between Augustinian and Reformed interpretations of the church as the elect communion (invisible) known to us now as a mixed body (visible). However, by embedding this understanding in the dynamic history of the covenant of grace, Reformed theology eschewed a dualistic (form-appearance) formulation. As even the statement from the Westminster Confession above demonstrates, the visible church has no less reality than the invisible church. They actually are not two churches but the church as it is known to God (already) and to us (already/not-yet). However, by lodging ecclesial being in God's electing grace, rather than in the extent to which local churches actually correspond to the consummated kingdom, the focus is on a kingdom that we are receiving rather than one that we are building or approximating through our own discipleship as we seek to mirror the Trinity.

The *en Christō* language throughout Ephesians (esp. chap. 1) is unmistakably concerned with participation, but it is the kind of *koinōnia* that obtains between covenant partners—who remain *partners* even in *union*, as the marriage analogy suggests. The husband and wife becoming "one flesh" can hardly mean fusion or assimilation. So the proper horizon of catholicity is the world of royal grants, marriages, families, and estate planning, not Plato's republic.

Also, in both Ephesians 4 and 1 Corinthians 8–14, the Supper (along with baptism and preaching) plays a critical role. In Ephesians, the communion that each of the elect enjoys with Christ (chap. 1) simultaneously creates on the horizontal register (to which Christ also belongs as head) a communion of saints that defies the divisions of both Athens and Jerusalem. In the work of the Spirit through the event of Word and sacrament, the church is not simply reminded or brought to a new awareness of its unity, but becomes more and more the catholic church in truth (1 Cor. 10:17).

This covenantal interpretation of the unity and catholicity of the church, which distinguishes the head and members while simultaneously recognizing their federative and mystical communion in Christ, has tremendous implications for ecclesial praxis. First of all, it challenges the widespread tendency today to allow rival catholicities to determine ecclesial character. All of us see things from our location, but for Christians the most decisive location is "in Christ." To be sure, we interpret reality within particular communities (ethnic, national, socioeconomic, generational, and so forth), but for Christians, again, the most decisive

37. Grenz, *Theology for the Community of God*, 623. While attributing this view to "the older Calvinists," his reference here is to the evangelical Baptist theologian Millard Erickson, *Christian Theology* (Grand Rapids: Baker, 1984), 3:1033.

community is the church—and not only the local church, but also the visible catholic church in all times and places. This point deserves further elaboration.

One Word, Many Languages

It has been frequently observed that whereas the Spirit descended on Babel in judgment to scatter the proud nations and divide their languages, the same Spirit descended at Pentecost in blessing to unite the peoples and give them a common tongue. However, it is apparent from Acts 2 that the diversity of languages was fully preserved at Pentecost. This point is emphasized throughout: "in the native language of each." "Amazed and astonished, they asked, 'Are not all these who are speaking Galileans? And how is it that we hear, each of us, in our own native language . . . about God's deeds of power" (vv. 4–8, 11b). Evidently, this gift of interpreting foreign languages was retained during the apostolic era (1 Cor. 12:10, 30; 14:2–4).

Much like modernity, the Promethean ambitions of those gathered on the plains to build a tower reaching to the heavens would create a hegemonic unicity (Gen. 11:1–9, whereas the Spirit who created a world full of diversity preserves it in that diversity and plurality. Those gathered near the temple at Pentecost who—"cut to the heart" by Peter's proclamation of the gospel—trusted in Christ that day were more perfectly *one* than any society, yet in a harmony of difference (Acts 2:37–41). The message that they heard was the same, but each heard it in his or her own language: "in our own languages we hear them speaking about God's deeds of power" (2:11). They were one because they *shared* the same things, not because they became *fused* into the same thing. Yet the story of which they were already a part (as Jewish converts) and the news that they heard was more unifying than any cultural differences that divided them. It was a plurality of languages that we encounter at Pentecost, not a plurality of gospels. There are not many lords, but one Lord; not many faiths, but one faith "once for all entrusted to the saints" (Jude 3); not many baptisms, but "one baptism" (Eph. 4:5); not many spirits, but one Spirit of truth (Eph. 4:4).

As we survey the contemporary ecclesial landscape, however, this account of catholicity seems to be reversed. Whereas an almost infinite diversity of doctrine and practice is tolerated, even celebrated, churches are becoming more hegemonic than ever with respect to politics, socioeconomic position, age, gender, and cultural tastes. "People like to become Christians without crossing racial, linguistic, or class barriers. This principle states an undeniable fact. . . . The world's population is a mosaic, and each piece has a separate life of its own that seems strange and often unlovely to men and women of other pieces."[38] McGavran anticipates the objection that this simply capitulates to cultural narcissism: "It is better, they think, to have a slow growing or nongrowing church that is really

---

38. Donald McGavran, *Understanding Church Growth*, ed and rev. C. Peter Wagner (Grand Rapids: Eerdmans, 1970), 163.

brotherly, integrated, and hence 'really Christian,' than a rapidly growing one-people church."[39]

Though clearly rejecting forced segregation on the basis of race, McGavran argues that before people can embrace true "brotherhood," they must become Christians, and since people become Christians more rapidly in culturally homogeneous units, we should do whatever it takes to serve that missional end.[40] South African theologians Allan Boesak and John de Gruchy argue that it was pietist missionaries who assumed this very principle when they planted "homogeneous" churches that inadvertently helped to bring apartheid into existence.[41]

Ecclesial apartheid is expanding, as each generation and demographic market is treated to its own study Bibles and devotional materials, small groups, and "worship experiences." Some of the leading megachurches with which I am familiar in southern California actually offer professionally choreographed theme-services based on musical preferences (1950s rock, Hawaiian, country, hip-hop, and alternative).

I have been increasingly impressed by the fact that wherever Christ is the focus of catholicity and Word-and-sacrament ministry is the means, a genuinely multicultural and multigenerational community is generated. However, where ethnic distinctiveness is prized over catholicity, the church easily becomes a reflection of a rival catholicity. This can happen in quite traditional churches, where cult and culture become confused. God's electing and redeeming grace forces us to redefine "outsiders" and "insiders," as we see so clearly exhibited in Jesus' ministry. Furthermore, if Jews had to get used to Gentiles in the ancient church, when the covenant community had been properly identified with a particular nation, then surely Gentiles themselves must embrace a catholicity defined by God's electing grace rather than our own preferences.

Embracing rather than eliminating cultural differences, the community generated by Pentecost is necessarily oriented toward a catholicity that expresses the end-time harvest of the nations. The fact that Paul's clearest teaching on the Supper is motivated by the practical problem of allowing socioeconomic differences to obtain in the communion of saints points up the similarities with our own age.

39. Ibid., 174.

40. Ibid., 174–75. C. Peter Wagner defends McGavran's approach in *Our Kind of People: The Ethical Dimensions of Church Growth in America* (Atlanta: John Knox Press, 1979).

41. Allan Boesak responds, "Manipulation of the word of God to suit culture, prejudices, or ideology is alien to the Reformed tradition" (*Black and Reformed: Apartheid, Liberation, and the Calvinist Tradition,* ed. Leonard Sweetman [Maryknoll, NY: Orbis, 1984], 87). According to John de Gruchy, Reformed churches were not segregated until the "revivals in the mid-nineteenth century" by holiness preacher Andrew Murray and pietist missionaries. "It was under the dominance of such evangelicalism," says de Gruchy, "rather than the strict Calvinism of Dort, that the Dutch Reformed Church agreed at its Synod of 1857 that congregations could be divided along racial lines." He adds, "Despite the fact that this development went against earlier synodical decisions that segregation in the church was contrary to the Word of God, it was rationalized on grounds of missiology and practical necessity. Missiologically it was argued that people were best evangelized and best worshipped God in their own language and cultural setting, a position reinforced by German Lutheran missiology and somewhat akin to the church-growth philosophy of our own time" (*Liberating Reformed Theology: A South African Contribution to an Ecumenical Debate* [Grand Rapids: Eerdmans, 1991], 23–24).

Within the history of American Protestantism (including our own Presbyterian churches), catholicity has been undermined more grievously by slavery and racism as well as by socioeconomic divisions. As these divisions are increasingly recognized as sinful, however, the solution is often to find *cultural* ways of negotiating and celebrating differences rather than by renewed attention to the *cultus*—that is, the ministry of the gospel, which creates ecclesial unity.

The current phase of ecclesial division is actually welcomed in the name of mission. It is not the catholicity of ethnic bonds or race. Though closely related to socioeconomic status, it is not exactly the same. Rather, it is the catholicity of the market. Not only separate churches, but also separate "churches-within-churches" are proliferating, each targeting its unique market.

In this context the church becomes a collection of consumers or tourists rather than a communion of saints and pilgrims. Hardly benign, the priority given to the invisible hand of the market is just as schismatic as the divisions of the early church. For all the appropriate lamentation concerning the denominational splintering of traditional Protestantism, individual choice and stylistic preferences threaten catholicity in our day not only between local churches but also within them. It is of the essence of marketing to attract consumers by appealing to the "felt needs" that are ostensibly unique to them, creating demographics defined by those consumer habits. If everyone were fairly similar in basic needs, there would be no motivation to purchase the panoply of ever-new accessories for one's ever-changing personality. The same logic that grounds personal salvation ultimately in one's own choice easily submits to the market-driven culture of choice. In effect, the covenant becomes a contract—both in its relation to God and in the communion of saints.

The same market forces that drive us to disposable identities and perpetual novelty (planned obsolescence) are tearing apart the fabric of genuine covenant community. Where it used to be said (and is still the case) that America's racial divisions were most evident on Sunday, it is increasingly the case that even families are more divided up into their market niches at church than anywhere else. Generational narcissism has become a publicly accepted form of self-preoccupation ever since the 1970s, and each generation is profiled in such literature in the most hyperbolic terms. When marketing and sociology developed the demographic known as "youth," the church created the "youth group." Today, it is quite possible for people entering college to have been raised in churches where they have never really been a part of the public services on the Lord's Day. Ensconced in their niche programs, from "children's church" to youth services, it is no wonder that more than half are reportedly unchurched by their sophomore year in college. Instead of regarding them as having abandoned church, we might perhaps wonder if they were ever fully a part of one. Years ago children learned the catechism with their parents at home and together in church before or after the service; then the American Sunday school movement became dominant, preparing the way for the "niching" of the community, ostensibly in the name of mission and outreach.

We have learned to think as never before in terms of the uniqueness of over-stereotyped generations. Where church divisions used to be lamented as differences over doctrine, they are now celebrated as "megachurch" and "emergent," as if each generation were an ex nihilo creation. As Timothy Gorringe reminds us, "'Community' in this world is a collection of individual consumers, who might change their preference from week to week."[42]

In the name of "incarnational ministry" and diversity, are we actually perpetuating a catholicity of the market that imposes cultural homogeneity while marginalizing unity in doctrine and church practice? One of the brilliant successes of the market is in convincing us that we are sovereign choosers even while, through its ubiquitous preaching and catechesis (media) and sacraments (advertising), it determines the horizon of our choices.

In the name of mission we can, as Barth warns, "actually separate the Churches." However, "the local community, with its local characteristics, cannot be basically and essentially another community in relation to others." In the New Testament, the plural term "churches" "does not speak of a plurality of Churches genuinely and radically different from each other," notes Barth. "It is one and the same community, separated only by geographical distance and what it involves. . . . Whatever we may understand by the seven churches of Asia Minor with their seven angels (Rev. 2–3), none of them has its own Lord or Spirit or Gospel."[43]

Catholicity does not depend on the similarity of our cultural tastes, consumer preferences, or political views. Nor does it depend on a similarity of our conversion stories, our progress in holiness, or even on our having identical formulations of every doctrine. Yet it does require a common confession (*homologein*—"same speech") concerning the triune God and the action of this God for our salvation in Christ: one Lord, one faith, one baptism.

We do not listen to the voice of Paul, Peter, or John because we have decided to privilege ancient Palestinian Jewish Christians. The church's catholicity thus does not derive from our privileging the voice of the apostles themselves in their persons, but only in their office, as we have access to the New Testament canon. For in their office, we hear the voice of God that gathers a people from every cultural demographic into a new location. "If with Christ you died to the elemental spirits [principles] of the universe, why do you live as if you still belonged to the world?" Paul asked the Colossians (Col. 2:20). "So if you have been raised with Christ, seek the things that are above, where Christ is, seated at the right hand of God" (3:1).

Nothing is more hegemonic and inattentive to otherness than demographic readings of Scripture. Referring to this as "chronological snobbery," C. S. Lewis nicely captured the essence of modern prejudice against the past, but it also can be applied to other forms of collective narcissism in which we try to conform the

---

42. Timothy Gorringe, *A Theology of the Built Environment* (Cambridge: Cambridge University Press, 2002), 164, from Frederick Tönnies, *Community and Society*, trans. C. Loomis (New York: Harper & Row, 1963), 165.
43. Karl Barth, *CD* IV/1:672.

church's faith and practice to our own experience. This is not to deny the reality of situated readings, but it is to insist that in the community spoken into existence by the Father in the Son through the Spirit, the readings that should be truly privileged are those that have been recognized by the communion of saints in all times and places, not just our own. Given our election, redemption, and all other gifts in Christ, why should we allow our churches to be defined by catholicities that are generated by this fading age?

Upbraiding the Corinthians for imposing secular habits of socioeconomic division to the communion of saints, the apostle to the Gentiles was appalled that Communion had been turned into a dinner party that excluded the poorer members. "What! Do you not have houses to eat and drink in? Or do you despise the church of God and humiliate those who have nothing?" (1 Cor. 11:22 ESV). Paul says that they had so disfigured the meal that "when you come together, it is not the Lord's supper that you eat" (v. 20 ESV). We might extend this reaction to include gatherings of the youth that exclude the elderly (or vice versa), and a variety of other cultural preferences. Do we not have our own homes and social networks for pursuing our tastes in music, style, politics, fashion, and hobbies?

The only way of transcending these rival catholicities that actually divide and conquer is by recognizing once again that genuine catholicity is determined by the Word of God, which relativizes all of our locations. Ironically, by carving the church into niche markets, emphasizing the ostensible uniqueness of each local culture, generation, ethnic, and socioeconomic status, we end up knowing more about ourselves and those who are like us than we do about the faith that we share with martyrs in China and Nigeria. Consequently, in all of this fascination with the context of our ministry, we are less likely to recognize the ways in which we systematically misinterpret that word.

However decisive for our interpretation and misinterpretation of Scripture, the experiences of our particular group are not a source of revelation but are the contexts within which our readings take place. The New Testament Gospels were obviously directed especially to specific groups, but they communicate the same gospel. Similarly, the epistles are addressed to "the church *in Corinth*" and elsewhere, but to "*the church* in Corinth," which was bound up with the churches in Jerusalem, Asia Minor, and Rome more than it was with its own neighbors. A Christian in Rome might be indistinguishable from fellow Romans in dress, cultural preferences, and even political convictions, yet a deeper catholicity bound the believer to fellow-Christians who might have quite different social affinities. We are united not by our demographic profile, but by being "baptized into one body—Jews or Greeks, slaves or free" (1 Cor. 12:13), and "we all partake of the one bread" (1 Cor. 10:17).

Culture and gospel do *not* contribute to a single act of divine speaking, because the gospel comes to us all *extra nos*. God has already accommodated his discourse to our creaturely finitude by employing ordinary languages and the most ordinary elements (water, bread, and wine) and actions (speech, bath, and meal). In these ways, God has made Christ accessible to people in every time and place. This is precisely why we need to hear and read Scripture together rather than in our niche groups, so that this catholicity, which is ours definitively in Christ, can be more fully realized among us. We locate ourselves most decisively "in Christ" when we share the same baptism, hear the same word of judgment and grace, pray and sing together, and receive together the body and blood of Christ, confessing our sins and our common faith. There we discover a community that we did not create or choose for ourselves, but we find ourselves incorporated into a kingdom of priests "out of every tribe and tongue and people and nation" (Rev. 5:9 NKJV).

In Israel's history, as Gregory Beale reminds us, "the emerging domination of ungodly kingdoms over the world is sometimes described with the imagery of the outgrowth of Eden's trees as a kind of parody. . . . Such unbelieving empires plant gardens to 'enjoy the aesthetic without the ethic'; they 'collectivize themselves . . . to seek a community without a covenant' (Gage 1984: 60–61)."[44] Without the securities of suzerainty treaties (having a *covenantal* relationship), life and death were managed either under *despotic* or *contractual* regimes dependent on the whim of rulers or the ruled, but not grounded in a transcendent ethical obligation. This is why the people's perennial demand for a king "like the other nations" is so tragic and untrusting of Yahweh: they want "a community without a covenant." I suggest that we find ourselves at this juncture today.

As much as is possible, given the profile of the neighborhoods that churches serve, each local church should be a visible expression of this catholicity that will one day be fully revealed. It is a place where grandparents worship together with their children and grandchildren, and it is once again the case that the older teach the younger by word and example, where there is a story larger, broader, and richer than the micronarratives defined by this fading age. Yet it is also a place where strangers are welcomed. In the public confession of sin and absolution; in the prayers, singing, and hearing of the Word; at the font and table—we not only *recall* that the most demographically decisive location is "in Christ"; we actually *become* located *there*. As the psalmist sings, "Lord, *you* have been our dwelling place in all generations" (Ps. 90:1; cf. Pss. 100:5; 102:12). "Under the sun"—that is, from the perspective of this fading age—"a generation goes, and a generation comes," and "all is vanity" (Eccl. 1:2–4), but *sub specie aeternitatis*, each generation of the covenant community belongs to the Lord, transcending itself by participation in the catholic body of Christ, whose "kingdom endures from generation to generation" (Dan. 4:34). "The unity of the Spirit in the bond of peace" that we are enjoined to maintain in Ephesians 4:1–6 must necessarily include this intergenerational fellowship.

Effort is required to maintain the bond of peace, especially when we are seduced into living as if other bodies, other spirits, other callings, lords, faiths, and baptisms vie for our ultimate allegiance. It requires humility, gentleness, and patience, as we read in those verses. Not only the young but also the old must love their fellow saints and seek to preserve a connection with the future as well

44. Ibid., 126, 129.

as the past. Covenantal succession requires patience on all sides. By settling for the truce of different niche groups and even worship services, we not only perpetuate ecclesial apartheid but also deprive ourselves and our group of the graces that enrich the whole body: the weak and the strong (Rom. 14:1–15:6; Gal. 6:1–10), the rich and the poor (1 Tim. 6:17–19), Jews and Gentiles (Rom. 15:7–21; Col. 3:11), men and women (Gal. 3:28), young and old (1 Tim. 5:1–10). Not because we all listen to the same music or share the same political agenda, but we find our true affinity because "we all partake of the one bread" (1 Cor. 10:17), have been "baptized into one body" (12:13), and embrace the same faith in one Spirit (Eph. 4:4–5). It was precisely because of worldly divisions that Paul warned the Corinthians to examine themselves before eating and drinking at the Lord's table (1 Cor. 11:27–34). Each local expression of the catholic church is under that solemn obligation to "be subject to one another out of reverence for Christ" (Eph. 5:21).

In what Barth called "the strange new world of the Bible," we find that instead of trying to make God's story fit the soap operas of our own life in this passing age, we become characters in the drama of redemption. It is the church's responsibility to stage local performances of God's "community theater" through concrete practices. Not only must the preaching regularly immerse us in the canon; we also must be catechized at home and at church in a common faith, in a story that gives decisive shape to the liturgy: not only the apostles' teaching and the Eucharist, but also "fellowship . . . and the prayers" (Acts 2:42). The goal even of the singing in our public and private worship, says Paul, is so that "the word of Christ [may] dwell in you richly" (Col. 3:16).

The covenant is not a grand concept, but a living reality. To say that the church is holy is to say that it is different—and its difference from the world is sustained by God's action (praxis), not simply by the theories or doctrines that are held. To say that the church is catholic is to say that particular churches in all times and places are united in a common confession and regulated by a common canon. Not the national flag but the pulpit, font, and table indicate where this catholic community exists. Just as the subjects of this covenantal body were chosen by God rather than by us, the means for sanctifying and unifying this body lie in God's hands.

Although we do not have a God's-eye perspective, we do belong to a community that is defined by the inbreaking of the age to come that relativizes all times and places, putting in jeopardy all of our cherished locations in this age. It even challenges our tendency to find our ultimate identity in our own denomination or tradition. While vigilant to uncover our own prejudices that work against it, we strive toward a catholic hearing of God's Word. From this perspective, we should not speak of a Reformed faith or an Orthodox theology or a Lutheran confession, but of a Christian faith, theology, and confession, from a Reformed, Orthodox, or Lutheran perspective.

The covenant gives us not only an ecclesiological theory, but also provides the concrete context for integrating faith and praxis. Contextual theologies and political theologies often assume that we know more than we do about our situation in this present age (based on our cultural analysis, which others may do better than theologians). It is remarkable how confidently preachers and theologians address the social, moral, economic, and political issues of the day in comparison with the false humility often displayed in proclaiming the doctrines of Christianity. As divided as churches are today by doctrine, they are more sharply separated by their respective ideologies about how to create a better world and maintain a more "relevant" mission. However, catholicity is an essential element of the community that any genuinely Christian mission serves. When the gospel unites us, there are no Republicans or Democrats, youth or elderly, rich or poor, healthy or sick, devotees of hip-hop or classical music, black, white, Asian, Hispanic, or other, but fellow sinners absolved by the one who has all authority in heaven and on earth to create his own demographic.

Covenantal Nurture: "To a Thousand Generations"

To interpret all of reality from the location of being in Christ, we must be sanctified by the Word of truth (John 17:17), which means at least in part that we are no longer to be conformed to the pattern of this world's way of thinking (Rom. 12:2). The covenant comes to us from outside of ourselves, but it draws us in. It comes to us by hearing and passively receiving, but it gives us tongues and it makes us servants to each other. Unconditionally guaranteed by grace as to its basis, the covenant nevertheless also calls for the appropriate response of repentance and faith and this response is not only made once but also throughout the Christian life, and not only by individuals but also by the church corporately.

As Robert Jenson points out, the distance that many feel between the biblical world and their own is more the fault of the church itself than the academy. "For the single most important cause of Scripture's alienation is that for the last twenty years the clergy of the American church stopped catechizing the neophytes of their congregation."[45] Not only formal classes, but also the liturgy and songs mediate the covenantal legacy from generation to generation.

The disruption of intergenerational catholicity has as much to do with a conservatism that ignores the needs of its youth as with a perpetual innovation that ignores the communion of saints. The point to be made against both tendencies is that the church is not a voluntary association of the old, the young, or the middle-aged, but a living branch of the Vine, which is spread throughout all times and places. Unlike the "house church," for example, as Bonhoeffer observes, the local parish church "is a piece of the world organized exclusively by the *sanctorum communio*."[46] The local church is not a gathering of a nuclear family with its circle of friends, but a strange assembly of spiritual relatives we may never have

---

45. Carl E. Braaten and Robert W. Jenson, *Reclaiming the Bible for the Church* (Edinburgh: T&T Clark, 1995), 91.
46. Bonhoeffer, *SC,* 230.

known, much less chosen, in our ordinary course of life. The local church, as part of the wider visible church, "for all its imperfection, is the guarantor of a relative unity of doctrine."[47]

At the same time, traditional churches must not treat their people as givens but as gifts, indeed as treasures that have been entrusted to their communion and care. Whenever the congregation is treated as an "audience" or "mass," Bonhoeffer reminds us, the problem of coming personally to profess the faith for oneself recedes behind the collective faith of the church.[48] Baptism is not only God's promise; it is also God's command to the whole church to assume its responsibilities to the child as agents of covenantal nurture.

> Thus the church-community as the community of saints carries its children like a mother, as its most sacred treasure. It can do this only by virtue of its "communal life"; if it were a "voluntary association" the act of baptism would be meaningless. This means, however, that infant baptism is no longer meaningful wherever the church can no longer envision "carrying" the child—where it is internally broken, or where it is certain that baptism will be the first and last contact the child will have with it.[49]

Bonhoeffer's comments not only serve to point up the critical difference between a contractual economy ("voluntary association") and a covenant community, but also to impress upon those of us who endorse the latter the danger of socialization without salvation. However, the answer is not to look outside of the covenant and its institutions that have been appointed by Christ for his people, but to renew a genuine covenantal piety and praxis that restores intergenerational integrity.

CATHOLICITY AS LOCAL AND UNIVERSAL

Nearly everything that I have proposed so far could be accepted within a range of views concerning the government or polity of the church. However, in this section I will explain why, in my view, presbyterian polity is the most appropriate expression of a covenantal ecclesiology.

The Church and the Churches in Contemporary Ecclesiologies

According to official Roman Catholic ecclesiology, just as the church's unity is a unicity determined by a hierarchical ministry with a single visible head, its catholicity is constituted by the relationship of particular (local) churches to that ministry. It is this perspective that we find elaborated by Joseph Cardinal Ratzinger (now Pope Benedict XVI). "The temporal and ontological priority lies

47. Ibid., 230–31.
48. Ibid., 239–40.
49. Ibid., 241.

with the universal Church; a Church that was not catholic would not even have ecclesial reality."[50] Catholicity is therefore an unambiguous empirical attribute, inasmuch as it is simply the *totus Christus* with the pope as its visible head. Thus the tension that we find in Augustine between the catholic church that is affirmed in faith (i.e., the unity of all the elect in Christ) and its visible communities in the present (i.e., particular churches) is resolved in favor of a one-to-one correspondence, with Rome as the center for human union with God. "A Church understood eucharistically is a Church constituted episcopally," Ratzinger continues.[51] Yet, against the East, he adds that this episcopal ministry itself depends on its relation to the pope as its visible head.[52]

The universal is therefore ontologically supreme. Unity equals unicity. It is this visible hierarchy that he has in mind when he offers the otherwise uncontroversial claim, "*Communio* is catholic, or it simply does not exist at all."[53] Further, according to Ratzinger, "The church is celebration of the Eucharist; the Eucharist is the church. These two do not stand next to one another, but rather are the same."[54] Thus, one truly receives this Communion (in both senses) only in the Roman Catholic Church.[55] In this way, both the natural and eucharistic bodies of Christ are assimilated to the ecclesial. The bishops in communion with the pope mediate the "whole Christ" to the whole church; therefore, the universal church (one) instantiates itself in various local churches (many).

The East has always suspected that Western papalism derives from faulty formulations of Trinitarian dogma. As we have already seen, Zizioulas reiterates this charge, emphasizing that it is the Spirit who not only brings about this communion (*koinōnia*), but *is* or *constitutes* this communion.[56] Because of the Spirit, Christ has a body—the church.[57] The event where all of these constituting factors converge is the Eucharist. If this is so, then we cannot say (as Rahner and Roman Catholic ecclesiology typically does) "that the 'essence' of the Church lies in the universal Church." Rather, "the one Christ event takes the form of *events* (plural), which *are as primary ontologically as the one Christ event itself.* The local Churches are as primary in ecclesiology as the universal Church. No priority of the universal over the local Church is conceivable in such an ecclesiology."[58] Eschatology and communion (which converge in the Eucharist) preserve the integrity of the one-and-many.

50. Joseph Cardinal Ratzinger, *Called to Communion: Understanding the Church Today*, trans. Adrian Walker (San Francisco: Ignatius Press, 1996), 44.

51. Ibid., 79.

52. Ibid., 79–80.

53. Ibid., 82.

54. Ibid., 42; Joseph Cardinal Ratzinger, *Principles of Catholic Theology: Building Stones for a Fundamental Theology*, trans. Mary Frances McCarthy (San Francisco: Ignatius Press, 1987), 55.

55. Ibid., 45.

56. John Zizioulas, *Being as Communion: Studies in Personhood and the Church* (Crestwood, NY: St. Vladimir's Seminary Press, 1985), 130.

57. Ibid., 131.

58. Ibid., 132–33.

If the Church is constituted through these two aspects of Pneumatology all *pyramidal* notions disappear in ecclesiology: the "one" and the "many" co-exist as two aspects of the same being. On the universal level this means that the local Churches constitute one Church through a ministry or an institution which composes simultaneously a primus and a synod of which he is a primus. On the local level, this means that the head of the local Church, the bishop, is conditioned by the existence of his community and the rest of the ministries, particularly the presbyterium. There is no ministry which does not need the other ministries; no ministry possesses the fullness, the plenitude of grace and power without a relationship with the other ministries.[59]

Further, eschatology keeps ecclesiology from becoming a mere affirmation of a historical institution.[60] Thus "the metropolis, an archdiocese or a patriarchate cannot be called a church itself, but only by extension, i.e., by virtue of the fact that it is based on . . . local churches which are the only ones . . . properly called churches."[61]

Zizioulas regards as disastrous the shift from the presence of a college of presbyters (presbyterium) being present at the Eucharist to an individual presbyter acting as head of a eucharistic community, since this development in essence denied the catholicity and unity of *all* orders in the community.[62] The bishop became "an administrator rather than a eucharistic president" and the presbyter became "a 'mass-specialist,' a 'priest'—thus leading to the medieval ecclesiological decadence in the West, and to the well-known reactions of the Reformation, as well as to grave confusion in the ecclesiological and canonical life of the Eastern Churches themselves."[63] All of this stands in contrast, he says, to the plural rule and representation that preserved the integrity of the celebration that constantly creates anew that local event (the church) that is itself "many" as well as "one."

Like Pope Benedict, Zizioulas recognizes that the earliest form of church polity was essentially presbyterian, with the bishop as "a co-presbyter" in "a college of the presbyterium."[64] In any case, "the eucharistic community envisaged in its parochial or even episcopal form is necessarily local. The principle 'wherever the eucharist is, there is the Church' risks suggesting the idea that each Church could, *independently of other local Churches*, be the 'one, holy, catholic and apostolic Church.'" Rome overidentifies catholicity with the *universal* church, while many Protestants seem to think that the *local* church exhausts the concept of church.[65] In this respect, Reformed interpreters will find much to

---

59. Ibid., 139.
60. Ibid., 140.
61. Ibid., 252–53.
62. Ibid., 250.
63. Ibid., 250–51.
64. Ibid., 195: "On the one hand [the bishop] was understood as a 'co-presbyter,' i.e. as one—presumably the first one—of the college of the presbyterium." "This is clearly indicated by the use of the term *presbyters* for the bishop by Irenaeus (*Haer.* IV 26:2). This should be taken as a survival of an old usage in the West, as it can be inferred from *I Clement* 44, 1 Peter 5:1, etc." (195 n. 85). In *Called to Communion* (122–23), Ratzinger acknowledges that *presbyteroi* and *episcopoi* are used interchangeably in the New Testament.
65. Ratzinger, *Principles of Catholic Theology*, 25.

commend in Zizioulas's attempt to stake out a middle ground between pyrami- dal and independent ecclesiologies.

Christology and pneumatology are mutually conditioning and surely consti- tutive. "The primary content of 'catholicity,'" according to Zizioulas, "is not a moral but a Christological one." "The Church is catholic, not because she is obe- dient to Christ, . . . because she does certain things or behaves in a certain way. She is catholic first of all because she is the Body of Christ. Her catholicity depends not on herself but on Him. She is catholic because she is where Christ is."[66] This means that "there is *no autonomous catholicity*, no catholic ethos that can be understood in itself. It is *Christ's* unity and it is *His* catholicity that the Church reveals in her being catholic." It is not something she possesses or some- thing she must attain, but the presence of Christ himself.[67]

At the same time, it is a *dynamic* catholicity that depends on the descent of the Spirit (*epiclēsis*).[68] If it were a matter merely of remembering (*anamnēsis*), it would depend on our own mental operation, but if it is an eschatological event, then it depends on the Spirit.[69]

> This means not only that human attempts at "togetherness," "openness," etc., cannot constitute the catholicity of the Church, but that no plan for a progressive movement towards catholicity can be achieved on a purely his- torical and sociological level. *The eucharistic community can only break through history but never be identified with it.* Its call to catholicity is a call not to a progressive conquest of the world but to a "kenotic" experience of the fight with the anti-catholic demonic powers and a continuous depen- dence upon the Lord and His Spirit. (emphasis added)[70]

The Reformation could only happen, says Zizioulas, because the medieval Western church had narrowly defined the being of the church to its history: specifically, the historic episcopate. There was no need to invoke the Spirit for the event of euchari- stic communion, since this history already guarantees its validity and efficacy.[71]

Representing a free-church perspective, Miroslav Volf restricts the definition of the visible church (properly speaking) to the local assembly. He pursues this with a carefully nuanced application of social Trinitarianism to ecclesiology.[72] In terms of structure, "the church is not a monocentric-bipolar community, however artic- ulated, but rather fundamentally a *polycentric community*."[73] Although I have my own reservations about the social doctrine of the Trinity, my principal concern here is that Volf draws too univocal an identity between divine (Trinitarian) and

66. Zizioulas, *Being as Communion*, 158.
67. Ibid., 159.
68. Ibid., 160.
69. Ibid., 160–61.
70. Ibid., 161.
71. Ibid., 185.
72. Miroslav Volf, *After Our Likeness: The Church as the Image of the Trinity* (Grand Rapids: Eerd- mans, 1998), 203–5.
73. Ibid., 224.

human (ecclesial) being, despite his caution against such a move. Whenever we approach ecclesiology as a way of identifying an ideal model of community, we may distort both the doctrines of the Trinity and the church in the process. Neither Volf nor those whom he critiques give adequate attention, in my view, to the dissimilarity in the analogy between Trinitarian perichoresis and the covenant community.

Furthermore, although Volf's careful study recognizes the significance of divine action through preaching and sacrament, the nature of the church is still too dependent on the action of the community. In Volf's conception, just as the sacraments depend on faith for their validity, catholicity depends too much on the subjective attitude of openness to other churches (exclusively local congregations in this model). Especially in the climate of seemingly intractable divisions, this is a commendable reminder that ecumenism begins with an extroverted orientation that recognizes the validity of the claim to ecclesial status by other bodies. However, as a principle of catholicity, it may make ecumenism depend too much on the piety of individuals and congregations and is too slender a thread for the connection of particular churches to the wider body.

From a more covenantal perspective, Christ's presence in the midst of "two or more" witnesses makes every local church a microcosm of the only holy, catholic, and apostolic church, which it could not be if it were an isolated community. The perfect realization of this visible unity does indeed await the consummation, yet along with personal sanctification, it is imperfectly realized even now and represents a goal toward which we should press, an indicative gift that drives an imperative task. The recognition of the not-yet keeps us from a perfectionistic ecclesiology that can only lead to despair and cynicism, given the actual fragmentation of the visible church. Free-church ecclesiologies caution us against jumping the eschatological gun in this regard, and Volf does this with remarkable skill. Furthermore, the worldwide fellowship of evangelical groups has often facilitated a remarkably successful cooperation of informal transdenominational and nondenominational efforts based on spiritual rather than institutional unity. However, as Dulles points out, a dualistic ecclesiology and eschatological reserve can become a cop-out for overcoming our divisions here and now.[74]

If free churches tend to underappreciate the reality of a visible ecclesial unity in the present, Volf is certainly correct to point out the threat of Rome's position at the other end: "The Second Vatican Council designated all other Christian communities besides the Catholic Church as non-catholic, including the Orthodox and Anglican churches (see *Unitatis redintegratio* 13, 17; Dulles, *Catholicity*, 132)."[75] He properly concludes that this is profoundly "uncatholic."[76] This actually was a critical argument in the Reformation, appealing to the ancient ecclesiastical consensus that any bishop who raised himself above the others in effect

---

74. Ibid., 148.
75. Ibid., 260 n. 4.
76. Ibid., 261.

violated catholicity and became a rogue shepherd, and it remains a bone of contention between Orthodoxy and Rome.[77] Volf points out the irony that while continuing to downgrade the ecclesial status of Christian bodies, Rome's own catholicity is now understood to move even beyond Christ (at least faith in Christ) to include non-Christian religions.[78] Unity prevails only by ranking Christian churches and other religions in a descending order on the ladder of ecclesial being. In contrast, Volf maintains that catholicity, like all other aspects of ecclesiology, must be understood "within a comprehensive *eschatological framework*."[79]

All of this is salutary—until he suggests that here and now at least there is only "the catholicity of local churches." Thus, for the time being at least, this "allows for no other church than the local church."[80] Volf's social Trinitarian model nudges him in the direction of an ecclesiology that privileges plurality over unity, so that the latter is not essential, at least on this side of the eschaton. Not even in the eschaton, however, can the church be essentially one even in its diversity if the unity of the Trinity itself is less ontologically "real" than its plurality.

If, as I point out below, the apostolic community understood the church as local and broader assemblies, then Pentecost has *already* given rise to a foretaste of that unity of the age to come. When restricting the church (1) to its local expression and (2) to a regenerate membership, independent ecclesiologies tend toward an underrealized eschatology with respect to the first and toward an overrealized eschatology with respect to the second, eliding the distinction between the invisible and visible church. The church is commissioned to approve professions of faith, not to execute a final separation of sheep and goats, weeds and wheat (Matt. 13:24–43). At the same time, independent congregations remind us of the priority of the local church as the concrete expression of covenantal membership and of the necessity for personal repentance and faith.

Covenant and Connectionalism

A covenantal ecclesiology challenges both realist/idealist as well as voluntaristic formulations of catholicity. As constituted "from above" by the always surprising and disruptive announcement of the gospel, the covenant community receives its catholicity along with its entire being *extra nos*, outside of itself, in spite of its own history of unfaithfulness. As constituted "from below" in history ("to a thousand generations"), catholicity is mediated through the faithful ministry of Word and sacrament, yielding a succession of faith from one generation to another across all times and places. Taking its bearings from both of these coordinates—the eschatological and the historical—a covenantal ecclesiology affirms that just as each believer must be joined to the visible body and each generation must be connected

---

77. Calvin appeals especially to Cyprian and Augustine on this point (*Institutes* 4.6.4, 13, 17; 4.7.1–17).

78. Volf, *After Our Likeness*, 263–64.

79. Ibid., 266.

80. Ibid., 270.

to those that precede and follow it, particular (local) churches must make "every effort to maintain the unity of the Spirit in the bond of peace" (Eph. 4:3) by ever wider and deeper solidarity that expresses itself in concrete, visible, and enduring structures.

This last point leads us to the especially controversial question of polity. The main outlines of a presbyterian polity can be seen in the Jerusalem Council in Acts 15, where a local church dispute was taken to the broader assembly of the church. It is striking that several times the report refers to "the apostles and the elders" as the decision-making body. Commissioners (including Paul and Barnabas) were sent from the local church in Antioch to the wider assembly, convened at Jerusalem. It was James rather than Peter who said, for his part, "Therefore I have reached the decision that we should not trouble those Gentiles who are turning to God" (v. 19). Still, the final verdict awaited the assent of the full assembly. "Then the apostles and the elders, with the consent of the whole church, decided to choose men from among their members and to send them to Antioch with Paul and Barnabas," to relate the written decision to that local church (vv. 22–29). Immediately we see the practical effects of this decision, as Paul, Timothy, and Silas "went from town to town" and "delivered to them for observance the decisions that had been reached by the apostles and elders who were in Jerusalem. So the churches were strengthened in the faith and increased in numbers daily" (Acts 16:4–5).

Elders are to be "worthy of double honor," although for this reason, "Do not ordain anyone hastily" (1 Tim. 5:17, 22). Qualifications for ministers and elders are clearly laid out in 1 Timothy 3:1–7, distinct from the office of deacon (vv. 8–13). So Paul can remind Titus that he left him "behind in Crete for this reason, so that you should put in order what remained to be done, and should appoint elders in every town, as I directed you," again listing the qualifications (Titus 1:5–9).

At the Jerusalem Council, the unity that the Spirit had established at Pentecost was preserved visibly not by the sacrifice of the one to the many or the many to the one, but by the consent of the many as one. The covenant community *functioned covenantally* in its outward and interpersonal government, in mutual submission rather than hierarchical unity or independent plurality. A covenantal conception of apostolicity seems to me at least to imply a connectional yet non-hierarchical polity: something like a presbyerian polity. The Second Helvetic Confession repeats some of the patristic quotes often appealed to by the Reformers. Besides Cyprian, Jerome is cited: "Before attachment to persons in religion was begun at the instigation of the devil, the churches were governed by the common consultation of the elders." Jerome goes so far as to suggest that the introduction of bishops as a separate order above the elders was "more from custom than from the truth of an arrangement by the Lord."[81] The significance of Peter in the apostolic college was never denied by the Reformers and the Reformed

---

81. Second Helvetic Confession 5.160–62, in *BC*, chap. 18.

confessions, yet it was pointed out that Christ gave the keys of the kingdom to all of the apostles equally, and it pertained to the confession of Christ as the Son of God (Matt. 16:19 with 18:18–20).

Although I regard presbyterian government as belonging to the well-being (*bene esse*) rather than the very existence (*esse*) of the church, it does seem most consistent with the covenantal ecclesiology that we find not only stipulated but also performed in the early church. Catholicity is expressed in the diversity of gifts bestowed on the church as an irreducible plurality, and yet within a connectional polity. Hence, Paul can move back and forth between the unity of the one body and its irreducible plurality. "For in fact the body is not one member but many" (1 Cor. 12:14 NKJV). There is an order of graces—gifts bestowed on office-bearers in the church, but no hierarchy of grace (vv. 27–31).

Especially given the recognition of Ratzinger and Zizioulas that presbyterian polity was the earliest working constitution of the apostolic community, I suggest that such polity (though often overlooked in recent evangelical and Pentecostal ecclesiologies) holds greater potential for transcending the choice between hierarchy and egalitarianism.

In a connectional polity, the church can indeed be well-described as a polycentric community, as Volf suggests. However, in independent or free-church polities, the church cannot really be, at least visibly, *a* polycentric community. It can only be a multitude of such communities: bodies of Christ, but not (at least for now) part of the one, visible, public body of Christ. This definition is further complicated by restricting the church to its local assemblies. Volf recognizes that both episcopal and independent models "underestimate the enormous ecclesiological significance of concrete relations with other Christians, relations through which every Christian becomes a Christian and in which that person lives as a Christian."[82] One side emphasizes purely objective conditions, while the other stresses subjective ones, but we require both. Free churches are correct to insist, with Volf, "We are the church!"[83] There is "one body" because the one Spirit has called us— Jew and Gentile—into one body: "one Lord, one faith, one baptism" (Eph. 4:4–5). Absent from such lists are "one pastor"; thus in Ephesians 4, the spoils of Christ's victory poured out on the church are a variety of evangelists, pastors, and teachers for the building up of the body of Christ in sound doctrine (vv. 7–14). Insisting that the church in its local and wider assemblies consist representatively of ministers and elders (following the repeated reference to the "apostles and elders" gathered at the Jerusalem Council), with elders being ordained rulers though not pastors, presbyterian polity avoids clericalism. Placing the spiritual leadership of the church in ministers and elders not only provides important checks and balances on ecclesiastical power; it also ensures that the title of "church" refers to the whole body and not simply to a magisterium of clergy, while nevertheless affirming the real authority of local and broader assemblies.

---

82. Volf, *After Our Likeness*, 134.
83. Ibid., 135.

Even in its tragic condition as a divided kingdom, the Spirit kept faith alive and a remnant preserved through the witness of the Old Testament prophets. Luther correctly perceived that the true church is the community of sinners that confesses its sins and receives forgiveness. Its holiness and catholicity are never a given, but always a gift, and always ambiguously and imperfectly evident in this age. As Barth expressed it,

> When has Christian ethics not wavered between pharisaical legalism and an antinomian libertinism, between a "spiritual" sectarianism and a complacent respectability, between a weary pietism and a feverish activism, between the attractions of conservatism and those of revolution (or perhaps only of Bohemianism)? When has it been the case that men could simply see the good works of Christians and had to glorify their Father which is in heaven (Mt. 5:16)? . . . The body of Jesus Christ may well be sick or wounded. When has it not been? But as the body of this Head it cannot die.[84]

The church is indeed the creation of the Word. In the face of our ecumenical challenges, only this confidence in the gospel can sustain our hope that the church elected, redeemed, called, justified, and sanctified by grace alone will indeed endure to the end.

---

84. Barth, *CD* IV/1:690–91.

Chapter Eight

Apostolicity

Historical Institution
and Eschatological Event

I have argued that holiness and catholicity converge in Jesus' petition "Sanctify them in the truth; your word is truth" (John 17:17). Thus, the measure and means of this sanctification are in the message entrusted to the prophets and apostles. Apostolicity, too, is guaranteed neither by the immanence of a historical office or personal experience, but by the Spirit's effective ministry of the gospel through the means appointed by Christ. The true church about which we have been speaking—the one, holy, catholic, and apostolic church—is "the congregation of all believers" (Augsburg Confession, art. 7; Belgic Confession, art. 27), "the communion of all the elect" (Heidelberg Catechism q. 54). Yet for the time being, the catholic church comes to visible expression in "particular churches, which are members thereof, . . . more or less pure, according as the doctrine of the gospel is taught and embraced, ordinances administered, and public worship performed more or less purely in them" (Westminster Confession 25.4).[1] As Paul Avis has observed, "Reformation theology is largely dominated by two questions:

1. The Westminster Confession, chap. 25.5, in *Trinity Hymnal*, rev. ed. (Atlanta and Philadelphia: Great Commission Publications, 1990), 863.

'How can I obtain a gracious God?' and 'Where can I find the true Church?' The two questions are inseparably related."[2]

.With apostolicity, therefore, we reach the closest intersection between the attributes of the church and its marks. The addition of discipline as a third mark in Reformed confessions underscores the fact that the church is both the consequence of an *eschatological event* generated through Word and sacrament and a *historical institution* with its enduring offices and church orders.[3] Both of these aspects are crucial for a biblical notion of a covenant community. After laying out that argument, this chapter builds the case for identifying the marks of the church (preaching and sacrament) as constitutive for a covenantal theology of mission.

HISTORICAL ORGANIZATION OR ESCHATOLOGICAL EVENT?

So far we have met two extreme tendencies. Bearing in mind that the contrast between "historical organization" and "eschatological event" highlights tendencies rather than hard-and-fast antitheses, it will suffice at least to provide a way of pointing up once again the potential of a covenantal approach.

Historical Organization

No longer the herald of grace, the medieval church regarded itself as the possessor of grace, dispensing it as it saw fit. In effect, the ambassador proclaimed itself the monarch; ecclesiology threatened to smother Christology, along with pneumatology and eschatology. Recalling the summaries in previous chapters, the organic analogies of the romantic era softened the post-Tridentine Roman Catholic view of the church as primarily a judicial institution with sovereign power. With a more organic conception, the church could be understood as always growing, yet always self-consistent (*semper idem*) and therefore, at least ultimately, unerring in its magisterial judgments.

2. Paul D. L. Avis, *The Church in the Theology of the Reformers* (Atlanta: John Knox Press, 1981), 1.

3. Representative of the Reformation confessions, the Belgic Confession (1561) elaborates the marks of the church:

> The true church can be recognized if it has the following marks: The church engages in the pure preaching of the gospel; it makes use of the pure administration of the sacraments as Christ instituted them; it practices church discipline for correcting faults. In short, it governs itself according to the pure Word of God, rejecting all things contrary to it and holding Jesus Christ as the only Head. By these marks one can be assured of recognizing the true church—and no one ought to be separated from it. . . . As for the false church, it assigns more authority to itself and its ordinances than to the Word of God; it does not want to subject itself to the yoke of Christ; it does not administer the sacraments as Christ commanded in his Word; it rather adds to them or subtracts from them as it pleases; it bases itself on men more than on Jesus Christ; it persecutes those who live holy lives according to the Word of God and who rebuke it for its faults, greed, and idolatry. These two churches are easy to recognize and thus to distinguish from each other.

In the modern Protestant variations, critical of either a sovereign canon or magisterium, the neo-Hegelian *totus Christus* took the form of an organic ecclesiology that located the unchanging *semen rationalis* in the religious experience of the community. It is no wonder, then, that Ernst Troeltsch could regard the church as a purely historical and therefore purely human institution alongside other social and cultural institutions.[4] Ironically, the divinized church of the neo-Protestant *totus Christus* ended in a secularized ecclesiology.

The tendency to substitute the church for Christ can be discerned in modern faith and practice across the ecclesial spectrum. Lesslie Newbigin cites a Protestant hymn by John Mason Neale often sung on Ember days:

> So age by age, and year by year,
>   His grace was handed on;
> And still the holy Church is here
>   Although her Lord is gone.[5]

"The Church seems here," Newbigin adds, "to have become a purely historical institution, the trustee of an absent landlord."[6]

As Barth pointed out, *ecclesia semper reformanda* (the church always being reformed), divorced from the rest of the slogan, "according to the word of God," identified the true church with modern progress—keeping up with the spirit of the age.[7] I would add that the drive in Protestant bodies to conform the gospel to the spirit of the age has often invoked the Spirit apart from and even sometimes against the Word in its activity of "always reforming." However, as Barth observes, "singing a new song" and "always being reformed" are only commendable goals if they are invitations to courageous and obedient faith rather than simply following the spirit of the age. It means that the church is always *being* reformed, not reforming itself, submitting itself to the judgment of God's Word and asking anew whether its confession and practice are in accord with Scripture.[8] Only in this way is any church truly apostolic.

Yet traditionalism also has its own way of looking away from Christ in reliance on the Spirit. While the creeds and confessions remain treasures to be defended, we easily forget that they serve rather than substitute for the living confession of Christ as we return in each generation to the original well from which they are drawn.[9]

---

4. Ernst Troeltsch, *The Social Teaching of the Christian Churches*, 2 vols., trans. Olive Wyon (New York: Harper & Brothers, 1960), esp. 1–38. However, the naturalistic presupposition is apparent throughout the impressive study.

5. Cited in Lesslie Newbigin, *The Household of God: Lectures on the Nature of the Church* (New York: Friendship Press, 1954; London: SCM Press, 1957), 83.

6. Ibid.

7. Barth, *CD* IV/1:705.

8. Ibid.

9. See Abraham Kuyper's critique of a dead conservatism, "Conservatism and Orthodoxy: False and True Preservation" (1870), alongside his critique of theological modernism, in *Abraham Kuyper: A Centennial Reader*, ed. James D. Bratt (Grand Rapids: Eerdmans, 1998), 65–86, 87–124.

Wherever the church looks away from its bodily ascended Lord, in constant dependence on the Spirit, it easily degenerates into a purely historical organization as the substitute (vicar) of Christ on earth. Once it has made this decisive move toward an immanentist ecclesiology, smothering eschatology, it is then easy also to identify this historical organization with a particular culture or civilization. By this standard, neither a self-satisfied conservatism nor an enthusiastic radicalism is an adequate response. The catholicity and apostolicity of the church can only be realized by reference to the canon of the Covenant Lord, as we today hear God addressing us in and through the words of the prophets and apostles, in the power of the Spirit.

The eschatological event provoked by the Spirit's gracious disruption of our ordinary ecclesial and personal existence always has priority, yet this work of the Spirit is not immediate or direct and is rarely even extraordinary in the sense of dissolving the historical structures, institutions, offices, and ministry of the church. Rather than merely bursting like fireworks above the historical-horizontal axis, the declarative and transforming Word of the Spirit charges that axis with truth and power from above, generating a historical body that is ever-renewed and ever being reformed. As *sacramental*, the Word breaks up and places the church in the middle of the conflict between the ages, sometimes even bringing the church to the point of having to question its own existence. Yet as *canon*, this Word endures from generation to generation, regulating the historical continuity of the contemporary church in any given place with the one holy, catholic, and apostolic church of all times and places.

As Lesslie Newbigin observes, Reformed theology, with its covenantal orientation, affirms just as strongly as Rome that the church is visibly incorporated into Christ. It therefore resists the tendency to collapse the visible into the invisible church or to regard the visible church simply as an event.

> When, on the other hand, the Church is identified simply with whatever society has continued in unbroken succession from the time of the apostles, then the flesh, not the Spirit, has been made determinative. There is in truth no "extension of the Incarnation," for His incarnation was in order to make an offering of Himself in the flesh "once for all." The fruit of that offering, of that casting of a corn of wheat into the earth, is the extension of His risen life to all who are made members of His Body in the one Spirit—until He comes again. . . . The fundamental error into which Catholic doctrines of the Church are prone to fall is . . . the error of *subordinating the eschatological to the historical.* (emphasis added)[10]

This is precisely what is at stake in recognizing that the church is the creation of the word. Newbigin judges:

> What seems to be implied in so-called Catholic definitions of the Church, however, is that while a Church may in other matters lose what belongs to

---

10. Newbigin, *The Household of God*, 82.

its essence and yet be accepted by God as a Church, a Church which loses its continuity with the undivided Church forfeits completely its character as part of the Catholic Church; that though a Church be besotted with corruption, bound to the world in an unholy alliance, rent with faction, filled with false teaching, and utterly without missionary zeal, God's mercy is big enough to cover these defects and they do not therefore destroy its claim to be regarded as part of the Church; but that though a Church be filled with all the fruits of the Holy Spirit, if it lack the apostolic succession it is no part of the Church and all the mercy of God is not enough to make it so.[11]

It all comes back to law and gospel, says Newbigin. Rome is correct "in insisting that the continuity of the Church is God's will," but "is wrong when [it] suggests that the doing of that will is the condition of our standing in His grace. As for the individual, so also for the Church, there is only one way to be justified, and it is to say, 'God be merciful to me a sinner.'"[12]

Accordingly, the gospel is the criterion for apostolicity, which means that because there is "one faith"—meaning the *fides quae creditur* (the faith that is believed)—there is historical continuity with the apostles. Not the one order in communion with one pastor, but "the faith that was once for all entrusted to the saints" (Jude 3) is the unbroken thread running from the prophets and apostles to us today. It is the gospel, revealed from heaven and proclaimed on earth in the power of the Spirit, that creates a visible link between the eschatological and the historical vectors of ecclesial existence.

Ancient Christian leaders of the East never accepted the supremacy of the Roman bishop. Some, like Cyprian, warned that any assertion of episcopal primacy would constitute schism. Even in the West such a privilege was rejected by Gregory the Great in the sixth century. He expressed offense at being addressed by a bishop as "universal pope": "a word of proud address that I have forbidden. . . . None of my predecessors ever wished to use this profane word [universal]. . . . But I say it confidently, because whoever calls himself 'universal bishop' or wishes to be so called, is in his self-exaltation Antichrist's precursor, for in his swaggering he sets himself before the rest."[13]

Therefore, it is impossible on historical grounds to require a definition of catholicity and apostolicity that is dependent on such acknowledgement. However, my concern at this point is more general. Aside from the question of papal authority or even apostolic succession through a valid episcopate, the deeper issue is whether the church is saved by law or gospel. Newbigin, who was a bishop in the Church of South India, contended, "The fundamental flaw" in making a valid episcopate essential to apostolicity "is that it forgets that the substance of the covenant is pure mercy, and that God retains His sovereign freedom to have mercy upon whom He will, and to call 'No People' His people when they that

11. Ibid., 85.
12. Ibid., 86.
13. Gregory I, *Letters* 1.75–76; 2.170, 171, 179, 166, 169, 222, 225; translation from *Nicene and Post-Nicene Fathers*, series 2, vol. 12.

are called His people deny their calling by unbelief and sin."[14] Newbigin rightly contends that a valid ministry of Word and sacrament *is* essential, but this does not require episcopal government.

Given the insistence of some, past and present, that presbyterian polity is essential to ecclesial being, the same point can be extended to any who would raise church order to the level of the gospel. Churches may rightly contend for one polity as more consistent with the New Testament and tradition, but to make it a sine qua non of ecclesial identity is in effect to substitute the church—perhaps even a single denomination—for the gospel itself, a move that, as Yves Congar laments, is actually made in Roman Catholic theology.[15] According to the Tridentine divine Cardinal Hosius, "The living gospel is the Church itself."[16]

Israel was a united church, but due to inner strife and apostasy, it divided into northern and southern kingdoms, with only a remnant preserved, and Judah itself followed Israel in breaking the covenant, provoking the exile. Mercifully, the church is not the living gospel, but the recipient of the good news that, despite its unfaithfulness, God will keep his promise. What remains inviolable is the "election of grace," a gift of God rather than a given of historical existence. There will always be a visible church with a valid ministry and public forms, but because this visibility is constituted by the Word and sacraments, any professing community can lose its connection to this valid apostolicity. Whether by privileging the visibility of a historical institution or the invisible power of the Spirit at work in the lives of its members, the church often loses its theocentric focus. Whatever the church is and does, it can only be catholic and apostolic to the extent that it is the site of the Trinity's disrupting and reorganizing grace.

Eschatological Event

It was against this anthropocentric trend in modern Roman Catholicism and Protestantism that Barth launched his epochal program. Redemption is concerned with God's action, not ours—whether individual or corporate, and consequently the church exists simply as a witness to divine action. Fearful of making God's grace a human possession, Barth seems hesitant to affirm that God ordinarily works through creaturely agency, although he may *commandeer, overwhelm, disrupt,* and otherwise use human words and actions as *witnesses* to revelation. Barth's actualist ontology underwrites this emphasis: "The Church is when it takes place."[17] "To speak of a continuation or extension of the incarnation in the Church is not only out of place but even blasphemous," he boldly and properly insists.[18]

However, where the conflation of Christology and ecclesiology in some modern theologies virtually eliminates the difference between divine and ecclesial

14. Newbigin, *Household of God,* 86.
15. Yves Congar, *I Believe in the Holy Spirit* (New York: Crossroad, 1999), 154.
16. Ibid., 153.
17. Barth, *CD* IV/1:652.
18. Ibid., IV/3.2:729.

agency, Barth virtually eliminates affinity. As we have already seen, distinctions often become dichotomies between God and humanity, the divine Word and human words, baptism with the Spirit and baptism with water. It is difficult to resist the impression that these dichotomies belong to the map of eternity and time, respectively.

Especially in the *Römerbrief*, the "kingdom of God" (apocalyptic and eschatological) is not only distinguished but is also set over against the visible church (historical and transient). The church's activity "is related to the Gospel only in so far as it is no more than a crater formed by the explosion of a shell and seeks to be no more than a void in which the Gospel reveals itself."[19] The church's words and actions "by their negation are sign-posts to the Holy One," never sacred themselves.[20] Barth refers to the Church of Esau and the Church of Jacob—not as two discrete entities, but as the one church in its observable and hidden forms. Where the Reformers insisted that the church was partly hidden and partly visible in this age, Barth identifies the visible church with the Church of Esau, "where no miracle occurs, and where, consequently, men are exposed as liars, precisely when they hear and speak about God."[21] "The Church of Esau is the realm where failure and corruption may be found, the place where schisms and reformations occur."

> But the Church of Jacob is capable of no less precise definition. It is the unobservable, unknowable, and impossible Church, capable neither of expansion nor of contraction; it has neither place nor name nor history; men neither communicate with it nor are excommunicated from it. It is simply the free Grace of God, His Calling and Election; it is Beginning and End.[22]

"Our speech is of the Church of Esau, for we can speak of none other," although we always keep in mind the reality of the Church of Jacob, upon which the Church of Esau depends for its own shadowy existence.[23] When the miracle occurs—when the purely natural community known as the Church of Esau hears and speaks the Word of God—"and this is the miracle!"—then "there is hidden in that historical moment the eternal 'Moment' of revelation and they are existentially what they are said to be. They are then—and here again is the miracle!—the invisible Church of Jacob."[24]

In this view, the relationship between the visible church and God's reign is tenuous. We are part of, cling to, and preserve the unity of the Esau-like church, Barth insists. However, "the work of the Church is the work of men. It can never be God's work."[25] "The Church is the Church of Jacob—only when the miracle

---

19. Karl Barth, *The Epistle to the Romans*, trans. Edwyn C. Hoskyns from the 6th ed. (London: Oxford University Press, 1933), 36.

20. Ibid.

21. Ibid., 341.

22. Ibid., 342.

23. Ibid.

24. Ibid., 343.

25. Barth, *The Epistle to the Romans*, 353.

occurs. Otherwise it is nothing more than the Church of Esau."[26] This would seem to question the very possibility of an actual church extending "from generation to generation" rather than simply moment by moment.

In terms of the secret of its being—"this spiritual character," "the community is the earthly-historical form of existence of Jesus Christ Himself." Ironically, Barth approaches the neo-Hegelian conflation of Christology and ecclesiology on this register. Yet this is to be distinguished from his "heavenly-historical form of existence . . . at the right hand of the Father."[27] In this connection, the church can only exist as purely secular in its empirical form and spiritual in the event of witnessing to Christ.[28] Invisible and visible refer not to two churches. Rather, "the one is the form and the other the mystery of the one and the self-same Church."[29]

If I am interpreting Barth correctly, the church as historical organization corresponds to the Church of Esau (form), while the church as eschatological event corresponds to the Church of Jacob (mystery). I will focus on two problems that I see with this formulation.

First of all, despite his own critique of natural theologies, Barth seems to assume that "secularity" is neutral, objective, descriptive science, when in fact the human sciences often exhibit a naturalistic bias that insists upon reducing the church to the plane of pure immanence. In other words, he seems to assume something like Troeltsch's theory of the visible and historical church as one worldly institution among others, yet affirms as its antithesis a *real* church that becomes manifest only in those elusive events when the church's witness actually corresponds to the revelation of Christ in his heavenly historical existence.

Second, and more significantly, Barth can only place the visible-historical form of the church on the "secular" side of the ledger upon the presupposition that God works and the church works, but these parallel tracks do not intersect, at least not to such an extent that the actions of preaching and sacrament can be considered means of grace. However, how can we reduce the visibility of the church to its secularity, since the institution of preaching, sacraments, offices, and order are directly established by Christ as the means by which the kingdom irrupts in this age, not only as a momentary event but also as a historical community? It is this second point that I want to challenge here, especially because it reflects assumptions commonly held at least implicitly by evangelicals, Pentecostals, and others in free-church or independent ecclesial traditions.

One often gains the impression that for Barth the *content* (revelation-as-reconciliation) is wholly divine and eternal, while the *form* is entirely human and historical. Although its invisibility escapes inspection, since it is the result of God's work alone, in its visibility the church is one social institution among others. As "secular," the form is neutral or at least adiaphora (indifferent). This

26. Ibid., 366.
27. Ibid., 661.
28. Barth, *CD* IV/1:652.
29. Ibid., 669.

assumption is often repeated in countless varieties with less sophistication, when outward forms are almost treated as the prison house of the soul. The message must be divinely authorized, but the visible form of the church—its polity, worship, and discipline—not only *involve* but also *are* from top to bottom matters merely of human judgment. The danger is that sanctification is regarded as applying only to the souls of individuals, but not to the visible body of Christ.

According to the "regulative principle" dear to Reformed Christians, the church cannot prescribe for true faith and practice anything that is not commanded in Scripture. In public worship, for example, there are *elements* (such as preaching, confession of sin, prayer, baptism, the Supper, singing, and almsgiving) and *circumstances* (such as the appointed time and order of services, liturgical forms, architecture, musical style, and so forth). Since they were indifferent, choices concerning the latter were left to sanctified wisdom, and churches were free to change them at their discretion, in the light of their time and place. Making everything in the church's worship and church order an element, even apart from any biblical warrant, is legalistic; making everything a circumstance, in spite of biblical command, is antinomian.

Barth certainly was no antinomian. However, his dualistic ecclesiology of the invisible Church of Jacob and the visible Church of Esau surrenders the latter to the presumed neutrality of the secular. What could be more obviously secular, he asks, than the outward form of the church in the Roman Empire or the Byzantine State?[30] We are both dependent and free in relation to all outward forms, he says. "In fact, all of these forms are employed in the church, *none of which is better adapted for the purpose than others*, and in these forms to be visibly what it is invisibly, namely, the Christian community or the community of Christ." He adds, "It may follow as its principle of order a monarchical, aristocratic or liberal and democratic constitution, or the model of a free association. . . . There is no sociological possibility—*for all are intrinsically secular*—which it must always select, *nor is there any which it must always refuse*" (emphasis added).[31] As a historical phenomenon, the church is entirely human (the Church of Esau), distinguished from God's act of electing, redeeming, and sanctifying (the Church of Jacob). On what basis could one then criticize, for example, the Constantinian perversion of Christ's ecclesial body?

As with other loci (such as revelation), it seems as if the vertical vector of eschatology, absorbed into an eternal moment, never actually crosses the horizontal vector of history. To characterize Barth's ecclesiology as "docetic" would be a mistake—or at least an oversimplification, especially in his later work.[32] The church is *more* than what is visible to the sociologist, historian of religion, and ethicist, but it is a worldly entity.[33] Its visibility is only part of the story—and consequently, we cannot exhaust the meaning of Christianity within the study

30. Barth, *CD* IV/2:740.
31. Ibid., 741.
32. Barth, *CD* IV/3.2:723.
33. Ibid., 723–26.

of religions.[34] However, that aspect of the church that renders it more than the object of sociological and historical analysis is not its external forms, rites, and order, but its witness—at least in those moments when such human and therefore sinful witness is commandeered by God.

Not only is ecclesiastical polity nonessential to the being of the church; for Barth, the very contention of Reformed churches (as other traditions) that Christ has prescribed a "sacred government" surrenders eschatology to history, evidence that the Reformed churches never sufficiently divested themselves of their Roman Catholic tendencies.

Pointing out the similarities between Barth and Hans Küng, Dulles counters that the empirical church is not simply the work of humans, distinct from the kingdom as the work of God. "At the outset it seems worthwhile to note that the term *ekklēsia* as used in the New Testament is an eschatological term. It means an assembly or convocation and more specifically the convocation of the saints that will be realized to the full at the eschaton."[35] However, far from passing away, as Barth holds, the church "will then truly come into its own. . . . The eschatological meals that Jesus celebrates with his disciples are a foretaste of the final messianic supper in the Kingdom of heaven. . . . Nothing suggests that the community of the disciples will be dissolved in heaven, when the twelve sit on thrones judging the twelve tribes of Israel."[36] The New Testament everywhere anticipates the consummation of the church's consummation, not its dissolution.[37] The distinction between *ecclesia militans* and *trimphans* is still important.[38]

On these points Dulles is closer at least to the traditional Protestant (at least Reformed) understanding of the church as more than a secular institution that happens to coincide at flash-point moments with the work of God. If the consummated reality is the abolition of the church, then how can its current existence be anything other than an *empty* sign?

As Lesslie Newbigin points out, Barth's interpretation goes beyond the Reformers (even Luther) when he sets the event of proclamation against the history of a covenant community. "The eschatological has completely pushed out the historical."[39] While it is true that Word and sacrament create and sustain the church, Newbigin rightly insists that "they do not create the Church *de novo*, or *ex nihilo*." After all, "every setting forth of the word and sacraments of the Gospel is an event in the life of an actually existing Christian church."[40] The semirealized eschatological event occurs each Lord's Day within the context of a covenant community extended through all times and places, bearing the marks of the church in a ministry entrusted (not surrendered) to its enduring offices. A

34. Ibid., 727.
35. Avery Dulles, SJ, *Models of the Church* (New York: Doubleday, 1974), 97–98.
36. Ibid., 98.
37. Ibid., 98–99.
38. Ibid., 99.
39. Newbigin, *The Household of God*, 50.
40. Ibid., 50–51.

covenant community takes time; it cannot be merely an event, much less a crater that is left behind by revelation. Both a people (*synaxis*) and a place (*ekklēsia*), an event and an institution, the visible communion today is connected historically to the apostles by the external marks of Word, sacrament, and discipline. Wherever God's Word is truly proclaimed and his sacraments administered according to Christ's institution in the world today, there is a church—not only as an eschatological event, but also as a part of Christ's body organically related to every other church in all other places and times.

This interpretation of the church as both a covenant-making and covenant-renewing event and a covenant community with its successive generations is also distinguished from John Zizioulas's view that the church exists only as a fully realized eucharistic event. As Volf points out, this represents not only an "over-realized eschatology," but also an "actualist ecclesiology," according to which "the church is an event that takes place unceasingly afresh, not a community structurally instituted in any permanent manner."

> Paul McPartlan interprets Zizioulas accurately when he writes that "nothing of Christ is carried into the present from the past; it is only received again in the present from the future." . . . The invisible church *is* the church that becomes visible in concrete assemblies. It is not quite clear, however, why the dispersed church is then to be called "church" at all in the proper sense of the term.[41]

At the same time, like Barth, Zizioulas reminds us that ecclesial existence is always a gift, never a given: "The epiclesis means ecclesiologically that the Church asks to receive from God what she has already received historically in Christ as if she had not received it at all, . . . as if history did not count in itself," including historical continuity with the apostles. "The Church needs the Pentecostal scene to be set again and again, each time she wants to affirm her apostolicity."[42]

I still think that this is an overstatement. The Pentecostal scene is not set again and again, but like the incarnation, atonement, and resurrection, is a constitutive and unrepeatable event in the church's past that continues to endow it with what it needs in the present. As I argue below, the apostolic era is qualitatively unique. Nevertheless, Zizioulas reminds us that apostolicity cannot be a matter simply of historical continuity; it must also be granted by the Spirit in order to be something other than a distinguished and ancient institution of this passing age.

Reflecting the Separatist more than the Puritan Congregationalist legacy, the traditions of independent Protestantism today often seem reticent to identify even the well-being of the church with any outward form. The work of the Spirit is often not only separated from but also contrasted with ecclesial forms and public rites. Even preaching is increasingly regarded in evangelical circles as an indifferent form

41. Miroslav Volf, *After Our Likeness: The Church as the Image of the Trinity* (Grand Rapids: Eerdmans, 1998), 102.

42. John Zizioulas, *Being as Communion: Studies in Personhood and the Church* (Crestwood, NY: St. Vladimir's Seminary Press, 1985), 185.

of communication. If other media teach, edify, or persuade more relevantly, then why should we feel constrained by this traditional form. Even the extraordinary work of the Spirit is often identified with the degree to which an event or experience is direct and immediate, circumventing creaturely agency. As Baptist theologian Dale Moody concludes, "The priority of the spiritual organism over the institutional organization is obvious in all this great theological stream."[43]

However essential the church may be for the purposes of edification and fellowship, it is not typically conceived in modern evangelical and Pentecostal circles as the motherly womb in which people come to faith through the ordinary means of grace. Even for those reared in the church, a radical experience of conversion is often expected *before* the effects of voluntary identification with the church can be realized. Writing against the "new measures" employed by his contemporary Charles Finney, John Williamson Nevin pointed out the contrast between "the system of the bench" (precursor to the altar call) and "the system of the catechism":

> The old Presbyterian faith, into which I was born, was based throughout on the idea of covenant family religion, church membership by God's holy act in baptism, and following this a regular catechetical training of the young, with direct reference to their coming to the Lord's table. In one word, all proceeded on the theory of sacramental, educational religion.

These two systems, Nevin concluded, "involve at the bottom two different theories of religion."[44]

Similar to the spirit-matter dualism of radical movements throughout church history, American revivalism has encouraged a dichotomy between the outward forms of the church—its polity, rites, liturgy, and confessions—as a merely human invention in contrast to the immediate work of the Spirit in the hearts of individuals. The church in its visible administration tends to be regarded as nothing more than an indifferent product of history: human traditions evolving out of pragmatic needs, but by no means to be regarded as divinely appointed means of grace.

Covenantal faith and practice, however, refuse to set the formal against the informal, the external and visible against the internal and invisible. The Trinity works within creation and history while never becoming assimilated. The Spirit works mysteriously, yet through visible structures and means. We are growing up into one body: a continuous succession of witnesses in history, and not simply individuals responding to God's supernatural acts of grace in our own ways.[45]

Apostolicity is guaranteed neither by immanent history nor by inner immediacy; it is a gift *from* above, *in* time and *across* time. On this point, as on the others that we have considered, only the ministry of the Spirit working through the

43. Dale Moody, *The Word of Truth* (Grand Rapids: Eerdmans, 1981), 441.
44. John Williamson Nevin, *The Anxious Bench* (London: Taylor & Francis, 1987), 2–5.
45. Newbigin, *The Household of God*, 77.

Word and the sacraments, maintaining discipline across the generations, is able to sustain this kind of integrated praxis.

Once again I think that Bonhoeffer plots exactly the right course here. "There are basically two ways to misunderstand the church," he writes, "one historicizing and the other religious; the former confuses the church with the religious community, the latter with the Kingdom of God." The first way rationalizes divine activity as the product of psychological or social-scientific structures, which "plainly is condemned by the saying in John's Gospel that 'You did not choose me, but I chose you' (John 15:16)." "The second misunderstanding does not take seriously the fact that human beings are bound by history; this means that historicity either is objectified and deified, as in Catholicism, or simply is regarded as accidental, as subject to the law of sin and death."[46] Since it is the creation of God's grace and not merely a worldly institution, the reality of the church cannot be deduced from sociological, cultural, or philosophical analysis, but must be received as a fact of revelation.[47]

APOSTOLICITY AND APOSTLESHIP

Marking the transition from the extraordinary ministry of apostles to the ordinary ministry of pastors, teachers, and elders, Paul instructs, "Timothy, guard what has been entrusted to you" (1 Tim. 6:20). "Hold to the standard of sound teaching that you have heard from me, in the faith and love that are in Christ Jesus" (2 Tim. 1:13). Neither Timothy nor his fellow ministers are expected to add to that deposit, but are told, "Guard the good treasure entrusted to you, with the help of the Holy Spirit living in us" (v. 14). Although the apostles were eyewitnesses of Christ, and Paul himself asserts his apostleship on the basis of having received it directly and immediately from Christ rather than from the church (Gal. 1:11–23), ordinary ministers, assisted by elders, must diligently teach and to refute anything that "is contrary to the sound teaching that conforms to the glorious gospel of the blessed God, which he entrusted to me" (1 Tim. 1:10–11). The distinction is qualitative, not quantitative. The apostles heard Christ directly, and their proclamation and writings were "breathed out" by the Spirit (2 Tim. 3:16), whereas we now, illumined by the Spirit, hear Christ through the word of the prophets and apostles, through the mouth of pastors and teachers.

While there were certainly unwritten traditions in the apostolic era that were nevertheless binding on those who received them, all of those traditions that are normative for the whole church in all times and places have been committed to the canon. Furthermore, the offices for which Paul provides instruction to Timothy, in transition from the extraordinary apostolic ministry to the ordinary

46. Dietrich Bonhoeffer, *Communio: A Theological Study of the Sociology of the Church*, vol. 1 of *Dietrich Bonhoeffer Works*, ed. Joachim von Soosten, English edition ed. Clifford J. Green and trans. Reinhard Krauss and Nancy Lukens (Minneapolis: Fortress Press, 1998), 125–26.
47. Ibid., 133.

ministry that Timothy signals, are those of bishop/pastor (*episkopos*), elder (*presbyteros*), and deacon (*diakonos*). While God "*gave* . . . apostles . . . [and] prophets" (Eph. 4:11) and the gifts of healing, languages, and prophecy were exhibited in the extraordinary ministry of the apostolic era, there are no instructions in these Epistles for the ordination of the apostles' successors to their office. Appeals either to a charismatic apostolicity in the papal office or in various individuals who throughout church history claim to be prophets of new revelations fail in my view to account for the difference between extraordinary events in the history of redemption and the "effective history" of those events, as the Spirit applies that accomplished redemption through the ordinary ministry. Just as the event to which the apostles bore witness is unique, unrepeatable, and completed, their office is extraordinary and unique in the church's history.[48] Paul describes himself as part of the foundation-laying episode in the church's history, adding, "For no one can lay any foundation other than the one that has been laid; that foundation is Jesus Christ" (1 Cor. 3:11). I take this to be a reference not only to the content but also to the historical-eschatological uniqueness of the apostolic ministry.

If this distinction is valid, no one can claim title to an apostolic office after this foundation-laying era. The church was actually warned against accepting those who were "disguising themselves as apostles of Christ" (2 Cor. 11:13). While living stones are continually being added to the temple, the edifice itself is "built upon the foundation of the apostles and prophets, with Christ Jesus himself as the cornerstone" (Eph. 2:20). As the person and work of the head is distinct from that of the members, the foundation-laying ministry of the apostles is different from the upbuilding ministry of their successors.

Where apostolic preaching became Scripture, our proclamation, faith, and practice stand in continuity with the apostles to the extent that they conform to that rule. To understand Scripture as canon, within its ancient Near Eastern background, is to recognize that, like the redemptive work to which it testifies, it cannot be revised by addition or subtraction (Deut. 4:2; Rev. 22:18–19). While interpretations are always subject to change, the norm has been given once and for all. Centuries after the theocratic covenant was made at Sinai, its sanctions were invoked on the transgressing partner. As the inhabitants of Judah were carried off to Babylon, they did not have to wrestle with any bridging of historical or hermeneutical distance between Sinai and exile. The exile proved that the covenant and its canon (i.e., the Sinai treaty) were fully in force. Yet so too was the Abrahamic covenant that pledged God's redemption in the fullness of time.

Similarly, the canon that witnesses to Jesus is the covenant that he ratified in his self-sacrifice. In its appeal to this canon and its practice of its stipulated rites, the church participates in the heavenly reality as servant rather than Lord of the

---

48. See esp. Richard Gaffin Jr., *Perspectives on Pentecost* (Phillipsburg, NJ: Presbyterian and Reformed Publishing Co., 1989).

covenant. Just as the Jesus history is qualitatively distinct from our own, the apostolic canon is distinct from subsequent tradition. One is definitive (revelation), and the other interpretive (illumination). The epicletic interim between Christ's advents is not an era of writing new chapters in the history of redemption.[49] Rather, it is a period in which the Spirit equips us for the mission between Acts and the Apocalypse—right in the mid-era of the ordinary ministry, with its new-covenant canon. Just as the church cannot extend the incarnation or complete Christ's atoning work, it cannot repeat Pentecost or prolong the extraordinary ministry of the apostles, but must instead receive this same Word and Spirit for its ordinary ministry in this time between the times.

APOSTOLICITY AND THE ORDINARY MINISTRY

In the light of my preceding arguments, we can say that a covenantal approach refuses the choice between the church as people or place. All of the people are priests, living stones being built into a holy sanctuary. Yet not all of the covenant people are ministers. All are sheep, but not all are shepherds under the Great Shepherd (as Paul especially argues in 1 Cor. 11–12). There are different gifts and different callings within the one body. Christ is the sole mediator between God and humanity (1 Tim. 2:5), but as we have seen from Ephesians 4, he has given apostles and prophets, evangelists, pastors and teachers to his body. These differing gifts generate special offices of ministry and oversight. However, such graces are not qualities (or, as in Roman Catholic terminology, bearing an indelible "character") sacramentally infused into ministers so that they might be elevated ontologically above the laity. They are simply gifts for particular offices. As Christ has promised, he has not left us "orphans" (John 14:18 NASB), but promises to be present by the Spirit through the ministry of the Word.

Admittedly, this is a difficult interpretation to affirm, especially since most of our modern translations (in contrast to older ones) render Ephesians 4:11–12 as follows: "The gifts he gave were that some would be apostles, some prophets, some evangelists, some pastors and teachers, to equip the saints for the work of ministry" (NRSV, but also essentially the same construction in other modern translations). However, there are good reasons for preferring the older translations (e.g., KJV), which render the verses, "And he gave some, apostles; and some, prophets; and some, evangelists; and some, pastors and teachers; for the perfecting of the saints, for the work of ministry, for the edifying of the body of Christ."

Reflecting the actual construction of the Greek, the older (KJV) translation draws three lines of purpose clauses from the offices given that newer translations obscure. The same persons who are given for the completion (not equipping) of

49. For this argument, see N. T. Wright, "How Can the Bible Be Authoritative?" *Vox evangelica* 21 (1991): 7–32.

the saints are also given for the work of ministry and edification of the body.[50] On this reading, Christ has given apostles, prophets, evangelists, pastors, and teachers for the ministry of the Word, which brings the whole body to unity, maturity, and completion in the truth. This is not to say that the body is *complete* in and through these offices alone, for there are other gifts mentioned elsewhere (esp. Rom. 12 and 1 Cor. 12). However, the focus here is restricted to that work of bringing unity and maturity to the body through sound doctrine.

Favoring this interpretation of Ephesians 4, Andrew Lincoln comments, "An active role for all believers is safeguarded by vv. 7, 16, but the primary context here in v. 12 is the function and role of Christ's specific gifts, the ministers, not that of all the saints. Rendering *katartismon* 'completion' has a straightforward meaning which does not require supplementing by a further phrase, and *diakonia*, 'service,' is more likely to refer to the *ministry* of the *ministers* just named." Thus, it is "hard to avoid the suspicion that opting for the other view is too often motivated by a zeal to avoid clericalism and to support a 'democratic' model of the Church."[51]

This is not a hierarchical model of the church, as Paul emphasizes in Romans 12:3–8 and 1 Corinthians 12:4–28. All believers have the same standing, but differing functions within the body. It is significant that the gifts mentioned in these passages include hospitality, giving, administration, and other acts of service, but Ephesians 4 only mentions Christ's gift of officers to his church for the good of the whole body. So the point is that in his ascension, Christ has given the ministry of the Word to his people as a gift. This does not mean that those who are not ministers are not gifted and called to love and serve each other, but that comes later, in verse 17 and onward through chapter 5. Before they serve, they are served. This underscores again the remarkable generosity of the church's victorious head, that he would make his people receivers first and active givers as a result.

While every member and every gift is needed in order for the body to be fully operative, the very life of the body depends on the faithful maintenance of the ministry of Word and sacrament. Not all members of the body can devote themselves exclusively to the Word and prayer, as Peter observed (Acts 6:2–7). When the apostles were freed for this work by the appointment of deacons, we read, "So

---

50. Our interpretation depends largely on whether we render *katartismon* in Eph. 4:12a "equip" and *eis* "for," or render them "complete" and "in." It is lexically possibly to render *katartismon* either "equip" or "complete" (also "train"). However, "completion" fits better with the logic of the argument, where the analogy is that of a body growing up into maturity. This occurs through Christ's gift of "evangelists, . . . pastors and teachers." Furthermore, this gift is given for the express purpose of "building up the body of Christ, until we all attain to the *unity of the faith* and of the *knowledge of the Son of God*, to [maturity], . . . so that we may no longer be children, tossed to and fro by every wind of *doctrine*" but instead be engaged in "speaking the truth in love" (Eph. 4:13–14 ESV, emphasis added).

51. Andrew Lincoln, *Ephesians*, Word Biblical Commentary 42 (Dallas: Word, 1990), 253; cf. T. David Gordon, "'Equipping' Ministry in Ephesians 4," *Journal of the Evangelical Theological Society* 37, no. 1 (March 1994): 69–78. It is also interesting to read John Calvin's commentary on this passage (*Commentaries on the Epistles of Paul to the Galatians and Ephesians*, trans. William Pringle [Grand Rapids: Baker, 1996], 277–86), especially since the more recent translation does not even occur to him. For this very reason, he seems to capture the flow of the passage's argument.

the word of God continued to spread" (v. 7). How much more do ordinary ministers, without the benefit of firsthand instruction from Jesus Christ, have need of proper training, study, and mutual admonition and correction in order to feed Christ's sheep?

Through this ministry, we are all recipients of the unity of the faith, the knowledge of the Son of God, and maturity in Christ. Therefore, that which we all possess jointly already in Christ (one God and Father, one Spirit, one Lord, one faith, one baptism) is preserved by Christ from generation to generation. On the basis of this gift of ambassadors, the other members of the body receive what they need to "no longer walk as the Gentiles do, in the futility of their minds" (v. 17 ESV) and to live out their calling in the world (vv. 18–24). They even participate in the service, not only as recipients but also as actors, "addressing one another in psalms and hymns and spiritual songs, singing and making melody to the Lord with [their] heart, giving thanks always and for everything to God the Father in the name of our Lord Jesus Christ, submitting to one another out of reverence for Christ" (Eph. 5:15–21 ESV).

There are significant practical implications for how we interpret this passage, since the rendering of more recent translations has made this passage the locus classicus for "every-member ministry," which in my view is effectively undermining the notion of the church as the creation of the Word. In his ascension, the Great King does not exercise tyranny over his subjects, but pours out gifts. The church is first of all lavished with grace, and only then can it be also active in love. The body of Christ, scattered in its secular vocations, will do many things for their neighbors that the church as a historical institution and eschatological gathering cannot accomplish and has not been commissioned to accomplish. If the purpose of the church as a divine institution is to do anything and everything worthwhile as a distinctively Christian activity, then there is no particular need for a distinct office of pastor and teacher. Yet if the unity, holiness, catholicity, and apostolicity—in a word, the *existence*—of the church is dependent on the Word, then this special office is indeed a gift of Christ's heavenly reign.

Therefore a pneumatologically rich ecclesiology should not be set over against an emphasis on the official ministry and its offices. As Bonhoeffer observes, "The church of Jesus Christ that is actualized by the Holy Spirit is really the church here and now. The community of saints we have outlined is 'in the midst of us.'"[52] The former is the "empirical church," not *in contrast to* a spiritual church or the kingdom of God, but that kingdom as it is visible to us now as things are.[53] The empirical church is not simply a religious community. "Rather, as a concrete historical community, in the relativity of its forms and in its imperfect and modest appearance, it is the body of Christ, Christ's presence on earth, for it has his word."[54]

---

52. Bonhoeffer, *Communio*, 208.
53. Ibid.
54. Ibid., 209.

Not only as a community (*Gemeinde*), but also a church (*Kirche*), the body is connected to its head in audible and visible bonds. For example, the Westminster Confession declares,

> The Lord Jesus, as king and head of his Church, hath therein appointed a government in the hand of Church officers, distinct from the civil magistrate. To these officers the keys of the Kingdom of Heaven are committed, by virtue whereof they have power respectively to retain and remit sins, to shut that kingdom against the impenitent, both by the word and censures; and to open it unto penitent sinners, by the ministry of the gospel, and by absolution from censures, as occasion shall require.[55]

Furthermore, broader assemblies are given authority to act in Christ's name subordinate to his word. Such decisions "are to be received with reverence and submission, not only for their agreement with the Word, but also for the power whereby they are made, as being an ordinance of God, appointed thereunto in his Word."[56] At the same time, the Confession notes that such bodies do err and, furthermore, "Synods and councils are to handle or conclude nothing but that which is ecclesiastical and are not to meddle with civil affairs which concern the commonwealth unless by way of humble petition in cases extraordinary."[57] The Word and the Spirit create a historical community, but precisely because they are Word and Spirit, they always put that community in question, breaking up its presumptuous autonomy, so that the event of Christ's action among us will not be assimilated to the history of this passing age.

Paul, whose letters Peter included under the category of "the scriptures" (2 Pet. 3:16), made a point of emphasizing that he received his apostolic commission directly from Christ and not from any leader, including Peter (Gal. 1:1–2:14). Nevertheless, both apostles subjected themselves jointly to the broader assembly. In this conception, it is recognized that particular churches can lose their connection with the apostolic church: as branches can be broken off, candlesticks can be removed when faithful witness (signified by the lampstands, as we will see) is no longer offered (implied in Rev. 2–3). Paul threatened as much in his stern remarks to the Galatians. Peter, James, and others who had been resistant to the mission to the Gentiles were brought along by the Spirit, through a process of mutual correction and admonition, defined by the gospel, which was beyond their command or control.

The same ecclesial head who creates his body by the gospel regulates it by his sovereign commands. Yet this direction from the church's one living head is mediated by the Spirit through a plurality of pastors and elders in assembly. If the apostles themselves were corrected by the Word, through mutual admonition, then surely the ordinary ministry can assume no greater authority. As Calvin points

55. Westminster Confession of Faith 32.1–2, in *BC*.
56. Ibid., 33.2.
57. Ibid., 33.4.

out in commenting on Ephesians 4, it is significant that this passage makes no mention of the papal office as essential to the unity of the church in faith and doctrine. "If he knew a primacy which had a fixed residence, was it not his duty, for the benefit of the whole church, to exhibit one ministerial head placed over all the members, under whose government we are collected into one body?"[58]

Ambassadors are not just witnesses; they are also restricted in their authority by the commission that they have received. As with the catholicity of the church, apostolicity is constituted by the ministry of the apostolic faith and is maintained by the assembly of ministers and elders together, over which Christ himself presides. Drawing on the Antiochene emphasis on "ambassadorship," Zizioulas points out that ministers receive grace *to serve others.* "This does not imply that the minister himself is not in need of that grace. The point is that he needs it precisely because he does not 'possess' it but gets it himself as a member of the community."[59] For this reason, Zizioulas suggests, we should be cautious about such terms as "vicar," as if it were "a representation of someone who is absent."[60]

> The fundamental implication of this is that there is no priesthood as a general and vague term, as it was to become later on in theology under the name of *sacerdotium.* . . . The true and historically original meaning of the term [priest] is this: as Christ (the only priest) becomes in the Holy Spirit a community (His body, the Church), His priesthood is realized and portrayed in historical existence here and now as a Eucharistic community in which His "image" is the head of this community offering with and on behalf of the community the Eucharistic gifts.

In this way, "the community itself becomes priestly in the sense of I Peter 2:5, 9," not by flowing from the priest, but resulting from the eucharistic gathering (synaxis) of the whole body.[61] As I argued in the previous chapter (appealing especially to Acts 15), even in the era of the apostles themselves, ecclesiastical power was not concentrated in one apostle or even in the apostolate collectively, but in the consensus of the "apostles and elders" in solemn assembly with "the consent of the whole church" (Acts 15:22). Distributed across the wider framework of pastors and elders from local assemblies who formed a broader assembly, this power reflected the diversity as much as the unity of Pentecost.

Apostolic succession, like all other attributes of the church, is therefore determined by the *content* of the church's ministry rather than by the historical succession of *persons* ordained to office. At the same time, those who minister in Christ's name must be called to that office by Christ, through the agency of the church: they cannot send themselves on the basis of an inward call alone, but must be sent, which again emphasizes the mission as concerned chiefly with heralding good news (Rom. 10:14–15).

58. Calvin, *Commentaries on the Epistles of Paul to the Galatians and Ephesians,* 280.
59. Ibid., 227–28.
60. Zizioulas, *Being as Communion,* 230.
61. Ibid., 231.

Analogous to the Father's sending of the Son, the sending of the Spirit by the Father and the Son, and their joint commission of the apostles, so pastors and elders are called and sent by the wider church to their local post, and the local church sends its representatives to its wider assemblies. Because they do not send themselves (any more than the Son or the Spirit sent themselves), and their commission from God is tested and validated by the church that bears the marks, their hearers can be assured that they are not speaking merely on their own authority when they bring good news. The ordinary ministers do not receive their gift and commission directly from God alone, but through "the laying on of the hands of the eldership [*presbyteriou*]" (1 Tim. 4:14 NKJV).

In view of these arguments, it becomes obvious that a covenantal ecclesiology stands between (1) a hierarchical model of apostolicity based on historical succession and (2) a democratic model based on private revelations, personal experience, or an inner call that may or may not be confirmed by the visible ministry of the church. In chapter 3 I noted the Reformers' argument that Rome and Radical Protestants similarly appeal to the Spirit and continuing revelation, and this observation has been substantiated in some recent Pentecostal interactions with Roman Catholic claims to a continuing apostolic office.[62] Nevertheless, the decisive difference between these positions is that Rome identifies this office with the pope, and Pentecostalism has traditionally evidenced suspicion of any attempt to bind prophecy and apostolicity to formal offices.

If church order is not the fountain of ecclesial identity, the message that is the true fountain nevertheless gives rise to a public order of faithful ministry and discipline. Each believer has been gifted for a particular function in the one body, but just as "the eye cannot say to the hand, 'I have no need of you,' nor again the head to the feet, 'I have no need of you,'" not everyone is an eye or a hand. "If the whole body were an eye, where would the hearing be?" (1 Cor. 12:12–26). The church is not, properly speaking, the magisterium or the ministerium, but the whole body. Yet as the Pastoral Epistles elaborate, the transferable aspects of the extraordinary apostolic vocation have been entrusted to the ordinary offices of pastors and elders. So we must avoid a legalism that subverts the unique authority of Christ and his Word by addition as well as an antinomian spirit of subtraction.

We are not saved by sound church order and discipline, but we are served by it. The forensic Word generates an effective, transformative, and regulated exis-

---

62. Amos Yong, *The Spirit Poured Out on All Flesh* (Grand Rapids: Baker Academic, 2005), 150–51. In seeking common ground with postconciliar Roman Catholic positions, Yong asks, "Insofar as the magisterium is led by the Spirit to serve the body of Christ and insofar as pentecostals (and other Christians) can discern such activity as being of the Spirit of God, is there any hindrance to pentecostals recognizing the provisional authority of the pope (or the episcopate) both as a symbolic re-presentation of the full realization of the apostolic message, the pleroma of Christ (cf. Eph. 4:11–13)?" (150). But how would any group of Christians be able to "discern such activity as being of the Spirit of God" except by reference to the Word, specifically the gospel? Obviously, this opens Pandora's box, evaluating the extent to which ecumenical consensus has been reached especially concerning justification. Yet it is significant that a shared conviction that the apostolic office remains in effect today might make Yong's invitation plausible among fellow pentecostals.

tence in history. The gospel, in other words, leads to obedience. Between the extremes of *divinizing* and *secularizing*, there is the *sanctification* of creaturely reality by the Spirit for the work of bringing about the perlocutionary effect of the gospel.[63] Drawing on Jesus' petition in John 17:17, we recognize that sanctification in the Word of truth not only draws together the themes of holiness and catholicity, but apostolicity as well.

MARKS AND KEYS: THE MINISTRY OF RECONCILIATION

If they are not lords and masters, ministers are also not merely facilitators, coaches, therapists, or entrepreneurs. They do not welcome the people to church as they might welcome them to their home. It is not their service, but God's. Thus, they begin by raising their hands in Christ's name to place his blessing on the people. As covenant attorneys, prophets and priests assured the people of God's favorable presence by this action. The Aaronic blessing, "The LORD make his face to shine upon you" (Num. 6:25) is equivalent to the phrases in which it is nestled: "The LORD bless and keep you" (v. 24); and "the LORD lift up his countenance [*pānîm*] upon you, and give you peace" (v. 26). These oral speeches are not merely generous, inspirational thoughts or even prayers. Ministering as diplomats of Yahweh, the priests actually place God's benediction on the people. It is a legal, covenantal action, a performative utterance that places the people under the blessings rather than the curses of the covenant. "So shall they *put my name upon* the people of Israel, *and I will bless them*" (v. 27, emphasis added).

Many other examples could be cited (such as Pss. 4:6; 34:16, 18, repeated in 1 Pet. 3:10–12), where we see this close connection between God's *face* and God's *nearness* in *ḥesed*, covenant faithfulness. It is through the incarnate Word himself—as archetypal prophet, priest, and king—that God places the covenantal blessing upon his people in the new covenant, as in the beatitudes (Matt. 5:1–11). Each of these pronouncements of blessing is an indicative rather than an imperative. The disciples are blessed not because they are poor in spirit, mourn, are meek, hungry, merciful, pure in heart, peacemakers, or are persecuted. Rather, these who *are* blessed by Christ are for that reason reviled by the world yet persevere in showing good to their enemies (vv. 11–12). They bless because they are already blessed.

Whenever the suzerain hands over his name to his vassal, he is pledging protection, friendship, and security. "Everyone who calls on the name of the Lord shall be saved" (Rom. 10:13, quoting Joel 2:32; cf. Acts 2:21). Like the issuance of the treaty itself, this invocation of the suzerain is accomplished not only through speech but also through participation in the ratification rite. "I will lift

---

63. In two recent books—*Holy Scripture: A Dogmatic Sketch* (Cambridge: Cambridge University Press, 2003), 5–41; and *Holiness* (Grand Rapids: Eerdmans, 2003)—John Webster has richly developed this theme.

up the cup of salvation and call on the name of the LORD, I will pay my vows to the LORD in the presence of all his people" (Ps. 116:13–14).

As in secular treaties, biblical rites are means of binding strangers to the sovereign who summons them to his communion. To become a covenant partner, the vassal-state was made a "son" of the suzerain, part of the imperial body of which he is the head. Hence, the relationship was to be exclusive, and the suzerain would look in jealous wrath upon back-room alliances with other lords. Within this frame of reference, Yahweh repeatedly announces, "I will take you as my people, and I will be your God" (Exod. 6:7; Jer. 24:7). Yet the keys both opened and shut. The covenant officers were also given the unpleasant task of announcing judgment: "Lo-ammi, . . . not my people" (Hos. 1:9), alongside the happy calling "to make ready a people prepared for the Lord" (Luke 1:17), even to announce to those who "once were not a people" that they are now "the people of God" (Rom. 9:25; 2 Cor. 6:16; Titus 2:14; 1 Pet. 2:10; Rev. 21:3).

In this in-between time, the business of the church is receiving and delivering the gift of salvation, not contributing to the gift, negotiating its terms, or determining its content. As minister rather than master of the Lord's house, the church is visible not only as a witness to but also as the semirealized inauguration of the kingdom to come. Since it is the era of gathering guests from the highways and byways to be seated at the heavenly banquet, the mission that the marks (Word, sacraments, and discipline) serve is that of opening and shutting doors. Jesus faulted the religious leaders of his day on this very point: "For you lock people out of the kingdom of heaven. For you do not go in yourselves, and when others are going in, you stop them" (Matt. 23:13). Jesus is not only the shepherd; he is also the "gate" of his sheep (John 10:7). This gate is flung wide now but is about to be closed by "the owner of the house." The insiders, who think that they have a right to sit at the table of the kingdom, will be outsiders, while those "from east and west, from north and south" gather at the feast with "Abraham and Isaac and Jacob and all the prophets in the kingdom of God." "Indeed, some are last who will be first, and some are first who will be last" (Luke 13:22–30).

The question of the marks of the church is therefore bound up with the subject of the keys, with its Old Testament backdrop. In Isaiah 22, Jerusalem's destruction is prophesied, and the self-seeking officials are denounced. They are a "disgrace to [their] master's house!" (v. 18). Therefore, God declares, "I will thrust you from your office, and you will be pulled down from your post." Instead, another will be installed. "I will place on his shoulder the key of the house of David; he shall open, and no one shall shut; he shall shut, and no one shall open. I will fasten him like a peg in a secure place, and he will become a throne of honor to his ancestral house" (vv. 19–23).

In that light, we overhear Jesus' announcement to Peter: "And I tell you, you are Peter, and on this rock I will build my church, and the gates of Hades will not prevail against it. I will give you the keys of the kingdom of heaven, and whatever you bind on earth will be bound in heaven, and whatever you loose on earth will be loosed in heaven" (Matt. 16:18–19). This office is extended to the whole

apostolate in chapter 18, when Jesus establishes the ecclesiastical court for the settling of disputes, where "whatever you loose on earth will be loosed in heaven"
(vv. 15–20).

At the end of Luke's Gospel, significantly, Jesus is progressively recognized by
his dejected disciples as the living Christ through his explanation of the Scriptures (Luke 24:6–8, 13–27) and the breaking of the bread (vv. 28–35), climax-
ing in his appearance in the midst of them, pronouncing, "Peace be with you"
(v. 36). And it is in the Apocalypse that a direct connection is made with Isaiah
22: "And to the angel of the church in Philadelphia write: These are the words of
the holy one, the true one, who has the key of David, who opens and no one will
shut, who shuts and no one opens" (Rev. 3:7). Similarly, in John 20, the resurrected Jesus breathes on his disciples, saying, "Receive the Holy Spirit. If you forgive the sins of any, they are forgiven them; if you retain the sins of any, they are
retained" (vv. 22–23). Anyone who receives the apostles receives Christ himself
(Matt. 10:40; cf. John 13:20).

According to the Reformed confessions and catechisms, this opening and shutting of the door that is nuclear to the church's mission is accomplished through
the three marks: the preaching of the gospel, the administration of the sacraments,
and discipline. In this way, Christ exercises here and now his ministry as prophet,
priest, and king. Herman Ridderbos points out the origins of the concept of apostle (*shaliach* [*šāliaḥ*]) in the power of attorney stipulated in the Jewish legal system. This heralding of the direct words of Christ himself "designates the content
of the gospel in its original, historically visible and audible form."[64]

Ever since the end of the apostolic era, an indirect calling of ministers through
the church continues this representational witness not only to Christ but also
from Christ. Through preaching, baptism, and admission (or refusal of admission) to the Communion, the keys of the kingdom are exercised. After all, it may
be said that the "binding and loosing" involved in church discipline is at issue in
every liturgical absolution, sermon, baptism, and Communion. On all of these
occasions, the age to come is breaking into this present age: both the last judgment and the final vindication of God's elect occur in a *semi*realized manner, min-
isterially rather than magisterially. The church's acts are not final—they do not
coincide univocally with the eschatological realities, but they are signs and seals.
Christ's performative speech is mediated through appointed officers.

The triumphant indicative ("All authority in heaven and on earth has been
given to me") is the basis for the imperative ("Go therefore and make disciples of
all nations, baptizing . . . and teaching," Matt. 28:18–20). This explains the link
between Christ's bestowal of the Spirit on the disciples along with the commission to mediate his royal authority. It is not in their persons but in their office
that they are ambassadors of the kingdom of Christ (2 Cor. 5:12; 5:18–6:2). The

64. Herman Ridderbos, *Redemptive History and the New Testament Scriptures*, trans. H. De Jongste, revised by Richard B. Gaffin Jr. (Phillipsburg, NJ: Presbyterian & Reformed Publishing Co.,
1963; 2nd rev. ed., 1988), 14.

ministry of reconciliation draws together the marks (Word, sacraments, and discipline) and further links the marks and mission of the church.

To summarize the logic, then, justification comes through faith; faith comes through hearing the proclamation of Christ; such proclamation is sent down from the heavenly sanctuary through an earthly emissary. This Paul contrasts with the logic of works-righteousness, according to which one ascends to heaven to acquire salvation. So the minister (*doulos, diaskalos*) is also a "herald" or "ambassador" to whom God has given "the ministry of reconciliation," and all for one purpose: "so that in him [Christ] we might become the righteousness of God" (2 Cor. 5:18–21). Although this is the particular office of ministers, it is precisely through their ministry that Christ makes all members witnesses who declare God's mighty acts more generally in their daily lives (1 Pet. 2:9). Even this language is borrowed from the world of ancient treaty-making, as Seyoon Kim relates, borrowing on C. Breytenbach's thorough study of the linguistic background of "reconciliation." The Greeks never used it "in a religious context for the relationship between God and human beings," but in the process of political or military peace-treaties. It is in this light that we recognize the import of Paul's invocation of such terminology as "'ambassadors' (*presbeis*) sent to 'petition' (*deomai*) or 'appeal' (*parakalein*) to warring parties for reconciliation."[65] This background is not idiosyncratic to Hellenism, but is the nearest vocabulary for expressing in Greek idiom the Old Testament covenant concept in its treaty-context.

Webster wisely reminds us that this ministry of reconciliation spoken of in 2 Corinthians 5 "is that which God *gave*." "That is to say, it is a matter of election or appointment. It does not spring into being as an activity of a busy imagined community with a lively sense of the need for alternatives to oppression and marginalization." "Reconciliation" is not a general work of improving the world for which the church has volunteered, but is "strictly derivable from the content of the church's proclamation of salvation."[66] This ministry of reconciliation is described as primarily speech, "the message of reconciliation" (v. 19), of which we are "ambassadors."[67] It is announcing the policy of Christ's regime, not using the name of Christ for whatever "reconciling" activities the church might find useful or important in the world.

An apostle is Christ's own representative, even if perhaps "an ambassador in chains" (Eph. 6:20). Even Timothy, who is a minister in the ordinary office rather than an apostle, is said to be "our brother and *God's coworker* [*synergon tou theou*] in proclaiming the gospel of Christ" (1 Thess. 3:2, author's trans.). Ministers in their office do serve Christ's own saving reign by his Word and Spirit—"God is

---

65. Seyoon Kim, "The Origin of Paul's Concept of Reconciliation," in *The Road from Damascus: The Impact of Paul's Conversion on His Life, Thought, and Ministry*, ed. Richard N. Longenecker (Grand Rapids: Eerdmans, 1997), 104. Cf. C. Breytenbach, *Versöhnung: Eine Studie zur paulinischen Soteriologie* (Neukirchen-Vluyn: Neukirchener Verlag, 1989).

66. John Webster, "Christ, Church and Reconciliation," in *Word and Church* (Edinburgh: T&T Clark, 2001), 222.

67. Ibid.

making his appeal through us" (2 Cor. 5:20a). Therefore, the call to be reconciled to God is made "on behalf of Christ" himself (v. 20b).[68] "As we work together with him [Christ], we urge you also not to accept the grace of God in vain. . . . See, now is the acceptable time; see, now is the day of salvation!" (2 Cor. 6:1–2).

The ministry of the keys includes discipline, which the Reformed confessions included as the third mark of the true church alongside preaching and sacraments. Ironically, for those who are fond of setting Luther and Calvin in opposition on the third use of the law (viz., guiding believers), Calvin only acknowledged the two marks in his writings, while Luther had included church discipline as a mark in *On the Councils and the Church*:

> Now where you see sins forgiven or reproved in some persons, be it publicly or privately, you may know that God's people are there. If God's people are not there, the keys are not there either; and if the keys are not present for Christ, God's people are not present. Christ bequeathed them as a public sign and a holy possession, whereby the Holy Spirit again sanctifies the fallen sinners redeemed by Christ's death, and whereby the Christians confess that they are a holy people in this world under Christ. And those who refuse to be converted or sanctified again shall be cast out from this holy people, that is, bound and excluded by means of the keys, as happened to the unrepentant Antinomians.[69]

While many Protestants, on both the political right and left, want to impose what they regard as a Christian discipline on the secular *polis* while virtually ignoring the concrete care and discipline of church members, for Paul this was exactly backward (1 Cor. 5:9–13).

Christ gave the keys to the church, to be administered by lawfully called and ordained servants, for the express purpose of both preserving the corporate body and its individual members against the ravaging effects of false teaching and practice, as well as false accusations. Members and officers must have access to due

---

68. Isaiah 49:8 in 2 Cor. 6:2: Is Paul the "Servant"? Mark Gignilliat, "2 Corinthians 6:2: Paul's Eschatological 'Now' and Hermeneutical Invitation," *Westminster Theological Journal* 67 (2005): 147–61:

> Paul's quotation of Isa 49:8 in 2 Cor 6:2 is an eschatological reading of the text in its plain sense that is faithful to its final canonical form and an invitation into the eschatological world of Isa 40–55 (66), a text that for Paul has abiding theological/eschatological significance for our understanding of Christ's person and mission. For Paul, the eschatological now of God's new redemptive activity by means of His Servant has been realized and is continuing to be realized in the person and work of Christ—in this sense, Paul really is "living in the Bible." That Paul identifies the Servant as part of the very identity of God (cf. Phil 2) and as fulfilled in the person and work of Jesus Christ (2 Cor 5:14–21) coupled with a typological clashing within such a close proximity (2 Cor 5:14–21 and 2 Cor 6:2) makes the position of Paul's identification of himself as the Servant untenable. (160)

69. Martin Luther, "On the Councils and the Church," in *LW*, vol. 41, *Church and Ministry III*, ed. E. W. Gritsch (Philadelphia: Fortress Press, 1966), 153; cf. David Yeago, "The Office of the Keys: On the Disappearance of Discipline in Protestant Modernity," in *Marks of the Body of Christ*, ed. Carl Braaten and Robert Jenson (Grand Rapids: Eerdmans, 1999), 95–123.

process in church courts. The point of a presbyterian polity is to spread the ministerial authority of the church out to the many, at the local level and with recourse to broader assemblies, rather than to place it in the hands of one pastor or circle of power.

In commissioning his disciples with the keys that are properly his own, Jesus explicitly announced a union of the sign (ministerial binding and loosing "on earth") and the signified (magisterial binding and loosing "in heaven"). God's sanctification of ordinary, creaturely action for divine, heavenly purposes means, on one hand, that the church's juridical authority is *ministerial rather than magisterial* and, on the other hand, that it is *more than witness.*

Barth goes so far as to say that the church and the world need Christ, and the church needs the world, but the world does not need the church.[70] The church's ministry may witness to Jesus' ministry, but does not convey it.[71] In my view, such statements go beyond the salutary warning to distinguish the head from the body, toward a wounding separation. While Barth offers critical correctives to the widespread tendency today to treat the church as a coredeemer with Christ, he does not take seriously enough passages that clearly authorize—indeed, command—the church through its ministers to act as ambassadors on his behalf (e.g., Matt. 16:19; 18:18–20; Rom. 10:8, 14–17; 2 Cor. 5:18–21). In 2 Corinthians 5, there clearly is an explicit distinction made between the reconciling work of Christ and the ministry of the church. The former is just as Barth interprets, "a definitive and self-contained event."[72] Yet there is also "the ministry of reconciliation" that is said to be "entrusted to us"—apostles and ministers (v. 18), as "ambassadors for Christ, since God is making his appeal through us" (v. 20).

For the reasons we have already encountered, Barth resisted the traditional Reformed affirmation that Matthew 16:19; 18:18; and John 20:23 refer to any representative and even ministerial power given to the church as such.[73] "Unless it neglects or corrupts its ministry, can it possibly use the keys of the kingdom of heaven committed to it to close the kingdom to men?"[74] Barth thinks that the Protestant scholastics (both Lutheran and Reformed) moved in a troubling direction when they spoke of the church in terms of a visible government: a sacred ministry (pastors, in Lutheranism) or a sacred classis/presbytery and synod/general assembly (Reformed). "Either way, the community is divided into two subjects, a smaller, superior, active and directly responsible, and a greater, subordinate, passive and only indirectly responsible, the mediaeval scheme thus being revived in a new clergy and laity."[75] "The Church" comes to be identified with its officers rather than with the people of God generally.[76]

70. Barth, *CD* IV/3:826.
71. Ibid., 835.
72. Barth, *CD* IV/1:76.
73. Ibid., 861.
74. Ibid.
75. Ibid., 765.
76. Ibid., 766.

To be sure, Barth does not deny the appointment of offices in the church.[77] However, it is difficult to see how these offices are *means through which Christ himself acts*. Barth judges, "Calvin's doctrine of the Church at the beginning of Book IV of the *Institutio* is in fact a very aristocratic doctrine of ecclesiastical office, or the ministry, or the administration of the word and sacrament, which was to be exercised by an exclusive and special class, and in which the community, represented by the elders and deacons ordained alongside the presbyters and deacons, could only incidentally play any active part."[78] According to this standard, it would be difficult to see how the apostles themselves could be exonerated from an "aristocratic" view since they certainly prescribed ordination for the ministry of Word and sacrament. There is, for example, the advice to Timothy to make sure that "the elders who rule well be counted worthy of double honor, especially those who labor in the word and doctrine" (1 Tim. 5:17 NKJV).

Surely Barth is not suggesting that ecclesiastical office be abandoned or that the qualifications in 1 Timothy 3 are elitist for describing a mature Christian who is above reproach, is learned in and holding firmly to "the mystery of the faith," and "apt to teach" as well as "to take care of God's church" (KJV). Furthermore, how can representation by elders and deacons—elected or nominated by the members—constitute aristocracy in the church any more than the election of representatives to a national congress or parliament? Are citizens rendered inactive because they do not hold public office? At least here Barth seems to assume, as many people do, that all of the work to be done by the church-as-people is to be done in the church-as-place—in other words, that "church work" (preaching, teaching, administering sacraments, leading in worship, and overseeing the health of the local church and its wider assemblies) is more honorable than the secular vocations of the other members. Yet is this not itself a form of clericalism? We have seen from Ephesians 4 that the ministry of pastors and teachers is to complete the saints with what is needed in order to be built up in one body and to love and serve their neighbors in their callings.

Turretin and other Protestant scholastics too closely identified the church with the mediation of Christ's personal reign, Barth thinks.[79] Although he allows that a minister is an "ambassador" to the world in the sense of offering testimony, he concludes that the official ecclesiology of Reformed confession and practice makes the minister an officer in a self-enclosed "institution of salvation for those who belong to it."[80] It leads, he says, to a "holy egoism" that is not truly missionary in intent.[81]

This infelicitous conception dominated the ecclesiastical landscape in Barth's time and place, especially as the established churches came to mirror the pyramidal and bureaucratic form of secular government. However, Barth's criticism

77. Ibid.
78. Barth, *CD* IV/3.1:33.
79. Ibid., 767.
80. Ibid.
81. Ibid.

targets the theory itself, not simply its distortions. Far from Barth's description, the churches of the Reformation carefully distinguished between *magisterial* authority (held by Christ alone) and *ministerial* authority (entrusted to the church), and between the *general* office of all Christians (the priesthood of all believers) and the *particular* office of pastors, elders, and deacons. However, it becomes clear that for Barth this is not a sufficient qualification. "It ought never to have been even admitted, let alone dogmatically formulated," he says, "that by the Church we are to understand, as in *parte pro toto*, certain persons or bodies which are exalted above the rest and particularly prominent and to that extent representative in its activity, both internally and externally."[82]

When the marks and the keys—in other words, ecclesiastical authority to act in Christ's name—are interpreted in a legalistic manner that fails to distinguish the head from its members, there is no doubt that the church loses its missionary impulse. Ministers become religious specialists whom we pay in order to keep the rest of us from having to be disciples and witnesses. However, when interpreted evangelically, the commission to bind and loose is synonymous with mission. It is the *authorization* to go, given by the one to whom all authority has been given, and to know that "whoever receives the one whom I send receives me; and whoever receives me receives him who sent me" (John 13:20). Although entrusted to officers in its formal, public assemblies, this commission includes, in its wider application, every member of Christ's body. The ministry of Word and sacrament prepares all believers not for the work of the ministry (of Word and sacrament), but for the work of Christians in the world.

THE MISSION OF THE CHURCH DEFINED
BY THE MARKS OF THE CHURCH

Although parsed somewhat differently, Roman Catholic and Orthodox ecclesiologies insist that the proper *ministry* (apostolic succession) guarantees the proper message and mission. Inconsistent with the logic of their own confession, Lutheran and Reformed churches often rest on their own purity of doctrine and (at least among the latter) church order. In this way, the *marks* become a new law by which the church seeks to justify itself rather than as the marching orders for mission in the world. Recent evangelical and Pentecostal movements have emphasized the *mission* as guaranteeing the ministry and the message.

I suggest that by locating the visibility of the church in the public marks of the preaching of the gospel and administration of the sacraments, these emphases are more fully integrated. Furthermore, it ensures that the indicative ("All authority in heaven and on earth has been given to me" [Matt. 28:18]) drives the imperative (Therefore, "go into all the world" [Mark 16:15]), instead of the reverse, which can only lead to another form of "holy egoism," as well as spiritual exhaus-

82. Ibid.

tion. The gospel not only determines the message, but also defines the ministry and mission of the church. In other words, Christ retains the sole authority to determine not only what we say in his name, but also what we do and how we do it, so that the mission is consistent with the message. The message determines the mission, but the mission delivers the message. We cannot choose between being doctrinal and being missional.

Thus, the marks define the mission. Preaching, baptism, and the Supper are means of grace—that is, God's acts of delivering Christ to us—rather than means of obedience. We certainly are also commanded as well as assured through these means, but obedience is the "reasonable service of worship" that we render "in view of the mercies of God" (Rom. 12:1 KJV). Indicatives come before imperatives. Prayer, offering our service and gifts, personal and family worship, Bible reading, fellowship with other believers, sharing the gospel with others—these are all important responses of gratitude, but they are not means of grace.

Sharing a common heritage in the revivalism of Charles Finney, to which I have already referred in previous chapters, American Protestants have trouble being *recipients* of grace. The church becomes an army of activists—social engineers, moral reformers, event planners, life coaches—rather than a theater of grace where God has the lead role. Given this orientation, it is not surprising that "means of grace" do not seem as relevant as practical methods of personal and social transformation, church growth, and daily problem-solving. Although the medieval church had extended the sacraments to seven, Protestantism today is brimming with alternatives to preaching, baptism, and Communion. These "new measures," or as Finney also called them, "inducements sufficient to convert sinners with," were simply practical implications of a basically Pelagian anthropology.[83] Apart from the conviction that the application as well as the accomplishment of redemption was God's work from beginning to end, none of us would have devised a religion whose chief methods of propagation were sermons, a bath, and a simple meal with remarkably meager quantities of bread and wine.

Concerning the complex of doctrines that Finney associated with Calvinism (including original sin, vicarious atonement, justification, and the supernatural character of the new birth), he concluded, "No doctrine is more dangerous than this to the prosperity of the Church, and nothing more absurd."[84] Not only was

---

83. Ironically, Finney held to an ex opere operato view of his own new measures that he would never allow to baptism and the Supper. As for the Pelagian charge, Finney's *Systematic Theology* (Minneapolis: Bethany House Publishers, 1976) explicitly denies original sin and insists that the power of regeneration lies in the sinner's own hands, rejects any substitutionary notion of Christ's atonement in favor of the moral influence and moral government theories, and regards the doctrine of justification by an alien righteousness as "impossible and absurd." Roger Olson, in his defense of Arminianism, actually sees Finney's theology as well beyond the Arminian pale (*Arminian Theology* [Downers Grove, IL: InterVarsity Press, 2006], 27). Thus, it is all the more remarkable that Finney occupies such a distinguished place among evangelicals, as the tribute to him in the Billy Graham Center (Wheaton, IL) illustrates. It is little wonder that American religion struck Bonhoeffer as "Protestantism without the Reformation."

84. Charles G. Finney, *[Lectures on] Revivals of Religion* (1835; revised, 1868; Old Tappan, NJ: Revell, n.d.), 4–5.

Finney willing to set aside the ordinary means of grace for extraordinary "seasons of revival"; he also insisted, "A revival is not a miracle." "There is nothing in religion beyond the ordinary powers of nature. It consists in the right exercise of the powers of nature. It is just that, and nothing else. . . . It is a purely philosophical result of the right use of the constituted means—as much so as any other effect produced by the application of means."[85] Find the most useful methods, "excitements sufficient to induce conversion," and there will be conversion. "God Has Established No Particular Measures" is the subheading of a chapter in his *Systematic Theology*. "A revival will decline and cease," he warned, "unless Christians are frequently re-converted."[86]

Toward the end of his ministry, as he considered the condition of many who had experienced his revivals, Finney wondered if this endless craving for ever-greater experiences might lead to spiritual exhaustion.[87] His worries were justified. The area where Finney's revivals were especially dominant is now referred to by historians as the "burned-over district," a seedbed of both disillusionment and the proliferation of esoteric sects.[88] If, as Bonhoeffer declared, American religion has been decisively shaped by "Protestantism without the Reformation," then Finney is its clearest spokesperson.

Citing numerous contemporary heirs, Michael Pasquarello goes so far as to suggest that Finney's approach itself represents a "practical atheism," according to which the success of Christian mission depends on human technique, style, planning, and charisma, "without having to surrender ourselves and our words to the presence and work of the Word and Spirit."[89] The Great Commission just said, "Go," says Finney. "*It did not prescribe any forms*. It did not admit any. . . . And [the disciples'] object was to make known the gospel in the *most effectual way* . . . so as to obtain attention and secure obedience of the greatest number possible. No person can find any *form* of doing this laid down in the Bible."[90]

On all of these counts, the Second Great Awakening represents a seismic shift that significantly determined the course of American Protestantism down to our own time, both mainline and evangelical. Whatever churches ordinarily do in the public service, Finney's "protracted meeting" was a media event. In many circles today, however, the protracted meeting has taken the place of that ordinary ministry. Even if we still gather together to hear a sermon, to pray and sing, to confess our sins, and receive the Supper, the real means of grace seem to lie elsewhere: in largely private spiritual disciplines or in well-planned and publicized events and enthusiastic movements.

85. Ibid.

86. Ibid., 321.

87. See Keith J. Hardman, *Charles Grandison Finney: Revivalist and Reformer* (Grand Rapids: Baker, 1990), 380–94.

88. See, e.g., Whitney R. Cross, *The Burned-Over District: The Social and Intellectual History of Enthusiastic Religion in Western New York, 1800–1850* (Ithaca, NY: Cornell University Press, 1982).

89. Michael Pasquarello III, *Christian Preaching: A Trinitarian Theology of Proclamation* (Grand Rapids: Baker Academic, 2007), 24.

90. Quoted in ibid.

With salvation placed in the hands of the rugged American individual, the only challenge was to find the appropriate spiritual, moral, and emotional technology for radical, visible, and immediate results. As exhibited in its sprawling empire of publishing, radio, television, music, political lobbies, and large-scale events, the evangelical movement gives every impression of being driven by a sense of mission that is tenuously connected to the divinely appointed message of the cross and means of grace. Especially in this context, we need to reintegrate the message, the marks, and the mission of the church.

The point that Wendell Berry makes in connection with contemporary approaches to our natural environment are analogous to ecclesial mission: "We must learn to grow like a tree," he says, "not like a fire."[91] He adds, "Our present 'leaders'—the people of wealth and power—do not know what it means to take a place seriously: to think it worthy, for its own sake, of love and study and careful work. They cannot take any place seriously because they must be ready at any moment, by the terms of power and wealth in the modern world, to destroy any place."[92]

Similarly, we seem too easily to forget that our churches are "real places" defined by the covenant of grace rather than by whatever ideologies or spiritual technologies that we think may save the world. American Protestantism has frequently identified the church as people in opposition to place to such an extent that the people are actually rendered homeless, restless drifters in a mall of designer spiritualities. In the most well-publicized "missional" efforts of the last thirty years, the focus has not been so much on identifying the church in terms of God's work for us but in our work for God or even our work for each other.

If more traditional ecclesiologies can marginalize the notion of the church as people in their emphasis on the church as place, movement-driven approaches risk making the opposite mistake. Dan Kimball, a thoughtful representative of the emerging-church movement, tells us that "it is actually impossible to 'go to church.'" Not only is the church not to be identified with the building (a salutary point); "nor is it the meeting" (a not-so-salutary point). Rather, "the church is the people of God who gather together with a sense of mission (Acts 14:27). We can't *go* to church because *we are* the church."[93] From this, Kimball draws the familiar contrast between evangelism (mission) and the marks of the church (means of grace):

> The excellent book *The Missional Church*, edited by Darrell Guder, makes the case that since the Reformation, the church unintentionally redefined itself. The Reformers, in their effort to raise the authority of the Bible and ensure sound doctrine, defined the marks of a true church: a place where the gospel is rightly preached, the sacraments are rightly administered, and church discipline is exercised. However, over time these marks narrowed the

91. Wendell Berry, *Sex, Economy, Freedom and Community* (New York: Pantheon Books, 1993), 13.
92. Ibid., 22.
93. Dan Kimball, *The Emerging Church: Vintage Christianity for New Generations* (Grand Rapids: Zondervan, 2003), 91.

definition of the church itself as a "place where" instead of a "people who are" reality. The word church became defined as "a place where certain things happen," such as preaching and communion.[94]

Kimball repeatedly contrasts *service* with *gathering*. The former emphasis, which he correlates with the megachurch (now considered "traditional" worship), is consumeristic: all about what I can get out of it. One can understand why younger Christians recoil at a narcissistic conception of "service," appropriately skeptical of the seeker-driven approach familiar in their own experience. However, what if *service* has an entirely different meaning?

One of the words that the New Testament uses for the event is *leitourgeia*, from which comes the word *liturgy*. It means service in the sense of ministering. That is considerably different from the church as service-provider in the technological sense of contemporary business. In short, there is no *gathering* until there is a *service*. There is no ecclesial going and giving until there is a hearing and receiving, no sanctification without justification, and no following of Christ apart from faith in Christ. However, it is *God* who is the server. God comes to us in the Word (preached, read, sung, prayed) and in the sacraments, to convict and comfort, to kill and make alive, to judge and to justify, to bring about the effects of Christ's completed work: not only justification, but also sanctification; not only faith, but also hope and love. There is a gathering—an *ekklēsia*—because there is a work of God through preaching and sacrament called the gospel, which does its work before we can get around to ours. In both traditional and contemporary forms of worship today, the emphasis seems to fall on our activity rather than on God's. Yet this fails to be genuinely evangelistic, either for Christians or others who might be present.

If we realize what God is doing through Word and sacrament—enacting a covenantal drama—then the public ministry becomes a living event rather than dead ritual. While revivalism from Finney to the contemporary church-growth movement has located "new measures" in pragmatic techniques, a new generation—understandably thirsting for a more transcendent orientation—looks for new means of grace in more mystical practices. For example, Brian McLaren writes,

> What I like about the sacramental nature of Catholicism is this: through learning that a few things can carry the sacred, we become open to the fact that all things (all good things, all created things) can ultimately carry the sacred: the kind smile of a Down's syndrome child, the bouncy jubilation of a puppy, the graceful arch of a dancer's back, the camera work in a fine film, good coffee, good wine, good friends, good conversation. Start with three sacraments—or seven—and pretty soon everything becomes potentially sacramental as, I believe, it should be.[95]

94. Ibid., 93.
95. Brian McLaren, *A Generous Orthodoxy* (Grand Rapids: Zondervan 2004), 225–26.

However, this is to confuse general revelation with special revelation. "The heavens are telling the glory of God" (Ps. 19:1), but only the gospel, delivered through the Word, baptism, and Eucharist, can tell the mercy of God in Christ's cross and resurrection. God's *good gifts* in creation raise our eyes in gratitude to the Giver, but God's *good news* (i.e., the gospel) is not latently present in smiles, graceful dancers, and good wine.

Wolfhart Pannenberg has noticed a similar tendency among Protestants in Germany today. Largely because the churches in which they have been reared have become unreflective about the meaning of baptism and the liturgy, many are looking for resources outside of the evangelical tradition—indeed, outside of Christianity. Pannenberg's counsel addresses both form-without-content traditionalism as well as eclectic spirituality:

> Christians need not feel ashamed or empty when looking at the splendours of eastern mysticism. We only have to recover the forgotten spiritual treasures of our own tradition. Where is the religious mysticism that surpasses the participation in the inner life of the Trinity that is made accessible to each baptized Christian and is actually realized in the experience of Christian prayer? We only have to become aware once more of the spiritual treasures we have been granted, especially in the sacraments of the Church. We have to overcome the superficial way of administering and attending the liturgy and the sacraments as if they were merely ancient forms of ritual. If they are not understood, their celebration quickly turns boring. But they carry divine life within themselves. It just waits to be rediscovered.[96]

"According to Luther," adds Pannenberg, "faith is trust in God that places us outside ourselves. It is the specifically Christian form of mystical experience, and it pervades all aspects of a Christian life."[97] Baptism is not just *initiation* into Christ's visible body, but the definitive event to which the Christian *returns daily* in repentance and faith. Preaching is not only doctrinal and moral instruction (although it includes these); it is also God's living and vivifying voice, through which the Spirit creates and sustains Christians and churches in their union with Christ. The Supper is not only our reaffirmation of our own ecclesial reality, but also God's reaffirmation of his covenant oath, which constantly generates, shapes, and defines that reality.

From the perspective of the marks of the church enunciated by the Reformers, neither conservative nor postconservative evangelicalism has sufficiently appreciated the point that *God* is the liturgist, the server, the evangelist who not only identifies both the plight and the solution but who wounds and heals. Once we make the outward forms of the church—its visibility—a matter of purely human origins, goals, methods, and aims, the *place* of grace vanishes like a mirage.

---

96. Wolfhart Pannenberg, "Baptism as Remembered 'Ecstatic' Identity," in *Christ: The Sacramental World*, ed. David Brown and Ann Loades (London: SPCK, 1996), 88.
97. Ibid., 86.

The *people* then become the means of grace, both Word and sacrament, by their "changed lives." In this view, the church's visibility consists in the service that its members perform within the local church rather than in the service that God renders to his people and then, through them, in the world via their vocations.

We must therefore resist the false choice between looking after the sheep already gathered through preaching, sacrament, and discipline (the marks) and reaching out to the lost sheep who have yet to hear and believe (the mission). The proper balance is found in Peter's Pentecost sermon: "The promise is for you, for your children, and for all who are far away, everyone whom the Lord our God calls to him" (Acts 2:39). Peter draws no contrast between ministering the gospel to covenant members (believers and their children) and mission to the world. Instead, there is an ever-widening circumference, as the ecclesial body expands through the apostolic teaching, the Supper, the fellowship, and the prayers (vv. 40–47). Confessional Protestants typically focus on the apostles' teaching; independent evangelicals and Pentecostals on fellowship and evangelism; more liturgical churches on "the breaking of the bread and the prayers," while more liberal churches concentrate on caring for material needs. However, a genuinely apostolic and therefore missional church will be intent on integrating all of these concerns. In the process, our churches will become not only more apostolic (the marks oriented toward mission) but more catholic as well.

The word brings conviction and conversion, of both the churched (those who are near) and the unchurched (those who are far). The church not only *makes* disciples; it also is the place where disciples *are made*, and not just once but throughout their Christian life. "For he is our God, and we are the people of his pasture, and the sheep of his hand" (Ps. 95:7). God is the focus, and the church is both his people and his pasture. The orderly worship of the saints gathered in weekly assembly for preaching, teaching, and witness *is* missional (1 Cor. 14:23–25). Since incorporation into Christ is simultaneously incorporation into his visible body, any emphasis on mission that separates evangelism from baptism and church membership is not only ecclesiologically deficient but also soteriologically deficient. Throughout Acts we see that the same means of grace (marks of the church) that were employed for the church's outreach were those that sustained and deepened the church's inreach. In other words, a church that properly cares for its members will simultaneously exhibit a concern for others who have yet to be incorporated into the body of Christ.

In spite of its profoundly mixed record of faithfulness to its commission, the ordinary ministry of the church (baptizing, catechizing, preaching, receiving the Supper, praying, singing, caring and comforting, admonishing and encouraging in fellowship, and finally, burying the dead in the hope of the resurrection) has yielded the most effective results even when considered on purely empirical grounds. Those who are deeply rooted in the mysteries of the gospel will not only be more confident but also more zealous to share their hope in the ordinary course of daily life. And they will also more eagerly encourage others to attend the public means of grace, where strangers are reconciled.

There is due place for doing the Word as well as hearing it, for serving as well as being served. However, when we know what we believe and why we believe it, fed richly on the indicatives of the gospel, we find ourselves filled with faith toward God and love toward our neighbor. Those who are properly suited with the belt of truth, the breastplate of righteousness, the shield of faith, and "the sword of the Spirit, which is the word of God," will also find themselves wearing "shoes for your feet" that "will make you ready to proclaim the gospel of peace" (Eph. 6:13–17). It is precisely by the church doing what it is commissioned to do for the people who have gathered in Christ's name that the church actually sets the stage for genuine conversation and conversion.

This means that a genuinely missional church should not only provoke a disrupting encounter with a holy and gracious God in its preaching and teaching, but also in the regular celebration of the Supper. Why should the Supper be celebrated so infrequently and, in many cases, at an evening service where visitors are less likely to attend (and therefore, to be offended, perplexed, convicted, or intrigued)? Although Calvin and other Reformers have argued that the Supper should occupy a central place alongside preaching, its strange absence from the regular gathering in many Reformed and Presbyterian churches not only impoverishes the saints; it also weakens the missional diet. It is the Eucharist, along with preaching and baptism, that not only generates a church in the first place, but also keeps its focus on Christ's presence in action as well as his absence in the flesh, generating our longing for his return.

Decades ago, Scottish minister H. H. William M. Cant argued, "Of course what our Lord has to say is not simply commands for another week, though worship will include these. . . . Yet before the imperatives . . . there must come the indicatives. He who is the risen One tells of what He has done for us."[98] Where in the service is this forgiveness and reconciliation given—even to lifelong believers? First of all, in preaching. Yet today, many ministers are suggesting that there are more meaningful ways of communicating the gospel, such as more "conversational" methods. But is this listening to the risen Lord or to the preacher and each other?[99] Do we come to church expecting Christ to raise the dead and the weak and feeble?[100]

> It is surely right, then, that the worshippers should come away from this worship, not only with a Gospel message for the individual, but [also] with a strong sense of having been made a member again of the one Holy Catholic and Apostolic Church, with a new awareness of being joined once more to the joyful believing and committed company of the whole Church in heaven and upon earth in whose fellowship they happily unite in the Lord's Prayer. If the transformation of life is a reality within the service of

98. William M. Cant, "The Most Urgent Call to the Kirk: The Celebration of Christ in the Liturgy of Word and Sacrament," *Scottish Journal of Theology* 40 (1987): 110.
99. Ibid., 113.
100. Ibid., 114.

the Word through the presence of the risen Lord, how much more in the service of the Word *and* Sacrament.[101]

Remembering Christ's death is a key part of the sacrament. "Yet it has to be said that it is very easy along this memorialist road to become a Pelagian—we remember what Christ has done for us in the past, we recall the wonder of His dying love for our sins, and then we seek to make our human progress. We very easily forget that the ability to make the response of dying and rising again comes from the ascended Christ through the Spirit."[102] Who can follow Christ until they are made more and more into members of his mystical body?[103] "This paschal mystery has two sides to it," Cant reminds us: "a descending and ascending movement, both *katabasis* and *anabasis*. . . . As we partake of the Table, we are lifted up into sharing in the glorified humanity of Christ, into sharing in the life of heaven."[104]

The word that is preached, taught, sung, and prayed, along with baptism and the Eucharist, not only prepares us for mission; it also is itself *the* missionary event, as visitors are able to hear and see the gospel that it communicates and the communion that it generates. To the extent that the marks define the mission and the mission justifies the marks, the church fulfills its apostolic identity.

101. Ibid., 115.
102. Ibid., 117.
103. Ibid., 119.
104. Ibid., 120–21.

PART THREE
DESTINATION
Royal Procession to Zion

Chapter Nine

Holy Land, Holy War

Preparing a Place

On a cold November day in 1095, Pope Urban II roused a Christendom plagued by internal wars to take up the cause of holy war against Islam. "If you must have blood," he exhorted, "bathe in the blood of infidels."[1] Substituting itself for its ascended Lord, the church assimilated a civilization to that ecclesial body. "Our divinely favored emperor," said the church father Eusebius concerning Constantine, "receiving, as it were, a transcript of the divine sovereignty, directs, in imitation of God himself, the administration of this world's affairs." With divine mandate, therefore, the emperor "subdues and chastens the open adversaries of the truth in accordance with the usages of war."[2] There were often lively debates as to whether the temporal and visible head of Christendom was the pope or the emperor; yet the medieval imagination was fed by an allegorization of Europe as Israel of old. Monarchs fancied themselves King David redivivus, driving out the Canaanites with their holy knights.

Though secularized by the logic of liberal democracy, the hijacking of Israel's national covenant as a metanarrative for the manifest destiny of supposedly

---

1. Robert Payne, *The Dream and the Tomb: A History of the Crusades* (New York: Stein & Day, 1985), 34.
2. Douglas Farrow, *Ascension and Ecclesia* (Edinburgh: T&T Clark, 1999), 115, from Eusebius, *Oration of the Emperor Constantine* 1.6–2.5.

Christian nations with a divine commission to extend their civilization and values continues unabated. This illicit invocation (taking God's name in vain) has proved useful for justifying colonialism and anticolonial revolutions, with Israel's exodus-conquest motif inspiring political speeches from Constantine to George W. Bush, from conservative Roman Catholics and Protestants to liberation theologians. Confusion of the kingdom of Christ with the theocratic kingdom of the old covenant, and then with whatever secular kingdom chooses to elect itself into divine favor—such confusion has provided the script for the most atrocious performances in Christ's name, from the Crusades to the massacre of natives, to apartheid in South Africa and genocide in Serbia.

No matter how different the cast each time, the roles of Joshua or David and the Canaanites are predictable. Today, in the United States, religious lobbies on the right and left continue to ally the cause of Christ with a particular political ideology and agenda, more certain of God's will concerning U.S. domestic and foreign policy, it seems, than of its own doctrine, ministry, and mission. Focusing on the challenges of secularism and Islam, evangelicals and Roman Catholics increasingly congeal around salvaging "Judeo-Christian" culture.[3] In a 2006 *Time* magazine article on the relation of Pope Benedict and Islam, conservative Catholic scholar Michael Novak explained concerning the pontiff: "His role is to represent Western civilization."[4]

At least in the United States, the culture wars, not to mention the "clash of civilizations" between the West and Islam, provoke nostalgia for this parody of the body of Christ. For millions of conservative Protestants in America today, biblical prophecy coalesces around the events unfolding today in the Middle East more than around the events that transpired there in the first century. Writing as "a Muslim to Muslims," Vincent J. Cornell has correctly observed, "Extremists on both sides feed on America's moral and eschatological obsession with the Holy Land. Both sides exploit the memory of the crusades."[5] He further notes that "Islam," for its own part, means "submission," not "peace."[6] Holy lands inevitably provoke holy wars. The first part of this chapter addresses the question of holy land; the second, holy war.

TEMPLE: ON EARTH AS IT IS IN HEAVEN

Instead of hallowing the land of origin, God was continually calling his people out of lands, dragging them across the desert like a nomadic dreamer, to inherit his territorial estate. Yet not even this land was God's ultimate dwelling place.

---

3. Former U.S. Senator Rick Santorum (Republican), a Roman Catholic, was listed as one of the most influential evangelicals by *Time* magazine, and the "Evangelicals and Catholics Together" initiative was led by conservative political writer and priest, Fr. Richard John Neuhaus.

4. David Van Biema and Jeff Israely, "The Passion of the Pope," *Time*, November 27, 2006, 46.

5. Vincent J. Cornell, "A Muslim to Muslims," in *Dissent from the Homeland: Essays after September 11*, ed. Stanley Hauerwas and Frank Lentricchia (Durham, NC: Duke University Press, 2003), 85.

6. Ibid., 86.

Even the temple-motif follows a covenantal plotline. However, as in other loci, the *type* of covenant theology one endorses makes all the difference.

From Sinai (Tent) to Zion (Temple)

Dominant in the narratives of Israel's march from Sinai to Zion is the notion that God *manifests* himself in particular places, not that he *dwells* there. Yahweh descends to Sinai in order to meet with the mediator of the vassal-state, only to make them pack up everything and keep on moving toward the goal.[7] Underscoring its covenantal character, Eichrodt notes that the "tent of meeting" is a "meeting-place," while the encroaching influences of Canaanite religion seduced Israel to erect its idolatrous "high places."[8] Even where Yahweh appears, he is concealed in his *kābôd*, "and this was to continue to be so, until the day in which the concrete historical fact of the revelation itself decreed its own independence of any holy place—when it reached its fulfillment in a Man who could say of himself: 'One greater than the Temple is here!'"[9]

The concept of the cosmic mountain is hardly unique to Israel's worldview. The motif can be found in cultures on every continent.[10] The Canaanite high places and Mesopotamian ziggurats that dotted Jacob's mental horizon when he received his vision in Genesis 28 attest to the significance of the human attempt to return to Paradise, to fuse cult and culture, ascending in self-confidence to take heaven by storm—despite the cherubim guarding the entrance with flaming sword.

The garden of Eden and "God's holy mountain" are correlated in Ezekiel 28:11–19, along with allusions to Adam while describing the king of Tyre's fall from his wisdom, beauty, and perfection.[11] So there is already a connection between the Adamic king (image-bearer) and the temple (image-bearer), both linked by the idea of glorious beauty.[12] Psalm 36:8–10 also equates the temple mount and Eden.[13] "In short, the Temple is intimately associated with creation," says Jŏn D. Levenson. "It is, in a sense, the gateway to life as it was meant to be, unlimited by death, eternal life, life *in illo tempore*, sacred time, always new, always just created."[14] Levenson quotes the sages, who intensified the biblical imagery: "Both [heaven and earth] were created from Zion."[15] So Zion takes on

---

7. Walther Eichrodt, *Theology of the Old Testament*, trans. J. A. Baker (Philadelphia: Westminster Press, 1961), 1:103.

8. Ibid., 104.

9. Ibid., 107; cf. Matt. 12:6, "Something greater than the temple is here."

10. Mircea Eliade, *Patterns in Comparative Religion* (Cleveland and New York: Meridian, 1958), 367–87; cf. Richard J. Clifford, *The Cosmic Mountain in Canaan and the Old Testament*, Harvard Semitic Monographs 4 (Cambridge, MA: Harvard University Press, 1972).

11. Ibid., 128–29.

12. On the significance of beauty as part of the *imago Dei*, see Michael S. Horton, *Lord and Servant: A Covenant Christology* (Louisville, KY: Westminster John Knox Press, 2005), 107–12.

13. Jŏn D. Levenson, *Sinai and Zion: An Entry into the Jewish Bible* (San Francisco: HarperSanFrancisco, 1985), 131.

14. Ibid., 133.

15. Ibid., 133, from *b. Yoma* 54b.

a cosmic, universal role that Sinai never did. "Not only Jerusalem and the land of Israel, but even the people of Israel can be designated as Zion," as in Isaiah 51:16 and Zechariah 2:10–11.[16]

As Levenson observes, Mount Zion is also Mount Moriah, identified with the site of various tests: Abraham's binding of Isaac and encounter with an angel (Gen. 22:2–14) and David's permission to see the Angel of Yahweh (2 Chr. 3:1; cf. 2 Sam. 24).[17] These events actually "serve as authorizations for the inauguration of the Temple on Mount Zion/Moriah."[18] Christians will also recall the significance of this place in the events of Jesus' life and will point out that, in addition to its association with Abraham and David, the vision of the angel of the LORD makes the site a significant foreshadowing of Christ, the greater Isaac who was actually sacrificed and the Son of David who inherited an everlasting throne.

Temple Typology

Redolent of creation, especially Eden as the beachhead of the kingdom of God, the temple is a miniature cosmos. Jewish and Christian interpreters generally agree on the Eden-tabernacle/temple typology.[19] Even the altar had to be made of natural earth (not of cut stones, Exod. 20:24–25 NASB). G. K. Beale has drawn similar conclusions, pointing out the ways in which the New Testament (esp. Rev. 21:1-22:5) incorporates the specific descriptions of the temple that we find, for example, in 1 Kings 6:20–22; 7:8–10; and Ezekiel 40–48.[20] First, the outer court of the temple "represented the habitable world where humanity dwelt," with its large washbasin and altar identified, respectively, as the "sea" (1 Kgs. 7:23–26) and "bosom of the earth" (lit., in Ezek. 43:14), as well as the "mountain of God" (lit., in Ezek. 43:16).[21] Next, there was the holy place, "emblematic of the visible heavens and light sources."[22] Symbolizing the heavenly bodies observable to the naked eye, the seven lights on the lampstand add to the cosmic imagery, which the Apocalypse picks up on as representing the seven churches and their seven heavenly angels, representative in both cases of covenantal witness.[23] Holy time (Sabbath) and holy space (temple) provide the coordinates for the covenant people, linking the theocracy to the original covenant of creation.

---

16. Levenson, *Sinai and Jerusalem*, 137.

17. Ibid., 94.

18. Ibid., 95.

19. Ibid., 139.

20. G. K. Beale, *The Temple and the Church's Mission: A Biblical Theology of the Dwelling Place of God* (Downers Grover, IL: InterVarsity Press, 2004).

21. Ibid.

22. Ibid., 32–33. Cf. E. Bloch-Smith, "'Who Is the King of Glory?' Solomon's Temple and Its Symbolism,' in *Scripture and Other Artifacts*, ed. M. D. Coogan, J. C. Exum, and L. E. Stager (Louisville, KY: Westminster John Knox Press, 1994), 183–94.

23. Ibid., 34–35.

Finally, there was the Holy of Holies, which "symbolized the invisible dimension of the cosmos, where God and his heavenly hosts dwelt."[24] Even the priest's own clothing was made of the same colored fabrics. Further, "the jewels on the priest's breastpiece, which were a small replica of the holy of holies, symbolized the earthly or heavenly cosmos, and the same jewels are part of the new city-temple in Revelation 21."[25]

In *Lord and Servant* (chap. 4) I explored the covenantal anthropology that funded Israel's concept of the *imago Dei*. This connection becomes even more obvious in the temple imagery that discloses the identity of a people as well as a place. Jewish and Christian interpretation has frequently recognized parallels between the accounts of creation and those of the temple's construction (Gen. 1:31; 2:1; 2:2; 2:3; respectively with Exod. 39:43; 39:32; 40:33; 39:43).[26] Yahweh subdues chaos and creates an ordered place as a sanctuary for dwelling with his people—a theme that we have already encountered in consideration of the relation between canon and covenant. "Accordingly, it is likely not coincidental that David initially conceived of building God a temple only after 'the LORD had given him rest on every side from all his enemies' (2 Sam. 7:1–6 [NASB]; following Levenson)." The building of the temple is undertaken by Solomon, since David did not yet have "rest on every side" and had himself been "a warrior," even shedding innocent blood (1 Chr. 22:8; 28:3). Like God's own enthronement in Sabbath rest after completing the work of creation, "God's dwelling in Israel's temple was conceived as the rest of a divine king who had no worries about opposition."[27]

Even the same Hebrew verbal form for God's "walking back and forth" are used of creation (Gen. 3:8) and the tabernacle (Lev. 26:12; Deut. 23:14; 2 Sam. 7:6).[28] "Cultivate it and keep it" in Gen. 2:15 (NASB) is elsewhere translated "serve and guard" in relation to the temple.[29] And like the subsequent temples, Eden has an eastern-facing entrance (Gen. 3:24; Ezek. 40:6).[30] The first cherubim are stationed at Eden's eastern gate, barring reentry after the covenant had been broken (Gen. 3:24), repeated in the account of the departure of the Glory and appointment of angelic guards in Ezekiel 28:14, 16.[31] The lampstand in the tabernacle and then later in the temple represents the tree of life.[32] So the temple exhibits a tripartite structure, representing the earth (land and sea), the visible heavens, and the majestic throne of God.

---

24. Beale, *The Temple and the Church's Mission*, 35.
25. Ibid., 39.
26. Ibid., 60–61.
27. Ibid., 62–63; citing Jön D. Levenson, *Creation and the Persistence of Evil: The Jewish Drama of Divine Omnipotence* (San Francisco: Harper & Row, 1988), 107.
28. Beale, *The Temple and the Church's Mission*, 66.
29. Ibid.
30. Ibid., 74.
31. Ibid., 70.
32. Ibid., 71.

The first sacred mountain (Ezek. 28:14, 16, with Exod. 15:17; Ezek. 40:2; 43:12; Rev. 21:10),[33] Eden also represents the first instance of a source of water nourishing the whole earth (Gen. 2:10–14; Ezek. 47:1–12; Zech. 14:8–9; Rev. 7:15–17; 22:1–2).[34] It is said in Genesis 2:10 that "a river flows out of Eden to water the garden," and again in Ezekiel 47:1 and Revelation 22:1–2, water flows out of the inmost sanctuary to renew the whole earth.[35] Ezekiel especially sees Eden as the first sanctuary (28:13–18). Connected by the *imago Dei* motif (glory, truth, righteousness, and beauty), there is also a close correspondence between Adam and the temple. *Jubilees* (160 BCE) offers a similar parallel of Adam and Israel, Eden and Zion, adding the picture of "Adam as a priest in an arboreal temple."[36] This centripetal expansion of the city of God from its central temple to the ends of the earth is repeated throughout the Scriptures. It begins with the creation commission: to rule, to subdue, and to expand God's glorious kingdom (Gen. 1:28; 2:15).

Not only the institution of the temple cult, but also its desecration, is treated as an echo of the fall in Eden. "Just as in the case of Adam, Israel's obedience within their 'garden of Eden' to the laws regulating the temple was a part of carrying out their renewed commission as a corporate Adam. Israel's land is explicitly compared to the garden of Eden (see Gen. 13:10; Isa. 51:3; Ezek. 36:35; 47:12; Joel 2:3) and is portrayed as very fruitful in order to heighten the correspondence to Eden (cf. Deut. 8:7–10; 11:8–17; Ezek. 47:1–12)."[37] Repeatedly, the nations erect parodies of the city of God, such as Babel, and once in the land, Israel too repeatedly sets up idolatrous altars on "every high hill and [under] every leafy tree" (Ezek. 20:28). All of this is "a sinful and perverted attempt to replicate the conditions of Eden for which only judgment could come."[38]

Hence, in the nation's disobedience, Israel's quarters are described in terms of the curse: a "barren" (Isa. 54:1–3) and "cramped space" (49:20). As the original curse threatens to return the earth to the darkness and void of chaos (Gen. 3:17–19) if it were not for God's common grace and the evangelical promise, the evacuation of the Glory from the temple leaves the land destitute of vitality, an uninhabited wasteland (Mic. 3:12), yet a remnant will be saved. The tree will be cut down, but "the holy seed shall be its stump" (Isa. 6:11–13 NKJV). The people will be the place. Even in the exile, far removed from the desecrated temple, God says, "Yet I have been a sanctuary for them a little while" (Ezek. 11:16).

In the end-time sanctuary, the Spirit will again be present in blessing, as in Haggai 2:5 and Zechariah 4:6–9—the latter alluding to Exodus 33:14–17, the Presence that goes with Israel.[39] God promises to make "the latter glory of this house . . . greater than the former" (Hag. 2:3–9 ESV), which certainly could not

---

33. Ibid., 72.
34. Ibid., 73.
35. Ibid., 74.
36. Ibid., 77–78.
37. Ibid.
38. Ibid.
39. Ibid., 115.

have been said of Herod's temple.[40] In the new age, according to Isaiah 66:21–23, "[God] will take [Gentiles] for priests and for Levites" (v. 21 ESV)."[41] "From new moon to new moon, and from sabbath to sabbath, all flesh shall come to worship before me, says the LORD" (v. 23). Like Noah's ark, all the nations will be gathered into this end-time temple (Jer. 3:16–18). Yet Isaiah 65:17–18 (with 43:18–19) implies that the old temple belongs to the old creation.[42] And for now, the rulers of the nations scheme against Yahweh and his Anointed (Ps. 2). Zechariah 1–2 along with Daniel 2 also points to this expanding and worldwide kingdom that will transcend any localized temple, and Beale offers examples from Second Temple literature that present the same vision.

The End-Time Temple

"Woman, believe me, the hour is coming when you will worship the Father neither on this mountain nor in Jerusalem" (John 4:21). A triple outsider, Jesus' conversation partner asks Jesus to weigh in on the age-old dispute between Jews and Samaritans over the correct sanctuary. In answering her query, Jesus relativizes both sites, not by a vague appeal to religious pluralism (see v. 22) but in reference to the eschatological moment that centers on him (vv. 23–26). In an age of typological signs, with blood running down altars, the smell of smoke and billowing incense, elaborate ritual, and the holy sanctuary itself, getting God's address right is of crucial importance. Yet "the hour is coming, and is now here," when redemptive history transitions from promise to fulfillment, from shadows to reality. From now on, true worship will be determined not by any religious edifice, but by whether it takes place in Jesus Christ as the holy place.

With each building of the temple on Mount Zion from tabernacle to first to second temples, there were successive expansions: first, the court of the women, then the court of Gentiles.[43] Indeed, even with the central temple in Jerusalem, Yahweh remained a nomadic deity, on his way to the fulfilled promise. However, Jesus Christ is described as "light for revelation to the Gentiles" (Luke 2:32 and Acts 26:23, alluding to Isa. 49:6). In Christ, there is no longer a court of women and a court of Gentiles. "For he is our peace; in his flesh he has made both groups into one and has broken down the dividing wall, that is, the hostility between us. He has abolished the law with its commandments and ordinances, that he might create in himself one new humanity in place of the two, thus making peace" (Eph. 2:14–15). "There is no longer Jew or Greek, there is no longer slave or free, there is no longer male and female; for all of you are one in Christ Jesus" (Gal. 3:28). The gospel will go out from Jerusalem (Holy of Holies) to Judea (the inner court) to Samaria and the ends of the earth (the court of the Gentiles).

40. Ibid., 116.
41. Ibid., 137.
42. Ibid., 141.
43. Ibid., 166.

Matthew 21 (and parallels) reports a series of acts performed by Jesus on the temple mount following his triumphal entry. Welcoming the "unclean" to the sacred precincts, Jesus nevertheless casts out the merchants. He forgives sins directly in his person, bypassing the temple altogether. Then, finding a barren fig tree along the road, he curses it, declaring, "May no fruit ever come from you again," and the tree immediately withers (v. 19). He then explains to the bewildered disciples that they will not only do the same, but will also "say to this mountain"—that is, to the temple mount, nothing less than the earthly Zion—"'be removed and be thrown into the sea,' and it will be done" (v. 21). Understandably, the religious leaders are appalled by such action and demand to know by what authority Jesus is presuming to do them.[44] *Bēt' 'Ēl* (Bethel, the house of God) is in the process of undergoing radical transformation, already anticipated by the prophets.[45] That Jesus saw himself as the gate of heaven, house of God, the Way itself, is clear enough in the Gospels, especially John. He is the stairway to heaven, with angels ascending and descending, as Jacob saw in his vision (Gen. 28:10–22 with John 1:43–51). Jesus is the Word who descends from heaven to pitch his tent on earth (John 1:4–9, 14), the house of God (2:19–21), the gate of heaven and stairway between heaven and earth (10:7; 14:6).

Gradually, it becomes clearer as events move closer to the crucifixion that Jesus is actually the end-time sanctuary. His body is the *axis mundi*, and his flesh is the temple curtain. "Who is this who even forgives sins?" demand the religious leaders concerning the one who is putting himself in the place of the temple, the sacrifices, and the priesthood (Luke 7:49). "Who is this who is speaking blasphemies? Who can forgive sins but God alone?" (5:21).

The old covenant, temple, sacrifices, along with the ceremonial and civil laws of the theocracy, die with Jesus on the cross and are left behind in his grave as the new sanctuary is raised on the third day. The climax of Jesus' trial before the Council is actually this report of destroying and rebuilding the temple. This leads the high priest to put the question to Jesus directly: "'Are you the Messiah, the Son of the Blessed One?' Jesus said, 'I am; and "you will see the Son of Man seated at the right hand of the Power," and "coming with the clouds of heaven."' Then the high priest tore his clothes and said, 'Why do we still need witnesses? You have heard his blasphemy!'" (Mark 14:57–64). As John relates the event in question, Jesus, after to his "cleansing" of the temple, announces, "Destroy this temple, and in three days I will raise it up" (John 2:19).

In Christ, according to the New Testament, the end-time temple made without hands has appeared in history. The temple curtain is torn from top to bottom, with its corresponding omens in the heavens, as the high priest enters not a copy but the true Holy of Holies with his own blood. No longer needed, the

---

44. Ibid., 179–80, citing N. T. Wright, *Jesus and the Victory of God* (Minneapolis: Fortress Press, 1996), 413–27.

45. All of this is treated with great skill in Wright, *Jesus and the Victory of God*, 413–27.

pictures are replaced by the reality. This is not by another attempt to renew the Sinai covenant: by becoming living stones in the end-time temple built by Yahweh himself, the people become the place: God's home. To the deputies of this last Adam, now invested in the robes and seat of glory, are given the keys of the kingdom (Matt. 16:18–19; 18:15–18; John 20:23, and Rev. 3:7, harking back to Isa. 22:22), and they are clothed in his righteousness.

In John's Apocalypse, the whole cosmos is the city, and the city is the temple. "Not only does the horizontal demarcation between the old temple and city disappear in the New Jerusalem," notes Kline, "but the vertical distinction between heavenly and earthly temples as well."[46] Not only the prophets and apostles, but also the whole people of God are now "caught up in the Spirit" to stand in the heavenly council, covered in priestly vestments, sent from the throne-room as witnesses.[47] In the New Testament, the glory of Christ's face (2 Cor. 4:6) reveals judgment from heaven. It is a Parousia-glory, as Jesus returns on the last day (Matt. 16:27; Mark 8:38; Luke 9:26).[48] In Hebrews 12, this Parousia-glory is identified with his voice (cf. Rev. 1:10–15).[49] In the heavenly worship scene of the Apocalypse, amid flashes of lightning and peals of thunder, flaming fires burn in front of the throne as the twenty-four elders are seated around God, and behind the throne the bow of judgment is no longer drawn but hangs in peace (Rev. 4:2–5).

In Revelation as well, then, the flaming torches are redolent of the church's witness, as at Pentecost. Christ's resurrection is regarded as the rebuilding of Israel's temple, a temple not built "by human hands" (Acts 7:48 ESV), "because believers have been 'circumcised with a circumcision made without hands, in the removal of the body of the flesh by the circumcision of Christ [i.e., his death]' (Col. 2:11)."[50] "Judaism highlighted this by saying that God would 'build the temple [of Exod. 15:17] . . . with his two hands' (*Mekilta de-Rabbi Ishmael, Tractate Shirata* 10.40–42)."[51]

Therefore, those who are united to Christ are not to compromise with the pagan cultus—in essence, grafting themselves onto other bodies (2 Cor. 6:16–18; cf. 2 Sam. 7, esp. v. 14). Our decaying bodies, like the moribund temple, belong to the old creation, yet they will be eschatologically restored in the new creation (2 Cor. 4:15–5:5). With Malachi 3–4 in the background, Paul sees the church as a vast temple built on Jesus Christ as its foundation (1 Cor. 3:11). Each believer is now the temple filled by the Glory-Spirit (1 Cor 3:16–17). At the same time, only by union with Christ are they "living stones" of the end-time sanctuary (1 Pet. 2:4). In this way, the gospel, as the tree of life, "is bearing fruit and growing in the whole world" (Col. 1:6), attributed throughout Acts to the fact that

46. M. G. Kline, *Images of the Spirit* (1980; repr., S. Hamilton, MA: self-published, 1986), 35.
47. Ibid., 94.
48. Ibid., 121–22.
49. Ibid., 122.
50. Beale, *The Temple and the Church's Mission*, 233–34.
51. Ibid., 235 n. 66.

"the word of God continued to increase" (Acts 6:7 ESV; 12:24; 19:20).[52] Although Christ alone in his very essence is the "image of the invisible God" (Col. 1:15), we "have put on the new self" and are therefore "being renewed to a true knowledge according to . . . [God's] image" (3:10 NASB).

None of the other places—including the temple in Jerusalem—is really permanent, because they cannot reconcile God and the covenant-violating congregation. The earthly Jerusalem even represents the covenant of law, Hagar, and bondage, while the heavenly Jerusalem represents the covenant of grace, Sarah, and freedom (Gal. 4:21–5:1). God's goal since creation has been to dwell in the midst of his people—that is, in blessing, as the source of communion, joy, peace, and righteousness. Yet the types and shadows could not bring about that Sabbath vision, and even if they could, they were routinely profaned by the covenant people. Zion, as we have seen especially from Levenson, represented the inviolable, permanent, unconditional, and gracious pledge of God, assuring God's covenant people that God's saving purposes stand above the vicissitudes of human obedience and disobedience. Going further than Levenson, however, on the basis of the New Testament we may say that the earthly Zion and its temple were also a temporary meeting place between God and humanity—now obsolete with the arrival of the permanent sanctuary (1 Tim. 2:5; Heb. 8:1–9:15; etc.).

ESCHATOLOGY AND COVENANT: "SPIRITUALIZING" THE PROMISE OF HOLY LAND?

Does the New Testament then "spiritualize" the Old Testament promise of a holy land? Revelation 21 envisions a new Jerusalem, with a loud voice crying from the throne, "See, the home of God is among mortals. He will dwell with them as their God; they will be his peoples, and God himself will be with them," wiping away their tears, "for the first things have passed away" (vv. 1–4). The water of life flows from the Alpha and Omega (v. 6). "I saw no temple in the city, for its temple is the Lord God the Almighty and the Lamb." Nor are sun or moon necessary, since the glory of God is its light "and its lamp is the Lamb" (vv. 22–23). But does not all of this talk of Christ as the temple, with believers as its living stones, downplay the corporeality and literal fulfillment of God's promise?

After the destruction of the second temple, Judaism increasingly shifted the concentration of its eschatological hopes from temple to Torah. "Not until the period of later Judaism," notes Eichrodt, "when piety underwent a transformation of the greatest consequence which turned the religion of Yahweh into a religion of observances, was there a threat that the soteriological character of the cultic actions might be obscured by the attempt to comprehend them all in the one-sided classification of works of obedience." This development, however, is

---

52. Ibid., 266.

alien to the intrinsic character of Old Testament cultic piety.[53] Nevertheless, without a land and a temple, Judaism came to regard the study and observance of Torah as a substitute.[54] The return of Yahweh after the exile, promised especially in Isaiah 52:7–10 and Ezekiel 43:1–7, has never been regarded by Judaism as having yet been fulfilled.[55]

This is where Christianity and Judaism parted ways. Where for Judaism the destruction of the temple and Diaspora existence merely extended the exile, Christians look to Christ as the end-time sanctuary. The New Testament (esp. Hebrews) calls Jewish Christians to persevere in this hope, refusing to return to the shadows of Sinai when they have arrived at Zion. This interpretation stands in considerable contrast to Orthodox Judaism and dispensational evangelicalism's expectations of a rebuilt temple and revived theocracy in Jerusalem.

At last, the people have become a place, where God dwells in peace, eventually giving rest from enemies on all sides. "What is the Citie, but the People? True, the People are the Citie" (Shakespeare, *Coriolanus*, act 3, scene 1). In Christ, a sanctuary is being raised from the rubble of this present age, and each believer serves as the icon of God to the others, "being transformed into the same image from one degree of glory to another; for this comes from the Lord, the Spirit" (2 Cor. 3:18). The gathering-together (*synaxis*) of the people in Christ and by the Spirit constitutes the end-time temple on the earth, the New Jerusalem-bride coming down out of heaven arrayed in wedding-day splendor.

Jewish theologian Michael Wyschogrod has no trouble accepting the identification of the people as place, but he is convinced that this requires a final restoration of the theocratic kingdom. According to both Orthodox Judaism and dispensational evangelicalism, the focus of future expectation is a renewal of the Sinai covenant: land, temple, sacrifices, and all. Until then, Jews must be willing to substitute study and observance of the Torah for the sacrifices and worship of the temple. Both the people and the place are holy. Although "the possession of the land promised to Israel is itself conditional, . . . as long as the people of Israel lives, its return to the land of promise is inevitable."[56] Judaism, he says, knows nothing of the Christian "dual citizenship," which distinguishes national and religious loyalties.[57] For Jews, because the election is unconditional, the loss of the land can only be a temporary divine punishment.[58]

Wyschogrod wonders how a religion that so emphasizes the realization of God's promises in the flesh (with the doctrine of the incarnation) could so spiritualize

53. Eichrodt, *Theology of the Old Testament*, 1:177.

54. N. T. Wright, *The New Testament and the People of God* (Minneapolis: Fortress Press, 1992), 228, quoting *m. 'Abot* 3.2.

55. Wright, *The New Testament and the People of God*, 269, citing Neh. 9:36–37.

56. Michael Wyschogrod, *Abraham's Promise: Judaism and Jewish-Christian Relations*, ed. R. Kendall Soulen (Grand Rapids: Eerdmans, 2004), 94; he develops this especially in "Incarnation and God's Indwelling of Israel," 165–78, as in "Incarnation," *Pro Ecclesia* 2, no. 2 (Spring 1993): 208–15.

57. Ibid., 95.

58. Ibid., 96.

the concept of the people of God, exchanging the election of the physical people of Israel (Jews) for a spiritual election.[59] After all, "were this election purely spiritual, were Israel a church instead of a people, it would not need a land."[60] Both the people and the place are essential in identifying God's presence, Wyschogrod concludes. "God has thus two dwelling places or addresses: the Temple and the people of Israel."[61] For Jews, God did not completely abandon the temple mount even after the exile. "But wherever a community of (ten) Jews gather, the divine presence is with them. Anywhere."[62] So for now, at least, God occupies the second address (the people) until the temple is rebuilt, according to Wyschogrod.

Yet the New Testament is not spiritualizing when it identifies the temple with Christ and the people of Israel with his body, any more than the Old Testament is spiritualizing when it promises Abraham children from all of the nations. The early Christian reaction to the destruction of the temple was not to look for a third one, with a revived Sinaitic theocracy, but to look to Christ as the reality to which these earthly institutions pointed. The contrast is not between what is tangible, embodied, and concrete versus what is ethereal, incorporeal, and abstract, but between a temporary and conditional covenant limited to one people (the Sinai covenant), and an eternal and unconditional covenant that includes Gentiles as well as Jews. The prophecy of a new covenant in Jeremiah 31 includes the enlargement of Jerusalem as a cosmic city in which righteousness is at home. Therefore, from a Christian perspective (esp. obvious in Hebrews), the concentration of eschatology on a geopolitical territory and a rebuilt temple not only turns the clock back to the exile, before Christ's advent, but also falls far short of the world announced by the Hebrew prophets. With the fulfillment of the new covenant, there arrives not merely a preservation of an ethnic people, but actually the resurrection of the dead and the life everlasting, a new creation with an international family. Wyschogrod quotes Franz Rosenzweig: "[Judaism] must be a blood community, because only blood gives present warrant to the hope for a future."[63] However, it is not that blood no longer binds in Christianity, but that it is the blood of Christ, signified and sealed in baptism, that is thicker—and wider—than the blood of ethnicity.

Jesus retains the connection to the land, as David Holwerda emphasizes. "The meek . . . will inherit the earth," not simply a slice of geopolitical territory (Matt. 5:5; Ps. 37:11).[64] As a result of this end-time fulfillment of the promise made to Adam and Eve and Abraham and Sarah, the new Zion cannot be contained within the present boundaries of the earthly land; it is therefore in the Apocalypse, a universal city (Rev. 21:22). Just as the prophets announced (Isa. 60:19), it will be a universal sanctuary illuminated by Yahweh (Rev. 21:23). The expectation is not that

59. Ibid., 98–99.
60. Ibid., 100.
61. Ibid., 169.
62. Ibid., 170.
63. Quoted in ibid., 128.
64. David E. Holwerda, *Jesus and Israel: One Covenant or Two?* (Grand Rapids: Eerdmans, 1994), 85.

there will be no earth, but that the whole earth will be full of the glory of God. The superiority of a temple made without hands lies not in an abstract preference for incorporeality, but in the fact that its "architect and builder is God" (Heb. 11:10).[65]

Both Orthodox Jews and Christians await the arrival of the promised Messiah, who will make all things new, but the gospel does this on the basis of a decisive series of events that have already occurred with his first advent, inaugurating the kingdom that cannot be shaken.[66] This time, as Moltmann observes, the march is from "Jerusalem to the ends of the earth (Acts 1.8), from Israel to the Gentiles, from the Gentiles to Israel again, and back to Jerusalem (Rom. 11.26)."[67] Ethnic Israel has not been forgotten or absorbed into a largely Gentile history; salvation comes from the Jews to the nations, and in Romans 9–11 Paul anticipates a great future regrafting of ethnic Israel onto the Living Vine.

Precisely because the New Testament (interpreting the Old) distinguishes the national election of Israel (realized at Sinai) from the unconditional election of people from every nation (promised to Abraham and realized in Christ), the church does not need a land. It does not even need a building, a square, or a shrine of any kind, much less a nation, a city, or a political action committee. It does not recognize any distinction between holy and profane sites. There are no sacred missions in the world today other than the Great Commission; Christians share with their non-Christian neighbors in the common curse of ordinary infirmities and injustice and in the common grace that enriches our life together. Although believers are in Christ, their vocations in the world are no holier than those of non-Christians. There are no Christian nations, and the New Testament does not include any blueprint for our transformation of secular kingdoms into holy ones.

The common is still a realm of God's remarkable kindness and blessing, with believers having no privileges to health, wealth, or happiness in this age (Matt. 5:45). Restraining evil, living as salt and light, and loving and serving our neighbors by our words and deeds, the actions of Christians become means of this common grace. However, like Abel, Noah, and Abraham, who "confessed that they were strangers and foreigners on the earth" and were "seeking a homeland," we too "desire a better country, that is, a heavenly one. Therefore God is not ashamed to be called their God; indeed, he has prepared a city for them" (Heb. 11:13–16).

HOLY WAR: PREPARING A PLACE

If, in our era of redemptive history, there is no holy land in a geopolitical sense, then can there be holy war? In this deeply divisive debate, the easiest answer is

---

65. Michael S. Horton, *Covenant and Eschatology: The Divine Drama* (Louisville, KY: Westminster John Knox Press, 2002), chap. 1.

66. See Jürgen Moltmann's excellent interaction on this point with Martin Buber in *The Way of Jesus Christ: Christology in Messianic Dimensions*, trans. Margaret Kohl (London: SCM Press, 1990; Minneapolis: Fortress Press, 1991), 30–31.

67. Ibid.

either to repudiate the "texts of terror" in the Bible or to invoke them for our own purposes. Consistent with my interpretation of holy land above, I suggest that this issue is complicated by a redemptive-historical account of the distinct covenants in which we encounter the theme of divine warfare.

Holy War in the History of Redemption

The association between holiness and war is not superficial in Scripture, as if Yahweh could be invoked for nationalistic goals and imperial ambitions. The idea is captured in the term for holy war: *ḥerem*—acts of devotion—which refers first of all not to the piety of the warriors, but to the judicial act of setting people, places, and things aside, either for salvation or judgment. It is part of the structure of the treaty itself: its sanctions of curse and blessing.

The theme of holy war is often treated as a static, timeless concept. When we are insufficiently attentive to the specific covenant and specific era in the history of the covenant that is in play in a given passage, the interpretive options seem rather easy: *reject* the passage as a "text of terror," or *invoke* it as if it were in force today.[68] In contrast to these options, I have found M. G. Kline's notion of "intrusion ethics" helpful.[69] The Day of the Spirit is a day of judicial verdict. As in the creation story, which opens with the scene of the Spirit hovering (or sweeping) over the face of the deep (Gen. 1:2), the division of time into "sevens" indicates the pattern of God's own creation-victory and entrance into his Sabbath session. In *Images of the Spirit*, Kline begins with Genesis 3:8, where God comes to Adam "in the *ruach* [Spirit] of the day." "This passage must be played fortissimo."[70] Far different from the romantic interpretation of cool breezes wafting through the garden as Adam and Eve revel in their communion with God and each other, the scene is one of judgment.

Then there is the contest between David and the Philistines. "On that occasion David's advance on earth was matched by (or better, corresponded to) Yahweh's advance above, the latter signalized by the 'voice' of marching over the tree-tops" (2 Sam. 5:24).[71] (See also Ezek. 1:4–28, esp. vv. 24–28.) We may also refer to the command given to Joshua to march around Jericho with his army for six days. "But the seventh day you shall march around the city seven times, and the [seven] priests shall blow the [seven] trumpets" as they bear the ark of the covenant (Josh. 6:1–4 NKJV). Yahweh promises that he will then cause the walls of Jericho to collapse (v. 5). The parallels with the Genesis creation narratives are obvious: "sixes" of judgment-work followed by a "seventh" of rest.[72]

---

68 Phyllis Trible, *Texts of Terror* (London: SCM Press, 2002).

69. M. G. Kline, *The Structure of Biblical Authority* (Grand Rapids: Eerdmans, 1975); cf. idem, *Images of the Spirit*, 98–102; idem, *Kingdom Prologue: Genesis Foundations for a Covenantal Worldview* (Overland Park, KS: Two Age Press, 2000), 128, 143–291.

70. Kline, *Images of the Spirit*, 98.

71. Ibid., 99.

72. Ibid., 109–10.

Thus, the Sabbath is an inbreaking of the age to come, an irruption (Kline's "intrusion") in which ordinary activity is suspended.[73] As the Day of the Lord is to time, holy war is to space. The same event is a calamity or deliverance (sometimes both), depending on which covenant is in play and one's relationship to and within it. Every divinely authorized campaign recorded in Israel's history is a prolepsis of the last day, and if Israel itself desecrates the covenant, it too will be caught up in the "Spirit of the Day" (just as Yahweh came to Adam and Eve after their disobedience in the spirit [ruach] of the day [Gen. 3:8]). The Spirit of the Day is the Day of Lord—God's arrival in judgment. "Woe to you who desire the day of the LORD!" Amos prophesies. After all, it will bring disaster far greater than the destruction of Jerusalem and the exile (Amos 5:18–20 NKJV). God "passed *over*" Israel in the destruction he brought about in Egypt, but will "pass *through*" Israel in judgment (v. 17, emphasis added). Although God passed through the halves alone in Genesis 15, when he made the covenant with Abraham, it now is Israel that is on trial in the Sinai covenant and in the wake of its thorough transgression; it is Israel that God causes to pass through the halves, bearing the sanctions of this national covenant (Jer. 34:18–20). Yahweh will even join Israel's enemies in battle (Jer. 21:3–10). Nevertheless, he will restore Israel through a remnant and draw the nations into it. "I will make you pass under the staff, and will bring you within the bond of the covenant. I will purge out the rebels among you, and those who transgress against me" (Ezek. 20:37–38a).

The concept of *ḥerem* war is not left behind when we cross the threshold of the testaments, although its meaning is no longer determined by the context of a typological theocracy. Kline notes, "Baptism is a sign of the *parousia* of the Spirit in judgment."[74] "At Jesus' birth, his identifying sign (*sēmeion*) was his clothing, the swaddling clothes, the garment of his humiliation, and his position, lying in a manger (Luke 2:12). At his coming again, the identifying (name-)sign of his exaltation will be the Glory-robe in which he is arrayed, his Spirit-clothing, and his position, standing in the heavens."[75] "Invested with the Glory-Name, he comes in the day of the Lord as the Spirit of the day."[76]

The original "delay of the *parousia*" immediately after the fall of humanity in Paradise mercifully delayed the decisive judgment, postponing the consummation, in order to establish a covenant of grace.[77] In the process, God not only exhibited his redemptive grace toward his covenant people but also displayed common grace as God's ordinary way of dealing with rebellious humanity. If those outside of the covenant enjoyed a stay of execution, including the ordinary joys of human experience, it was because of God's ultimate purposes in the

---

73. I prefer "irruption" to "intrusion" because of the modern cosmological assumptions often associated with the latter term (specifically, that when God acts in history directly and miraculously, he is somehow trespassing on his own property).

74. Kline, *Images of the Spirit*, 125.

75. Ibid., 128–29.

76. Ibid., 131.

77. M. G. Kline, *The Structure of Biblical Authority*, rev. ed. (self-published, 1989), 155.

covenant of grace. Just as the delay between Christ's two advents creates an eschatological interim of peace before judgment, the protevangelium of Genesis 3:15 announced a delay of the consummation that opened up space for redemption and common grace.

However, at signal points in redemptive history, there is a fresh era of divine "intrusion," disrupting the usual order of common grace with previews of the Day of the Lord at the end of history. "The identification of the new covenant with the consummation keeps pace with the stages in the exaltation of the Son of Man; and while we see him sitting on the right hand of power, we have not yet seen him coming in the clouds of heaven. Hence, there is not yet a corresponding antitype for every element of Old Testament typology," Kline adds. Some, like the sacrificial imagery, are fulfilled, but others await future fulfillment.[78]

From where we stand in redemptive history, then, believers' attitudes toward unbelieving neighbors is determined by common grace, not by either taking judgment into our own hands or by basing this neighbor-love on any illusion of universal participation in God's saving grace.[79] Through the appointed *cultus*, they participate in the prelibations of the age to come; in the *culture*, members of the covenant of grace share with unbelievers in the common curse and common grace of this time between the times. They pray for their enemies and obey their pagan rulers rather than attempt to drive them out and establish a holy culture. Even the ordinary ministry of the church seems deceptively uneventful in comparison with the extraordinary era of Joshua, the kings and prophets, Jesus and his apostles. Yet, in the Spirit, it is the time in which the Lord is planting and growing his worldwide vineyard for the final harvest.

In this era of common grace, neither salvation nor judgment is fully consummated. Nevertheless, the now-exalted Jesus will judge the earth in righteousness. John the Baptist pointed to this judgment entrusted to Jesus (Matt. 3:11–12). Jesus warns against the whole body being cast into hell (5:30); no prophet or apostle spoke so vividly and repeatedly of the last judgment (8:10–12; 13:40–42, 49–50; 22:13; 24:51; 25:30; Luke 16:19–31). Whatever can be said for such references in the parables having to do with an immanent judgment for Jesus' contemporaries, in the Olivet discourse he has a future assize in mind. "When the Son of Man comes in his glory, and all the angels with him, then he will sit on the throne of his glory" (Matt. 25:31). Echoing Isaiah 2 (as well as Isa. 11), Jesus says that the nations will appear before the Son of Man in judgment, and all will be separated, as sheep and goats, "into eternal life" and "into eternal punishment" (Matt. 25:41, 46). If we have trouble with Joshua and his campaigns, we should be still more unsettled by Jesus.

We encounter the same solemn expectation in the Epistles. Paul writes, "But by your hard and impenitent heart you are storing up wrath for yourself on the day of wrath, when God's righteous judgment will be revealed." For the wicked

78. Ibid., 157.
79. Ibid., 161.

and unbelieving, "there will be wrath and fury, . . . anguish and distress" (Rom. 2:5, 8–9). First Thessalonians 5 warns that "the day of the Lord will come like a thief in the night," just when everyone is proclaiming peace and security (vv. 1–3). This event of salvation-and-judgment will be as final as it is sudden, "when the Lord Jesus is revealed from heaven with his mighty angels in flaming fire, inflicting vengeance on those who do not know God and on those who do not obey the gospel of our Lord Jesus. These will suffer the punishment of eternal destruction," Paul says, "separated from the presence of the Lord and from the glory of his might, when he comes to be glorified by his saints and to be marveled at on that day among all who have believed, because our testimony to you was believed" (2 Thess. 1:7–10). Elsewhere we read that Sodom and Gomorrah "serve as an example by undergoing a punishment of eternal fire," and false teachers are "wandering stars, for whom the deepest darkness has been reserved forever" (Jude 7, 13). Second Peter 3:7 speaks of "the day of judgment and destruction of the godless."

The Apocalypse requires its own special treatment of the theme of holy war, but a few examples will suffice. With the opening of the sixth seal, the powerful and wealthy of all the earth who have feared no mortal, call "to the mountains and rocks, 'Fall on us and hide us from the face of the one seated on the throne and from the wrath of the Lamb; for the great day of their wrath has come, and who is able to stand?'" (Rev. 6:15–17). This is followed by the vision of the bowls of wrath, the fall of the great Babylon, symbol of the earthly city in all of its infamous pride, injustice, and immorality, not to mention its persecution of the saints (Rev. 16–18). Finally, Babylon—symbolic of the human attempt to rise up in pride against the Lord and his Messiah—is judged and destroyed, with the saints singing, "'Hallelujah! The smoke goes up from her forever and ever'" (19:1–3).

After this the rider on the white horse defeats the beast and its armies, followed by a thousand-year interim, which I take (in amillennial fashion) to refer symbolically to the present era between Christ's advents. Finally, Satan is "thrown into the lake of fire and sulfur, where the beast and the false prophet were, and they will be tormented day and night forever and ever" (Rev. 19:11–20:10). The dead are then judged. "This is the second death, the lake of fire" (20:14–15). It is the finality of this holy war that ushers in the finality of the new heavens and earth, where there is no longer any judgment, war, pain, suffering, or oppression. And it is there, finally, where the tree of life yields its fruit for the healing of the nations (Rev. 21–22).

So there is no general principle of holy war to either deny or invoke. The question is our present location in redemptive history. This is the hour of salvation. For now, then, James and John—and any number of their kindred souls today—are rebuked for invoking the final judgment on the village that spurned their preaching of the kingdom, even though this was appropriate for the theocratic era, as it will be on the last day (Luke 9:52–55).[80] The imprecatory (judgment-invoking)

---

80. Ibid., 162.

psalms too, on the lips of those who lived in the "intrusion ethics" of the theocracy, typological of the last day, are appropriate in their time, as they will be in the last judgment. They may be spoken, even sung, by the royal psalmist who prefigured the messianic judge of the earth. Yet they are out of place on the lips of Christians today, guided as we are not by the ethics of intrusion but by the ethics of common grace.[81] The old covenant was not wrong, but is now obsolete.

Therefore, for nations or churches to invoke passages of holy war in this time, when Christians render to Caesar what is Caesar's and to God what is God's, is to jump the eschatological gun and to take the last judgment into their own hands. Even ungodly rulers can be considered "God's minister" of common justice (Rom. 13:1–7 NKJV). It is intriguing that when Paul appeals to Philemon to welcome instead of punish Onesimus, his runaway slave, and charge any wrong to his own (Paul's) account, he does not invoke the law of Moses, but acknowledges the legal jurisdiction of the secular court. Even in a hostile pagan context, Paul does not offer a political or military strategy for holy war but commands obedience to and respect for the secular authorities. It is striking that so much detail is provided for the concrete praxis and structure of the visible church—especially its ministry and offices—in comparison with the lack of any clear agenda for reforming social structures.

Appealing to divine promises of land or final justice would avail nothing in the court of common grace and common justice. This is not because modern, "enlightened" nations (responsible, it must not be forgotten, for the greatest atrocities in the history of human violence) have advanced beyond superstition, but because God—in the person of Christ—has announced a delay of his judgment and therefore a space for repentance. Even the unrepentant, therefore, benefit from this divine patience, even though they exploit the delay as evidence that it is a myth (2 Pet. 3:3–13).

No one can read Jesus' unyielding commands to love enemies and endure persecution without recognizing the contrast with the commands in the old covenant to accomplish thorough destruction of Israel's idolatrous neighbors who perpetually raided others nearby and offered their children in sacrifice to Baal. Allowing the violence and idolatry of the pagan nations occupying his land to reach their consummation, Yahweh finally executed judgment through his servant Israel (Gen. 15:16; Deut. 9:4–5). Yet if Israel imitates its neighbors, it too will suffer the same consequences: "Like the nations that the LORD is destroying before you, so shall you perish, because you would not obey the voice of the LORD your God" (Deut. 8:20; cf. Lev. 26).

The land is not Israel's, but God's, and eviction is always a live option for the holy nation as well as God's enemies. Yahweh not only claims that the land belongs to him; he also adds, "for you are strangers and sojourners with Me" (Lev. 25:23 NKJV). Not even the Holy Land is a permanent dwelling place for God with his people.

81. Ibid.

Only a thoroughly theocentric point of view can recognize the justice in the action commanded by God. Michael Wyschogrod points out,

> Immanuel Kant, in commenting on Psalm 79:5–7, in which he finds "a prayer for revenge which goes to tarrying extremes," can dismiss with contempt a writer who comments, "The Psalms are inspired; if in them punishment is prayed for, it cannot be wrong, and we must have no morality holier than the Bible," and instead hurl the following rhetorical question which, for Kant, obviously settles the issue: "I raise the question as to whether morality should be expounded according to the Bible or whether the Bible should not rather be expounded according to morality."[82]

Wyschogrod properly directs our attention to a theocentric rather than anthropocentric interpretation. However, what Kant *and* the commentator he rebukes both assume is that these imprecatory psalms are timeless ethical principles, to be rejected or invoked, rather than covenantally determined texts of judgment that are conditioned by their location in redemptive history. It is hardly a neutral, objective, and unbiased verdict that determines whether these passages are texts of terror rather than texts of justice. Once more, if we refuse to accept the justice of these prolepses of final judgment in Canaan, we will have even greater difficulty with the teaching of Jesus and the apostles.

Since Israel itself was a mixed multitude when it came up out of Egypt, comparisons of these wars to ethnic cleansing and genocide are wide of the mark. So when God commands such destruction in these texts, there is no hint of any suspension of the ethical as such. As terrifying as these prolepses indeed are, they always fall far short of the Parousia-judgment that might with justice have fallen on all of humanity after the fall or at any point since. As Paul indicates, the whole race is "storing up wrath" for the day of judgment (Rom. 1:18; 2:5), yet for now it is the day of salvation and of common grace.

Other examples of intrusion ethics (i.e., the suspension of common-grace law) include the "sacrifice" of Isaac and the marriage of Hosea.[83] Thus there is in God's economy a time for judgment and a time for both salvation and sharing the common ills and blessings of our neighbors. "When our Father shall say, 'It is done,' we must listen to his voice," writes Kline. "But if we are listening to him today, we are still seeking by his grace to be good Samaritans."[84]

In my view, this interpretation keeps us from treating the *ḥerem* or holy-war traditions of the old covenant (anticipated on a fuller scale in the New Testament) either as wrong or as legitimately invoked in the current era of redemptive history. Representing the former view, C. S. Cowles defends a nearly Marcionite opposition between the God of the Old Testament versus the God of the New

---

82. Wyschogrod, *Abraham's Promise*, 101, quoting Immanuel Kant, *Religion within the Limits*, trans. T. M. Greene and H. H. Hudson (New York: Harper & Row, 1960), 101.
83. Kline, *The Structure of Biblical Authority*, (1989), 168–69.
84. Ibid., 171.

Testament.[85] He observes that these texts have been used throughout church history to justify "the mass destruction of human beings," but he seems to assume that they actually do serve that purpose.[86] "No longer should Christians define God as the 'God of Abraham, the God of Isaac and the God of Jacob' (Ex. 3:6), as important as they were in salvation history, but as the 'Father of our Lord Jesus Christ, the Father of compassion and the God of all comfort' (2 Cor. 1:3). . . . If this is the case, then God is not like the first Joshua, a warrior, but like the second, the Prince of Peace."[87] "What Jesus was introducing was nothing short of an entirely new rewrite of Jewish theology," radically revising—even contradicting—Old Testament texts as he preached.[88] "The God portrayed in the Old Testament was full of fury against sinners, but the God incarnate in Jesus is not."[89] Jesus' "command to 'love your enemies' (Matt. 5:44) represents a total repudiation of Moses' genocidal commands and stands in judgment on Joshua's campaign of ethnic cleansing."[90] According to Cowles, "This hermeneutical change was so radical and offensive to unbelieving Jews that they hounded Jesus to the cross, stoned Stephen while accusing him of speaking 'words of blasphemy against Moses and against God' (Acts 6:11), and harassed Paul to the end of his days."[91] Since Jesus has come, we are under no obligation to justify that which cannot be justified, but can only be described as *pre-Christ, sub-Christ, and anti-Christ*" (emphasis added).[92]

Blanket condemnations or invocations miss the subtlety and drama of God's unfolding purposes. Furthermore, Cowles fails to account for Jesus' own teaching concerning a future judgment far greater than any yet witnessed, over which he will personally preside (e.g., Matt. 20:1–16; 21:44; 22:13; 24:1–25:46; and parallels). Not only is Yahweh described as a warrior in the Old Testament; the Prince of Peace of Revelation 19:11–15 also is full of "wrath," "judges and makes war," with "a robe dipped in blood," striking down the nations.[93] Further, despite his intention to stop short of a Marcionite antithesis between the God of the Old Testament and the God of the New Testament, Cowles's conclusions seem to leave us with precisely that choice. However, he does not wrestle with the New Testament insistence—from the lips of Jesus himself—that Christians worship the God of Abraham (Matt. 22:32; cf. Acts 3:13; 7:32).[94]

Nevertheless, Jesus' constant proclamation is of a kingdom that in its present phase is manifested solely by absolution of sinners and their incorporation into the mystical and visible body of Christ. He has "all authority in heaven and on

85. C. S. Cowles, "The Case for Radical Discontinuity," in *Show Them No Mercy: Four Views on God and Canaanite Genocide*, ed. C. S. Cowles, et al. (Grand Rapids: Zondervan, 2003).
86. Cowles, "The Case for Radical Discontinuity," 17.
87. Ibid., 23, referring to Walter Brueggemann, *Theology of the Old Testament* (Minneapolis: Fortress Press, 1977), 107.
88. Cowles, "The Case for Radical Discontinuity," 24.
89. Ibid., 28.
90. Ibid., 33.
91. Ibid., 34.
92. Ibid., 36.
93. Eugene H. Merrill, "Response to C. S. Cowles," in Cowles, *Show Them No Mercy*, 49.
94. Ibid.

earth" (Matt. 28:18), yet uses it for the time being to reconcile rather than drive out his enemies. Following his own course from humiliation to exaltation, the kingdom moves from the cross and grace in the present to power and glory at the end of the age.

The "marks" of the church (Word, sacrament, and discipline) alone constitute the visibility of Christ's reign in this present age, unlike the visibility of all other earthly regimes. In the Sermon on the Mount (Matt. 5), the tables of the theocratic polity are turned. Whereas the covenantal blessing was held out as a *reward* for obedience in the old covenant, the kingdom polity of the new covenant *begins* with the blessings (Beatitudes). Where the former, delivered by Moses on his mount, requires the sharpest divisions between "clean" (Jew) and "unclean" (Gentile), holy war against God's enemies, and exact retribution (*lex taliones*), in *his* Sermon on the Mount, Jesus tells us that he has come not to set this law aside but to fulfill it. He is hardly a softer Moses. Now, adultery and murder are discerned in the heart, the loopholes in the law for divorce are sewn up, oaths are forbidden, excessive injustice is to be requited with excessive charity, and enemies are to be loved, in imitation of God, who cares for the just and the unjust alike. It is obvious that this is not the theocratic era of God's immediate judgment through human emissaries.

This kingdom is given no commission to use physical force or violence (even to promote civic legislation to be enforced), but is certainly forbidden from doing so even at the cost of martyrdom. Its subjects may die for the faith, but not kill for it. While "sons of thunder" may wish to execute divine judgment in this era, Christ commands his followers simply to proclaim the kingdom, baptize, and teach; to share in fellowship, prayer, and material care, and to celebrate the eucharistic meal through which, along with the Word, the Spirit is forging a new covenant community. Growing together until the final harvest, the wheat and weeds, sheep and goats, are often indistinguishable within the visible church.

Yet as a sign, the church does exercise judgment within its own ranks. Thus the prime objective of 1 Corinthians is to restore proper discipline on the basis of the gospel, regulated by the moral law. Apostolic authority is challenged, sects emerge, social divisions are allowed to interrupt the new bonds of unity established in Christ, sexual immorality and class warfare defile even the celebration of the Supper, and believers are adopting the habits of a litigious society even between each other. So Paul commands the church to exercise discipline in its own ranks and not to judge those outside (1 Cor. 5:9–13; 6:9–11). Furthermore, the church keeps the future judgment on the world's radar screen, while nevertheless announcing rather than invoking it.

The kingdom does not come in such a way, says Jesus, that one says, "'Look! Here is the Messiah!' or 'There he is!'" (Matt. 24:23). For now, the kingdom is hidden; on the last day it will be cataclysmic. "For as the lightning comes from the east and flashes as far as the west, so will be the coming of the Son of Man" (24:27). Just as in its present manifestation (new birth), the kingdom does not come to ameliorate all social ills but to introduce an entirely new order; the Spirit is freely working in ways imperceptible to the world at large (John 3:3–8).

Among the many implications of this interpretation is the reminder that in this phase of redemptive history, the vocations of Christians as citizens in the kingdoms of this age are distinct from their vocation as citizens of the city of God. We gather as the synaxis of the covenant people to receive a foretaste of the eschatological Sabbath, but we scatter to occupy our common stations in the world. The kingdom of God is "coming down from heaven" (Rev. 21:2, with Heb. 12:28) not, like Babel, ascending to the heavens from earthly ambition. Faith and coercion, cult and culture, the kingdom of Christ and the kingdoms of this age—these for now are completely distinct: all ruled by Christ, but in different ways. Public policies are legislated and enforced, while the policies of the kingdom of Christ in this era are proclaimed and enacted through the means of grace and the discipline of the church.

Spiritualizing the Holy-War Theme?

The theme of holy war in the theocracy is drawn upon by the New Testament, but within a distinct politics. No more than in consideration of the land is the theme of holy war "spiritualized," according to this approach. The overtly military recognition of Yahweh, "Through You we push down our enemies" (Ps. 44:4 NKJV), can now be heard in the light of Jesus' declaration that "the gates of Hades will not prevail against" the church to whom Christ has given the keys to bind and loose (Matt. 16:18–19). Similarly, Paul's appeal to believers to put on "the whole armor of God" prepares them for the real battle that the holy wars foreshadowed; each piece of that armor is connected with the kingdom of grace—delivering the gospel through the church's ministry—rather than by physical violence (Eph. 6:10–17).

Like the holy-land theme, the holy-war motif is not forgotten or allegorized; instead, it is given its proper interpretation in the present administration of God's covenantal economy. Only if we no longer believe that the contest between death and life, judgment and justification, the tyranny of sin and liberation to serve the living God no longer belong to the "real world" can we conclude that this represents a quietistic approach.

On one hand, there is a tendency to internalize such passages in quasi-gnostic fashion, reducing them to a purely subjective battle within the individual, to conquer the body and its passions and aspire to pure spirit. There is too much of the cosmic, public, courtroom imagery drawn from the prophets to justify this sort of interpretation of Ephesians 6 (which explicitly appropriates Isa. 59). On the other hand, we may so identify the "spiritual forces of evil in the heavenly places" with certain political and economic systems that the claim that "our struggle is not against enemies of blood and flesh" is turned on its head. In any case, Ephesians 6 points us to the Word, the gospel, Christ's righteousness, truth, and salvation as the equipment for the battle that is conducted by the church.

The cosmic struggle that dominates the story from Genesis 3 to the Apocalypse is that war between the serpent and his seed and the woman and hers. That the cosmic warfare envisioned by the New Testament is not ethereal or irrelevant to earthly realities is clear enough already in the history of this battle between the serpent and the woman as inaugurated in Genesis 3:15. It is seen in the crisis already between Cain and Abel. Since everything now (after the protevangelium) turns on the advent of the serpent-defeating Messiah, the battle strategy concentrates on the elimination of that promised "seed of the woman." Yet God raises up Seth in the place of slain Abel, and the kingdom continues to march toward its messianic goal. Eventually, the Sethites intermarry, threatening absorption of the covenantal line in terms of both the false worship of the nations and the end of the messianic seed (Gen. 6). Yet Noah and his family are left and continue the story (6:9–9:28). Immediately after the covenant with Noah, however, sin threatens, leaving Canaan cursed and Shem blessed, with the promise that God will "make space for Japheth" in the "tents of Shem" (9:25–27). Later in the narrative, we find even the line of the Shemites assimilated into the worship of the moon, with Abram and Sarai called out to belong to Yahweh (Gen. 12). Leaping ahead to the cry of the children of Abraham in Egypt, we encounter the contest between Yahweh and the serpent, as the latter is personified in Pharaoh.

Even in the land, Israel itself becomes the theater of this cosmic battle, not only in the holy wars that drive out the nations but also in the wickedness of Israel's own rulers, which again threatens the covenant, both in terms of its religious integrity and in terms of the messianic lineage. Often this line of succession is hanging by a single thread. Queen Athaliah enters the temple to learn the source of the commotion, only to be astonished that a young Joash has escaped her massacre of the royal family (2 Kgs. 11:13–14); this scene parallels the fury of the outmaneuvered dragon in Revelation 12. Under Joash's reign, the high places and sacred pillars erected to Baal are destroyed, and the temple is repaired, yet he eventually turns away from the Lord and is killed (2 Chr. 24:17–25).

In all of these episodes, it becomes clearer that the question of the kingdom does not turn on the "willing or running" of its would-be inaugurators. Joash turns out to be as bad a king as many of the others. Yet he was the ancestor of the messianic Son of David. The story behind all of these stories is the cosmic battle commenced in Eden, which reaches its climax in the massacre of the male infants by Herod (Matt. 2:13–23). The "exile" in Egypt and repatriation to Nazareth already announce that even in his youth, this unique child is recapitulating Israel's history, and in so doing, the triumph of the "seed of the woman" over the serpent and his human agents is being accomplished. In Jesus' outlook, the opposition of his own people to the kingdom that has belonged to them but whose title they have now forfeited is really a playing out of this cosmic battle (Matt. 23:33–35). Even Peter's attempt to dissuade Jesus from the cross can be treated by Jesus as the voice of Satan (16:23).

In this light, Luke 10 makes greater sense. Just as Moses had appointed seventy elders, Jesus sends seventy disciples to go "on ahead of him in pairs to every town and place where he himself intended to go" (v. 1). It is instructive that seventy nations are named in Genesis 10 and that the sending of disciples in pairs (as in the commissioning of the Twelve in Mark 6:7) fulfills the requirement of "two witnesses" for confirming any testimony (Deut. 17:6).

First, as the commander of this force, Jesus tells the seventy, "See, I am sending you out like lambs into the midst of wolves" (v. 3). This is hardly the sort of speech that we encounter in the military campaigns of the theocracy's holy wars, yet it is consistent with the present phase of this kingdom. Their only weapon (they cannot even bring an extra pair of sandals) is their witness to Christ. "Whatever house you enter, first say, 'Peace to this house!' And if anyone is there who shares in peace, your peace will rest on that person; if not, it will return to you" (vv. 5–6).

Once more we encounter the primary meaning of the keys of the kingdom: to open and shut the gates of heaven through the preaching of the gospel. Like a herald bringing the good news of a truce, the seventy are to declare the kingdom of God as a peace treaty. Without scruples, they are to share in whatever meals are set before them, cure the sick, "and say to them, 'The kingdom of God has come near to you'" (vv. 8–9). If the townspeople reject the message, the heralds are to tell the people that they wipe off even the dust on their feet "in protest against you. Yet know this: the kingdom of God has come near" (v. 11). After all, the presence of the kingdom is good news for those who receive it, yet the worst possible news for those who reject it. "I tell you," Jesus adds, "on that day it will be more tolerable for Sodom than for that town" (v. 12).

The presence of the eschatological kingdom demands an immediate answer, but final vindication and judgment await the Parousia of the King in person. These seventy witnesses will bear this message, pronouncing the covenant curses (woes) on the rebellious cities, yet leaving the execution of judgment in God's hands at the end of the age. "Whoever listens to you," says Jesus, "listens to me, and whoever rejects you rejects me, and whoever rejects me rejects the one who sent me" (vv. 13–16).

Then we hear the report of the seventy and Jesus' response:

> The seventy returned with joy, saying, "Lord, in your name even the demons submit to us!" He said to them, "I watched Satan fall from heaven like a flash of lightning. See, I have given you authority to tread on snakes and scorpions, and over all the power of the enemy; and nothing will hurt you. Nevertheless, do not rejoice at this, that the spirits submit to you, but rejoice that your names are written in heaven." (vv. 17–20)

A chapter later, Jesus announces,

> But if it is by the finger of God that I cast out the demons, then the kingdom of God has come to you. When a strong man, fully armed, guards his castle, his property is safe. But when one stronger than he attacks him and overpowers him, he takes away his armor in which he trusted and divides his plunder. Whoever is not with me is against me, and whoever does not gather with me scatters. (Luke 11:20–23)

That there is a real war going on is hardly in doubt, and to imagine that this story is less real or less significant than the "wars and rumors of wars" reported to us every day is yet another sign that we have forgotten the theocentric focus of the plot. Furthermore, this conflict may even cost the witnesses their lives in battle. Nevertheless, it is prosecuted by means of Word and Spirit, not in the flesh, through military conquest.

It makes all the difference whether we understand the journey of Jesus to Jerusalem (i.e., his messianic kingdom) in terms of the cross and resurrection or as a restoration of the theocracy. Interpreting the royal march according to the latter, James and John wanted to call fire down on the Samaritan village that rejected Jesus and his preaching (Luke 9:51–54). "But [Jesus] turned and rebuked them. Then they went on to another village" (vv. 55–56).

A final judgment is neither denied nor executed in the ministry of Jesus and his apostles, but it is announced, and for those who receive the good news, the verdict of that last day is not left in doubt. *Christus Victor* meets *Agnus Dei*; the conquering King and the substitutionary Lamb are one and the same in this unique person and his kingdom. Jesus responds to the elation of the seventy at being able to subdue even the demons (in the language of treading on serpents, redolent of Gen. 3:15) with the even greater news that their names are written in heaven. The "strong man" may be bound, and consequently the extraordinary ministry of Jesus and his disciples is succeeded by the ordinary ministry of Word and sacrament. Yet our warfare "against the rulers, against the authorities, against the cosmic powers of this present darkness, against the forces of evil in the heavenly places" continues unabated (Eph. 6:12).

As throughout the history recounted above, the cosmic battle is waged through earthly agents: personal and institutional; religious and social; cultic and cultural; rhetorical and political. Yet the church knows the real enemy behind these penultimate agents; the real war behind the wars of the headlines, in our homes, and in our hearts. Whatever skirmishes may require our responsible action in the kingdoms of this age, the church is the only institution entrusted with a commission to plunder the evil empire that its Captain has already defeated. "Indeed, we live as human beings, but we do not wage war according to human standards; for the weapons of our warfare are not merely human, but they have divine power to destroy strongholds. We destroy arguments and every proud obstacle raised up against the knowledge of God, and we take every thought captive to obey Christ" (2 Cor. 10:3–5).

Wherever human beings are seduced into deeper self-confidence and away from the proclamation of Christ and his kingdom, the battle lines are drawn. This means that the church itself is a primary theater of this cosmic battle. In 2 Thessalonians 2, Beale observes, "Paul is saying that even now the false teachers that have been prophesied by Daniel and Jesus (cf. Matt. 24:4–5, 23–24, etc.) are now with us. This means that the end-time 'great tribulation' has begun in part. The prophecy of the 'apostasy' and coming of 'the man of lawlessness' into the temple of the new covenant church has begun to be fulfilled."[95]

---

95. Beale, *The Temple and the Church's Mission*, 288.

When we put all of these passages together, we can see a larger outline emerging. In his earthly ministry, Jesus was binding the strong man and looting his stolen goods, so that now whatever is bound and loosed on earth is bound and loosed in heaven (Matt. 16:19). Finally cast out of heaven once and for all, where he accused the church day and night, Satan is "cast down" even as Christ is raised up. Yet, as Revelation 12 reminds us, though this is good news for the church triumphant (the saints gathered in heaven), it is ominous for the church militant (the saints alive on the earth). More Christians have been martyred for their testimony to Christ in the last fifty years than in all of the combined centuries of persecution.[96] State persecution of Christians continues unabated even in many of those nations now cooperating with the United States in its War on Terrorism.

While citizens of liberal democracies may find it difficult to take this contest between the serpent and the woman seriously, brothers and sisters in other parts of the world—where the gospel of the kingdom is rapidly spreading despite (and in part, because of) persecution—are acutely sensitive to the war of the ages. In all of these passages, the real headline is the triumph of the Lamb through his own person and work and through the testimony of his witnesses. In other words, the big story is about the gospel and its progress in the world.

The entire order of Gentile power and submission in the fallen world no longer obtains in the kingdom of Christ, as Jesus not only taught and exemplified but also brought about in his own humiliation and exaltation. He proved that in this story, at least, we have a Lord—the only lord who really *is* Lord of all, as a servant of all. When *this* King declares war, the captives leap for joy. It is the Year of Jubilee, the liberation day of the world from its bondage to decay, oppression, and violence. Even the oppressors are being saved during this era. Genuine repentance and reconciliation are at work in the world.

Nevertheless, in the Olivet discourse Jesus explains that the Son of Man will come in glory and power at the end of the age. "You will see the Son of Man sitting at the right hand of Power and coming on the clouds of heaven" (Matt. 26:64; Mark 14:62; Luke 22:69). There was a partial realization of this in the vision of Stephen the Martyr (Acts 7:56), which preconversion Paul approved (8:1), as also in the vision of Paul on his way to another campaign against the believers in Damascus (9:1–6). Yet we still await the second part of that manifestation, his "coming on the clouds of heaven," marking the transition from grace to glory. Just as the renewal is occurring in its own order (justification and rebirth now, glorification and resurrection then), so too the judgment is first of all forensic—the announcement of God's Word to the nations—and then one day executed visibly on the stage of history by the returning Messiah in glory.

No more than in its treatment of the holy-land theme is the New Testament "spiritualizing" the motif of holy war. Rather, it is finally going to the root of all evil and injustice in the world. Death itself is a divine judgment for covenant-

---

96. David B. Barrett, "Annual Statistical Table on Global Mission," *International Bulletin of Missionary Research* 18 (1994): 25.

breaking humanity, yet once its sting (the law's condemnation) is removed, resurrection life beyond the grave is assured. With the resurrection of Christ as the "firstfruits" of the whole harvest, the consummation cannot be converted into a myth of the soul's ascent; it is the renewal of the cosmos beyond the reach of sin and death (Rom. 5:12–21; 6:23; 1 Cor. 15:56).

Far from "spiritualizing," this phase of the holy war—like the holy land—is both deeper and wider in its renewal of creation. The renewal that begins with the Spirit's work of raising those spiritually dead is consummated with their bodily resurrection. In the end, not only souls but also bodies will be saved; and not only humans but also the whole creation (Rom. 8:18–25).

Even the most mundane questions that we confront in our secular polis ultimately are connected to the problem of sin and death. As William Willimon observes, "Ford Motor Company spends more on employee health care each year than on steel. The whole world has become a hospital. I'm saying that *death* is pulling our strings."[97] Therefore, to talk about the problem of sin and death is hardly to take flight from the problems of this world; it is, rather, to take them more seriously than we usually do. Every event where the Spirit mediates union with Christ through Word and sacrament is another violent disruption of the kingdom of evil, refusing to let death have the last word.

As I argued at length in *Covenant and Salvation*, the forensic aspect of judgment and deliverance is the most generative force in the covenantal ontology. Sin and salvation are first of all judicial matters that create their own moral, physical, and historical domains. That is why Jesus comes not to clip the branches, but to pull up the tree by its root: to fulfill all righteousness, absolve and bless the brokenhearted, bear the curse, rise in conquest, and ascend to intercede for us in the heavenly courtroom. Along the way, Jesus announces a future judgment and consummated rest, which will occur at the end of the age. Signs of this consummation break out in Jesus' ministry, but the most decisive fact is his absolution of sinners.

Far from spiritualizing or allegorizing this holy war, the writer to the Hebrews reminds us that we have come not to Mount Sinai and the theocratic order of bloody sacrifices, but to Mount Zion "and to Jesus, the mediator of a new covenant, and to the sprinkled blood that speaks a better word than the blood of Abel" (Heb. 12:22–24). In that comparison we see a glimpse of the difference between the violence in Christ's self-offering and that violent sacrifice of others that demands retribution. Christ's blood speaks a better word than the blood of Abel precisely because while Abel's blood cried out from the ground for vengeance (Gen. 4:10–11), Christ's blood cries out from the Holy of Holies for mercy.

It is therefore not the kingdom of Christ but the kingdoms of this age that spiritualize the theme of holy war and holy land, in service to imperial, nationalistic,

97. William H. Willimon, *The Intrusive Word: Preaching to the Unbaptized* (Grand Rapids: Eerdmans, 1994), 10–11.

or liberationist aspirations. It is this spiritualization—or better, allegorization—that is so deadly, precisely because, as an allegory instead of a historically contextualized event, it can be appropriated and invoked by anyone, anytime, anywhere. Human blood will still be shed in wars, some of which we may still properly call just, but only blasphemously call sacred, interminable, or final. We are living a drama in the West today that is essentially the result of having never repudiated Christendom. First, we allegorized the story of Israel's theocracy. Biblical allusions were still required for the myth to work. Note how easily the ascent of mind coalesces with the Enlightenment myth of progress in William Blake's boast:

> I will not cease from Mental Flight,
> Nor shall the Sword sleep in my hand
> Till we have built Jerusalem
> In England's green and pleasant Land.[98]

Despite his aspirations, however, Jerusalem was never built in England, and the sun did set on the British Empire, as it has or will on every other.

From Babel to the modern age, parodies of the city of God have organized themselves from a powerful bureaucratic center, outward into centrifugal patterns to establish ever-greater "living space" (*Lebensraum*), subsuming difference into the expanding homogeneity of empire. The Third Reich appealed to ancient Germanic mythology as precedent for "uniting" all the separated Germanic peoples of Europe. Already in the late nineteenth century, Ernst Moritz Arndt could rhapsodize,

> Where is the German's Fatherland?
> Is it Swabia? Is it the Prussian land?
> Is it where the grape grows on the Rhine?
> Where sea-gulls skim the Baltic's brine?
> O no! more great, more grand
> Must be the German's Fatherland![99]

In the more recent Balkan conflict, the Serbs appealed to the "Greater Serbia" as the horizon of their eschatological expectation. For many American Christians, however, the mission of the United States is more transcendent. Given our history as a "melting pot" of ethnicities, we may bristle at rhapsodies on blood and land. Nevertheless, we too celebrate God's having "crowned our good with brotherhood from sea to shining sea" and identify Christ's Parousia-judgment with the

98. William Blake, *Milton* [prefatory poem], in *The Complete Writings of William Blake*, ed. G. Keynes (Oxford: Oxford University Press, 1966), 480.

99. Ernst Moritz Arndt, "Was ist des Deutschen Vaterland?" in *The Poetry of Germany*, trans. Alfred Baserkville (Baden-Baden, 1876), 150–52, quoted in Yi-Fu Tuan, *Space and Time: The Perspective of Experience* (Minneapolis: University of Minnesota Press, 1977), 177.

salvation, preservation, and advance of the Union in the "Battle Hymn of the Republic."[100] Puritans and Transcendentalists rhapsodized the sacred errand into the wilderness and leaders of the Social Gospel movement of the Gilded Age spoke of America's covenant with God to "Christianize" and civilize "lesser peoples" of the earth in terms that would make today's purveyors of faith-based war blush.[101]

In all of these ways, we move the pointers intended by the old covenant to Christ and draw them around our own nations, causes, or aspirations. In our day, "empire" spreads through the conquest of the market, until the whole earth is filled with the glory of Mammon—a global supermarket of desire. The depersonalized, disembodied flows of the invisible global market represent, in consummate form, a true spiritualization of eschatology.

Yet the kingdom of Christ expands in this age through suffering and cross, proclaiming Christ in the tangible, material, and ordinary means of Word and sacrament. Overlooked in the headlines of this fading age, this nucleus of the new humanity exists in fellowship, prayer, and mutual support even of temporal necessities, so that no brother or sister will be left to starvation or homelessness in body or soul. The result is a new nation, united together by blood indeed, but by the "blood of the new covenant, which is shed for many for the remission of sins" (Matt. 26:28 NKJV). Every nation and empire in this age is a version of Cain's city, in which believers dwell and share with their neighbors in the common curse and common grace of life "under the sun." A city frequently shaken and poised for retaliation, Babylon builds towers *reaching the heavens* only to have them pulled down in judgment at the last. By contrast, the city of God *descends from heaven*, like a bride adorned for her groom (Rev. 21:2). On the basis of the resurrection of Jesus as the prolepsis of that light of glory, we can patiently endure our inability to understand God's judgments.

In the meantime, we proclaim peace from city to city, warning of the judgment to come without invoking it. There are not two rival deities, but distinct covenants and eras that give us our coordinates for interpreting these texts. Instead of driving the nations out of his holy land at present, Yahweh is gathering them to his Son; even those who refuse to come are preserved, and they even flourish for the time being. It is this divine care, common to all people, that Jesus summons us to imitate (Matt. 5:45). Neither salvation nor judgment rests in our

100. George Hunsinger, *Disruptive Grace: Studies in the Theology of Karl Barth* (Grand Rapids: Eerdmans, 2002), 42. "Witness, for example," George Hunsinger observes, "the recently issued document entitled 'Christianity and Democracy: A Statement of the Institute on Religion and Democracy.' The report begins and ends with the words 'Jesus Christ is Lord,' while shamelessly confessing: '. . . we believe that America has a peculiar place in God's promises and purposes.'" It is telling that the drafters felt compelled to add, "'This is not a statement of national hubris.'" Conservatives and liberals may allegorize (and thus confuse Christ's kingdom with geopolitical regimes) in conflicting ways, but the hermeneutical tendency is roughly the same.

101. Garry Wills, *Head and Heart: American Christianities* (New York: Penguin Press, 2007), 391–95.

hands, but the Day of the Lord is the next great event on the eschatological horizon. "The Lord is not slow about his promise, as some count slowness," we are reminded, "but is patient with you, not wanting any to perish, but all to come to repentance. But the day of the Lord will come like a thief. . . . Yet, in accordance with his promise, we wait for new heavens and a new earth, where righteousness is at home" (2 Pet. 3:9–10, 13).

Chapter Ten

Consummation

The Eucharistic Liturgy of the Kingdom That We Are Receiving

We have encountered B. A. Gerrish's conclusion that "the entire oeuvre of John Calvin may be described as a Eucharistic theology," with "the holy banquet as the liturgical enactment of the themes of grace and gratitude."[1]

This volume began with the ascension of Christ, the forerunner, and it ends with the arrival of the whole church in his train. The church here and now finds its faith, hope, and love in that productive though precarious interim between his bodily ascension and its own. I began this series by advocating the significance of covenant and eschatology as the lens for integrating biblical, systematic, and practical theology. Concluding this work, as well as the four-volume project of which it is a part, this chapter argues that a covenantal theology is necessarily a liturgical theology and that the eucharistic economy is not only the heartbeat of ecclesial fellowship, but of reality itself.

---

1. B. A. Gerrish, *Grace and Gratitude: The Eucharistic Theology of John Calvin* (Minneapolis: Augsburg Fortress Press, 1993), 52; cf. Owen F. Cummings, "The Reformers and Eucharistic Ecclesiology," in *One in Christ* 33, no. 1 (1997): 47–54.

THE THANKSGIVING PARADE: A ROYAL PROCESSION
FROM SINAI TO ZION

There certainly are many ways to summarize the history of revelation from creation to fall to redemption and finally to consummation. Yet one prominent
theme is the eucharistic parade: a royal procession from work to Sabbath.

Given the lead part in this covenantal liturgy of antiphonal response, humanity was created in God's image. God speaks creation into being, and against the
backdrop of the "void and darkness" in Genesis 1:2, there are the six days of creation, meant to be understood, I believe, not as literal twenty-four hour periods
but as day-frames that correlate the creation of each domain with its ruler.[2] Days
1 and 4 announce the creation of light and its ruling luminaries to rule day and
night. Days 2 and 5 give us the creation of sky and water along with their respective rulers: birds and fish. Finally, on days 3 and 6 we have the creation of land
and vegetation, ruled by animals and humans. It is given humans to rule the
whole creation under God, not in waste and exploitation, but in service, imitat-
ing the Creator's own pattern of work and rest—the rest of an enthroned
monarch who has no enemies and has completed the mission.

So the creation account is like a pyramid, with humanity as its crown. Humanity was "crowned . . . with glory and honor. . . . You have made him ruler over
the works of your hands; you put everything under his feet" (Ps. 8:5–6). Echoing God's own pattern of creation-work and celebratory rest, God's covenant
partner was to lead the vast creation-parade through the "six days" of eucharistic
labor and conquest and then by right enter the everlasting land of promise.

This is the parade of the creature-kings, behind their human archruler, as they
pass before the review of the Great King enthroned in Sabbath majesty. Alan
Richardson points out, "Whether plant, tree, sun, moon, star, bird, or fish—
everything performs its duly ordained liturgical office, like the priests and Levites
of the sanctuary in their appointed courses. And finally, man, as the arch-priest
and crown of the whole created order, exercises dominion under God in this vast,
cosmic theocratic empire, in which everything that happens redounds to the
glory of God."[3] The destination was immortality and confirmation in righteousness and peace in God's own everlasting Sabbath time and place, with the
tree of life as its sacrament.

Eden was a holy city, yet it was intended merely to be the beachhead for the
universal kingdom of God on earth, with God as the Great King dwelling in the
midst of his people. Therefore, the goal from the beginning was not the perpet-
uation of ordinary life and history, much less a sacred cycle of birth-death-rebirth,

2. M. G. Kline, *Kingdom Prologue: Genesis Foundations for a Covenantal Worldview* (Overland
Park, KS: Two Age Press, 2000), 38–40; cf. Mark D. Futato, "Because It Had Rained: A Study of
Genesis 2:5–7, *Westminster Theological Journal* 60 (1998): 1–21.
3. Alan Richardson, *Genesis 1–11: The Creation Stories and the Modern World View* (London: SCM
Press, 1953), 55.

but the extension of God's law of love and righteousness. From the very beginning, then, there was a grand project to be accomplished, a trial to be successfully completed, a mission to be fulfilled. Created not merely as biological individuals who are naturally self-absorbed, human beings were designed for extroverted, ecstatic, and goal-oriented existence defined by God's covenant.

Not only were the earthly paradise and the human trial intended as an analogy of God's own work of creation and entering as conqueror into his Sabbath glory; the mutiny of Lucifer in heaven was being played out in God's city as well. Breaking away from the royal procession from Eden to Zion, with creation in his train, the human viceroy led a detour into a cul-de-sac of enmity, vanity, and frustration—and death as the sanction for covenantal disobedience. This time, instead of answering back, "Here I am," the covenant partner responded to God's approach ("Adam, where are you?") with fearful silence. No longer exercising a legitimate royal office that leads all of creation into the everlasting peace of God's kingdom, humanity now leads a parade of terror across the earth: Cain, Lamech, Nimrod; and the empires of Babel, Egypt, Persia, Greece, and Rome centralize this mutiny. Psalm 2 portrays the kings of the earth breaking their bonds and shaking their fists in the face of Yahweh and his Messiah. Instead of being God's analogy and servant, humanity wanted to be the creator and master.

Paul vividly captures the tragedy of the condition in which all of us are born as royal office-bearers who have gone our own way, with *ingratitude* as the heart of the rebellion (Rom. 1:18–22). Suppressing the truth in unrighteousness, humanity invests enormous energies in creating idols that can be manipulated and controlled in place of the Creator, who can only be thanked. Confused, distorted, disfigured, and subject to debilitating decay, the nonhuman creation was subjected to futility not by its own will but by the decision of its representative head (Rom. 8:20).

So God began a new parade—to the typological land of rest in Canaan and, with Christ's advent, to Zion itself. As in the creation story itself, God descends to "set up house," transforming space (a wilderness wasteland) into a habitable place for divine-human fellowship (Isa. 45:18). Just as Yahweh in creation led an exodus from "void and darkness" to habitable terrain for covenantal fellowship, so he repeats this march by liberating his enslaved people and leading them through the desert to Mount Sinai and then finally to Mount Zion. Time becomes history, oriented toward the Sabbath consummation, typologically identified with arrival in Canaan; space becomes place.

With profound insight, Jŏn D. Levenson develops this theme of Yahweh's march (Israel in tow) out of Egypt to Sinai and then on to Zion, concentrating first on the theme of "YHWH's home in no man's land."[4] Psalm 68 (probably dated somewhere between the thirteenth and tenth centuries BCE) is a war

---

4. Jŏn D. Levenson, *Sinai and Zion: An Entry into the Jewish Bible* (San Francisco: HarperSanFrancisco, 1985), 19.

psalm, calling upon Yahweh: "Father of orphans and protector of widows," to rise up and scatter his enemies (vv. 1–5). "God gives the desolate a home to live in; he leads out the prisoners to prosperity, but the rebellious live in a parched land" (v. 6). The following verses recount a march through the wilderness led by "the God of Sinai," where the camp is fed and its thirst quenched by Yahweh himself (vv. 7–10). "The Lord gives the command; great is the company of those who bore the tidings: 'The kings of the armies, they flee, they flee!' " while the women divide the spoils (vv. 11–14). The high mountains look upon the mountain of God with envy (v. 16). Rich with a combination of martial and liturgical elements, the verses that follow "record a march of YHWH from Sinai, a military campaign in which the God of Israel and his retinue . . . set out across the desert."[5]

As important as Sinai is in the march, it lies midway between Egypt and Canaan (Zion). It is a covenant of law, prescribing the work to be done, rather than the Sabbath rest; the place of trial rather than the place of victory and consummated blessing. The focus shifts from Sinai to Zion, for example, in Psalm 97 (cf. Deut. 33:2; Pss. 50:2–3; 68:8–9). "The transfer of the motif from Sinai to Zion was complete and irreversible, so that YHWH came to be designated no longer as 'the One of Sinai,' but as 'he who dwells on Mount Zion' (Isa 8:18). . . . The transfer of the divine home from Sinai to Zion meant that God was no longer seen as dwelling in an extraterritorial no man's land, but within the borders of the Israelite community."[6] And in the Zion traditions, "there will emerge something almost unthinkable in the case of Sinai, a pledge of divine support for a human dynasty."[7]

Thus, the march from Sinai to Zion also speaks of a progress in covenantal history from conditionality and temporality to unconditional and everlasting blessing.[8] The heavenly Zion (unlike the earthly one) exists "by his grace alone."[9] This is why Jeremiah 7 faults those who "have taken the cosmos out of the cosmic mountain," turning it "into a matter of mere real estate. They do not long in joy and awe for the mountain."

> Why should they? They are standing on it. The edifice on Mount Zion does not correspond to the gate of heaven; it *is* the gate of heaven. In other words, they have lost the sense of the delicacy of relationship between the higher and lower Jerusalem, and have assumed that the latter always reflects the former perfectly.[10]

I have argued (esp. in part 1 of *Covenant and Salvation*) that this failure to see the earthly Zion as merely a type or foreshadowing of the heavenly Zion that

---

5. Ibid., 19. Levenson concurs with W. F. Albright's dating of this psalm to the 13th–10th centuries BCE.
6. Ibid., 91.
7. Ibid., 92.
8. Ibid., 165.
9. Ibid., 166.
10. Ibid., 169.

would descend from heaven is the result of confusing the Abrahamic and Sinaitic covenants (see esp. the allegory in Gal. 4).

Elaborating Levenson's summary in the light of Christ, we may say that the incarnation, obedience, and death of Christ take place in the "desert" of human rebellion, not in the promised land of consummated rest. In this work, the last Adam, which is the true Israel, recapitulates the history of the broken covenant and fulfills it. Because of this, there remains the promise of a holy land and a holy rest, a new creation that is effected by the Word of God (Heb. 4:1–13) as it is mediated through preaching and sacrament (Heb. 6:4–19). The march from Sinai to Zion, aborted by Adam and Israel, is at last completed by Jesus Christ: those who look to Christ, Jews and Gentiles, have arrived not at Sinai but at Zion: the heavenly Jerusalem in festive assembly (Heb. 12:18–24). With Christ's fulfillment of the work of new creation-and-conquest, all prior history—including the Sinai theocracy—now belongs to the old order that is "passing away," "fading," "becoming obsolete." Christ's resurrection has inaugurated the age to come, so that the Abrahamic promise—and Israel's commission to the world—can finally be fulfilled. As Jenson finely puts it, "By Jesus' Resurrection occurring 'first,' a sort of *hole* opens *in* the event of the End, a space for something like what used to be history, for the church and its mission."[11]

GETTING THE JOURNEY RIGHT

It was just at this place in the story that Israel misunderstood the journey. Zealously getting its house in order so that Messiah could arrive to drive out the Romans, truly end the exile, and inaugurate his reign, Israel, especially under the leadership of the Pharisees, concentrated on renewing its vows that were made at Sinai. Rather than follow in the train of the Messiah to the heavenly Zion, the disciples themselves were expecting a mere revival of the earthly types and shadows. In other words, the goal was the restoration of the old covenant and its geopolitical theocracy and the unhindered purity of its cultic and ceremonial practices.

So now in the ministry of Christ, the scene in Eden is reset, with the Servant in the garden being confronted by the serpent, who challenges God's Word and promises a path of power and glory that circumvents the command and the cross. Yet this time, the Servant rebuffs the illicit offer, refusing to satisfy his hunger with an inappropriate use of his power (turning stones to bread) and submitting himself entirely to the Word of God. "It is written, 'One does not live by bread alone, but by every word that comes from the mouth of God'" (Matt. 4:4). It is Jesus, not the Father, who is being put to the test (4:7). Jesus is not a means to an end, a Messiah who simply reestablishes Israel's place in history; he is the end: the goal, the consummation, the center of history itself.

11. Ibid., 85.

As Jesus drew closer to Jerusalem, his teaching and action became increasingly clear and, to that degree, perplexing to the disciples. We see this especially in Mark's Gospel. Chapter 8 reports that after Jesus began to explain how he would be crucified and raised after three days, "Peter took him aside and began to rebuke him" (vv. 31–32). This is the same Peter who, in a preceding verse, declared Jesus to be the Messiah (v. 29). Doubtless, Peter shared the common view of his day that the Messiah would be crowned in Jerusalem, not crucified. Yet because Peter was unwittingly repeating Satan's temptation to a theology of glory rather than the cross (Mark 1:12–13; cf. Matt. 4:1–11 and Luke 4:1–13), Jesus, "turning and looking at his disciples, . . . rebuked Peter and said, 'Get behind me, Satan! For you are setting your mind not on divine things but on human things'" (Mark 8:33). After this, Jesus explained what it means for him to give his life for others (vv. 34–38). Again, in chapter 9, Jesus repeats the announcement of his impending death and resurrection (vv. 30–31). "But they did not understand what he was saying, and were afraid to ask him" (v. 32).

In Mark 10, Jesus repeats this a third time. "They were on the road, going up to Jerusalem, and Jesus was walking ahead of them; they were amazed, and those who followed were afraid." This is hardly the triumphal entry they were expecting back in Galilee. "He took the twelve aside again and began to tell them what was to happen to him, saying, 'See, we are going up to Jerusalem, and the Son of Man will be handed over, . . . and after three days he will rise again'" (vv. 32–34). Then in the following verses, James and John petition Jesus to allow them to sit on his right and left hand in his glorious enthronement at Jerusalem (vv. 35–37). "But Jesus said to them, 'You do not know what you are asking. Are you able to drink the cup that I drink, or be baptized with the baptism that I am baptized with?' They replied, 'We are able'" (vv. 38–39). They could only say this because they still misunderstood the journey. The story that unfolds from there is full of disappointment as well as intrigue: Peter, who triumphantly cuts off the arresting soldier's ear in defense of his Messiah, who rebukes him for it (Matt. 26:51–54; John 18:10–11), nevertheless denies him three times in fear for his own life (Mark 14:66–72).

Finally, Luke reports that after the resurrection, Jesus met two dejected disciples along the road to Emmaus. Just before this encounter, two angels had told the women at the tomb, "'He . . . has risen. Remember how he told you, while he was still in Galilee, that the Son of Man must be handed over to sinners, and be crucified, and on the third day rise again.' Then they remembered his words, and returning from the tomb, they told this to the eleven and to all the rest" (Luke 24:1–9). Now Jesus himself appears to the two disciples on the road, asking them why they are downcast, and they tell him what has occurred, concluding, "But we had hoped that he was the one to redeem Israel" (v. 21). They had the journey wrong. "Then he said to them, 'Oh, how foolish you are, and how slow of heart to believe all that the prophets have declared! Was it not necessary that the Messiah should suffer these things and then enter into his glory?' Then beginning with Moses and all the prophets, he interpreted to them the things about himself in all the scriptures" (vv. 25–27).

First the cross; then glory. After fulfilling all righteousness, enduring the judicial test of the "six days" (see above), Jesus Christ was enthroned beside the Father, not only as the only-begotten Son, but also as the last Adam. Therefore, the road to Jerusalem was a royal march to victory, but through Golgotha. No longer a sign of promised blessing for obedience, the Sinai covenant was the mountain that no one could climb but Jesus alone. Because of its violation, Sinai was the symbol now of death and judgment, but its sanctions were borne by the one who fulfilled its stipulations, "erasing the record that stood against us with its legal demands. He set this aside, nailing to the cross. He disarmed the rulers and authorities and made a public example of them, triumphing over them in it" (Col. 2:14–15).

Like most of their contemporaries, the disciples wanted to go back to Sinai, with Jesus as their captain, but Jesus knew that this was the cross that they could not bear—the cross that instead he would bear in their place. Because the disciples had misunderstood the destination—something far greater than a renewal of the Sinai covenant and actually redemption from the curses of that covenant— they missed the journey. That is why the risen Lord explains all the Scriptures, with himself at the center. At last, they finally recognize him and his words in the breaking of the bread (Luke 24:28–35).

As we saw in chapter 1 (above), even in the moments leading to the ascension the disciples could still gather to inquire of Jesus, "Lord, is this the time when you will restore the kingdom to Israel?" (Acts 1:6). Only after Pentecost is this question no longer asked, while the disciples are empowered as apostles of the Word to the ends of the earth.

Everything turns on getting Jesus' journey right. With Peter, we may want to rebuke Jesus for speaking of his crucifixion—especially when opportunities seem so ripe for a kingdom of glory here and now. We may have joined him on the royal procession to Jerusalem because we thought he was going to redeem and rule in a kingdom that is quite different from the one that seems actually to have arrived. Only when the Stranger meets us on the way, explaining the Scriptures and breaking the bread, do we recognize him as the host of the feast. Farrow explains that in terms of the larger story: "The outwards spiral of the apostolic mission is the ripple in the sea that marks the upwards passage of Jesus to receive what was promised."[12] "News of his coronation in heaven (still hidden from view) has reached earth in the pandemonium of Pentecost," and Peter's sermon is not on the Spirit or Jesus' resurrection, but on the ascension.[13] Pentecost is the echo of the victory parade in Psalm 68 (esp. v. 18), and this fits well with the motif of the cosmic mountain and "pattern of ascent and descent" in the flood, Babel, Sinai, tabernacle, Zion, Davidic throne.[14]

As G. K. Beale notes, Luke's genealogy works backward from Jesus to Adam, ending in 3:38: "the son of Adam, the son of God."

12. Douglas Farrow, *Ascension and Ecclesia* (Edinburgh: T&T Clark, 1999), 23.
13. Ibid., 25.
14. Ibid., 27.

Jesus, as true Israel, is the micro-Israel who has replaced the macro-national Israel. Hence, years are reduced figuratively down to days. Each response by Jesus to Satan is taken from a response by Moses to Israel's failure in the wilderness (Deut. 8:3 in Matt. 4:4; Deut. 6:16 in Matt. 4:7; Deut. 6:13 in Matt. 4:10). Jesus succeeds in facing the same temptations to which Israel succumbed. . . . That Eden's temptations are in mind is apparent from Mark's comments that after Jesus successfully endured the temptations in the wilderness, "he was with the wild beasts, and the angels were ministering to him" (which shows that he, in fact, was the promised one of Ps. 91:11–12, and compare 91:13).[15]

Even before Golgotha, then, Jesus Christ was winning our redemption and restoring the eucharistic liturgy on behalf of his ungrateful people. His active obedience is therefore as crucial soteriologically as his passive obedience.

AFTER FASTING, THE FEAST; AFTER THE SACRIFICE, THE EUCHARIST

The rulers of this age require their people to sacrifice themselves for the honor of the crown or for ideals, patriotism, or national interests. This ruler offered himself as the sacrifice to end all sacrifices. Even in terms of Israel's covenant, as great as the sacrifice of atonement indeed was, it is only part of the story that makes this drama something more than a parade of *forgiveness*; it actually restores the *eucharistic* economy. This point deserves some elaboration.

Leviticus 1–5 records the elaborate legislation governing the sacrificial system, which can be generally grouped into two categories: *sacrifices of atonement* (or guilt offerings) and *sacrifices of thanksgiving* (or thank offerings). The animal sacrifices for human fault could never replace the eucharistic (thankful) life of covenantal obedience and love for which God created humanity. It is not the offering of *representative sacrifices*, but the offering of *oneself in thanksgiving* that is God's delight: "Let us come into his presence with thanksgiving" (Ps. 95:2). "Enter his gates with thanksgiving, and his courts with praise. Give thanks to him, bless his name" (100:4). Referring to those whom God has redeemed, the psalmist exhorts, "Let them thank the LORD for his steadfast love, for his wonderful works to humankind. And let them offer thanksgiving sacrifices, and tell of his deeds with songs of joy" (107:21–22).

The animal sacrifices, both of atonement and thanksgiving, were never ends in themselves. The psalmist could even declare, "Sacrifice and offering you do not desire, but you have given me an open ear. Burnt offering and sin offering you have not required. Then I said, 'Here I am; in the scroll of the book it is written of me. I delight to do your will, O my God; your law is within my heart'" (40:6–8; cf. 51:16). Mediating God's dispute with his people, the prophets repeat

15. G. K. Beale, *The Temple and the Church's Mission: A Biblical Theology of the Dwelling Place of God* (Downers Grove, IL: InterVarsity Press, 2004), 172.

the psalmist's refrain against those who dare to bring their sacrifices while violating his covenant (Hos. 6:6; Amos 4:4; Mal 1:8). Jesus takes up the theme as well (Matt. 9:13).

Attributing such statements as Psalm 40:6–8 to antipriestly polemic misses the point that the psalmist is pointing to Christ, the one who is not only a guilt offering (providing the basis for forgiveness), but actually renders at last the covenantal faithfulness (a thank offering) that humanity in Adam has failed to yield.

That is how the writer to the Hebrews interprets it. No New Testament writer is more eager to highlight the significance of Christ's expiatory guilt offering. Yet his point (consistent with the psalmist's), is that what is required is not only a guilt offering greater than bulls and goats, but also something greater than a *guilt* offering. Although it made temporary provision by directing faith to the reality it signified, the guilt offering always highlighted the negative breach that required satisfaction. In other words, we might say, it never transcended the debt economy. If these sacrifices would have actually remitted all of their guilt for the course of their entire lives, the worshiper would not have to return home after the Day of Atonement still burdened by "any consciousness of sin" (Heb. 10:2). "But in these sacrifices there is a reminder of sin year after year. For it is impossible for the blood of bulls and goats to take away sins" (vv. 3–4). This, I maintain, is what the psalmist had in mind when he recognized the weakness of the old covenant sacrificial system.

But the writer to the Hebrews has still more in mind. Although Jesus Christ's self-offering actually provides the forgiveness that the temple cult foreshadowed, he provides something greater still. He can only bring the debt economy to an end if somehow he is not only the representative sin-bearer but also the representative law-fulfiller. Yielding the obedience that is better than sacrifice, Jesus was not only without personal sin but also positively fulfilled all righteousness.

Forgiveness is good, but obedience is better. God delights in forgiving debts, but his deepest joy—actually his requirement—is the faithful love and obedience (*ḥesed*) of the image-bearing covenant servant. Only a sacrifice of thanksgiving that God accepts—an obedient life—can resume the eucharistic parade and carry the new creation with him into his own glory. He accomplishes this for us not by offering an example, nor simply by offering a sacrifice for guilt, but by offering in our own humanity the thankful life for which we were created.

This interpretation makes the most sense of the fuller argument in Hebrews 10:

> Consequently, when Christ came into the world, he said, "Sacrifices and offerings you have not desired, but *a body* you have prepared for me; in burnt offerings and sin offerings you have taken no pleasure. Then I said, 'See, God, I have come *to do your will*, O God' (in the scroll of the book it is written of me)." When he said above, "You have neither desired nor taken pleasure in sacrifices and offerings and burnt offerings and sin offerings" (these are offered according to the law), then he added, "See, I have come to do your will." *He abolishes the first in order to establish the second.* And it is by God's will that *we* have been sanctified *through the offering of the body of Jesus Christ once for all.* (Heb. 10:5–10, emphasis added)

Therefore, it is not simply that Jesus has transcended the temporary sacrifices of the old covenant; he has also transcended the sacrificial economy altogether—not by abolishing it, but by fulfilling it. And he has not only fulfilled the debt economy but has also established a eucharistic economy on the basis of his own perfect obedience, by which we are being sanctified.

In holding together Christ's active and passive obedience, the writer is able to connect Christ's representative "Here I am!" to his propitiatory sacrifice: he is both the perfect eucharistic offering of obedience and the perfect sacrifice for sin. Together, this total life of living before the Father in the Spirit and giving himself up for the guilty becomes "a fragrant offering and sacrifice to God" (Eph. 5:2). This "Here I am!" is the proper covenantal and liturgical response, and Jesus offers it in word and deed not only for himself but also representatively for us.

Christ as the New Adam leads his covenant people in a triumphant procession into the promised *shalom*. As a result of our union with Christ, therefore, we too can be designated a fragrant sacrifice—and our lives, though still full of corruption, can nevertheless become eucharistically oriented.

> But thanks be to God, who in Christ always leads us in triumphal procession, and through us spreads in every place the fragrance that comes from knowing him. For we are the aroma of Christ to God among those who are being saved and among those who are perishing; to the one a fragrance from death to death, to the other a fragrance from life to life. Who is sufficient for these things? (2 Cor. 2:14–16)

The language of being led by Christ in "triumphal procession" underscores the covenantal, representative character of this economy of grace. Now Psalm 68 makes a deeper impression:

> With mighty chariotry, twice ten thousand, thousands upon thousands, the Lord came from Sinai into the holy place. You ascended the high mount, leading captives in your train and receiving gifts from people, even from those who rebel against the LORD God's abiding there. Blessed be the Lord, who daily bears us up; God is our salvation. Our God is a God of salvation, and to GOD, the Lord, belongs escape from death. But God will shatter the heads of his enemies, the hairy crown of those who walk in their guilty ways. . . . Your solemn processions are seen, O God, the processions of my God, my King, into the sanctuary. . . . Because of your temple at Jerusalem kings bear gifts to you. . . . Trample under foot those who lust after tribute; scatter the peoples who delight in war. . . . Sing to God, O kingdoms of the earth; sing praises to the Lord, O rider in the heavens, the ancient heavens; listen, he sends out his voice, his mighty voice. Ascribe power to God, whose majesty is over Israel; and whose power is in the skies. Awesome is God in his sanctuary, the God of Israel; he gives power and strength to his people. Blessed be God!" (Ps. 68:17–35)

While we ourselves cannot render an adequate sacrifice of thanksgiving any more than an offering for guilt, the perfume of Christ's living and dying runs down his face to every part of his body. Even the stench of sin clinging to our best works is overpowered by this scent. It is not at all surprising, then, that Hebrews 10—announcing the sufficiency of Christ's atoning sacrifice—leads us to the parade of witnesses from Abel to Daniel in chapter 11.

This argument does not *subvert* the debt economy (sacrifice of atonement), but *fulfills* it so that something still greater can be accomplished: the restoration of a new creation in Christ as true covenant partners in a eucharistic liturgy. In the debt economy, worshipers are constantly reminded of their sin—even in the process of being forgiven. Yet with the perfect sacrifice for sin finally offered, the conscience is cleansed so that a parade of worshipers may finally ascend the hill of the Lord and stand in his holy place clothed in the righteousness of the King of Glory. Moving through guilt, always under grace, the goal of this economy is to create a parade of gratitude, led by the second Adam, the faithful Israel, who leads us in joyful procession.

In view of the triumphant indicatives—"God's mercies"—as enumerated throughout Romans, Paul issues the imperative "to present your bodies as a living sacrifice, holy and acceptable to God, which is your spiritual worship" (12:1). No longer offering dead sacrifices of atonement, believers offer their own bodies as living sacrifices of thanksgiving, in a "spiritual worship" that goes far beyond the bloody altars of the old covenant. Jesus Christ alone offered a sufficient sacrifice for sin (Heb. 5:1; 9:26; 10:12), and this brings to an end any notion of debt in our relation to God.

Therefore, the line from the hymn "Come, Thou Fount" that says, "Oh! To grace, how great a debtor, daily I'm constrained to be," makes the wrong connection. Debt is the wrong correlate to grace. We can never be debtors to grace: "Who has given a gift to him, to receive a gift in return? For from him and through him and to him are all things. To him be the glory forever. Amen" (Rom. 11:35–36). We were once debtors to the law, but in Christ we are justified. Therefore, there is no debt relation to God whatsoever through faith in Christ. "Through him, then, let us continually offer a sacrifice of praise to God, that is, the fruit of lips that confess his name" (Heb. 13:15). Or as we find it in 1 Peter 2:5, "Like living stones, let yourselves be built into a spiritual house, to be a holy priesthood, to offer spiritual sacrifices acceptable to God through Jesus Christ."

This interpretation draws together the themes of creation, redemption, and consummation. Psalm 24 begins, "The earth is the LORD's and the fullness thereof" (KJV); this is established not only on the basis of God's universal sovereignty in creation, but also on the basis of the incarnation, life, death, and resurrection of the Lord who became the servant of the covenant. The age to come, says the writer to the Hebrews, has been subjected not to angels, but to humanity.

> As it is, we do not yet see everything in subjection to them [human beings], but we do see Jesus, who for a little while was made lower than the angels, now crowned with glory and honor because of the suffering of death, so that by the grace of God he might taste death for everyone. It was fitting that God, for whom and through whom all things exist, in bringing many children to glory, should make the pioneer of their salvation perfect through

sufferings. For the one who sanctifies and those who are sanctified all have one Father. For this reason Jesus is not ashamed to call them brothers and sisters, saying, "I will proclaim your name to my brothers and sisters, in the midst of the congregation I will praise you." And again, "I will put my trust in him." And again, "*Here am I and the children whom God has given me*" (Heb. 2:8–13, emphasis added)

Christ is not only the object of thanksgiving in this passage, but also the human liturgist, the Servant of Yahweh who is more fully human than any one of his siblings who benefit from his service.

Nothing belongs to us; there is nothing to be acquired, either for our earthly or heavenly welfare, but only to be gratefully received and shared with others. In this passage, Jesus is not only the one who has passed the grueling ethical test that humanity (including Israel) has failed; he has also entered the sanctuary with a worshiping throng in thanksgiving. Sanctified in him, those who are carried in his train are joyfully acknowledged in the heavenly congregation as his brothers and sisters. The "Here I am" of full obedience has finally been rendered. He has done it alone, yet he is not alone in his victory.

We need not "redeem" the culture in order to love and serve our neighbor. Christ has already taken care of the salvation of the creation, of which he is the firstfruits. The Christ who descended has also ascended as Lord over all: "The earth is the LORD's, and the fullness thereof" (Ps. 24:1 KJV). Leif Grane richly expresses the import of this verse:

> The world is neither mine nor the government's, nor is it merely the result of the working together of its different laws. But it is God's, which includes these laws and institutions and me and whatever may be the decisive person, or thing, in our world and time. . . . As to the features of reality, one may put it sloppily this way: Because God is the proprietor of our reality, its immeasurability and inconsistency are God's problem and not ours; and if there is anybody at all able to solve it, then it is God alone. Therefore we leave it to him.[16]

Far from rendering us aloof or disinterested in the concerns of this age, this confidence in God's sovereign grace means, "*We are free to realize our tasks.*"[17] In this way, the question of my own freedom and independence "has become penultimate." "'Hands, channels, and means'—even dictators and CEOs all have to execute, willy-nilly, God's will. Therefore, whatever they connive at or do, it will 'work together for good' (Rom. 8:28). It is not allowed to bind or free me. Rather, I am a free person, at least with regard to creatures. For we have this in common: we all together are 'the Lord's.'"[18]

---

16. Klaus Schwarzwäller, "The Bondage of the Free Human," in *By Faith Alone: Essays on Justification in Honor of Gerhard O. Forde,* ed. Joseph A. Burgess and Marc Kolden (Grand Rapids: Eerdmans, 2004), 50–51.

17. Ibid.

18. Ibid.

Thus, God remains Lord over creation and redemption, culture as well as cult, society as well as the church, but in different ways. Through the mask of ministers in their office of proclamation and sacrament, and the witness of all believers to God's saving action in Christ, as well as through the vocations of believers and unbelievers alike—through it all, God still cares for his world, both in saving grace and common grace. Even though he draws us into the parade of thanksgiving, using us as his means of loving and serving creation, "the earth is the LORD's," not ours. Those who are being gathered into Christ's thanksgiving parade are therefore defectors from the parade of sin and death who acknowledge, with the first answer of the Heidelberg Catechism, "I am not my own, but belong both in body and soul, in life and in death, to my faithful Savior Jesus Christ, who has fully paid for all my sins and has freed me from the tyranny of the devil."

Psalm 24 does not hold out to us a goal toward which we must strive, but a procession that we are to join. It cannot properly be turned into an allegory of our spiritual, moral, mystical, or intellectual ascent. This liturgy does not give us a higher self, but puts our old self to death and raises us with Christ, clothed in his righteousness and delighting in his grace. No longer trying to draw God into our parade of consumerism and self-fulfillment, we are finally drawn by the Spirit into God's parade of grace and gratitude. Christ's life was a liturgy of atonement and thanksgiving: the funeral march and the wedding dance. But because he made it to the summit, having passed the grueling ethical test, there is nothing left for us but praise. It is not our place to incarnate God's presence, redeem, or save the world, but to witness to the one who has done all of this for us. We do not follow in Christ's unique footsteps (*imitatio Christi*), but in the train of that victory that he alone accomplished (*Christus Victor*).

Freed from trying to be an acceptable *sacrifice of atonement* before God, we can now be means and masks of God's service to our neighbors—a fragrant *offering of thanks*. God's sacrificial action in Word and sacrament is always redemptive, while ours is always responsive: eucharistic. Even our imperfect works are warmly received not as a service that we render to God, as if we could complete Christ's work, but as means through which God serves our neighbors. Our prayers are received not for their virtue but because as they ascend, the Father recognizes the fragrance of his Son. "For as soon as God's dread majesty comes to mind," Calvin reminds us, "we cannot but tremble and be driven away by the recognition of our own unworthiness, until Christ comes forward as intermediary, to change the throne of dreadful glory into the throne of grace."[19] We can all pray with the psalmist, "O Lord, open my lips, and my mouth will declare your praise. For you have no delight in sacrifice; if I were to give a burnt offering, you would not be pleased. The sacrifice acceptable to God is a broken spirit; a broken and contrite heart, O God, you will not despise" (Ps. 51:15–17).

Swept into Christ's train, neither our worthiness nor unworthiness counts for anything. Nor are we enslaved by this present age to wander aimlessly in the

---

19. John Calvin, *Institutes* 3.20.17.

nihilistic consumerism of Vanity Fair, but are liberated to join the eucharistic procession that is already in progress, until one day we join our voices with the rest of redeemed creation. Even now we begin to realize the chief end of our existence: in the words of the Westminster Shorter Catechism, "to glorify God and to enjoy him forever."

The Lord of the church assures us that he has gone to the Father to prepare a place for us, "a city that has foundations, whose architect and builder is God" (Heb. 11:10). That is what the covenant is all about: "I will be your God, and you will be my people" (cf. Exod. 6:7). "I will dwell in your midst" (Zech. 2:11). Even now, through Word and sacrament, the Spirit turns a house into a home, anonymous space into a "a broad place" (Ps. 118:5), as a foretaste of our everlasting homeland.

In the Apocalypse the vision of the heavenly kingdom is a restored liturgy, with every part of creation performing its ordained role and singing the part for which its tongue was created. It is a universal city without walls or temple, for the Lord surrounds it in safety, and the Lamb is its sanctuary. At last, the symphony resounds throughout the cosmos that is not only restored creation but also consummated empire, led by the faithful liturgist who is both Son of God and Son of Adam:

> Praise him, sun and moon; praise him, all you shining stars! Praise him, you highest heavens, and you waters above the heavens! . . . Kings of the earth and all peoples, princes and all rulers of the earth! Young men and women alike, old and young together! Let them praise the name of the LORD, for his name alone is exalted; his glory is above earth and heaven. He has raised up a horn for his people, praise for all his faithful, for the people of Israel who are close to him. Praise the LORD! (Ps. 148:3-4, 11-14)

LET US THEN KEEP THE FEAST: PASSIVE RECEIVERS (SALVATION) AND ACTIVE DISTRIBUTORS (DOXOLOGY)

In *Christ* (but in Christ alone) as its representative head, the church receives the unilateral divine gift and returns it reciprocally with absolute purity, so that there is nothing left to offer God by way of debt. Yet Christ's personal and vicarious offering is far from disinterested benevolence; it binds together his sacrifice for others with his own self-interest, self-love, and desire for his own happiness. We are again reminded of Calvin's comment that "the highest honor of the Church" is that "until He is united to us, the Son of God reckons himself in some measure imperfect." "What consolation is it for us to learn that not until we are along with him does he possess all his parts, or wish to be regarded as complete!"[20] Even as host, Christ is one of the sharers in the feast, who enjoys the company of his

---

20. John Calvin on Eph. 1:23 in *Commentaries on the Epistles of Paul to the Galatians and Ephesians*, trans. William Pringle (Grand Rapids: Eerdmans, 1957), 218.

guests. We are therefore to set our eyes on "Jesus the pioneer and perfecter of our faith, who *for the sake of the joy that was set before him* endured the cross" (Heb. 12:2, emphasis added). Jesus has freely made his own joy dependent on our fellowship with him, in an everlasting exchange of gratitude to God.

Yet the church can never repeat this action, even asymmetrically; it can only be the effect of Christ's perfect return of thanks. As *recipient* of this covenantal exchange between the Father and the incarnate Son, the church lives in an economy of gratitude rather than either sacrifice or as an extension of Christ's atoning work. *Believers are passive receivers of the gift of salvation, but they are thereby rendered active worshipers in a life of thanksgiving that is exhibited chiefly in loving service to our neighbors.*

There is no divine gift that fails to issue in doxology, no faith that does not yield the fruit of good works. This is why Reformed churches have typically referred to their public services as "dialogical," expressing the asymmetrical yet genuine partnership of covenantal fellowship. Although the priority always lies with God's address ("the mercies of God"), praise and thanksgiving are our reasonable response, and finding nowhere else to go, this doxology generates enormous energy for our service to our neighbors. Here, the logic of the market (debt) is disrupted by the eucharistic logic of grace (gratitude), a covenantal feast that participates proleptically in the marriage supper of the Lamb. When our weekly worship is ordered and informed by this covenantal giving-and-receiving, however, our lives in the world can more easily and reasonably take the same kind of shape.

Notice especially the two crucial points made in 2 Corinthians 1:19–20: "For the Son of God, Jesus Christ, whom we proclaimed among you, . . . was not 'Yes and No'; but in him it is always 'Yes.' For in him every one of God's promises is a 'Yes.' For this reason it is through him that we say the 'Amen,' to the glory of God." It is Jesus Christ alone, as the unique and solitary covenant representative, whose return is equal to the demand, and he fulfills it, thus bringing the debt economy to an end for all of his coheirs. Not even the Father and the Spirit do what the Son does here. Although he shares our nature, he is isolated from all other human beings who have or will ever live as he hangs on the cross. Nevertheless, he puts a new economy in its place, so that "through him" we can "say the 'Amen,' to the glory of God." The Gift has been given; therefore, we are free to give thanks to God and to give our good works to our neighbor.

Until people are persuaded that God is the fountain of all of our good, and that he has left no part of our salvation to them, Calvin insists, "they will never devote themselves wholly, truly, and sincerely to him."[21] Grace inspires gratitude. "There is . . . an exact parallel in this respect between piety and faith," notes Gerrish. Only because of the forgiveness of sins that comes from Christ can the uneasy conscience ever be assured that God is indeed good and the source of all good.[22]

21. Calvin, *Institutes* 1.2.2.
22. Ibid., 3.3.19.

From God alone, therefore, all good and perfect gifts come to the world and are then distributed by us for the feast. The church is the *place* where sinners are receivers, yet it is also the *people* who are scattered to fulfill their common callings. In the latter, the church has no dominion. It cannot command the covenant community to embrace particular political ideologies, policies, parties, or politicians. It can only witness to the kingdom of grace, not inaugurate the kingdom of glory. Hence, Calvin as well as Luther refers to "two kingdoms" that must be kept distinct in the present age, although the believer participates in both.[23]

Gustav Wingren nicely summarizes Luther's concern with the neighbor as the recipient of the believer's good works. Instead of living in monasteries and committing their lives in service to themselves and their own salvation, or living in castles and commanding the world to mirror the kingdom of Christ, Luther argues, believers should love and serve their neighbors through their vocations in the world, where their neighbors need them.[24] "God does not need our good works, but our neighbor does."[25] When we offer our works to God, we simultaneously "attempt to depose Christ from his throne" and neglect our neighbor, since these works "have clearly been done, not for the sake of [our] neighbor, but to parade before God."[26] God descends to serve humanity through our vocations, so instead of seeing good works as our works for God, they are now to be seen as God's work for our neighbor, which God performs through us. That is why both orders are upset when we seek to present good works to God as if he needed them. In contrast, when we are overwhelmed by the superabundance of God's gracious gift, we express our gratitude in horizontal works of love and service to the neighbor.

This view of vocation had numerous implications for social life.[27] "In his *Treatise on Christian Liberty*, the main thought is that a Christian lives in Christ through faith and in his neighbor through love."[28]

> In faith, which accepts the gift, man finds that it is not only "heaven that is pure with its stars, where Christ reigns in his work," but the earth too is clean "with its trees and its grass, where we are at home with all that is ours." There is nothing more delightful and lovable on earth than one's neighbor. Love does not think about doing works, it finds joy in people; and when something good is done for others, that does not appear to love as works but simply as gifts which flow naturally from love.[29]

The regime of grace is therefore not in conflict with that of creation, but fulfills it. The commandment to love, Luther insists, is *lex naturae*.[30] Yet that law writ-

23. Calvin, *Institutes*, 4.20.1–3.
24. Gustav Wingren, *Luther on Vocation*, trans. Carl C. Rasmussen (Philadelphia: Muhlenberg Press, 1957; repr., Evansville, IN: Ballast Press, 1994), 2.
25. Ibid., 10.
26. Ibid., 13, 31.
27. Ibid., 36.
28. Ibid., 42.
29. Ibid., 43.
30. Ibid., 44.

ten on the conscience in creation is, in living letters by the Spirit, engraved on the heart of those who are swept into the new creation.

Under the law, in Adam, one is trapped in the cycle of sin and death, resentment and despair, self-righteousness and self-condemnation. Yet under grace, in Christ, one is not only justified apart from the law but is also able for the first time to respond to that law of love that calls from the deepest recesses of our being as covenantally constituted creatures. It is not the law itself that changes, but our relation to it, that makes all the difference.

A new day has dawned on this side of the resurrection, and that is why the law no longer takes on an awful specter, exciting sin and leading to judgment. As we read in 1 John 2:7–14, this new relationship to the law is eschatologically defined, in terms of our being in Christ and Christ's being in us. The law of love is "no new commandment," we read, yet in another sense it is

> a new commandment that is true *in him and in you*, because *the darkness is passing away and the true light is already shining*. Whoever says, "I am in the light," while hating a brother or sister, is still in the darkness. Whoever loves a brother or sister lives in the light, and in such a person there is no cause for stumbling. . . . I am writing to you, little children, because *your sins are forgiven* on account of his name. I am writing to you, fathers, because *you know him* who is from the beginning. I am writing to you, young people, because you have *conquered the evil one*. I write to you, children, because you know the Father. . . . I write to you, young people, because you are strong and *the word of God abides in you*, and you have overcome the evil one. (emphasis added)

Just as the gospel directs us outside of ourselves to the divine Stranger who meets us in peace and reconciliation, it frees us for an extroverted piety that is no longer obsessed with either self-condemnation or self-justification. It enables us to concentrate not on the inward process of infused habits and our own moral progress, but to turn our attention outward to the fellow strangers all around us. The forensic ontology I have recommended is extrospective, turning our gaze upward to God in faith and outward to our neighbor in love.

Freedom, in the economy of this fading age, means self-possession and self-determination, the ability to choose for oneself apart from any external constraints. The gospel, by contrast, exposes this autonomous freedom as the original bondage of a humanity "curved in on itself." "But what is this strange gift of evangelical freedom?" asks John Webster.

> It is a *strange* gift because it can only be known and exercised as we are converted from a lie—the lie that liberty is unformed and unconstrained self-actualization. It is *evangelical* because it is grounded in the joyful reversal and reconstitution of the human situation of which the gospel speaks. We may define it thus: In evangelical freedom I am so bound to God's grace and God's call that I am liberated from all other bonds and set free to live in the truth. "The law of the Spirit of life in Christ Jesus has set me free from the law of sin and death" (Rom. 8.2).[31]

31. John Webster, *Holiness* (Grand Rapids: Eerdmans, 2003), 92–93.

Yet in the context of North America, which Bonhoeffer described as "Protestantism without the Reformation," these insights are often muted at best. Radical grace and radical forgiveness are inconceivable, Bonhoeffer said, apart from a radical sense of sin that comes from the criticism by the word. Yet this is just what American Christianity has never experienced. "Because of this the person and work of Christ must, for theology, sink into the background and in the long run remain misunderstood, because it is not recognized as the sole ground of radical judgment and radical forgiveness."[32]

Interpreting Lutheran ethicist Paul Lehmann, Philip G. Ziegler adds,

> An ethic of justification will be one that "takes seriously the activity of the God who acts," since the advent of justification establishes the reality—the moral field—within which the question of ethics is to be firmly set. Justification, says Lehmann following Calvin closely at this point, is that act of God by which our "true position in the world—as a pilgrim between creation and redemption—is put within the orbit of [human] knowledge and behaviour in the world." It is the task of Christian ethics therefore to raise the question of the good and the right in light of the "disconcerting consequences" of God's gracious action for the human creature in Jesus Christ.[33]

"The repentance that flows from faith in this regard, transforms worry about *virtue* into desire for *obedience*, the strictures of *duty* into the gift of *vocation*."[34]

Even more than in the original creation, God's unilateral gift sets into motion an intrahuman exchange. God is in no need of our service, since it is he who gives life, breath, and everything else (Acts 17:25). Instead of trying to complete Christ's work, the goal of believers and the church corporately is simply to sing the "Amen." Instead of trying to transcend nature and history, grace redeems and restores creation. We are not made more divine, but more truly human.

Cheered on from the stands by "so great a cloud of witnesses," we "run . . . the race that is set before us, looking to Jesus the pioneer and perfecter of our faith, who for the sake of the joy that was set before him endured the cross, disregarding its shame, and has taken his seat at the right hand of the throne of God" (Heb. 12:1–2). Because we worship not on Mount Sinai, but on Mount Zion, with teeming hosts in festive assembly, we enter the Holy of Holies without fear (vv. 18–27). We are not called to build a kingdom or transform the kingdoms of this world into the kingdom of Christ, and this is precisely why we are liberated finally to place our full confidence in God and to love and serve our neighbor. "Therefore, since we are *receiving* a kingdom that cannot be shaken, let us give

32. Philip G. Ziegler, "Justification and Justice," in *Justification: What's at Stake in the Current Debates*, ed. Mark Husbands and Daniel J. Treier (Downers Grove, IL: InterVarsity Press, 2004), 119, citing "Protestantism without the Reformation," in Bonhoeffer, *No Rusty Swords: Letters, Lectures and Notes, 1928–1936*, ed. Edwin H. Robertson, trans. Edwin H. Robertson and John Bowden (London: Collins, 1965), 92–118.

33. Ibid., 129.

34. Ibid.; cf. Gene Edward Veith, *God at Work* (Wheaton, IL: Crossway Books, 2002).

thanks, by which we offer to God an acceptable worship with reverence and awe; for indeed our God is a consuming fire" (vv. 28–29, emphasis added).

Not only a unilateral moment, but also a gift that keeps on giving, this forensic word of pure grace transfers us from the realm of scarcity tending to death, and into the realm of abundant excess of resurrection life. This *is* the *shalom*, savory morsels of which we have already tasted in the body of Christ, in anticipation of the feast that awaits us in the everlasting Sabbath day. In the words of the eucharistic liturgy, "Christ has died. Christ is risen. Christ will come again. Therefore, let us keep the feast!"

To conclude this project, I suggest that we dare speak of God, God's reconciliation of the world in Christ, the church, and the new creation, because God has declared it to the world and made us his witnesses. Our lips stammer, not because there is too little to tell with any confidence, but that there is too much. We halt not before a void but before the majesty of God. If we fumble for words, it is not because we have accepted the thesis that the noumenal is inaccessible to thought or because the reality of God is unspeakable, or because all claims to transcendence are acts of violence. After all, we have heard and accepted the report that the Word was made flesh and pitched his tent among us. Rather, we stutter precisely because of what we have seen and heard.

"If 'silence' stands at the end of negative philosophical theology because the darts of all concepts and words fall to the ground before finding their mark," wrote Hans Urs von Balthasar, "a different silence stands at the end of Christian theology: that of adoration, which is likewise struck dumb by reason of the exceeding measure of the gift given."[35] In the words of T. S. Eliot's *Four Quartets*, "We shall not cease from exploration. And the end of all our exploring will be to arrive where we started and know the place for the first time."[36]

---

35. Hans Urs von Balthasar, *Theologik*, vol. 2 (Einsiedeln: Johannes-Verlag, 1985), 98.
36. T. S. Eliot, *The Four Quartets* (1944; London: Faber, 2000), "Little Gidding," V.

Index

Abraham
  migration of, 101–2
  promise to, 103
Abraham, William J., 90
absence, metaphor for covenantal relationship, 100
Absolute Spirit, 157
Achtemeier, Elizabeth, 71
action
  divine and human, distinction between, 42–43
  vs. presence, 108–9
Adam, Karl, 156–58
Adam and Eve, arraignment of, after the fall, 59
After Our Likeness (Volf), 181–84
agency, human, prioritized over divine, 74–75
alternative faith communities, 178
American religion
  gnostic nature of, 77
  as Protestantism without the Reformation, 250, 306
  revivalism in, 232
animal sacrifices, significance of, 103
Apocalypse
  as holy war, 275
  vision of heavenly kingdom in, 302
apostolicity
  covenantal conception of, 218
  as gift, 232–33
  guarantee of, 221
apostolic offices, extraordinary and unique in church history, 234–36
apostolic succession, determined by content of church's ministry, 239
Aquinas, Thomas, 7
  on Christ's ascension, 7
  on presence of Christ in sacrament, 108

on sacrament making people holy, 106–7
Arndt, Ernst Moritz, 286
ascension
  becoming part of gospel, 2
  causing eucharistic tension, 2, 4
  effect of, on Platonism and early Jewish eschatology and cosmology, 5
  as expansion of the body of Christ, 163
  function of, in the Epistles, 2–3
  giving "docetic" interpretation, 3–4
  most direct account of, 1–2
  redefining historical Jesus, 12
  remedying marginalization of, in theology, 3
  revealing power of new life, 4
  significance of, in Christian thought, 5–13
  transforming people into the body of Christ, 30–31
  treatment of, in history of interpretation, 3
Ascension and Ecclesia (Farrow), 3
ascent of mind, 5, 7–8, 11, 52, 61, 162, 286
Athanasius, 133
  on the ascension, 5–6
  on man becoming God, 5
Auerbach, Erich, 54
Augsburg Confession, 46
Augustine, 23, 70, 74
  on the ascension, 5–6
  calling the Supper the "bond of love," 140
  on Christ's presence at the Supper, 131, 132
  on hearing, 54
  nothing realized fully in the present, 145
  on *totus Christus*, 6, 155–56
  transforming light metaphor, 52–53
  on Word of God as a sign, 46
  on Word of God beginning internally, 46
aural analogies, difficulty in promoting over visual analogies, 52

Austin, J. L., 38–39, 109
Avis, Paul, 221–22

baptism
    as action of Trinity, 117
    baptized coming under God's judgment, 104
    children's, 117
    circumcision related to, 112–15
    conveying no benefit or blessing, 112
    dispute over, 111–12
    eschatological nature of, 104–6
    as God's command for church to assume
        responsibilities, 212
    as God's work, 116–19
    as human act, 112
    linked to preaching and catechesis, 50
    linked to the Word, 119
    reality of, embracing by faith, 115
    as response, 118
    role of, 253
    as sign and seal of righteousness, 119
    as sign of membership in covenant commu-
        nity, 143–44
Barna, George, 78, 170n.98, 177–78
Barth, Karl, 24, 33–34, 61, 74n.10, 88, 89,
    171
    assuming secularity as science, 228
    on baptism as human act of response,
        118–19
    belief that everyone already united in Christ,
        174
    on Christ's humiliation and exaltation, 173
    on church as place of repentance, 98
    on Church of Esau and Church of Jacob,
        227
    on church's holiness and catholicity as a
        gift, 220
    claiming that Reformation substituted
        preaching for the Mass, 142
    commitment of, to visible church, 171
    critique of pietism, 171, 173–74
    distinguishing between Christ and church,
        171–72
    distinguishing between church's content and
        form, 228–29
    dualistic ecclesiology of, 229
    eschewing Reformed sacramentalism, 142
    identifying the visible church, 227
    on individuals transitioning from wrath to
        grace, 174

monistic tendency in Christology of,
    172–73
not denying appointment of church officers,
    247
promoting Christology's objectivity and par-
    ticularity, 175
on Reformed churches surrendering escha-
    tology to history, 230
on Reformed ecclesiology leading to holy
    egoism, 247
separating divine and creaturely agency, 142
on separating the churches, 207
on speaking of continuing incarnation of the
    church, 226–27
on Supper and community, 143
turning attention back toward Jesus, 172
underscoring discontinuity of Jesus-history
    and church history, 173
view of the sacraments, 171–72
wariness of tendency to enclose Christ, 143
warning about collapsing Jesus Christ into
    the church, 175
on the world not needing the church, 246
Barth, Markus, 121
Baudrillard, Jean, 66–67
Bavnick, Herman, 39
Bayer, Oswald, 45–46, 47
    on efficacy of God's institutions, 196
    on Luther's view of hearing and seeing, 54
Beale, Gregory K., 209, 262, 283, 295
Being as Communion (Zizioulas), 164
Belgic Confession, 110, 117, 128, 130, 222n.3
believers
    active and passive roles of, 303
    deification of, 5
    goal of, 306–7
    priority of, over priority of the church,
        85–86
Benedict XVI, 158. See also Ratzinger, Joseph
Berger, Peter, 89
Berkhof, Louis, 111
Berry, Wendell, 251
Beza, Theodore, 41
Bible, the
    as church's book, 82–83
    concern of, 67
    as servant of self-creation, 76–77
    as sourcebook, 67–68
biblical faith
    attention paid to God's descending to us, 54

oriented toward proclaiming happenings, 54
biblical rites, as means of binding strangers to
    the sovereign, 242
biblical tradition, sacred space and time in,
    60–61
Blake, William, 286
Bloom, Harold, 74n10, 77
Blumenberg, Hans, 51–53, 64
body of Christ, use of, as metaphor, 188
Boesak, Alan, 205
Boman, Thorlief, 54n.72
Bonhoeffer, Dietrich, 50–51, 168–70, 306
    church and members both elected, 201
    on importance of being participants in God's
        action, 81
    on importance of church's collective faith,
        212
    on infant baptism, 186
    on the local parish church, 211–12
    on preacher's intention, 196
    ways of misunderstanding the church, 233
Boniface III, 8
Breytenbach, C., 244
Brunner, Emil, 171
Bucer, Martin, 126, 135n.56, 138
Bulgakov, Sergei, 23
Bullinger, Heinrich, 126
Bultmann, Rudolph, 171
burned-over district, 250
Butin, Philip Walker, 99, 129, 150, 202
Byzantine theology, 7

Called to Communion: Understanding the
    Church Today (Ratzinger), 160
Calvin, John, 74, 91, 197
    on absence and availability of Christ, 147
    on baptism as action of Trinity, 117
    Christology of, 135–36
    on the church's uniting with us, 186
    on communication of Christ's energies,
        133, 137
    complaining about pope and Anabaptists, 72
    on devotion to God, 303
    doctrine of union, 134–35
    emphasizing God's condescension to the
        human condition, 137
    eucharistic piety of, 140
    eucharistic theology of, 136
    facing eschatological issues of Supper
        directly, 133

focused on economy of grace, 126
following Ockham's logic, 145
on frequency of Communion, 137–39
on God and the gospel creating the
    church, 91
on God's coming to mouths and tongues
    of sinners, 77
on God's Word, 40–41
grace mediated through the sacraments, 143
on the highest honor of the church, 302
on humanity, 124
language for the church as less reactionary
    than Barth's, 175
locating church's catholicity in election, 200
marks of the true church, 245
moving from ascension to Eucharist, 10
others' defense of his eucharistic theology,
    149–52
on the preached Word, 47–48, 71
refocusing attention on Christ's absence and
    economy of redemption, 10
refusing contrast between inner and outer
    Word, 48
refusing to separate sign and signified, 126
reiterating Chalcedonian formula on pres-
    ence, 146
role of, in shaping Reformed Eucharistic
    teaching, 126
on sacraments as divine gifts, 117
on sacraments bringing clearest promises, 99
on scripture making no mention of papal
    office, 239
service of, as liturgy of Word and sacrament,
    110
on the Supper, what is received, where, and
    how, 125–35
theology of, described as Eucharistic,
    124–25
on two kingdoms, 304
versions of enthusiasm, 84
warning against faith in solitude, 89–90
zeal of reconciling Lutheran and Reformed
    churches, 134
canon, the
    Grenz's functionalist view of, 86–87
    proper understanding of, 83–84
Cant, William M., 255–56
Catholic Church. See Roman Catholic entries
catholic church, Westminster Confession
    defining, 202–3

catholicity
  depending too much on openness to other
    churches, 216
  determined by Word of God, 208
  full realization of, 209
  horizon of, 203
  intergenerational disruption of, 211–12
  requiring common confession, 207
  undermining of, 206
  understanding within ecclesiological frame-
    work, 217
Christ
  allowing space for repentance, 276
  ascension of, in redemptive-historical con-
    text, 1–5
  assimilated to holiness of his body, 192
  body of, as metaphorical character, 183
  as corporate personality, 165
  creating historical community, 33
  distinguishing true body of, from the visible
    church, x
  effecting ecclesial unity through the Supper,
    140
  as end-time sanctuary, 269
  experiencing union with, 298
  gifts of, preserved from generation to genera-
    tion, 237
  guilt offering of, 297
  imitation of, 85
  incorporation into, 254
  ministry of, resetting Edenic scene, 293
  as new Adam, 298
  no need for bodily return of, x
  as only subject of salvific activity, 182–83
  in our midst as different from bodily return
    of, 107
  presence of, mediated by the Spirit, 13–30
  proclamation of, as primary means of
    grace, 58
  remembering death of, as part of Sacrament,
    256
  as representative head in a covenant, 185,
    187
  risen, distributing spoils of his conquest, 31
  as saving part of Scripture, 41
  union with, occurring as common participa-
    tion of different members, 187
  workings of, 137
  See also Jesus, Jesus Christ
Christianity, parting ways with Judaism, 269

Christian Neoplatonism, 61
Christians, state persecution of, 284
Christian suffering, 22
Christian theology, recognizing dissonance
    between Hellenistic and biblical interpre-
    tations, 52
Christology, merging with ecclesiology, 12, 156
Chrysostom, John, 131, 135
Church, the
  acknowledging its own ungodliness, 90
  always on receiving end in relationship with
    Christ, 31
  applying market principles to, 178–79, 180
  aristocratic constitution of, 157–58
  as army of activists, 249
  assimilated into world by preaching another
    gospel or corrupting sacraments, 199
  becoming the body of Christ, 15–16,
    151–52
  bonded to body and head, 238
  business of, as receiving and delivering gift
    of salvation, 242
  called by Christ and controlled by his
    Spirit, 33
  catholicity of, 200–201
  as Christ's ongoing incarnation in the world,
    161, 162
  community created by the gospel, 50
  as covenant, ix—x
  covenantal approach to, 185
  as creation of the Word, 37–40, 45–46, 79
  effectiveness of ordinary ministry of, 254–55
  emerging as social institution with juridical
    power, 9–10
  empirical, not simply a religious community,
    237
  as eschatological event, 228
  filling Jesus' void, 160
  formed by individuals, 177
  goal of, 306–7
  growth of, attributed to the Word, 44
  as historical organization, 224, 228
  holiness coming to, 191, 193
  as human body of risen Jesus, 167
  as human institution, 223
  as incarnation of Christ in the faithful, 157
  identifying with progress, 223
  identity of, 73
  imagining itself as substitute for absent Lord,
    152

invisible, 170, 200
life of, dependent on faithfully maintaining
    ministry of Word and sacrament, 236–37
losing missionary impulse, 248
marks of, 249, 279
ministry of, as means of divine action,
    91–92
mission of, defined by the three marks,
    243–45, 248–56
mission's success tied to witness in Christ,
    196
modern practice of, accepting that religion is
    self-projection, 89
as mother of the Word, 82
need of, to yield to the Spirit, 24
not equal to God's Word, 96
not sacred in and of itself, 227
as object of redeeming action, 29–30
offices in, as gifts from Christ, 31
as offspring rather than origin of gospel,
    93–94
as passive recipient or active agent of
    redemption, 198–99
as place of repentance, 98
preferring reigning to witnessing, 27
promise-driven, 94
receiving grace, 92
receiving unilateral divine gift, 302–3
reducing visibility of, to secularity, 228
reflecting the Light of the world, 191
relation to the Word and implications for
    office of pastor and teacher, 237
role of, to supply serving opportunities,
    179–80
as servant rather than Lord of the covenant,
    234–35
simultaneously exclusive and inclusive, 158
sinless, 195–96
as source of grace, 8
sources for holiness of, 194
standing in place of historical Jesus, 12
standing under God's judgment and
    grace, 95
substituting for Christ, 148–49, 223
tempted to idolatrous substitutions for
    Christ, 13
as theater of cosmic battle, 283
unable to provide what Trinity does, 199
understood as unerring in magisterial
    judgments, 222

unregenerate members of, as beneficiaries of
    Spirit's activity, 197
viewing itself as Jesus' replacement, 6
viewing source of its existence, 73
visibility of, 158, 227, 229–30, 248
visible and invisible, 202
Church and World (von Balthasar), 159
churches
    creating niches within, 206, 208
    increasing hegemony of, 204–5
    losing connection with apostolic church, 238
    marketing of, 206–7
church-growth movement, 252
Church of Esau, 227, 229
Church of Jacob, 227, 229
church order, raising to gospel level, 226
church work, related to work of secular mem-
    bers, 247
circumcision, related to baptism in Christ,
    112–15
circumcision-baptism, apart from Christ,
    115–16
Cities of God (Ward), 145, 163–64
city of God, parodies of, 286
Clark, Gordon, 40n.6
Clowney, Edmund, 19–20
communicative theory, convergence with
    Reformed conceptions of Word and sacra-
    ment, 109
Communion. See Supper
community
    converging with individual, 86
    generated from interpersonal communica-
        tion, 67
community romanticism, 197
confessions, serving living confession of Christ,
    223
Congar, Yves, 159–60, 226
consumer society, nihilistic eros of, 59
conversion
    as ecclesial experience, 195
    source of, 78
Cornell, Vincent J., 260
corporeality, transcended, 148
corpus triforme, 8–9
cosmic battle, waged through earthly agents,
    283
cosmic Christ, 12
cosmic Christology, 162
cosmic mountain, motif of, 261

covenant, the
  appropriate response to, from individuals
    and church, 211
  contrasting new and old, 276
  as living reality integrating faith and praxis,
    210–11
  placement relative to, 100
  providing context for prophet's actions,
    42–43
  words and signs bound in, 113
covenantal approach
  challenging individualism, 198
  refusing choice between church as people or
    place, 235
covenantal ecclesiology
  challenging certain formulations of catholic-
    ity, 217–18
  position of, 240
covenantal faith, avoiding dualisms, 232
covenantal *koinonia*, 169
covenantal meals, significance of, 120
covenantal model
  affirming unity and difference as essential to
    church, 201
  interpreting unity and catholicity of church,
    203–4
covenantal speech, 45
covenantal thinking, linked to hearing, 62–63
Covenant and Eschatology (Horton), ix, 3
Covenant and Salvation (Horton), ix, 133, 198,
  285
covenant community
  market forces tearing apart, 206, 208
  requirements for biblical notion of, 222
  uniting generations, 209–10
covenant theology
  on church's holiness, 194–95
  emphasizing linguistic construction of real-
    ity, 61
  intra-Trinitarian concept of, 13
  offering different account of sign-signified
    relation, 100
  potential of, for renewal of theology, ix
Cowles, C. S., 277–78
Cranmer, Thomas, 139
creation
  consummation as goal of, 15
  covenantally constituted, 58
  interdependent with new creation, 14
creation story, 94, 290

creeds, serving living confession of Christ, 223
cross, theology of, 69
cultural difference, embracing, 205
culture, reciprocal relationship with gospel, 87
Cummings, Owen F., 124
Cyprian, 91
Cyril of Alexandria, 131, 134, 135

Dabney, R. L., 140n.73
debt economy, 298
Deddens, Karl, 141
de Gruchy, John, 205
Deleuze, Gilles, 66–67
de Lubac, Henri, 8–9, 156, 159, 160
Derrida, Jacques, 52, 67, 69
  on messiah's arrival, 75
  on sign-signified relation, 100
Descartes, René, 57, 65
descent-ascent-return pattern, 2, 7–8
Dillard, Raymond, 16–17
Dionysius, 164
disciples
  concentrating on Jesus' divinity, 5–6
  office of, granting position as ambassadors of
    the kingdom, 243–44
  personal lives of, related to recognition of
    Christ's identity, 29
  relationship with Jesus, 29
dislocation, 105
dispensations, doctrine of, 193
dogma, as drama, 40
drama, metaphor of, for expressing interplay
  between eschatology and history, ix
Dulles, Avery, 188, 216, 230
Duns Scotus, 9

East, impressions of Western papalism, 213
Eastern Orthodox ecclesiology, 164–66
ecclesial apartheid, 205, 210
ecclesiological universalism, 162
ecclesiology
  being allowed to redefine the gospel, 92–93
  errancy of conflating Christology with,,
    226–27
  independent, 180–81
  linking with soteriology, ix
  prioritized over soteriology, 168
  secularized, 223
  Western, requiring absent Christ, 9
ecstatic movements, 11

ecumenism, depending too much on individual and congregational piety, 216
Eden
    as beachhead for universal kingdom of God on earth, 290–91
    characteristics of, 263–64
    cosmic battle commenced in, 281
Edwards, Jonathan, 144
Eichrodt, Walther, 261, 268
election
    related to covenant of grace, 116
    upholding unity and plurality in Christ, 201
Eliot, T. S., 307
emergent movement, 91
Emerging Church movement, 12
Emerson, Ralph Waldo, 76
Enlightenment, 51–52
    effect of, 75
    placing sovereign authority in the self, 72–73
    reducing senses to vision, 55
    relationship with pietism, 73–74
episcopate, flaw in making essential to apostolicity, 225–26
Epistle to the Romans, The (Barth), 172
Erickson, Millard, 112
eschatological event, occurring each Lord's Day, 230–31
eschatology
    converging with communion in the Eucharist, 213
    hearing and, 66–68
    spiritualization of, 287
eschaton, visible church and catholic church identical in, 200
essence-energies distinction, Eastern, 133, 136–37
Eucharist
    defining, relative to time, 144–45
    distinct from Mass, 127
    as human work, 138
    overrealized eschatology of, 22–23
    subjective individualism of, 6–7
    See also Supper
eucharistic economy, restoring, 296
eucharistic parade, 290
Eusebius, 259
evangelical ecclesiology, 176–83
evangelicalism, 12, 251
    American, difficult to categorize, 111

approach of, to sacraments, 111
contractual view of union and communion, 170–71
dispensational, focus on renewal of Sinai covenant, 269
dominant view of Supper in, 143
emphasizing mission, 248
Grenz's assessment of theology of, 84–87
individual nature of, 194
losing sight of God's role in church, 253–54
preaching in, regarded as indifferent communication form, 231–32
precedence of human choice and agency in, 171
theology of, 228
theology of youth groups, 77
view of justification, 92–93
evangelicals
    defending church as active agent of redemption, 198
    focus of, 254
evangelism
    contrasted with marks of the church, 251–52
    task of, 91
every-member ministry, undermining the notion of the church, 237
exemplarist atonement doctrine, 162
exodus story, 94

faith
    arising from inner experience, 85
    arising in covenantal gathering of fellow hearers, 50
    coming through hearing, 47
    contrasted with idolatry, 59
    created by the Spirit and through the Word, 44
    as gift of the church, 160
    as private matter, 180
    related to sacraments, 116
    vs. faiths, 74
Farrow, Douglas, 3–5, 170
    appealing to Calvin, 125
    on church's view of itself, 6
    on cosmic Christ, 13
    criticism of Ward, 150
    on ecclesiology becoming irrelevant, 7–8
    on ecclesiology moving along an absolutist course, 9–10

Farrow, Douglas (*continued*)
  on eucharistic ambiguity, 189
  on growing dominance of icons, 8
  on Schleiermacher, 11–12
  on Spirit presenting absent Jesus, 26
  on turning from earthly Jesus to cosmic
    Christ, 7
Feast of Tabernacles, 17
feasts, in Siniatic economy, 17
Feuerbach, Ludwig, 12, 60, 76
Fichte, Johann Gottlieb, 156, 168
finite, source of evil, 157
Finney, Charles G., 78, 178–79, 249–50
Fletcher, John, 11n.43, 193
flood narrative, Spirit present in avian form,
    13–14, 15
Four Quartets (Eliot), 307
Franke, John, 87
Franklin, Eric, 3
free-church ecclesiology, 170, 216
free-church polity, working against polycentric
    community, 219
free-church theology, 228
Freud, Sigmund, 60, 76

generations, overstereotyping of, 207
Geneva Catechism, 95
Germany, trends among contemporary Protes-
    tants in, 253
Gerrish, B. A., 40, 109, 110, 124–27, 140,
    289, 303
gifts, pattern of receiving and passing on, 32
glory, theology of, 68–69
Gnosticism, 13
God
  action of, making the sacraments, 107–8
  baptism as work of, 116–19
  call of, beginning migration of God's people
    to their homeland, 101–2
  characterized differently in Old and New
    testaments, 278
  covenantal view of presence of, 100–101
  goal of, 268
  hostility to, 76
  as idol, 67
  manifesting himself in certain places, 261
  marginalizing voice of, 80
  needing the world for self-realization and
    completion, 157
  placing covenantal blessing on people, 241

presence of, 101, 191
  promising to meet us in covenant of grace,
    193
  remembering synonymous with acting, 102
  speech of, 39–40, 88–89, 101
  working through Word and sacraments,
    90–91
  See also God, Word of; the Word
God, Word of
  alleged contrast with the Spirit, 43
  freely spoken in time, 42
  giving us back our voice, 97
  living and active, 43–44
  See also the Word
God-consciousness, central theme of, resulting
    in less focus on Jesus' presence, 11
Gogarten, Friedrich, 171
Gore, Charles, 166
Gorringe, Timothy, 166, 167, 207
Gospel, the
  counterintuitive nature of, 73, 77–78
  creating knowledge, assent, and trust, 40
  as criterion for apostolicity, 225
  defining ministry and mission of the
    church, 249
  delivery of, in Word and Sacrament, 68
  exposing autonomous freedom, 305
  as intrusion among people, 79
  leading to obedience, 241
  as life-giving part of God's Word, 41
  messages antithetical to, 68
  need to bring into the world, 32
  reciprocal relationship with culture, 87
  self-sufficiency of, 93
  space separating people from, 77–78
grace
  coming from the church, 8
  confidence in, 300
  covenant of, x, 101, 116
  differing understandings of, 106–7
  establishing covenant of, 273–74
  limiting means of, 111–12
  as metaphysical substance, 108
Grane, Leif, 300
Great Awakening, 75
Great Commission, as only contemporary
    sacred mission, 271
Greater Serbia, 286
Greek culture, changes in, from Homeric era to
    Plato, 55

Gregory the Great, 225
Grenz, Stanley, 84–86, 112
   on congregational ecclesiology, 176–77
   on covenantal perspective challenging individualism, 198
   on Reformed treatment of visible/invisible church, 203
Grudem, Wayne, 111
Guder, Darrell, 251

Harnack, Adolf von, 83
Hauerwas, Stanley, 82, 83, 96, 166
hearing
   effects of, 54
   eschatology and, 66–68
   linked to covenantal thinking, 62–63
   related to promise and fulfillment, 64
   von Balthasar on, 65–66
Hebrews, restating Old Testament journey motif, 3–4
Hebrew Scriptures, hearing and seeing in, 64
Hegel, G. W. F., 12, 92–93, 156–57, 162, 166, 168
Hegelian monism, preventing community, 201
Heidelberg Catechism, 48, 59, 99, 109–10, 200, 301
Heidelberg Disputation, 68
Henry, Carl F. H., 40n.6
Heraclitus, 53
Herrmann, Wilhelm, 74
historical community, created by Word and Spirit, 238
Hobbes, Thomas, 185
Hodge, A. A., 130
Hodge, Charles, 134
Holiness
   coming to the church, 191, 193
   for people of God, 192
Holwerda, David, 270
holy egoism, 247–49
holy land, geopolitical absence of, 271
holy war
   change in meaning with change in testaments, 273
   early, comparing to modern conflicts, 277
   in history of redemption, 272–80
   spiritualizing theme of, 280–88
   treated as static, timeless concept, 272
Homer, 54–55
Hosius (Cardinal), 226

house-church movement, 170n.98
human experience, centrality of, 75
human history, becoming obsolete after ascension, 4
Humani generis, 192
humanity-divinity dualism, carried over into ecclesiology, 7
humans, taking bait of false prophets, 27
human witness, presence of divine witness in, 26
Hunsinger, George, 143
Hunter, James Davison, 77n.23
Hütter, Reinhard, 28, 143n.90

icons
   growing dominance of, 8
   limitation of, 67
   provoking vision, 69
idealism, price of, 169
idolatry
   contrasted with faith, 59
   motivation for, 63–64
   worshipers providing all the speech, 59–60
idols, speakers and, 59–63
images, prohibition of, in Judaism and the New Testament, 65
Images of the Spirit (Kline), 272–73
incarnation, undoing ascension by replacing, 12
incarnational, more frequent use of term, 166–67
incarnational ministry, 207
individual, converging with community, 86
infant baptism, covenantal view of, 186
infusion, as wrong category for God's gracious action, 108
ingratitude, at heart of rebellion against God, 291
inner light, as theme, 51
intrusion ethics, 272, 276–78
intuition, 52
Irenaeus, 74, 135
   concentrating on economy of grace, 5
   confronting gnostic dualism, 52–53
   stressing the ascension, 5
Israel
   dividing a united church, 226
   feasts of, 103–4
   focus of, on word of God, 63
   misunderstanding journey to Zion, 293
   quarters of, described, 264
   as Spirit-filled community of witnesses, 25

James, William, 161
Jenson, Robert, 92–93, 96, 131, 166, 167–68, 211
Jerome, 218
Jerusalem Council, 218
Jesus
    announcing union of sign and signified, 246
    becoming increasingly perplexing to his disciples, 294–95
    coinherence of work of, with the Spirit, 19
    as end-time sanctuary, 266
    entering into promised land, 17–18
    as firstfruits of new creation, 4
    human attributes of, transferred to church, 6
    information available about his voice, 66
    looking away from, as natural reflex, 170
    preparing disciples for Pentecost, 20
    preparing disciples for real absence, 28–29
    present in and as the church, 163
    recognizing Lord and Spirit in, 19
    referring to the spirit as another Advocate, 20
    resurrection of, opening hole in event of the end, 293
    as the Spirit's gift, 19–20
    story of, following sequence of Israel's feasts, 104
    transcending sacrificial economy, 298
    See also Christ, Jesus Christ
Jesus Christ
    completing march from Sinai to Zion, 293
    as marketing specialist, 78
    substituting church and Spirit for, 24
    See also Christ, Jesus
Jesus-history, divergence from our own, 4–5
Jesus of history, interest in, 157
Joachim of Fiore, 11, 23
John the Baptist, 21
John Paul II, 158
Judaism
    parting ways with Christianity, 269
    shifting eschatological hopes from temple to Torah, 268
    Sinai prevailing over Zion in, 64–65
judicial missions, in Old Testament, anticipating New Testament events, 14–15, 17
Jüngel, Eberhard, 198
justification, evangelical view of, 92–93

Kant, Immanuel, 55, 73–75, 277
Kärkkäinen, Veli-Matti, ix, 199

Kearney, Richard, 100–101
Kelsey, David, 82n.46
Kerr, Nathan R., 151
Kierkegaard, Søren, emphasizing looking outside self, 88
Kim, Seyoon, 244
Kimball, Dan, 180, 251–52
kingdom of Christ, confused with theocratic kingdom of the old covenant, 260
kingdom of God, the
    forbidden from using force, 279
    hidden nature of, 279
    spreading in holiness, 192
Kline, M. G., 14–15, 94, 267, 277
    on being united with Christ, 104
    on Christ's crucifixion as perfecting of circumcision, 114
    on intrusion ethics, 272–74
Knox, John, 138
Küng, Hans, 230

law
    humans' changing relation to, 305
    vs. gospel, 74–75
Lehmann, Paul, 306
Leith, John H., 47–48
Lennon, John, 75
Levenson, Jôn, 62–64, 261–62, 268
    on Sinai prevailing over Zion in Judaism, 64–65
    on Yahweh's march from Egypt to Zion, 291–92
Lévinas, Emmanuel, 67, 101
Lewis, C. S., 207
liberal churches, focus of, 254
liberal Protestantism, predictability of, 74
Lifton, Robert Jay, 89
light
    metaphor of, 51–53
    return to, 52
Lincoln, Andrew, 236
Lindbeck, George, 82
local churches
    as guarantor of doctrinal unity, 212
    pursuing catholicity, 202
Locke, John, 55
Loisy, Alfred, 167
Lord and Servant (Horton), ix, 263
Lundin, Roger, 70

Luther, Martin, 74
    on church as mouth-house, 76–77
    comparing metaphors of hearing and seeing,
        53–54
    conception of the Supper, Christology, and
        cosmology, 125–26
    correct perception of true church, 220
    faith as trust in God, 253
    leading recovery of emphasis on church as
        creation of the Word, 45–46
    marks of the true church, 245
    nominalist univocalism, 162
    overrealized eschatology of, 133
    on primacy of speech, 46
    theology of glory, 68–69
    on two kingdoms, 304
    warning against faith in solitude, 89–90
Lutheran-Reformed consensus, 141n.81
Lutherans, view of the Supper, 142

Machen, J. Gresham, 74n.10
MacIntyre, Alisdair, 83
Marion, Jean-Luc, 69, 133, 145
Marx, Karl, 76, 80
Mati'ilu, 103, 108, 120
Mattes, Mark C., 92–93, 168
Maximus, 7, 164
McCarthy, Dennis J., 103
McCormack, Bruce, 134
McGavran, Donald, 204–5
McLaren, Brian, 111, 252
McLoughlin, William, 75
McPartlan, Paul, 231
medieval church, dispensing grace, 222
Metzger, Paul Louis, 88
Meyers, Robin R., 78–79
Milbank, John, 7n.24, 23–24, 61, 83,
        143, 163
    appraisal of late medieval Roman Catholic
        theology, 144–45
    defending logic of transubstantiation, 148
    on incoherence of Calvin's sacramental the-
        ology, 149
    sacraments reduced to badge of membership,
        144
    totus Christus in writings of, 161–62
mind, ascent of, 5–6, 11
Minear, Paul, 188
ministry
    office of, 244

proper, guaranteeing proper message and
        mission, 248
Missional Church, The (Guder), 251
mixed assembly, 202
modernity
    flight from authority, 83
    metaphorics of vision over hearing, 62
Moltmann, Jürgen, 11n.43, 271
Moody, Dale, 232
Mount Moriah, 262
Mount Sinai, role of, 262
Mount Zion, role of, 261–62
Moyter, J. A., 42
mundane problems, related to sin and
        death, 285
Müntzer, Thomas, 11n.43, 72
Musculus, Wolfgang, 135n.56

Neale, John Mason, 223
Neoplatonism, 52–53
Nevin, John Williamson, 232
Newbigin, Lesslie, 187, 223
    on Barth's interpretation of church's posi-
        tion, 230
    on church incorporated into Christ, 224–25
    episcopal government nonessential for valid
        ministry of Word and sacrament, 226
    objecting to notion of anonymous Christian,
        193–94
    substance of covenant as mercy and grace, 197
new covenant, prophecy of, 270
New Hermeneutic, 45n.21
Newman, John Henry, 166
New Testament
    anticipating church's consummation, 230
    spiritualizing promise of a holy land?, 268–71
Newton, Isaac, 55
Nicholas of Cusa, 9
Nietzsche, Friedrich, 12, 60, 76, 89
Noah, covenant with, 102
nominalist ontology, 149
Novak, Michael, 260

Oakes, Edward T., 70
obedience, trumping forgiveness, 297–98
old covenant, paling in comparison to new
        covenant, 65
Oliver, Simon, 147
Ong, Walter, 54–58, 66, 73
On the Councils and the Church (Luther), 245

ontological xenophobia, 88, 161
oral culture, role of past in, 54–55
ordinances, 111–12
O'Regan, Cyril, 11n.43, 157
Origen, 5, 52
Orthodox Judaism, focus on renewal of Sinai
    covenant, 269
Osiander, 137

Pannenberg, Wolfhart, 92, 253
Parmenides, 51
Parousia, becoming part of gospel, 2
Pasquarello, Michael, 250
Passover, 17
    as sign, 105
    significance of, 120–21
Paul, two ages of, 3
Pentecost (Feast of Weeks), 14, 17, 204
    causing church to become part of the story, 30
    forecasting unity of age to come, 217
    generating community of Spirit-empowered
        testimony, 32
    new episode in economy of grace, 24–25
    Peter's sermon at, 254
    Spirit and judgment connected in Peter's ser-
        mon at, 16
    Spirit at, 18
    transforming people into the body of Christ,
        30–31
    as unrepeatable event, 231
Pentecostals
    ecclesiology of, 176–83
    focus of, 254
    movements of, emphasizing mission, 248
    suspicious of binding prophecy and apos-
        tolicity to formal offices, 240–41
    theology of, 194, 228
personal faith, importance of, 112
personal response, having no effect on Word
    and sacraments, 184
Philo, attempting to translate hearing into
    seeing, 53
Pickstock, Catherine, 7n.24, 152, 163
pietism, 73–74, 75
Placher, William, 72
Plato, 51, 54–55
Platonism, 67, 157–58
Pneumatology, eschatological character of, 164
postmodernity, representation becoming reality
    in, 66

poststructuralism, 67
preaching
    bringing about extralingual reality, 106
    causing canon to become grace, 46
    importance of, 46–48, 51
    as means of grace, 116
    role of, 253
presbyterian polity
    consistent with covenantal ecclesiology, 219
    most appropriate expression of covenantal
        eschatology, 212, 214–15
    point of, 246
    seen in Jerusalem Council in Acts, 218
presence
    Aquinas's view of, 146
    as metaphor for covenantal relationship, 100
    vs. action, 108–9
Preston, Geoffrey, 168
private Christianity, 180–81
promise, Spirit of, 13–18
prophets
    authorized to speak living and active word, 42
    protesting against idols, 59
Protestantism, offering many alternatives to
    preaching, baptism, and Communion,
    249
Protestantism, American
    on guard against sacerdotalism, 139–40
    identifying church as people, 251
    trouble receiving grace, 249
Protestantism, Radical, 47, 112
Protestants
    confessional, focus of, 254
    confusing local church with church, 214–15
protracted meeting, 250
Pseudo-Dionysius, focusing on individual and
    ecclesial ascent, 7
public ministry, as living event, 252–53
public worship, elements and circumstances
    of, 229

Radical Orthodoxy, 7n.24, 12, 67, 143, 166
    approach of, to Eucharist, 143–52
    defending church as active agent of redemp-
        tion, 198
    totus christus in, 161–62
Rahner, Karl, 9, 156, 158, 193
ratification ceremonies, 103
Ratzinger, Joseph, 160–61, 164–65, 181,
    183, 187

recognizing early working of presbyterian polity, 219
on Roman Catholic's catholicity, 212–13
See also Benedict XVI
Reardon, Bernard, 75
reconciliation, ministry of, 241–48
redemption
covenant of, 28
drama of, 40
redemptive history, 273–75
Reformation
churches of, 248
emphasis on devocalizing the universe, 73
public worship during, becoming verbal event, 45
questions dominating theology of, 221–22
recovering Hebraic understanding of reality and speech, 45
restoring Supper to practical prominence, 138
reform Catholicism, 156–59
Reformed churches, social impact of eucharistic teachings, 140–41
Reformed confessions
emphasis on preached Word, 47–48
on sacraments as divine gifts, 117
Reformed orthodoxy, on what is contained in the Supper, 131
Reformed—Roman Catholic dialogue, 37–38, 141n.81
Reformed theology
on church's holiness, 195
covenantal orientation of, 224
dialogical nature of, 303
distinguishing between visible/invisible church, 203
rejecting visible representations of deity, 69–70
understanding of sacramental presence, 108
on what is received in the sacrament, 128–29
Reformed tradition, understanding of grace, 107
Reformers
distinguishing sacraments from written and preached Word, 142–43
Word of God coming from outside in, 46–47
regulative principle, 229
religion/spirituality, 75
resurrection, interpretation of, as going to heaven, 3

revelation
occurring as conversation between God, church, and culture, 87
summarizing history of, 290–93
Revisioning Evangelical Theology (Grenz), 84–87
revivalism, 73, 75
revivals, endless craving for, 250
Revolutionaries, 170n.98, 177–78
Richardson, Alan, 290
Ricoeur, Paul, 60, 61
Ridderbos, Herman, 121–22, 243
Roberts, Hywell, 139
Roman bishops, ancient Christian leaders not accepting supremacy of, 225
Roman Catholic Church, 47
claims of, to continuing apostolic office, 240
ecclesiology of, 212–15
as realization of the kingdom of God, 156
on source for church's holiness, 194
theology of, substituting church for gospel, 226
Romanticism, European, 75
Rome, overrealized eschatology of, 133
Römerbrief, 227
Roof, Wade Clark, 77n23
Rosenzweig, Franz, 270
royal investiture, covenantal history of, 15
Ryrie, Charles, 111

Sabbath, as inbreaking of age to come, 273
sacrament, containing earthly signs and heavenly realities, 131
sacramentalism, of Reformed tradition, 142
sacraments, the
calling for appropriate response of partners, 112–13
coming from God's action, 107–10
effect of, added to baptism and Eucharist, 110–11
as God's means of effecting dislocation, 105
infusing grace into the participant, 106–7
making people holy, 106
as means of grace, 116
Reformed theology's understanding of, 108
Reformed view of, 112
as treaty ratification, 101–6
understood as work of the believer, 111
view of, having ecclesiological and soteriological implications, 112

sacrificial system, categories of, 296–97
salvation, coming from outside ourselves,
    79–80
salvation-and-judgment, 274–75
sanctification, as claim made by triune God,
    191
sanctuary, end-time, 264–65
Sauter, Gerhard, 94–95
Sayers, Dorothy, 40
Scheeben, M. J., 23n.74
Schleiermacher, Friedrich, 33, 166, 185
Schmemann, Alexander, 136
Schopenhauer, Arthur, 62
Scripture
    as dead letter, 40, 42, 43, 47
    demographic readings of, 207–8
    as product, 83
    as record of faith community's encounter
        with God, 86
Second Great Awakening, 250
Second Helvetic Confession, 48, 49, 126, 218
Second Vatican Council, role of church accord-
    ing to, 159–60
seeing, related to promise and fulfillment, 64
self
    creating divinity from, 76
    crucifying and burying in baptism, 76
    idolatrous position of, 78–79
self-transformation, continual process of, 89
service
    contrasted with gathering, 252
    ministering sense of, 252
signs, function of, in covenantal economy, 102
sign and signified
    analogical relation between, 175
    confusing, 143–52
    relation between, 104
Sinai, symbol of death and judgment, 295
Siniatic economy, feasts in, 17
Smit, Laura, 149–51
Smith, Christian, 77
Smyth, John, 184
sola scriptura, 83
    degenerate present-day versions of, 96
    as product of modern foundationalism, 87
    protests against, 93–94
    transferred to domain of private
        spirituality, 91
soteriology, linking with ecclesiology, ix

sound
    binding people in an existential
        relationship, 56
    enveloping nature of, 57
speakers, idols and, 59–63
speech
    covenantal, 58–71
    importance of, in covenantal context, 55
    primacy of, assuming illusion of presence,
        52n.62
speech-act theory, 109
Spinoza, Baruch, 157
Spirit, the
    as Advocate, 20, 24–25
    alleged contrast with the word, 43
    associated with glory cloud and wind, 14, 15
    in avian form, 13–14, 15
    causing restlessness within us, 22
    Christ's presence mediated by, 13–30
    close relationship with eschatology, 19–20
    clothing us with Christ, 15
    coinherence of work of, with Jesus, 19
    conflation of, with the Son, 23
    connecting us to Christ's past, present, and
        future, 21
    contrasted with ecclesial forms and public
        rites, 231–32
    creating bond between sign and reality
        signified, 41
    as divine witness, 14, 15
    enhypostasis of, 23–24
    equal actor in economy of grace, 24–25
    extroversion of, pertaining to church's
        relationship to the world, 33
    generating communion with Christ, 22
    guide to destination of the Son, 26
    identified with sanctification, 16
    inbreathing of, making humanity a living
        being, 16
    indwelling the community, 161
    Jesus and, 18–25
    as Jesus' gift, 20–21
    leading into all truth, 28
    linked to Jesus-history in economy of
        grace, 17
    as mediator of Christ's persona and work, 18
    merging with the church to fill Christ's
        absence, 162
    ministry of, 28

as missionary sent from Father and Son, 27–28
outpouring of, associated with last days and age to come, 15
at Pentecost, 18
permanently indwelling temple-people, 29
presence of, announcing turning of epochs, 21–22
present when Christ is present, 25–26
of promise, 13–18
reduced to spirit of the community, 160
related to judgment, 15, 16–17
results of, separation from Christ, 23–24
revealing economy of grace, 28
role of, in the Supper, 130
sent to convict, 26–27
setting church apart to receive Word and sacraments, 196
as source of hearing and speaking of prophets, apostles, and ministers, 49
trading places with Christ, 26
transforming created space into covenantal place, 14
transforming mission field into the mission-ary, 31–32
treating as substitute for absent Christ, 22–23
spirit-matter dualism, 232
spiritual election, 270
spirituality, inward nature of, 85
spiritualization, 6
Supper, the
close connection between nature and efficacy of, 138–39
communicating Christ's presence and work, 136
in covenantal context, 119–23
creating communion of saints, 203
efficacy of, 135–41
eschatological understanding of, 132
as fissure in the present age, opened by the Spirit, 133
frequency of, 137–41, 255
as human act, 112
linked to preaching and catechesis, 50
Reformed view of, 112
reversing order for real and the sign, 148–49
role of, 253
as sacrifice, 139

as sign, 105–6, 107
turning into theatrical display, 145, 147–48
what is received at, 125–28
and where it is received, 131–35
Systematic Theology (Finney), 250

Teilhard de Chardin, Pierre, 166
Temple, the
associated with creation, 261
early Christian reaction to destruction of, 270
end-time, 265–66
as miniature cosmos, 262–63, 267
successive expansions of, 265
Teresa of Avila, 198
Tetrapolitan Confession, 138–39
third age, vision of, 11
Third Reich, 286
Tillich, Paul, ix, 51, 86
time, division into sevens, 272–73
Tocqueville, Alexis de, 75
Tönnies, Frederick, 185
Torrance, T. F., 134
totus Christus, 6, 22, 61, 84
appearance of, in Radical Orthodoxy, 161–62
as Christ with the church, 167
eclipsing ascended Christ and individual believers, 162
eschatological orientation of, 186
holiness and catholicity flowing from, 192–93
identity between Christ and church com-plete in, 155–56
incompatible with solus Christus, 183
recent Protestant ecclesiologies and, 166–70
sharing contractual outlook with Protestant individualism, 185
transcendence, domestication of, 72
transubstantiation
applied to ecclesial body, 159
placing Christ in church's possession, 8
Treaty and Covenant (McCarthy), 103
Treatise on Christian Liberty (Luther), 304–5
Trent, following Ockham's logic, 145
Trinitarianism, social, 215–16, 217
Trinity, as pure relations, 161
Troeltsch, Ernst, 223
Turretin, Francis, 247

two histories, hermeneutical significance of, arising after resurrection, 4–5

Unam Sanctam (Boniface III), 8
United States, groups in
  perceptions of mission, 286–87
  speaking for God's will, 260
Urban II, 259

Van Mastricht, Peter, 144n.95
Vatican I, 192
Vatican II, widening its ecclesiology, 192n.3
Vermigli, Peter Martyr, 135n.56, 138
vision
  metaphor of, in Western philosophy, 51–53
  words assimilated to, 57
Vitiello, Vincenzo, 101–2
Volf, Miroslav, 22, 160–61, 181–84, 187
  on free-church ecclesiology, 176
  on free-church polity, 219
  on the local church, 184
  pointing out threat of Vatican II to Catholicism, 216–17
  restricting definition of visible church, 215–16
  universal church as eschatological reality, 182
  on Zizioulas's overrealized eschatology, 231
von Balthasar, Hans Urs, 6, 65–66, 142, 159, 307
  on Barth's approach to theology in event and history, 174–75
  commending Dionysian mysticism of Middle Ages, 193
von Rad, Gerhard, 60
Vos, Geerhardus, 114

Wainwright, Geoffrey, 198
Wandel, Lee Palmer, 138
Ward, Graham, 143, 163–64
  on contemporary culture offering secular eschatology, 145
  criticism of, 149–50
  misrepresenting Calvin, 146–47
  on reducing Eucharist to theatrical spectacle, 145
  viewing ascension as displacement, 148
Way of Opinion, The (Parmenides), 51
Webb, Stephen H., 39, 45, 53n.69, 66, 73

accent on immanence rather than God's transcendent presence, 80
  on Reformation view of Word in preaching and liturgy, 97
  sacraments as more than verbal, 106
  sound's effect on people, 88
Webster, John, 81, 83, 91, 166–67
  on authority of Scripture, 95–97
  on Barth's treatment of baptism, 118
  on churches' treatment of God, 92
  on gift of evangelical freedom, 305
  on grace as movement of relation, 107
  on ministry of reconciliation, 244
Wesleyan triangle, 86
Westminster Confession, 49, 196, 202, 221, 238
Westminster Directory for Public Worship, 139
Westminster Larger Catechism, 49, 128, 139
Westminster Shorter Catechism, 76–77, 107–8, 302
Westminster Standards, 139
Westphal, Merold, 88, 105, 162–63
Williams, Rowan, 105
Willimon, William, 77–80, 285
Wingren, Gustav, 304
Witten, Marsha, 180
Wittenberg Concord, 126
Wittgenstein, Ludwig, 83–84
Wollebius, Johannes, 131, 135n.56, 139
Wolterstorff, Nicholas, 108–9
word
  coming before light, 52
  inner, creating inner church, 73
  internal vs. external, 73–75
  light illuminating, 53
  necessity of experiencing within community, 77
  priority of, over the sacred, 61
Word, the
  as act of creation, 41–42
  alternative to theocentric and Trinitarian concept of, 39
  baptism linked to, 119
  captivity of, to inner self, 52
  church as mother of, 82–83
  church needing to recover confidence in sacramental, 70–71, 81–82, 224
  created by community experience, 86
  as the effect of personal presence and lively activity, 38

grounded in the Son and Spirit, 43
immanentizing of, 84
inability to set church against, 50
keeping church from being assimilated into
    passing history, 92
keeping in social-ecclesial context, 90
liberating quality of, 97–98
as living and active energy, 39
as means of grace, 68
power of, lying in ministry of the Spirit,
    48–49
priority of, over the church, 94–95
as second person of the Trinity, 38
as source of creation, judgment, and
    redemption of history, 44
transcendence of, doubly threatened, 86
treated as dead letter, 40
as vital energy and normative constitution, 49
See also God, Word of
word-event, theology of, 45n.21
words
    human, as God's breath, 38–39
    losing ability to generate community, 67–68
    power of, in oral culture, 57
Word and sacrament, human response to, 301
works-righteousness, 244
worship, in proper manner, 60

Wyschogrod, Michael, 269–70, 277

Yong, Amos, 11n.43, 87, 193, 240n.62

Ziegler, Philip G., 306
Zizioulas, John, 22, 133, 164–66, 181–83
    on church existing as fully realized
        eucharistic event, 231
    on ecclesial existence as a gift, 231
    on ministers receiving grace to serve
        others, 239
    on primary content of catholicity, 215
    recognizing early working of presbyterian
        polity, 219
    on Western papalism, 213–14
Zwingli, Ulrich
    assumption of, that Christ's deity does all
        redemption work, 136
    on baptism, 118
    on Christ's bodily presence at the Supper, 131
    directing faith to ascend the earthly, 137
    disagreement with Calvin on communica-
        tion of reality, 128
    dualistic view of spirit and matter, 125–26
    on God's using material means to convey
        spiritual blessings, 142
    underrealized eschatology of, 133

CPSIA information can be obtained
at www.ICGtesting.com
Printed in the USA
FSOW04n0747120216
16849FS